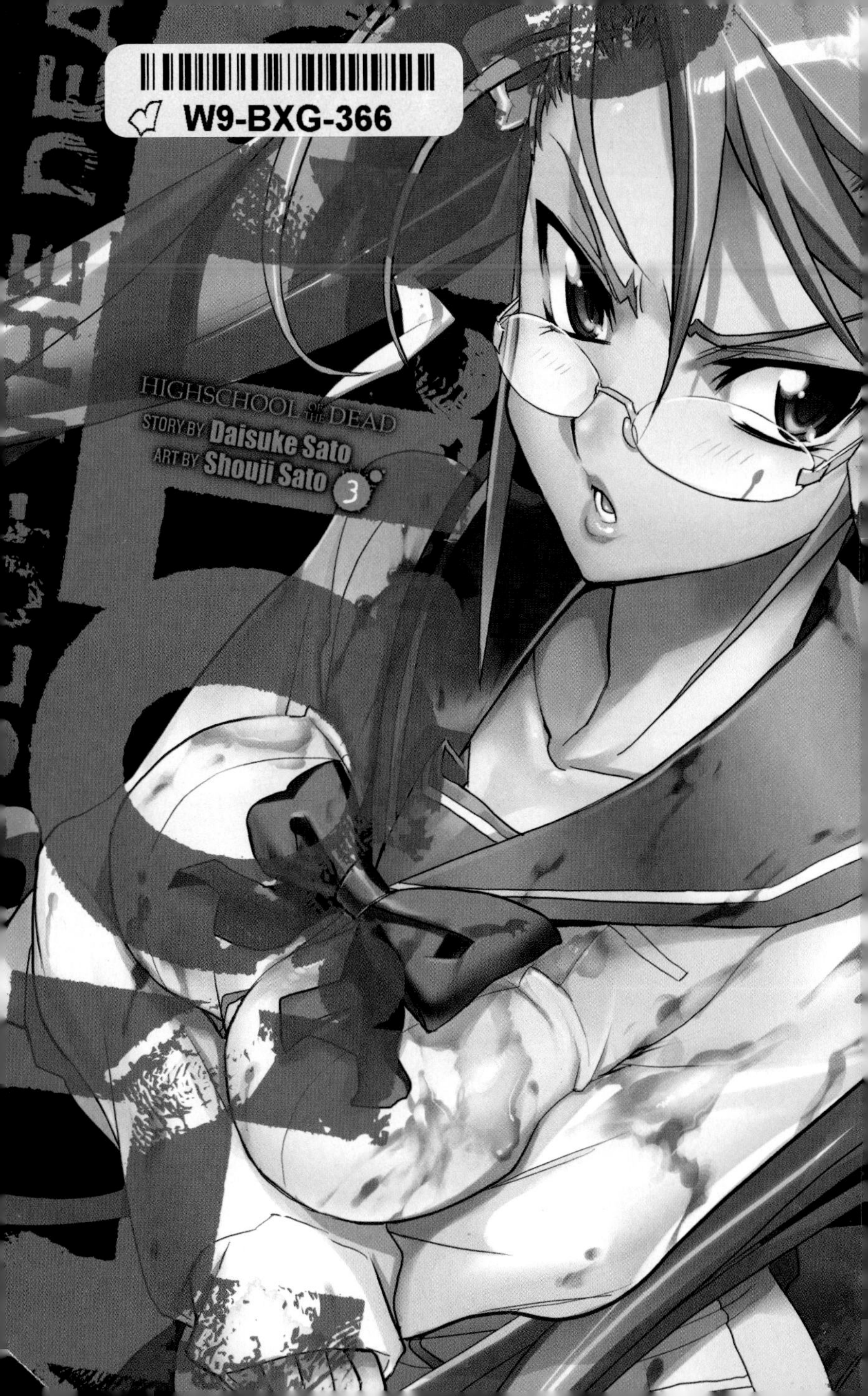
HIGHSCHOOL OF THE DEAD
STORY BY Daisuke Sato
ART BY Shouji Sato
3

CONTENTS

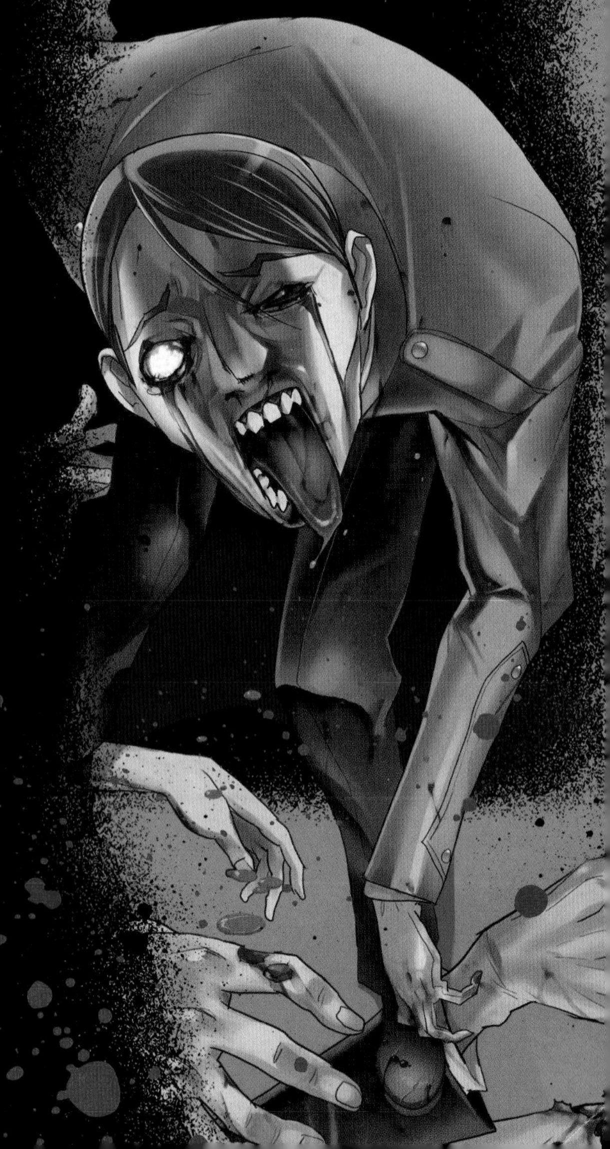

List of Weapons

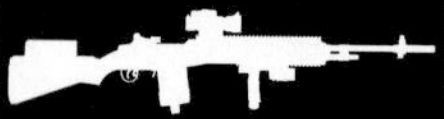
[SPRINGFIELD M1A1]

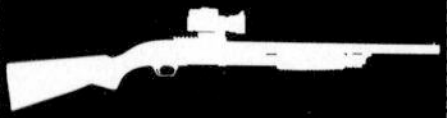
[ITHACA M37]

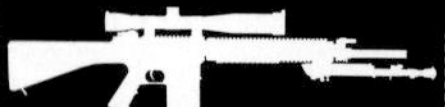
[KNIGHT'S SR-25 SERIES, ARMALITE AR-10 V]

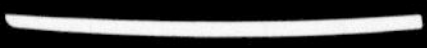
[WOODEN SWORD]

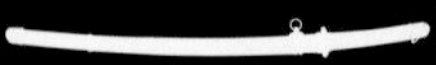
[MURATA BLADE]

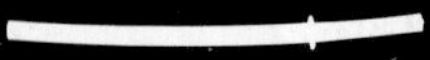
[SATSUMA-MADE DOUTANUKI]

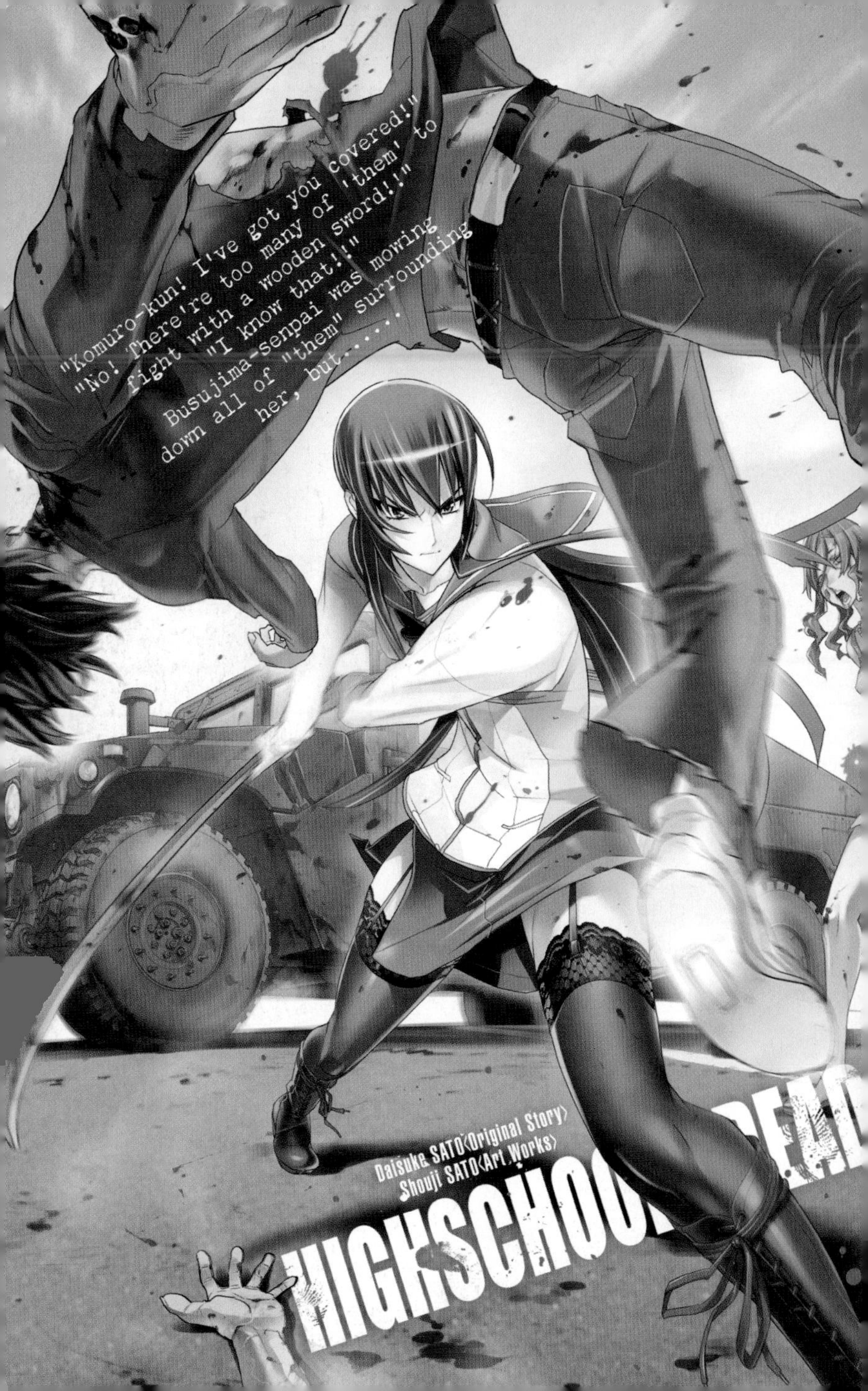
"Komuro-kun! I've got you covered!"
"No! There're too many of 'them' to fight with a wooden sword!!"
"I know that!!"
Busujima-senpai was mowing down all of "them" surrounding her, but.....
Daisuke SATO<Original Story>
Shouji SATO<Art Works>
HIGHSCHOO

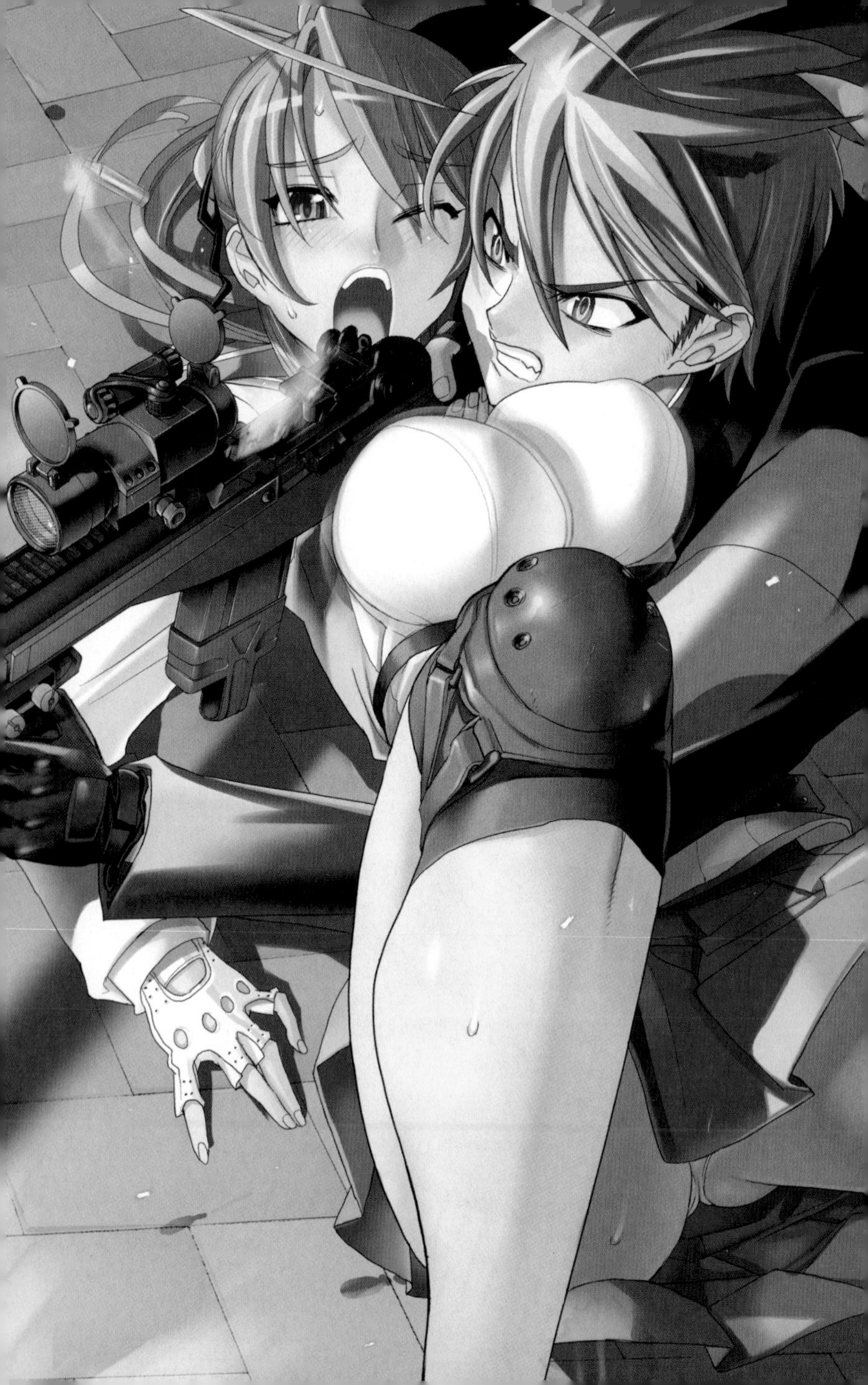

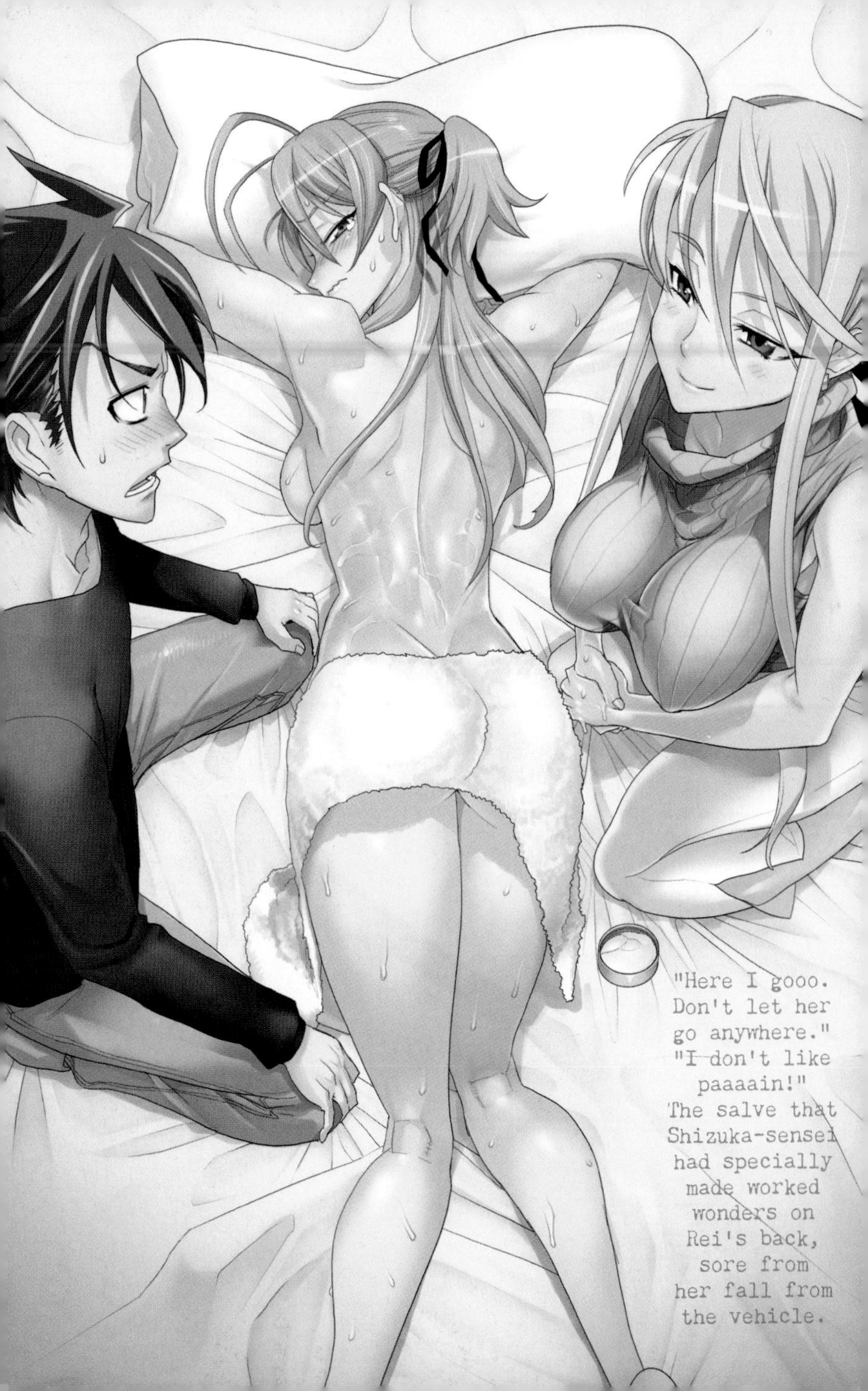
"Here I gooo. Don't let her go anywhere."
"I don't like paaaain!"
The salve that Shizuka-sensei had specially made worked wonders on Rei's back, sore from her fall from the vehicle.

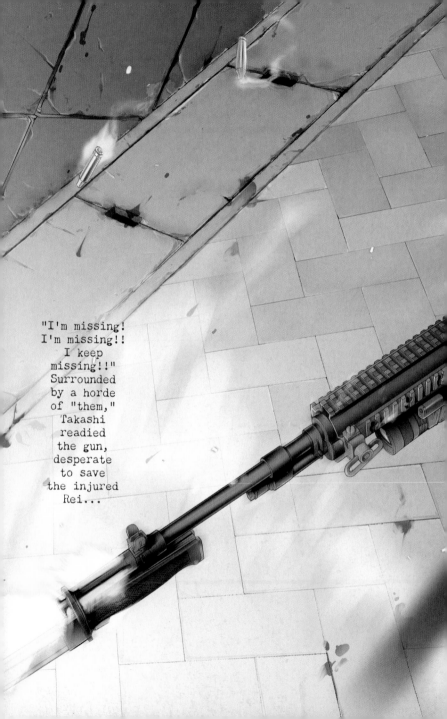

"I'm missing!
I'm missing!!
I keep
missing!!"
Surrounded
by a horde
of "them,"
Takashi
readied
the gun,
desperate
to save
the injured
Rei...

HIGHSCHOOL OF THE DEAD

3

STORY BY

Daisuke Sato

ART BY

Shouji Sato

That was the day our once
peaceful world fell apart. A second-
year at the private school Fujimi High,
Takashi Komuro gets away from "them"
when they suddenly storm his campus,
making it to the school roof along
with his best friend, Hisashi Igou,
and childhood crush, Rei Miyamoto.
However, along the way, Igou gets
bitten and dies, only to come back as
one of "them," forcing Takashi to
put Hisashi to rest.

Takashi and Rei team up with other
survivors — namely fellow classmates
Saya Takagi and Kouta Hirano; a
third-year master of the sword, Saeko
Busujima; and the school nurse, Shizuka
Marikawa — and escape from the school.
However, Rei so adamantly opposes a
teacher, Shidou, joining their group
that she and Takashi end up taking a
different route than their friends.

Rei is attacked by a huge man at a
gasoline station, but Takashi rescues
her and equips himself with a handgun
he retrieves from the body of a police
officer. The two then manage to join up
with their friends, who have broken off
from Shidou's group. Together they seek
shelter in the empty home of a police
force friend of Marikawa-sensei's where
they ride out the night. In the middle
of the night, Takashi sees a little girl
being attacked by "them" and succeeds
in mounting a rescue. However, the crew
finds that they themselves have to
flee for their lives.

ACT.8 **Alice in Dead land.**

THERE WAS ALSO THIS ENDING THAT WE HAD NO WAY OF FORESEEING.

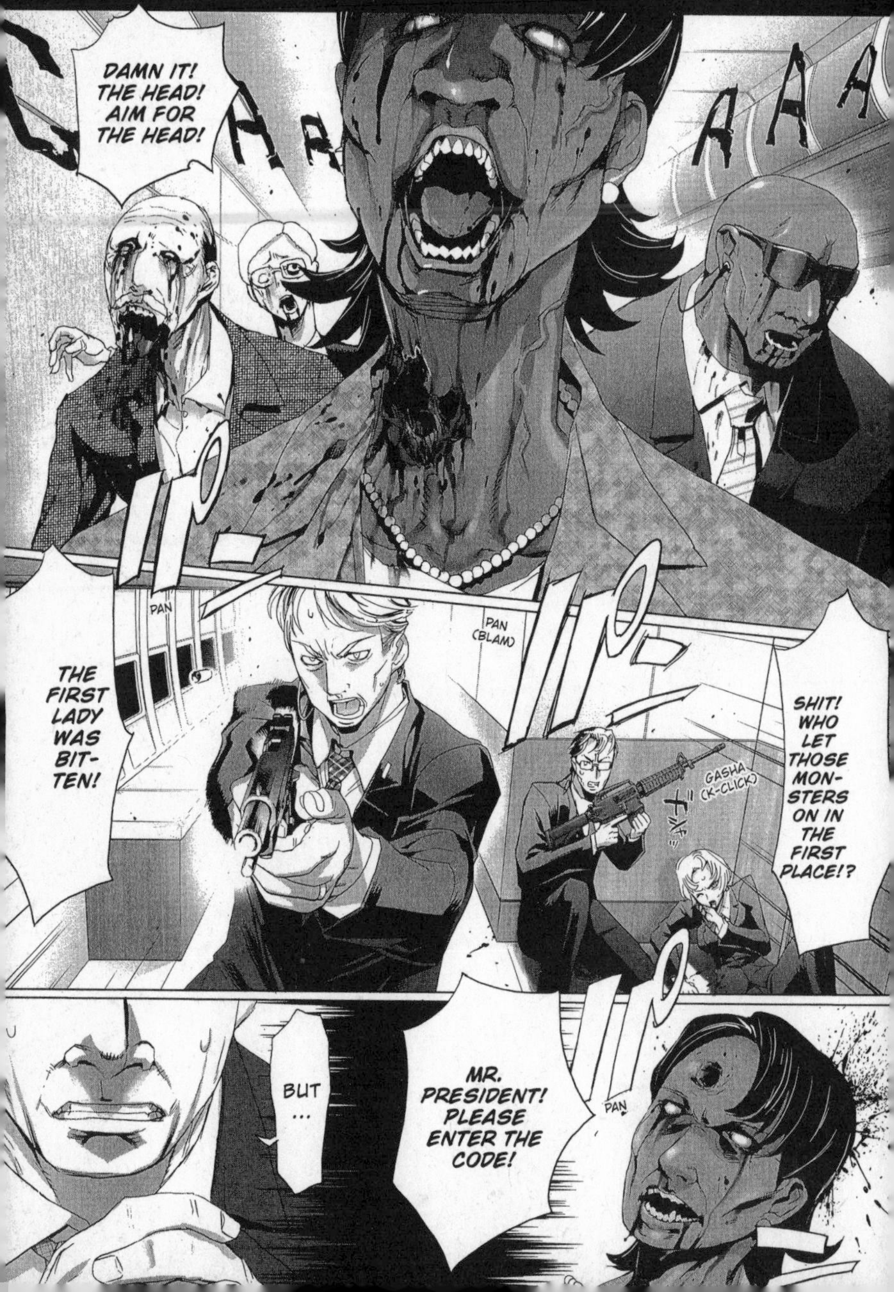
DAMN IT! THE HEAD! AIM FOR THE HEAD!
SHIT! WHO LET THOSE MON-STERS ON IN THE FIRST PLACE!?
GASHA (K-CLICK)
PAN (BLAM)
PAN
THE FIRST LADY WAS BIT-TEN!
PAN
MR. PRESIDENT! PLEASE ENTER THE CODE!
BUT ...

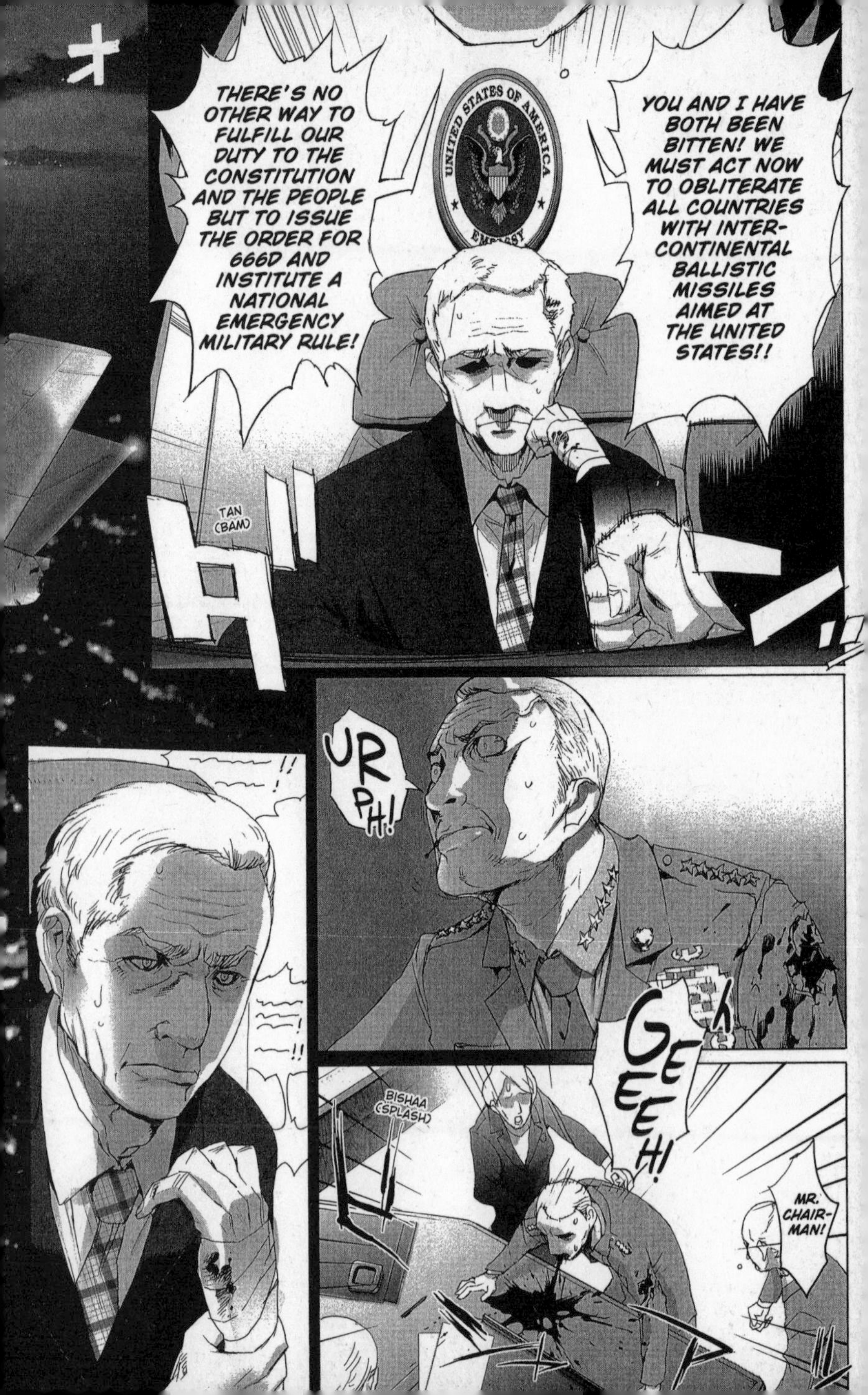
YOU AND I HAVE BOTH BEEN BITTEN! WE MUST ACT NOW TO OBLITERATE ALL COUNTRIES WITH INTER-CONTINENTAL BALLISTIC MISSILES AIMED AT THE UNITED STATES!!
THERE'S NO OTHER WAY TO FULFILL OUR DUTY TO THE CONSTITUTION AND THE PEOPLE BUT TO ISSUE THE ORDER FOR 666D AND INSTITUTE A NATIONAL EMERGENCY MILITARY RULE!
TAN (BAM)
URPH!
GEEEH!
BISHAA (SPLASH)
MR. CHAIR-MAN!

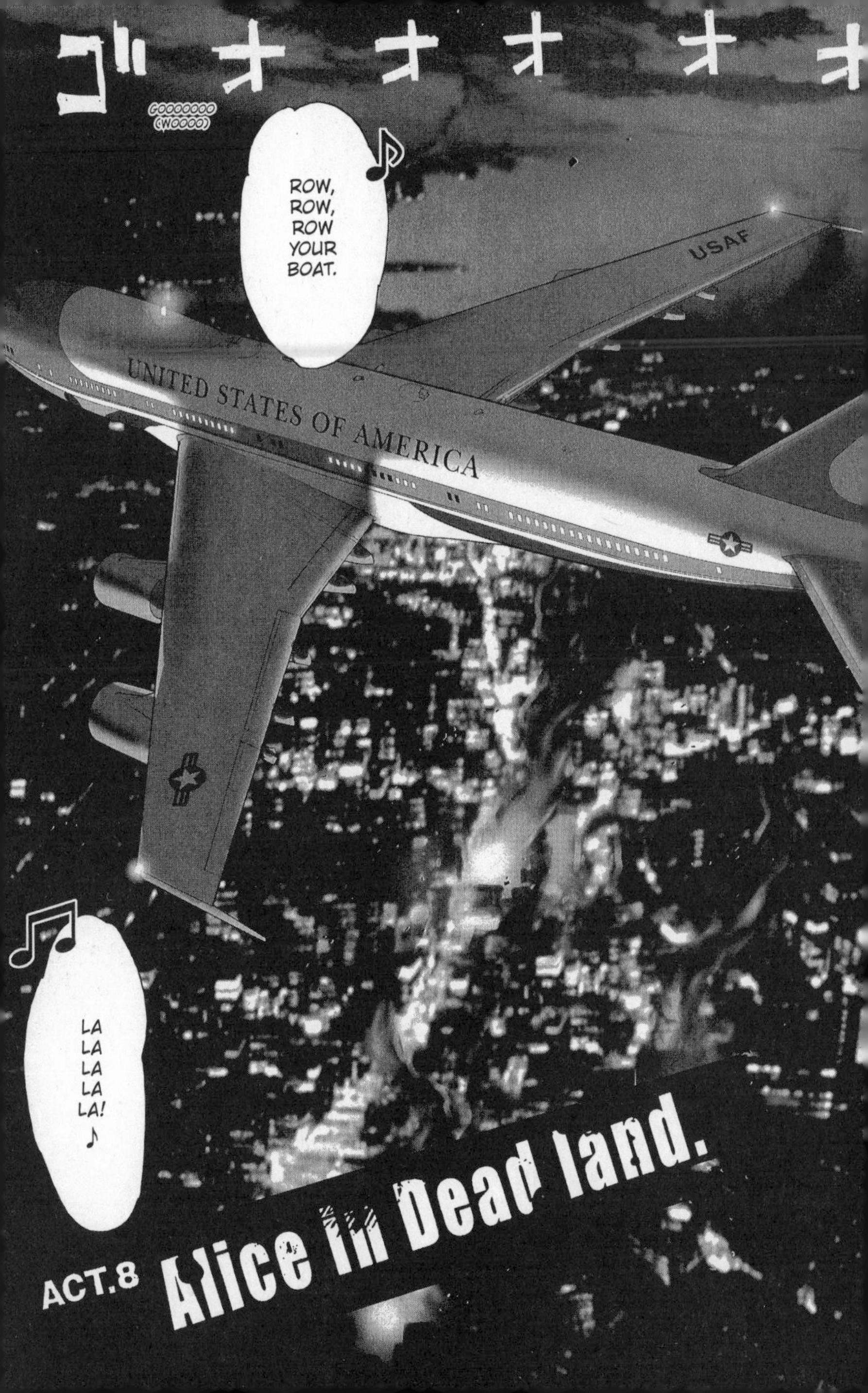

ゴオオオオオ
GOOOOOOO (WOOOO)
ROW, ROW, ROW YOUR BOAT.
USAF
UNITED STATES OF AMERICA
LA LA LA LA LA! ♪
ACT.8 Alice in Dead land.

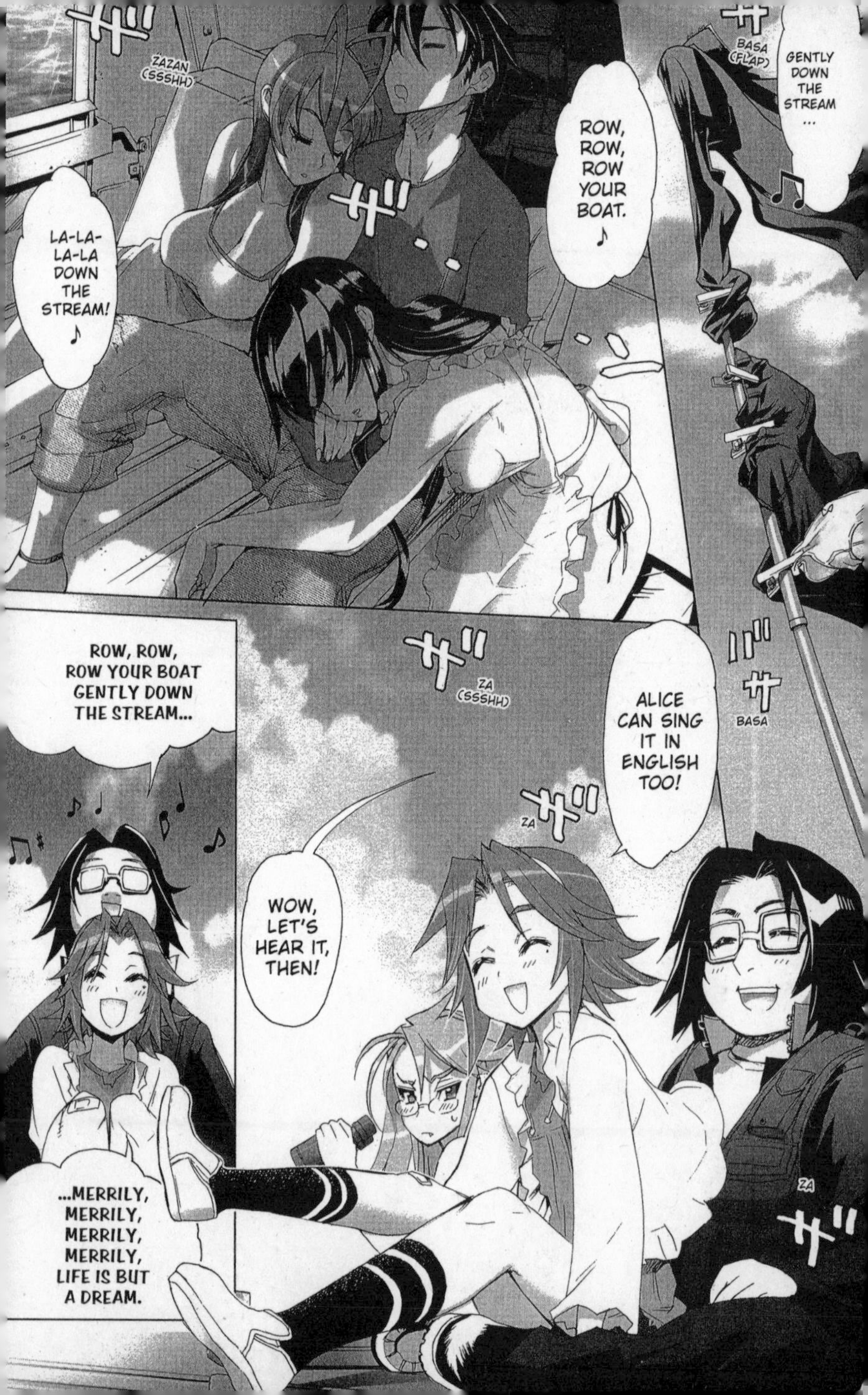
BASA (FLAP)
GENTLY DOWN THE STREAM ...
ZAZAN (SSSHH)
ROW, ROW, ROW YOUR BOAT. ♪
LA-LA-LA-LA DOWN THE STREAM! ♪
BASA
ALICE CAN SING IT IN ENGLISH TOO!
ZA (SSSHH)
ZA
WOW, LET'S HEAR IT, THEN!
ZA
ROW, ROW, ROW YOUR BOAT GENTLY DOWN THE STREAM...
...MERRILY, MERRILY, MERRILY, MERRILY, LIFE IS BUT A DREAM.

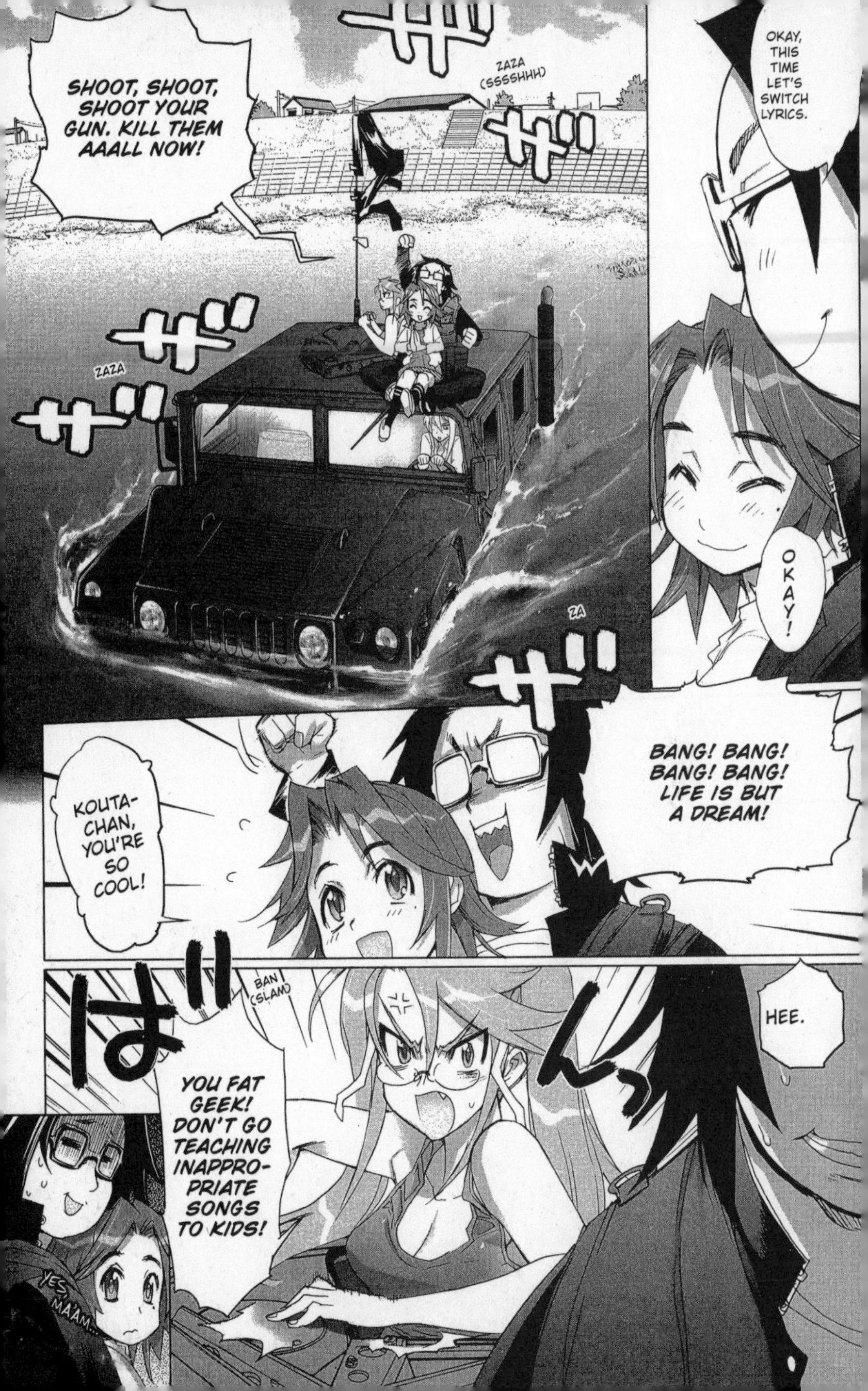
OKAY, THIS TIME LET'S SWITCH LYRICS.
OKAY!
SHOOT, SHOOT, SHOOT YOUR GUN. KILL THEM AAALL NOW!
ZAZA (SSSSHHH)
ZAZA
ZA
BANG! BANG! BANG! BANG! LIFE IS BUT A DREAM!
KOUTA-CHAN, YOU'RE SO COOL!
HEE.
BAN (SLAM)
YOU FAT GEEK! DON'T GO TEACHING INAPPRO-PRIATE SONGS TO KIDS!
YES, MA'AM...

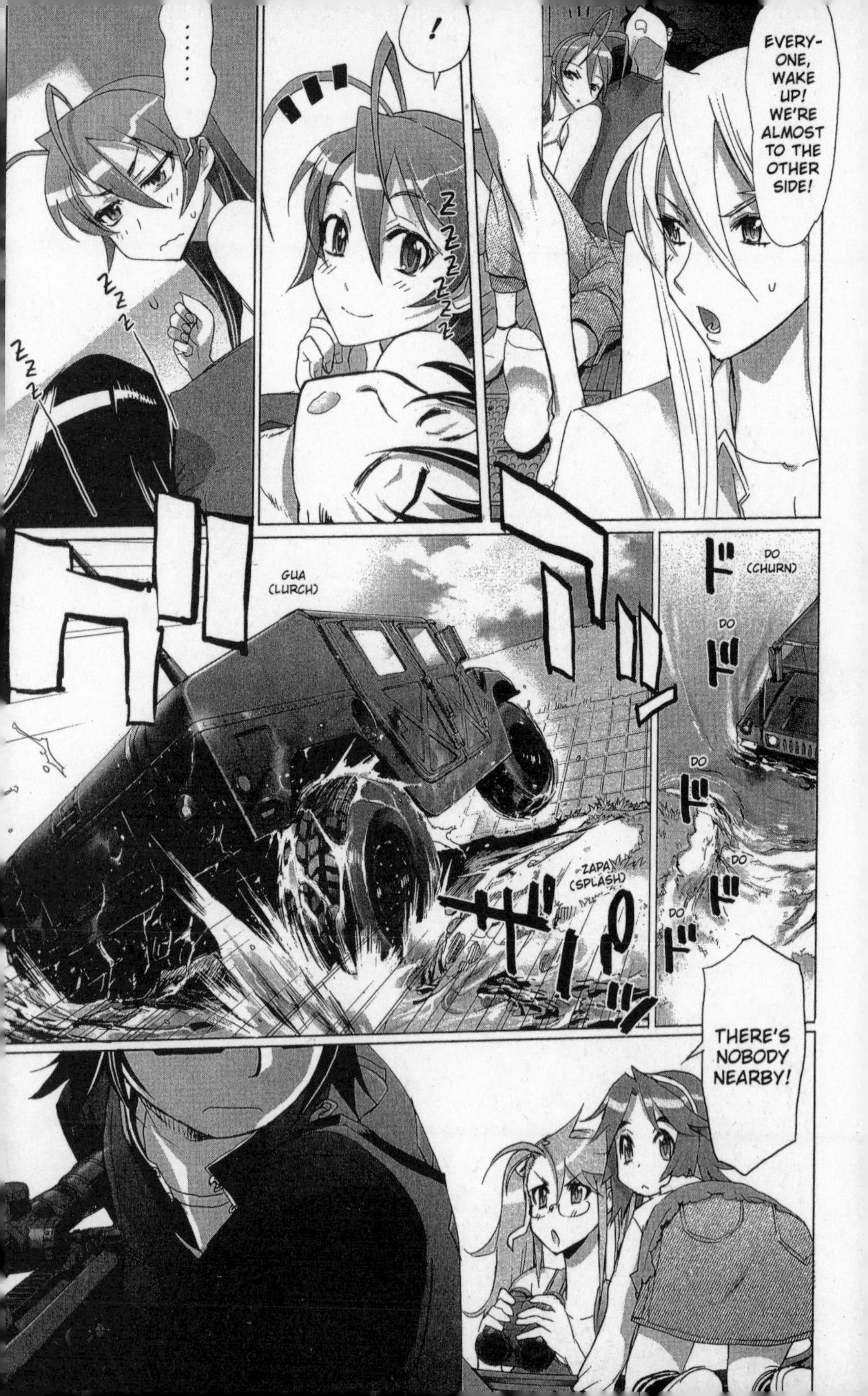
EVERY-ONE, WAKE UP! WE'RE ALMOST TO THE OTHER SIDE!
!
ZZZZZZ
......
ZZZ
ZZZ
DO (CHURN)
DO
DO
DO
DO
GUA (LURCH)
ZAPA (SPLASH)
THERE'S NOBODY NEARBY!

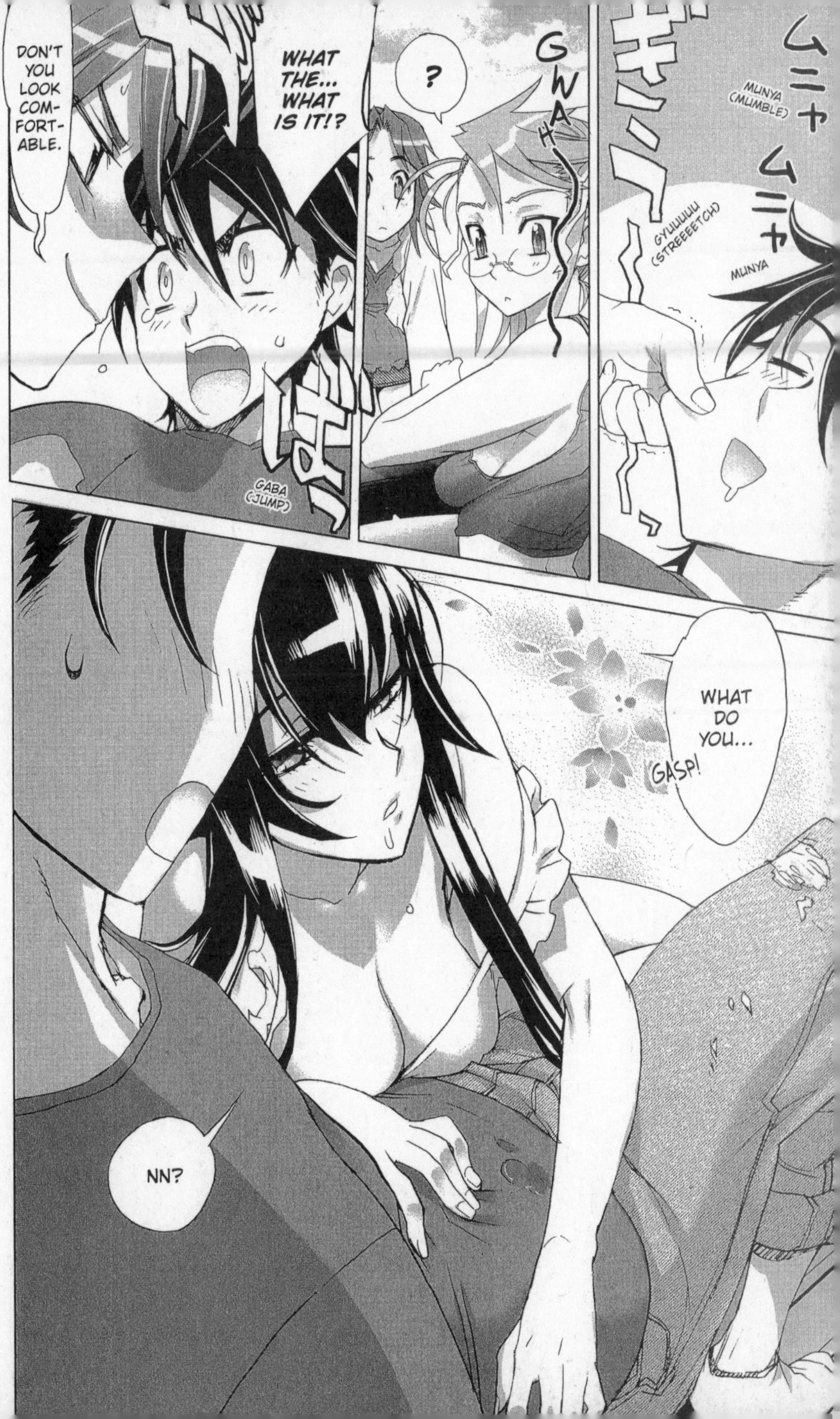
ムニャ
MUNYA (MUMBLE)
ムニャ
MUNYA
GYUUUUU (STREEEETCH)
GWAH
?
WHAT THE... WHAT IS IT!?
DON'T YOU LOOK COM-FORT-ABLE.
GABA (JUMP)
WHAT DO YOU...
GASP!
NN?

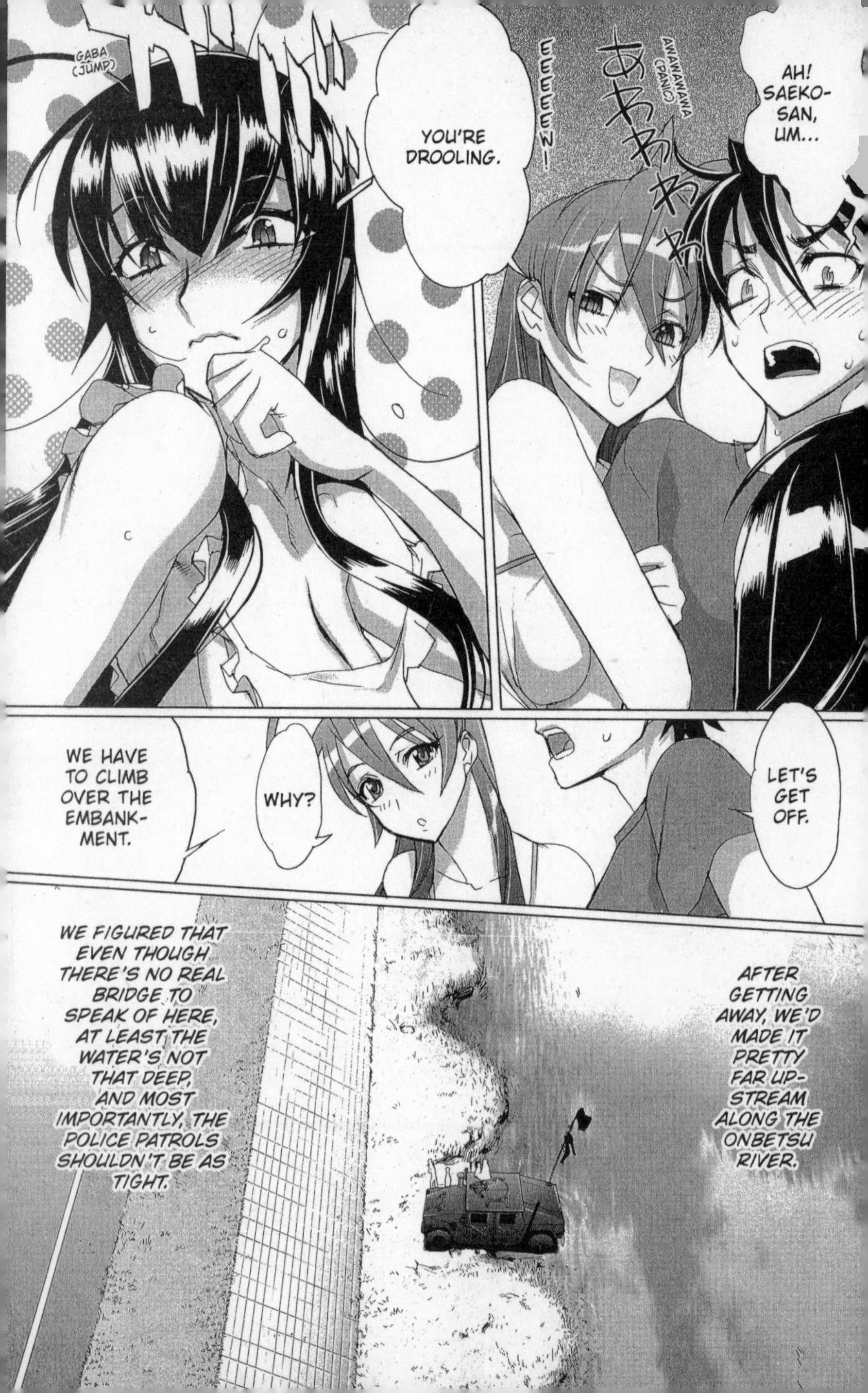
AH! SAEKO-SAN, UM...
AWAWAWAWA (PANIC)
EEEEEEW!
YOU'RE DROOLING.
GABA (JUMP)
LET'S GET OFF.
WHY?
WE HAVE TO CLIMB OVER THE EMBANKMENT.
AFTER GETTING AWAY, WE'D MADE IT PRETTY FAR UP-STREAM ALONG THE ONBETSU RIVER.
WE FIGURED THAT EVEN THOUGH THERE'S NO REAL BRIDGE TO SPEAK OF HERE, AT LEAST THE WATER'S NOT THAT DEEP, AND MOST IMPORTANTLY, THE POLICE PATROLS SHOULDN'T BE AS TIGHT.

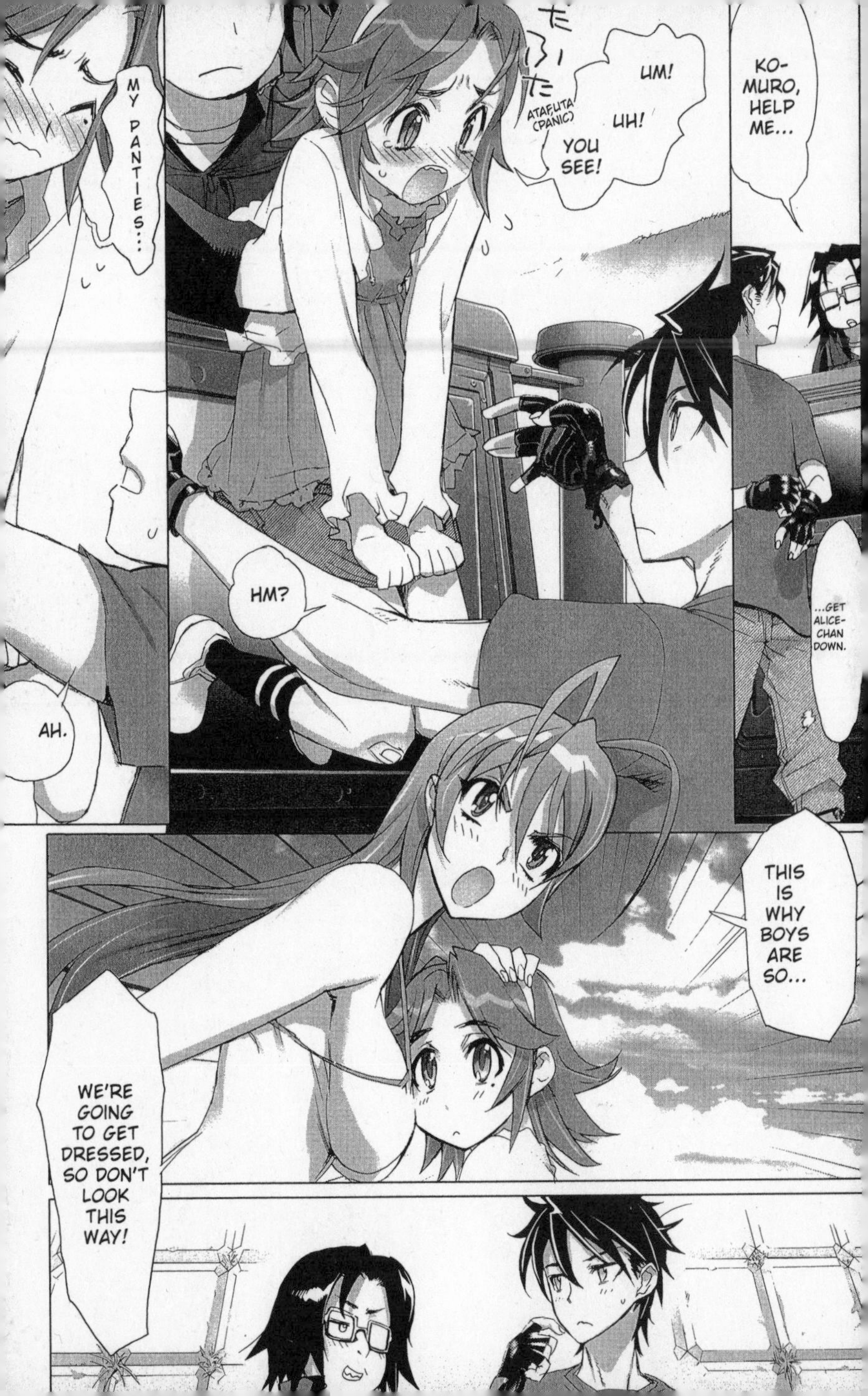
KO-MURO, HELP ME...
...GET ALICE-CHAN DOWN.
UM!
UH!
YOU SEE!
ATAFUTA (PANIC)
HM?
MY PANTIES...
AH.
THIS IS WHY BOYS ARE SO...
WE'RE GOING TO GET DRESSED, SO DON'T LOOK THIS WAY!

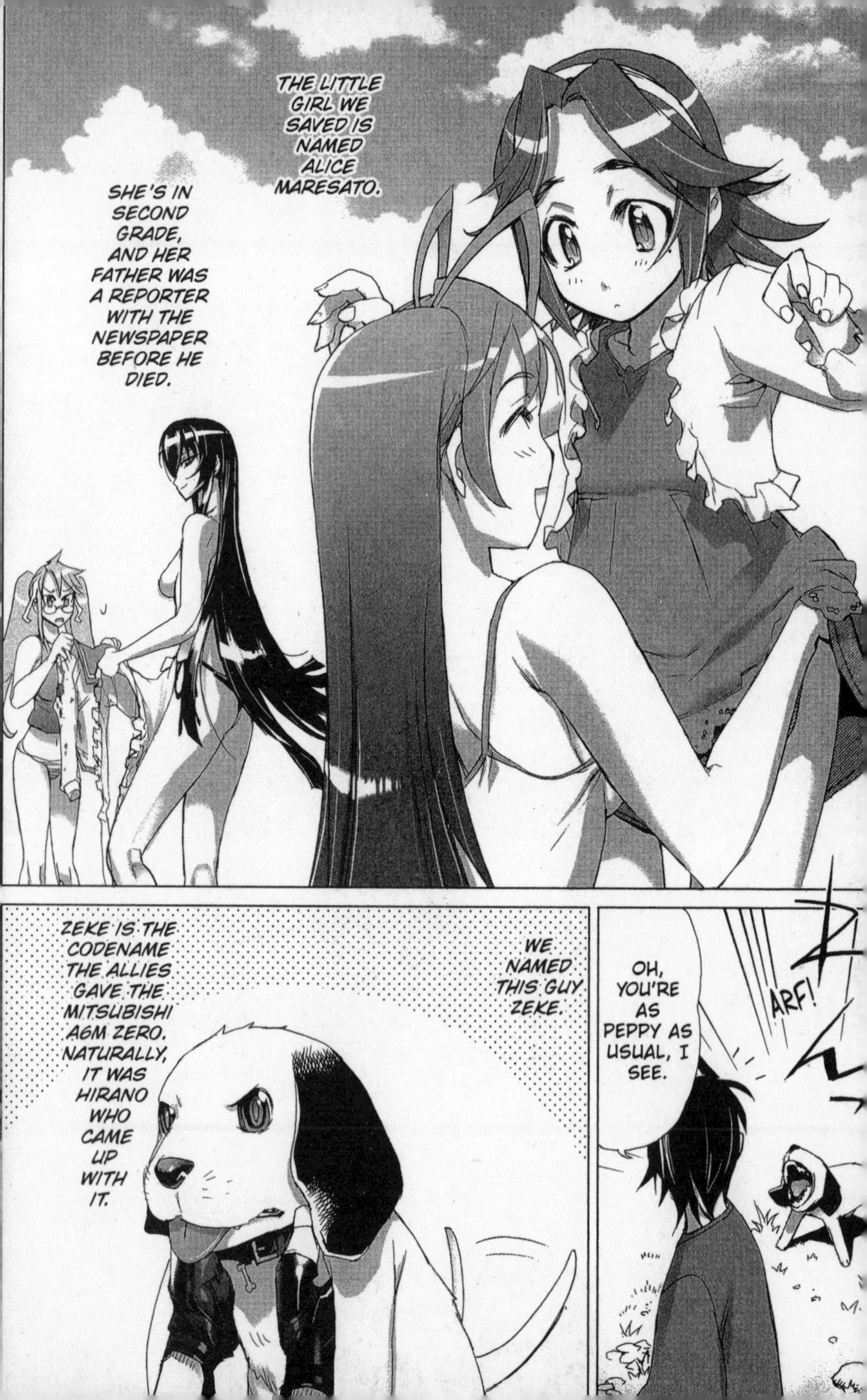
THE LITTLE GIRL WE SAVED IS NAMED ALICE MARESATO.
SHE'S IN SECOND GRADE, AND HER FATHER WAS A REPORTER WITH THE NEWSPAPER BEFORE HE DIED.
ARF!
OH, YOU'RE AS PEPPY AS USUAL, I SEE.
WE NAMED THIS GUY ZEKE.
ZEKE IS THE CODENAME THE ALLIES GAVE THE MITSUBISHI A6M ZERO. NATURALLY, IT WAS HIRANO WHO CAME UP WITH IT.

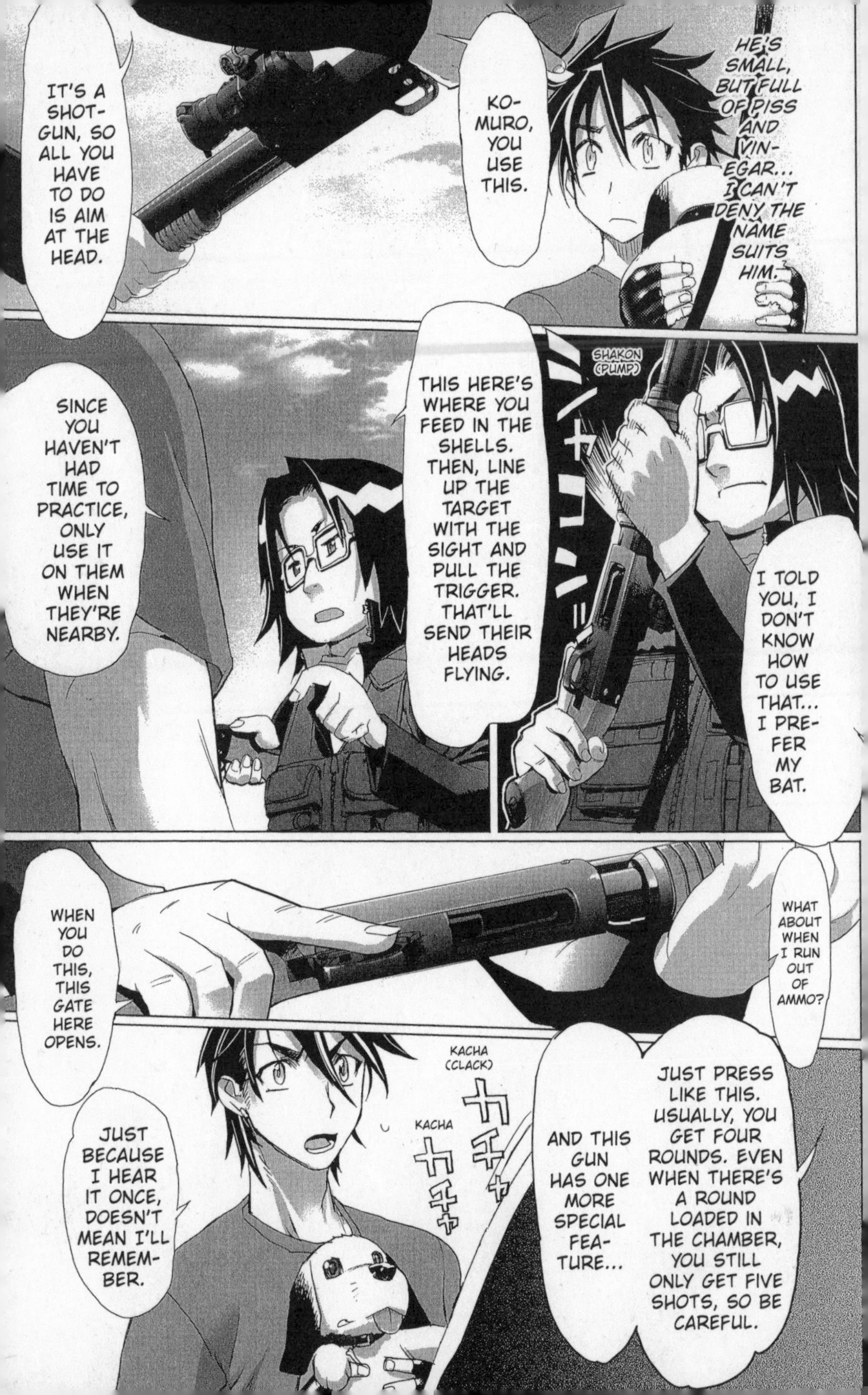
HE'S SMALL, BUT FULL OF PISS AND VINEGAR... I CAN'T DENY THE NAME SUITS HIM.
KOMURO, YOU USE THIS.
IT'S A SHOTGUN, SO ALL YOU HAVE TO DO IS AIM AT THE HEAD.
I TOLD YOU, I DON'T KNOW HOW TO USE THAT... I PREFER MY BAT.
SHAKON (PUMP)
THIS HERE'S WHERE YOU FEED IN THE SHELLS. THEN, LINE UP THE TARGET WITH THE SIGHT AND PULL THE TRIGGER. THAT'LL SEND THEIR HEADS FLYING.
SINCE YOU HAVEN'T HAD TIME TO PRACTICE, ONLY USE IT ON THEM WHEN THEY'RE NEARBY.
WHAT ABOUT WHEN I RUN OUT OF AMMO?
WHEN YOU DO THIS, THIS GATE HERE OPENS.
JUST PRESS LIKE THIS. USUALLY, YOU GET FOUR ROUNDS. EVEN WHEN THERE'S A ROUND LOADED IN THE CHAMBER, YOU STILL ONLY GET FIVE SHOTS, SO BE CAREFUL.
AND THIS GUN HAS ONE MORE SPECIAL FEATURE...
KACHA (CLACK)
KACHA
JUST BECAUSE I HEAR IT ONCE, DOESN'T MEAN I'LL REMEMBER.

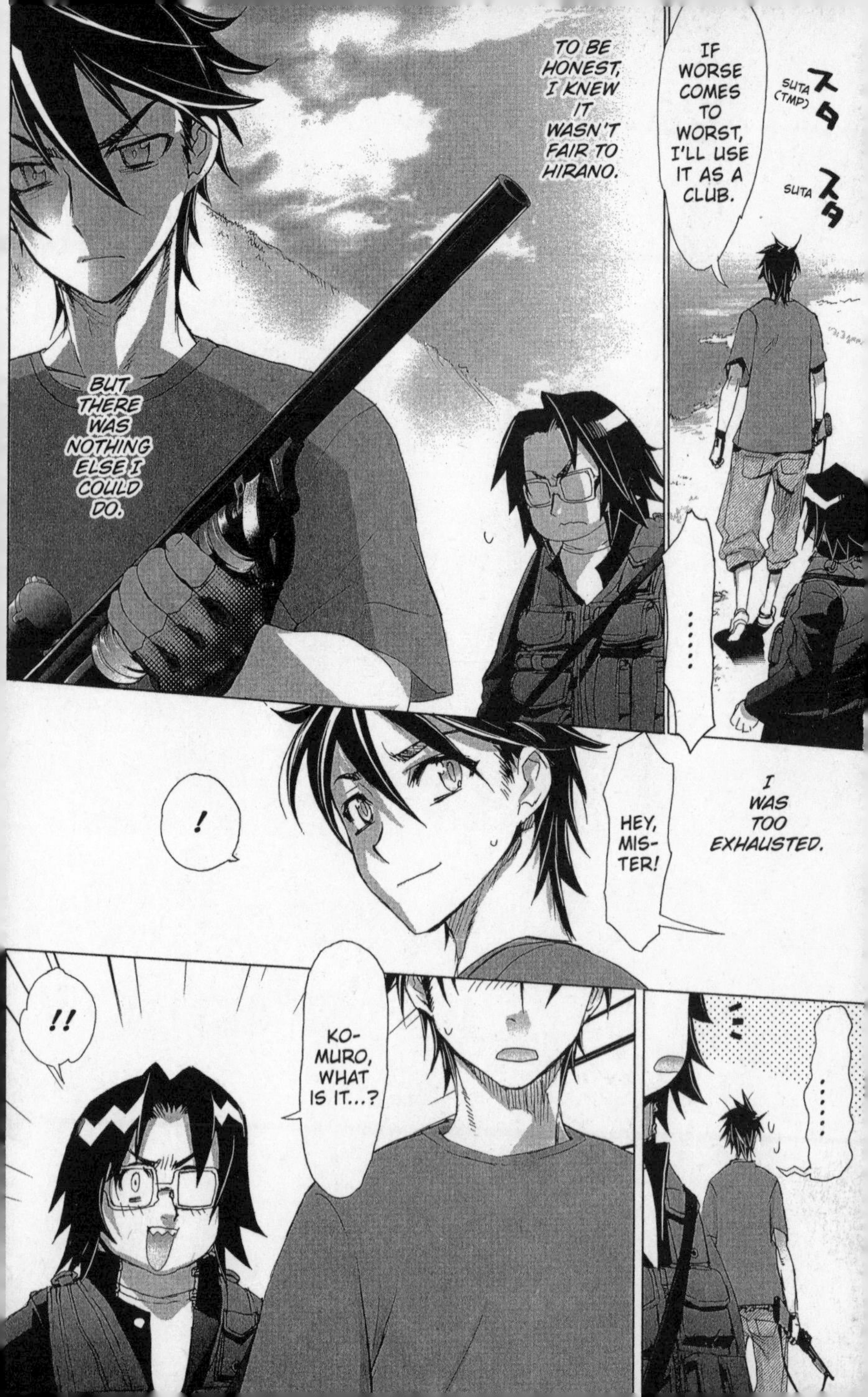
IF WORSE COMES TO WORST, I'LL USE IT AS A CLUB.
SUTA (TMP) スタ
SUTA スタ
......
TO BE HONEST, I KNEW IT WASN'T FAIR TO HIRANO.
BUT THERE WAS NOTHING ELSE I COULD DO.
I WAS TOO EXHAUSTED.
HEY, MISTER!
!
......
KO-MURO, WHAT IS IT...?
!!

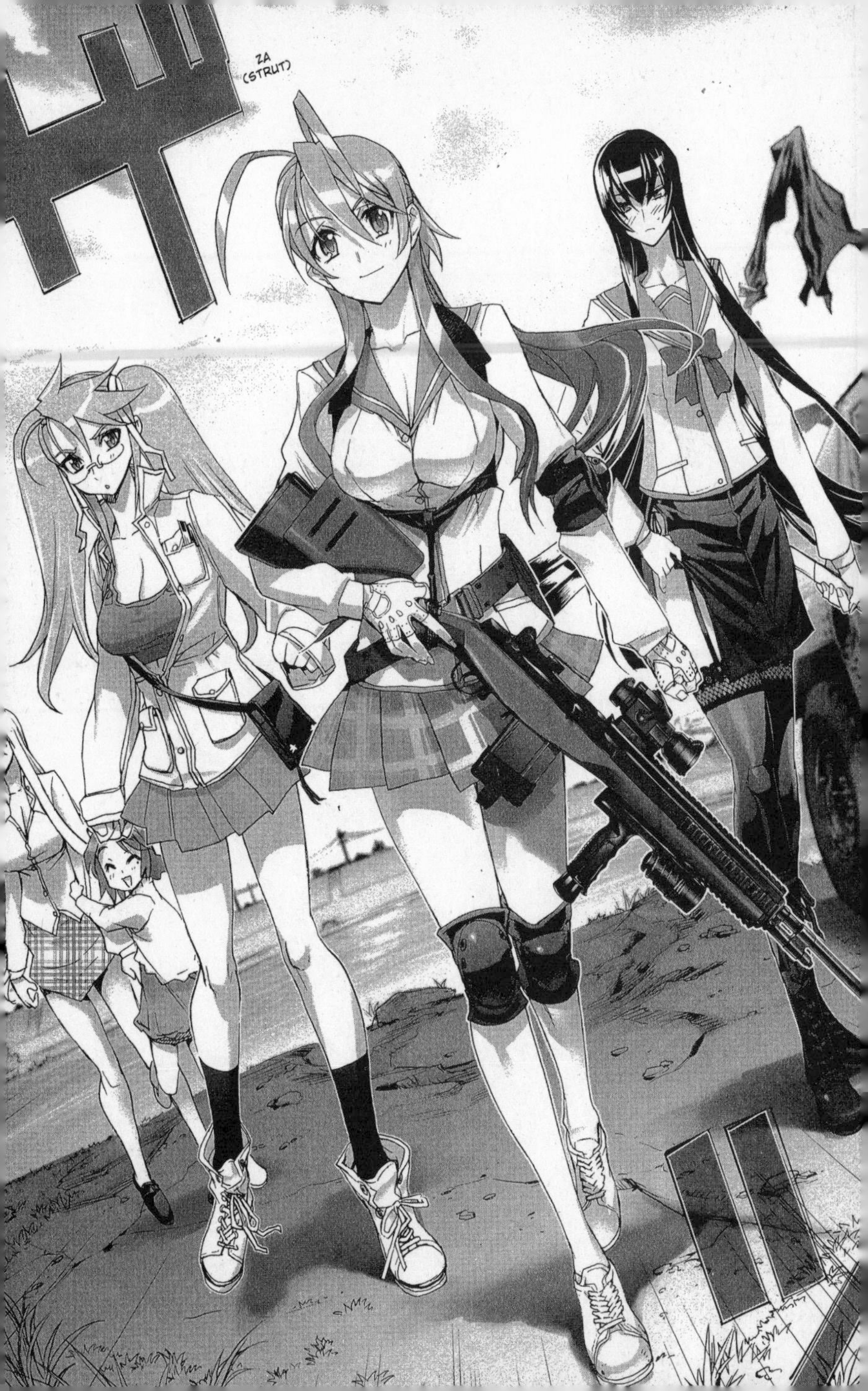
ZA
(STRUT)

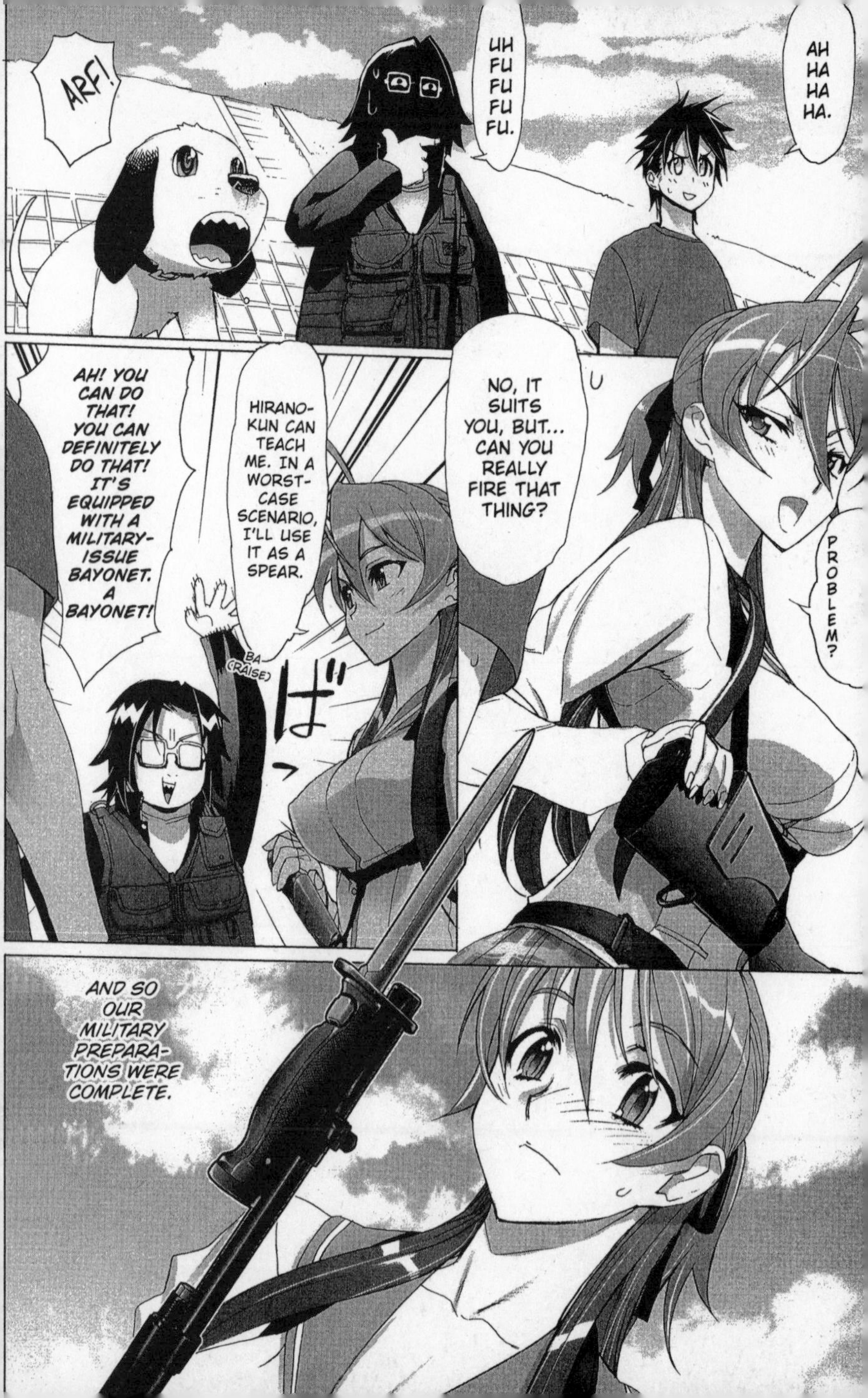
AH HA HA HA.
UH FU FU FU FU.
ARF!
PROBLEM?
NO, IT SUITS YOU, BUT... CAN YOU REALLY FIRE THAT THING?
HIRANO-KUN CAN TEACH ME. IN A WORST-CASE SCENARIO, I'LL USE IT AS A SPEAR.
BA (RAISE)
ば
AH! YOU CAN DO THAT! YOU CAN DEFINITELY DO THAT! IT'S EQUIPPED WITH A MILITARY-ISSUE BAYONET. A BAYONET!
AND SO OUR MILITARY PREPARATIONS WERE COMPLETE.

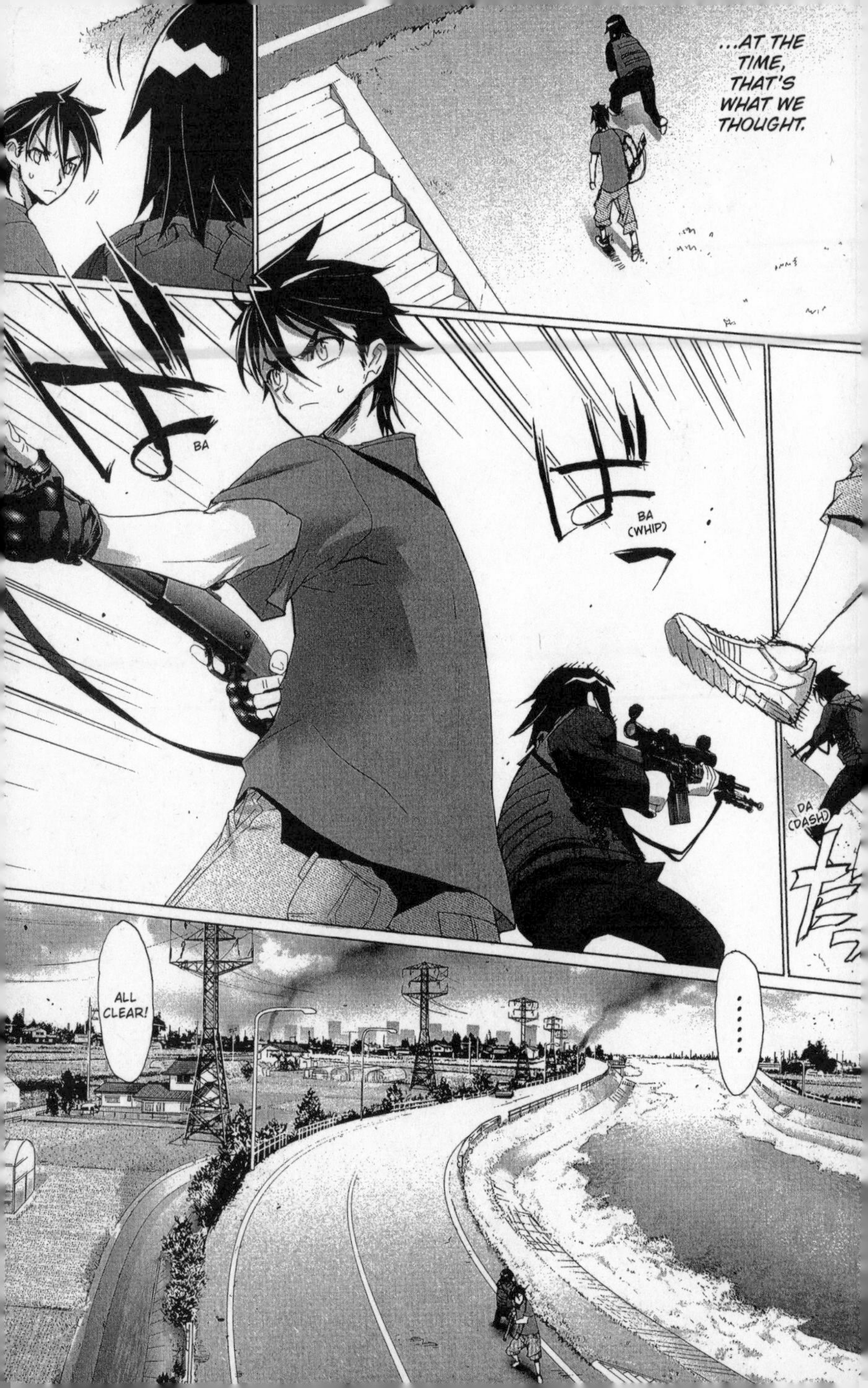
...AT THE TIME, THAT'S WHAT WE THOUGHT.
DA (DASH)
BA (WHIP)
BA
......
ALL CLEAR!

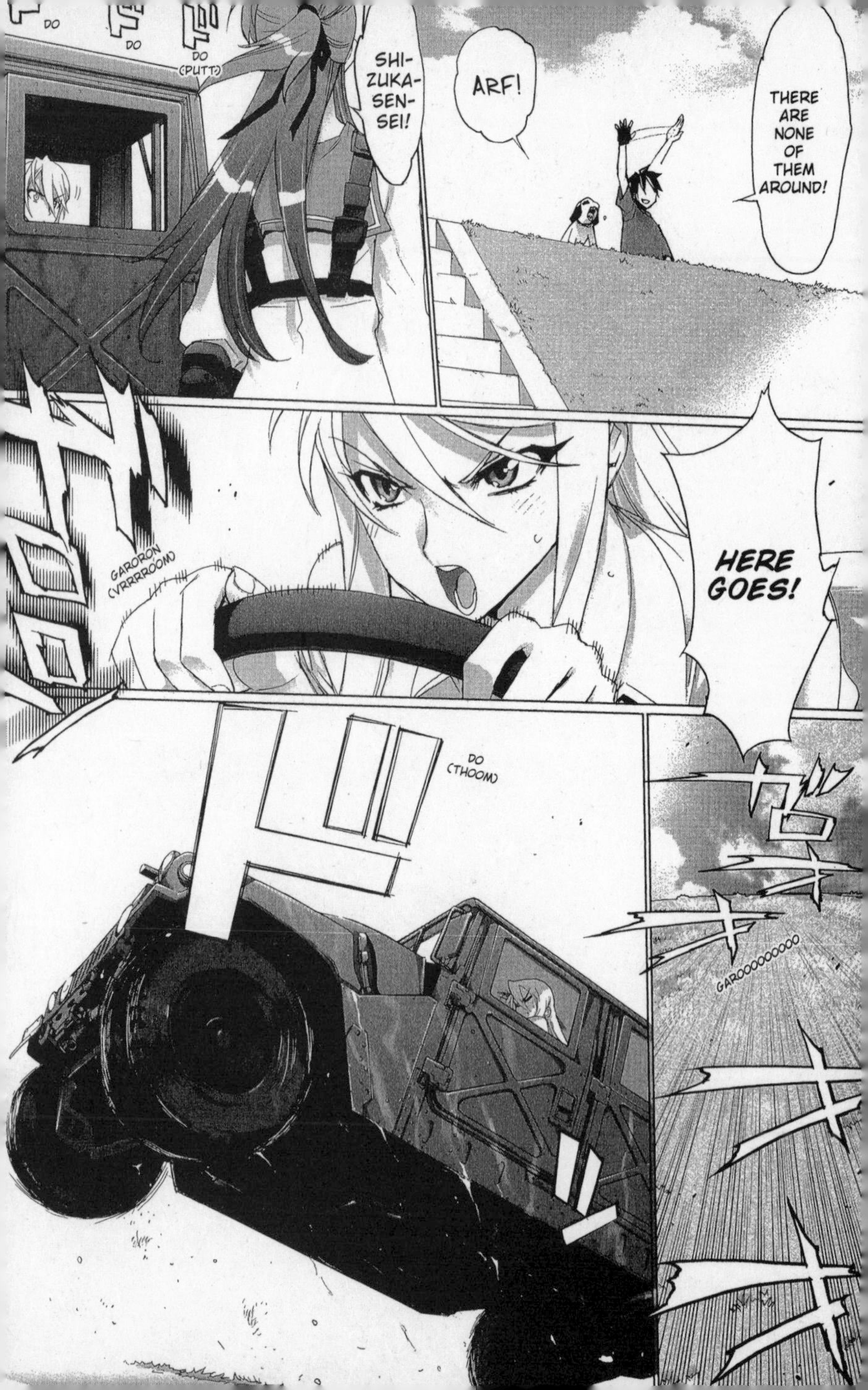
THERE ARE NONE OF THEM AROUND!
ARF!
SHI-ZUKA-SEN-SEI!
DO
DO
DO (PUTT)
HERE GOES!
GARORON (VRRRROOM)
GAROOOOOOOOOO
DO (THOOM)

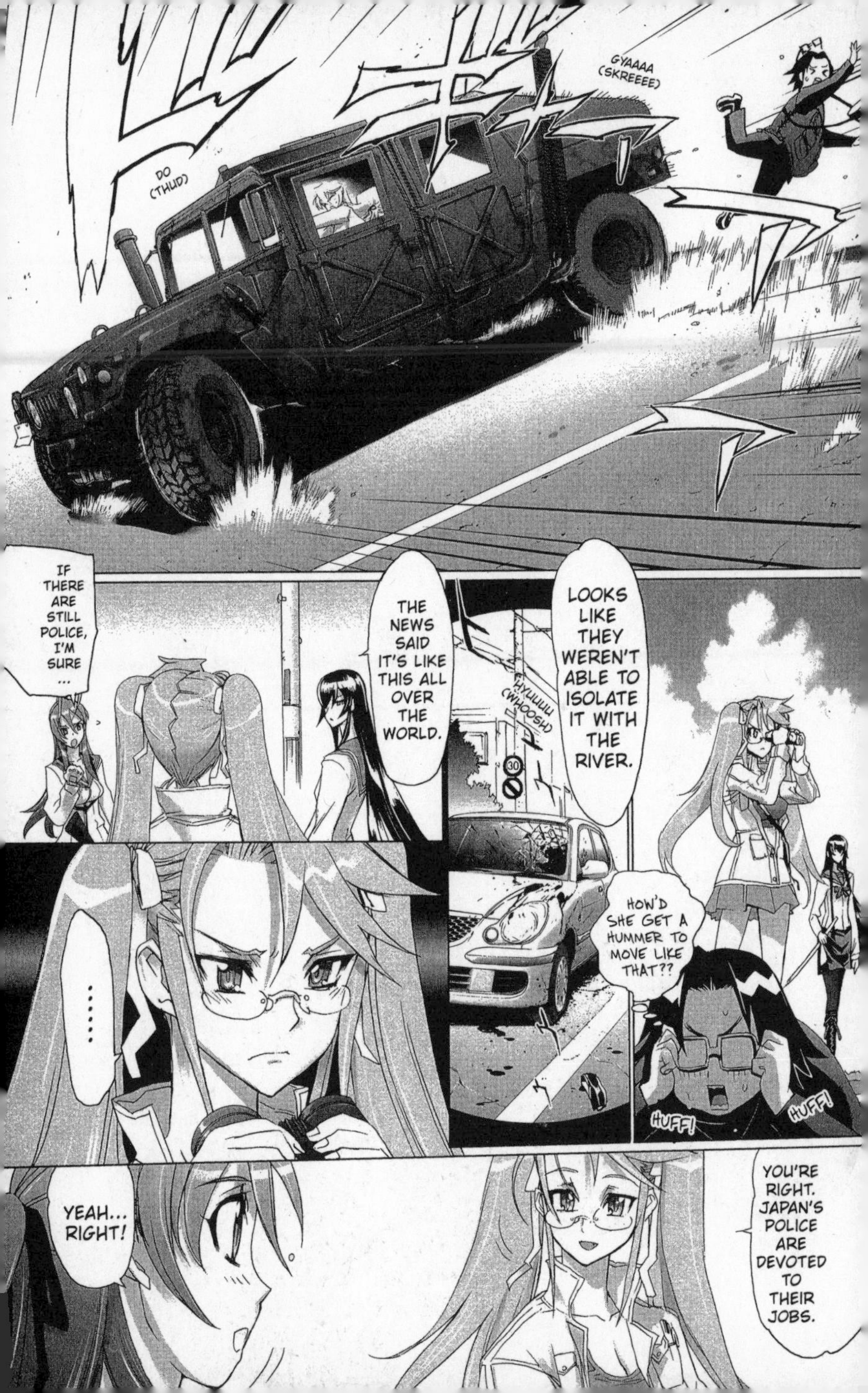
GYAAAA (SKREEEE)
DO (THUD)
LOOKS LIKE THEY WEREN'T ABLE TO ISOLATE IT WITH THE RIVER.
HYUUUU (WHOOSH)
THE NEWS SAID IT'S LIKE THIS ALL OVER THE WORLD.
IF THERE ARE STILL POLICE, I'M SURE ...
HOW'D SHE GET A HUMMER TO MOVE LIKE THAT??
HUFF!
HUFF!
......
YOU'RE RIGHT. JAPAN'S POLICE ARE DEVOTED TO THEIR JOBS.
YEAH... RIGHT!

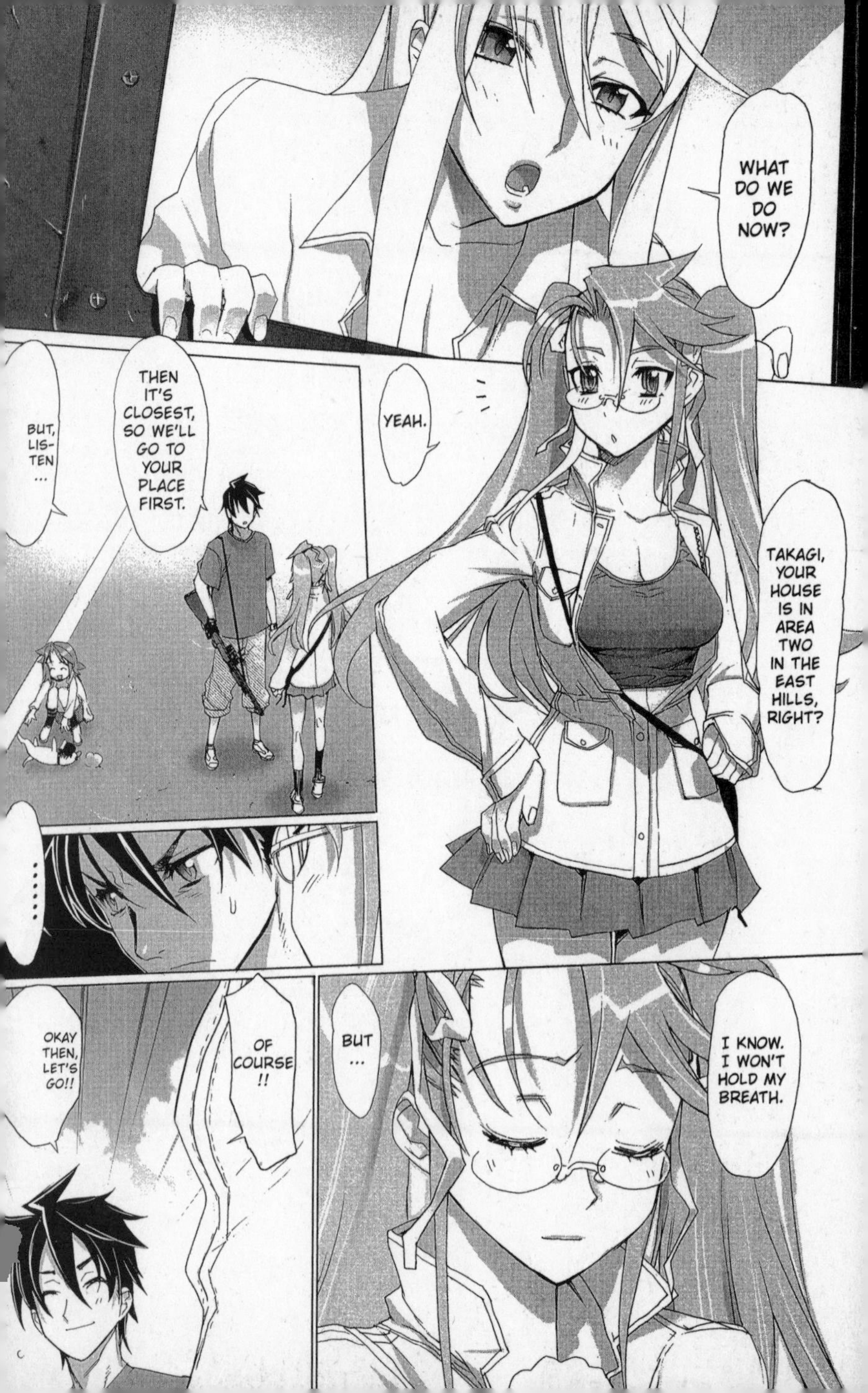
WHAT DO WE DO NOW?
TAKAGI, YOUR HOUSE IS IN AREA TWO IN THE EAST HILLS, RIGHT?
YEAH.
THEN IT'S CLOSEST, SO WE'LL GO TO YOUR PLACE FIRST.
BUT, LIS-TEN ...
......
I KNOW. I WON'T HOLD MY BREATH.
BUT ...
OF COURSE !!
OKAY THEN, LET'S GO!!

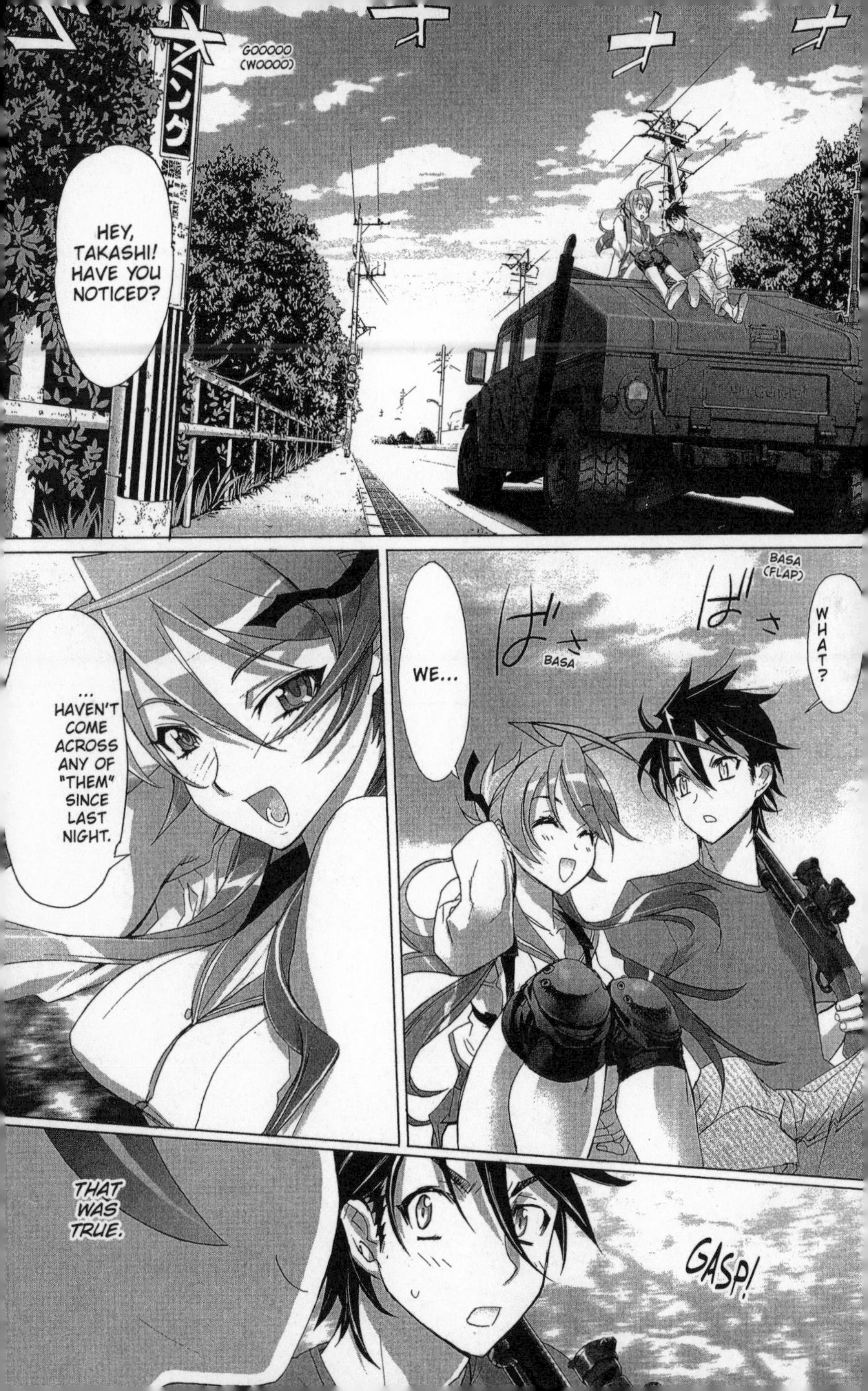
GOOOOO (WOOOO)
HEY, TAKASHI! HAVE YOU NOTICED?
BASA (FLAP)
WHAT?
BASA
WE...
... HAVEN'T COME ACROSS ANY OF "THEM" SINCE LAST NIGHT.
GASP!
THAT WAS TRUE.

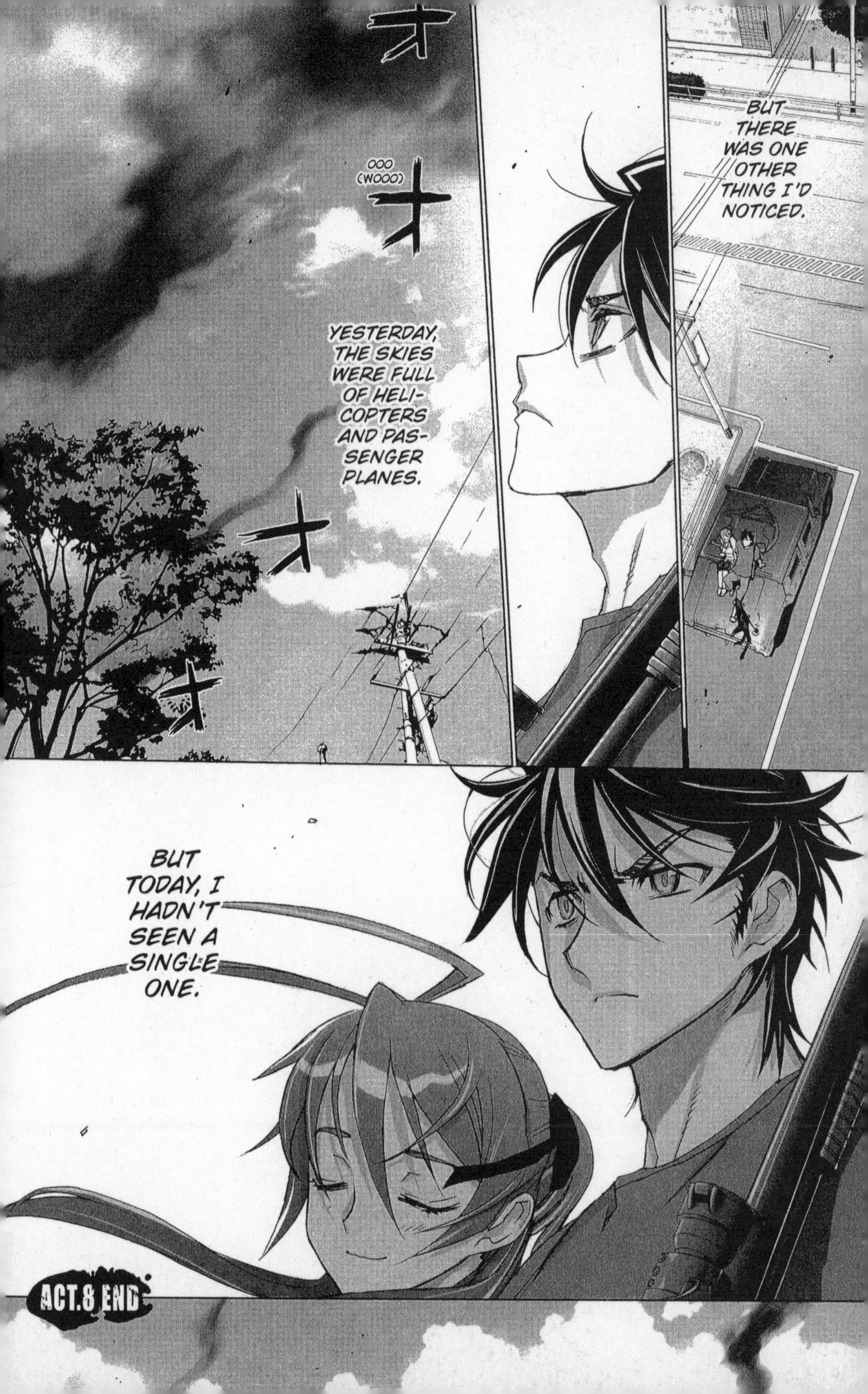
BUT THERE WAS ONE OTHER THING I'D NOTICED.
OOO (WOOO)
YESTERDAY, THE SKIES WERE FULL OF HELI-COPTERS AND PAS-SENGER PLANES.
BUT TODAY, I HADN'T SEEN A SINGLE ONE.
ACT.8 END

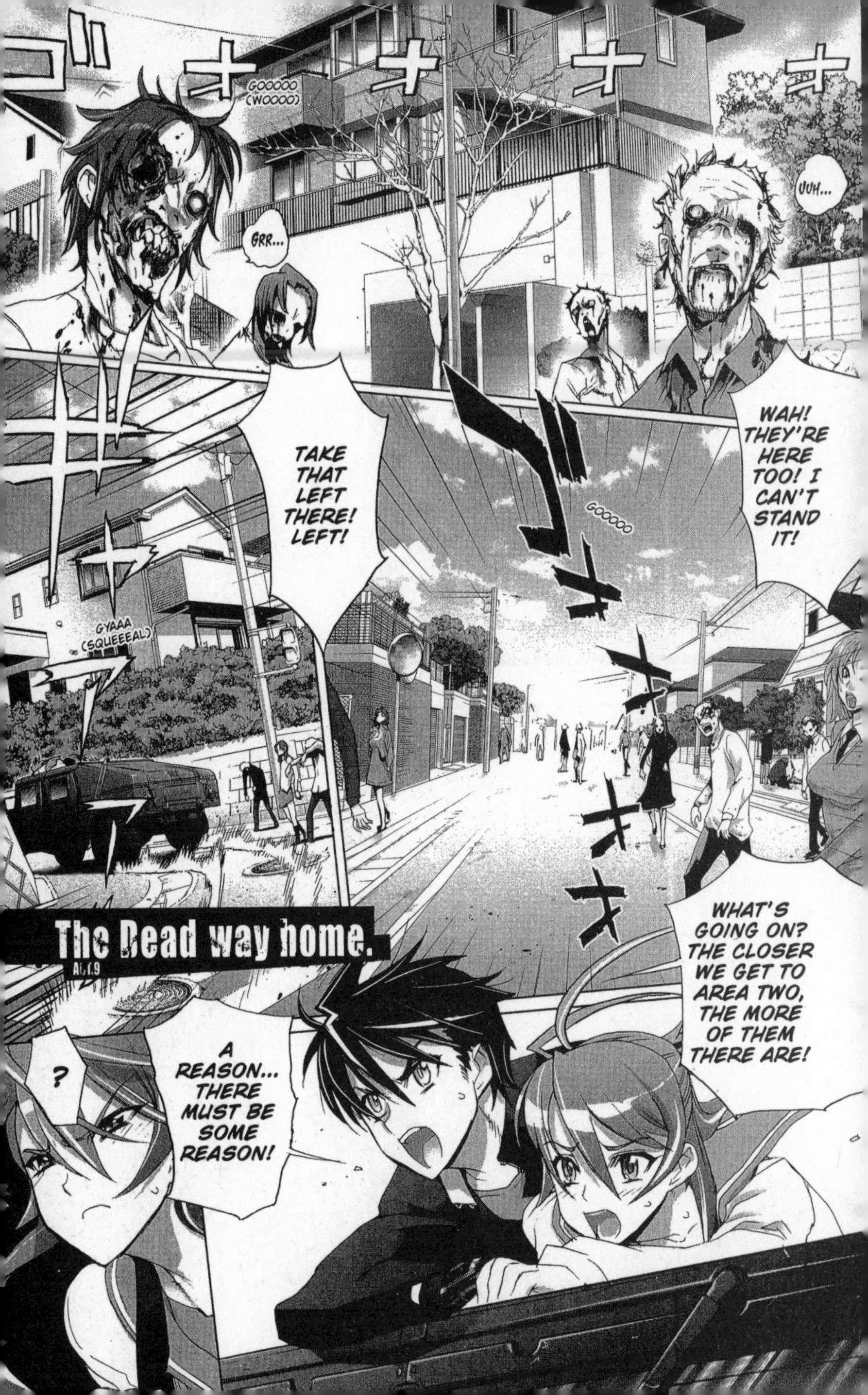
UUH...
GOOOOO (WOOOO)
GRR...
WAH! THEY'RE HERE TOO! I CAN'T STAND IT!
GOOOOO
TAKE THAT LEFT THERE! LEFT!
GYAAA (SQUEEEAL)
The Dead way home.
ACT.9
WHAT'S GOING ON? THE CLOSER WE GET TO AREA TWO, THE MORE OF THEM THERE ARE!
A REASON... THERE MUST BE SOME REASON!
?

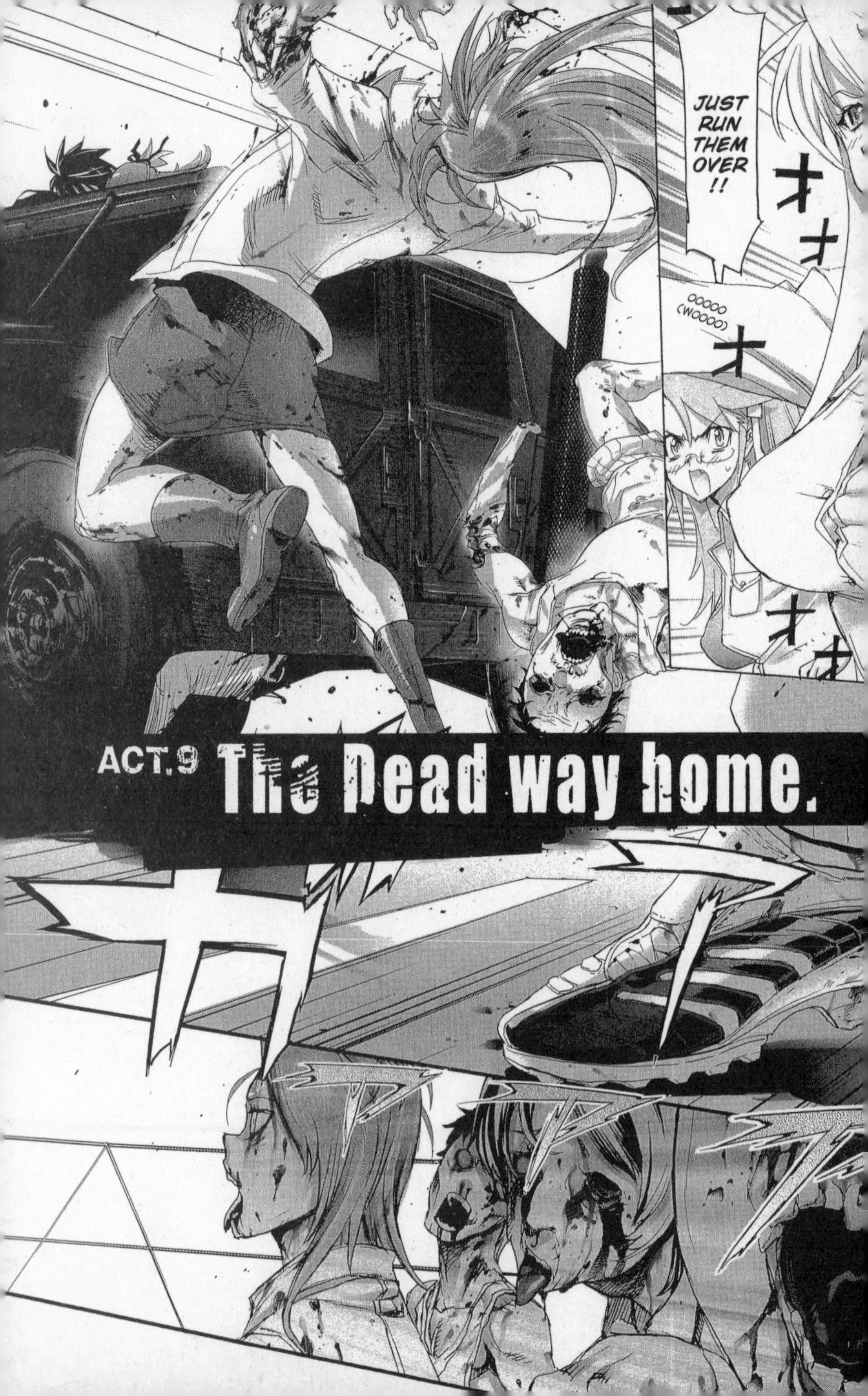
JUST RUN THEM OVER !!
OOOOO (WOOOO)
ACT.9 The Dead way home.

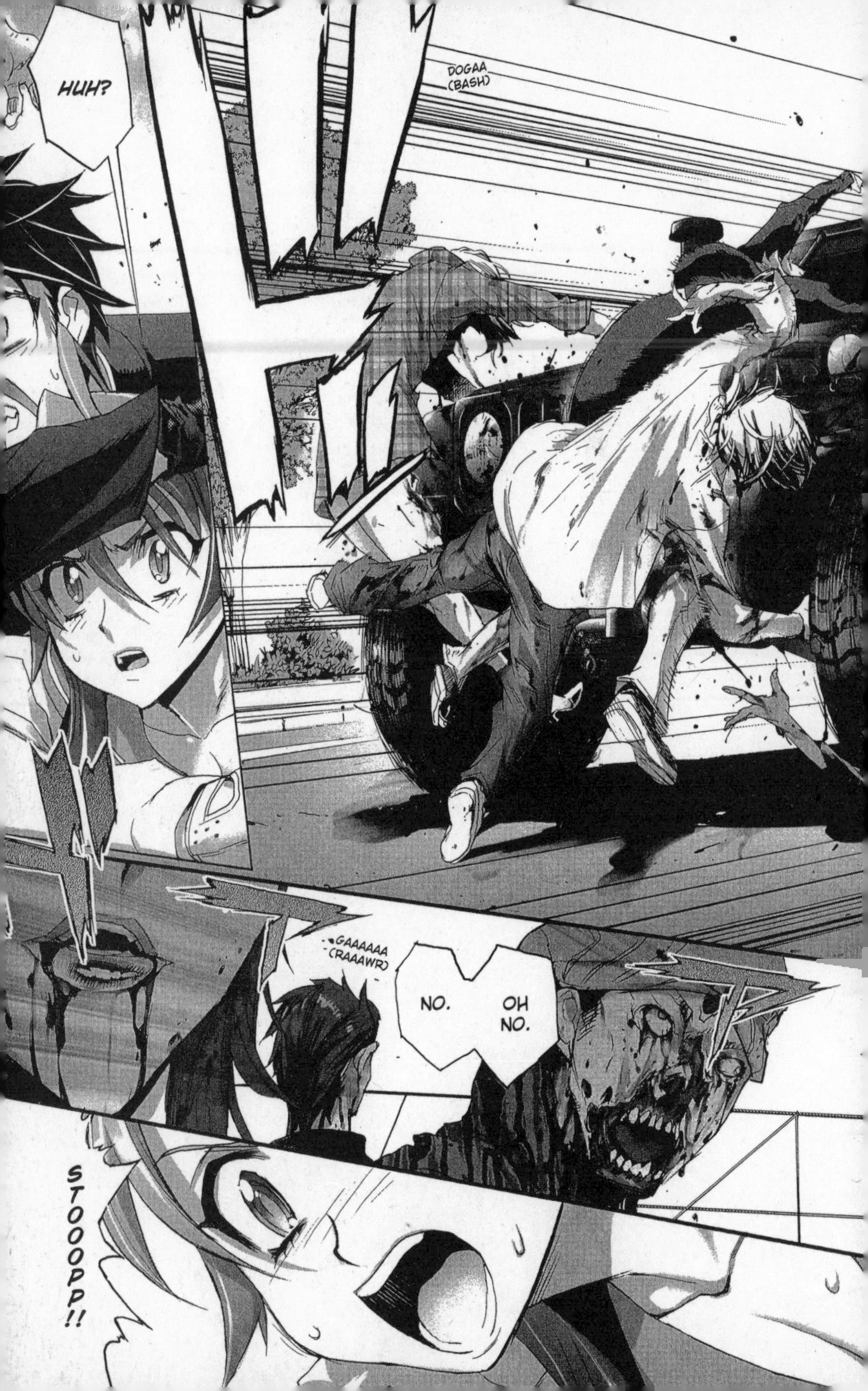
DOGAA (BASH)
HUH?
GAAAAAA (RAAAWR)
NO. OH NO.
STOOOPP!!

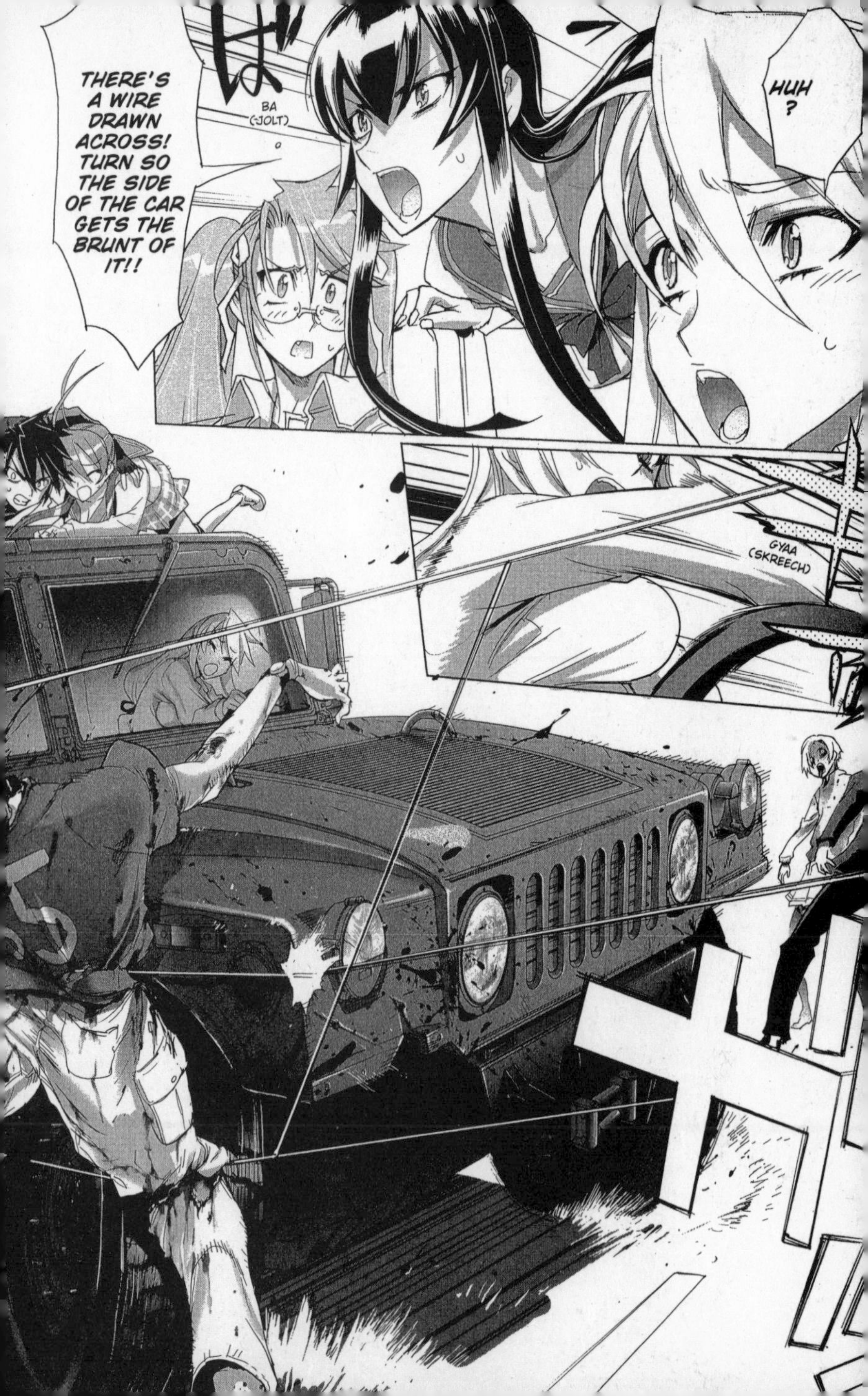
HUH ?
BA (-JOLT)
THERE'S A WIRE DRAWN ACROSS! TURN SO THE SIDE OF THE CAR GETS THE BRUNT OF IT!!
GYAA (SKREECH)

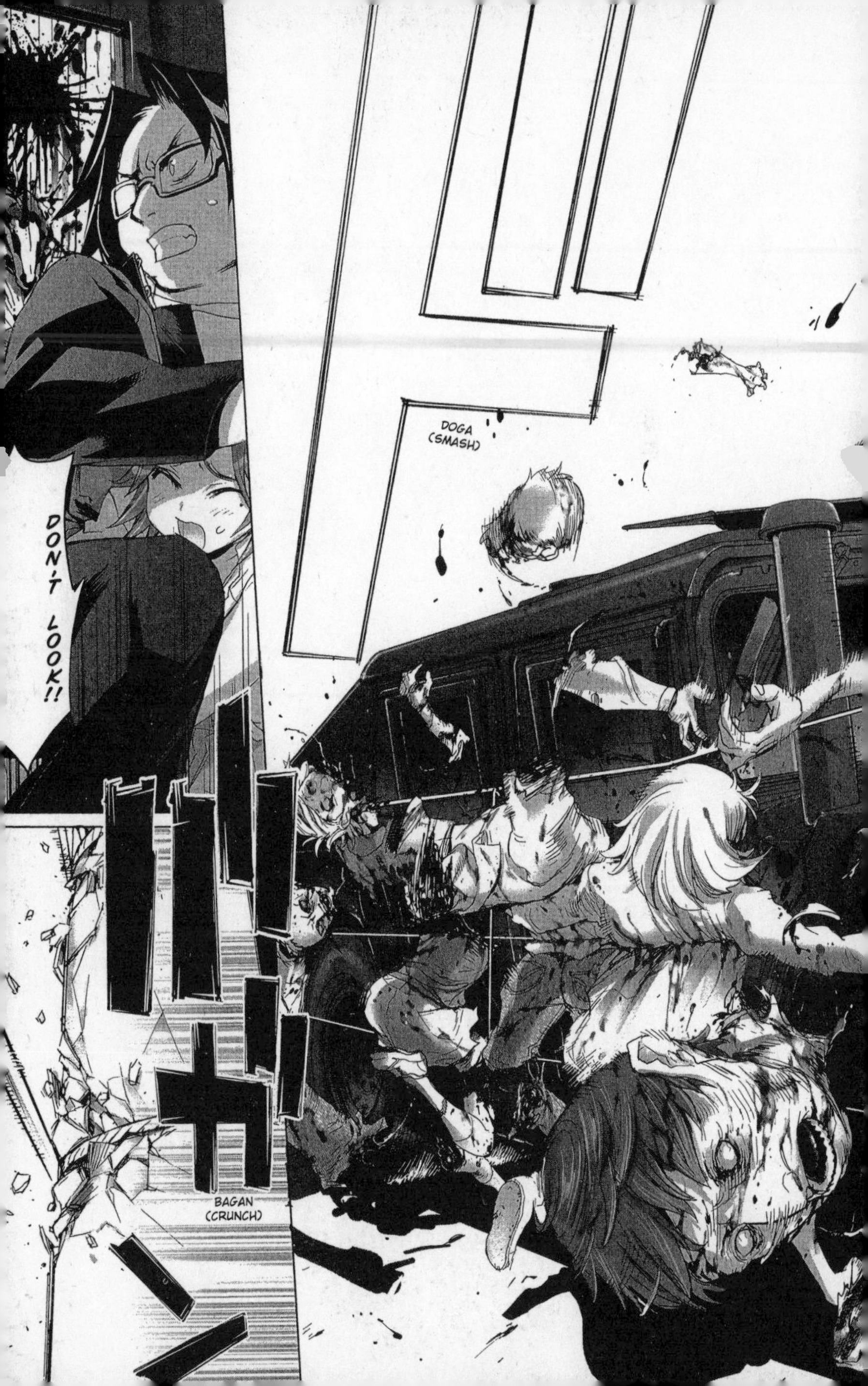
DOGA (SMASH)
DON'T LOOK!!
BAGAN (CRUNCH)

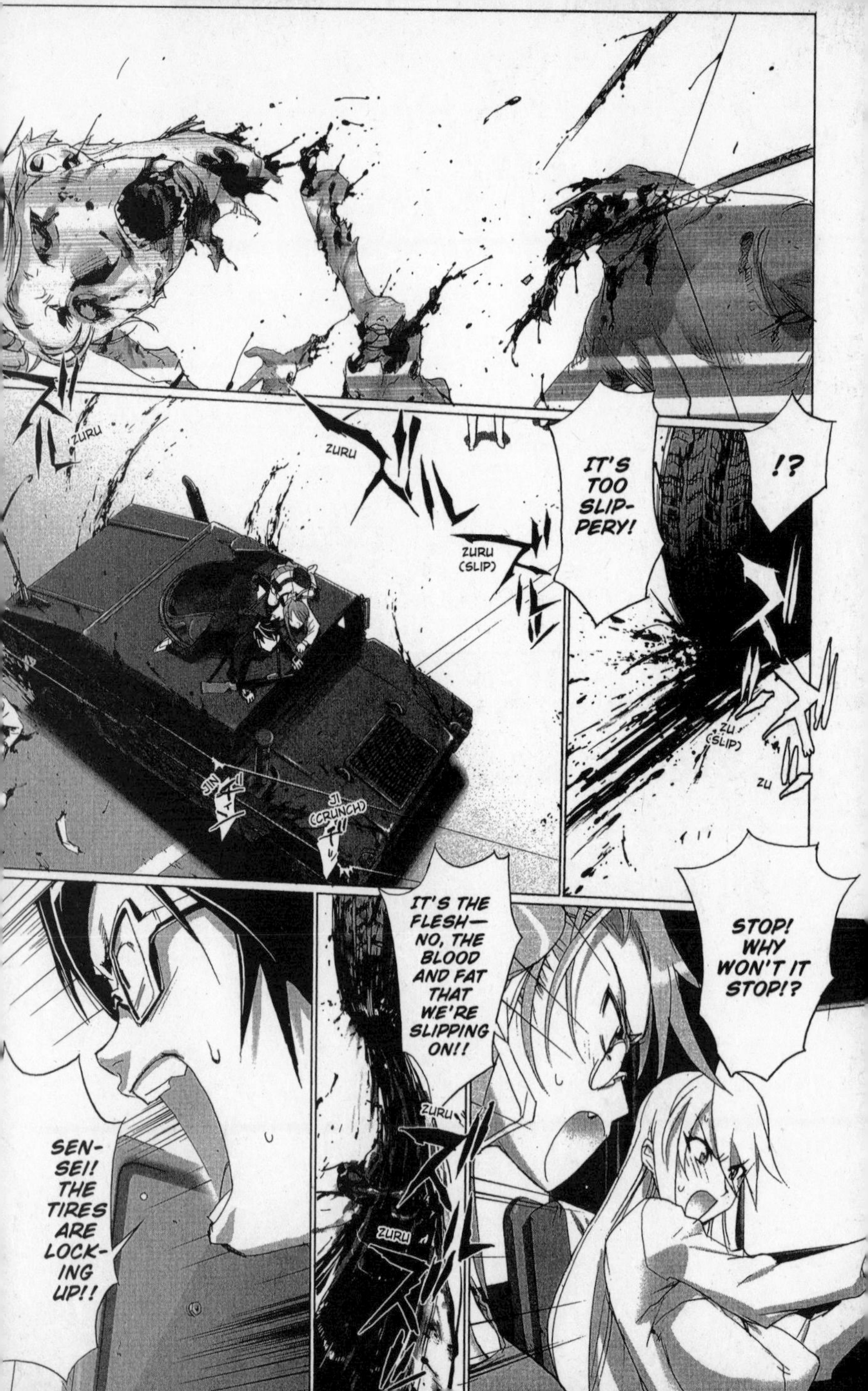
!?
IT'S TOO SLIPPERY!
ZU (SLIP)
ZU
ZURU
ZURU
ZURU (SLIP)
JI (CRUNCH)
JIN
STOP! WHY WON'T IT STOP!?
IT'S THE FLESH— NO, THE BLOOD AND FAT THAT WE'RE SLIPPING ON!!
ZURU
ZURU
SEN-SEI! THE TIRES ARE LOCKING UP!!

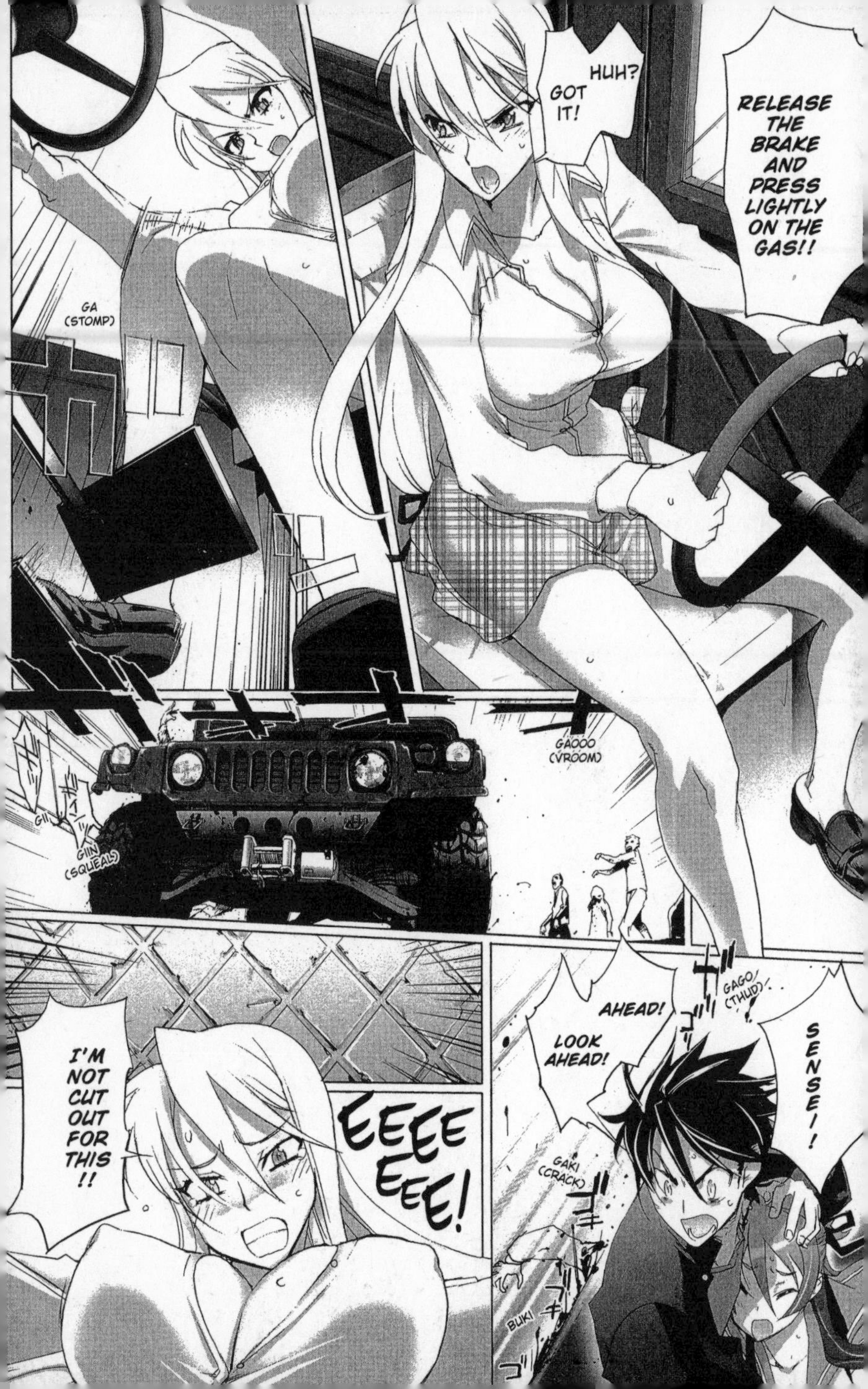
RELEASE THE BRAKE AND PRESS LIGHTLY ON THE GAS!!
HUH?
GOT IT!
GA (STOMP)
GAOOO (VROOM)
GII
GIIN (SQUEAL)
SENSE!!
GAGO! (THUD)
AHEAD!
LOOK AHEAD!
GAKI (CRACK)
BUKI
EEEE EEE!
I'M NOT CUT OUT FOR THIS!!

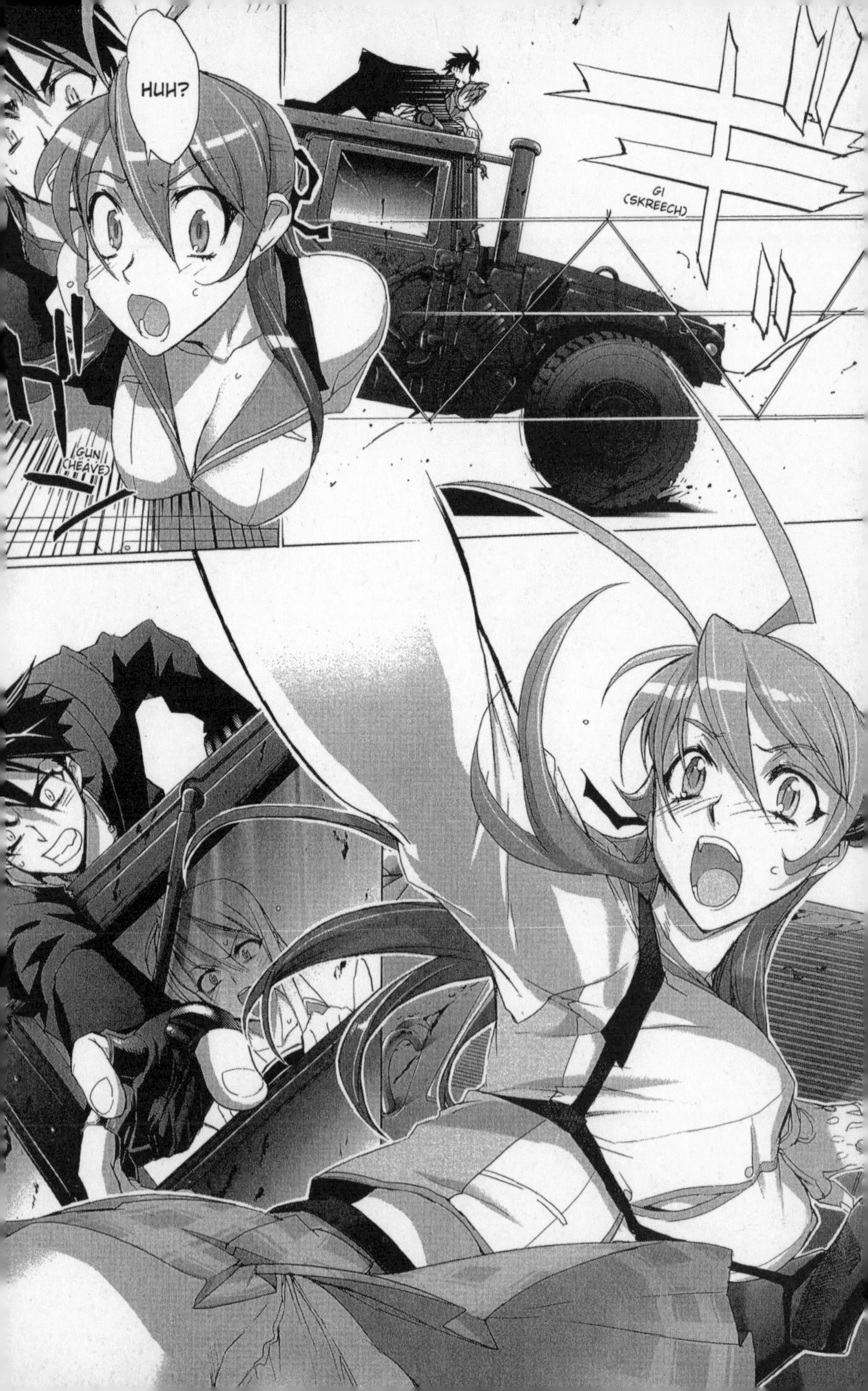
GI
(SKREECH)
HUH?
GUN
(HEAVE)

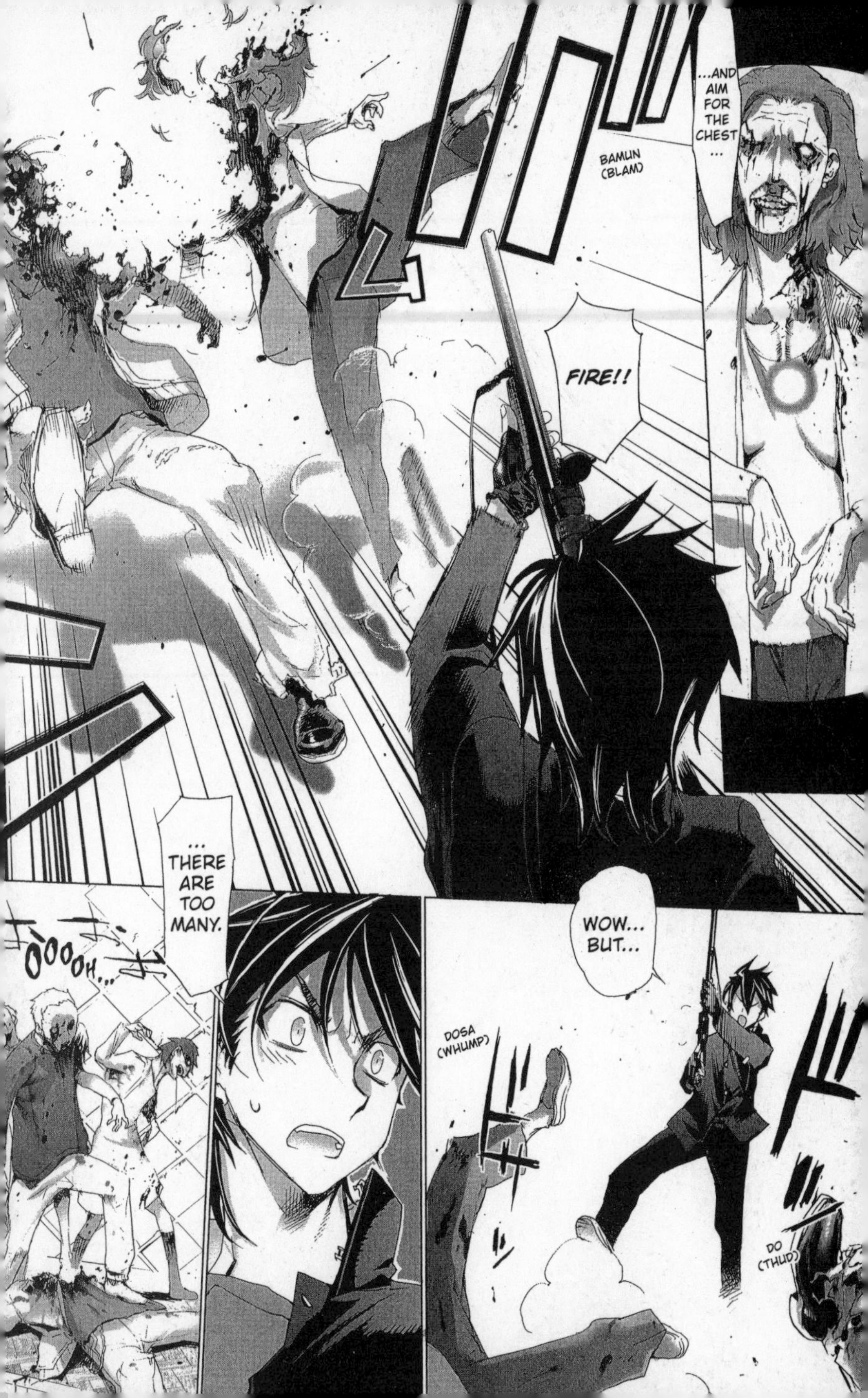
...AND AIM FOR THE CHEST...
BAMUN (BLAM)
FIRE!!
WOW... BUT...
DO (THUD)
DOSA (WHUMP)
... THERE ARE TOO MANY.
ÒOOOH...

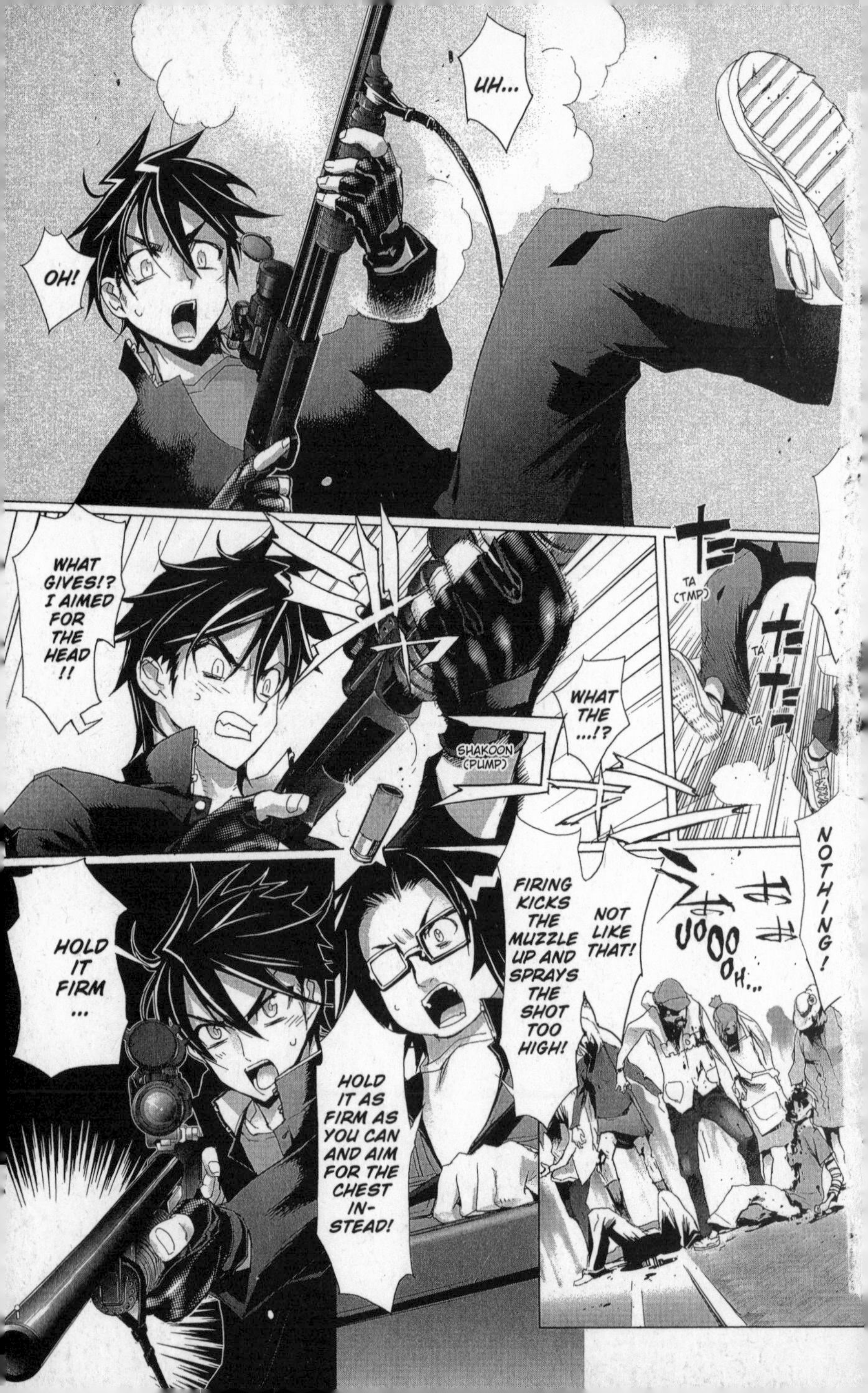
UH...
OH!
TA (TMP)
TA
TA
WHAT THE ...!?
SHAKOON (PUMP)
WHAT GIVES!? I AIMED FOR THE HEAD!!
NOTHING!
UOOOOH...
NOT LIKE THAT!
FIRING KICKS THE MUZZLE UP AND SPRAYS THE SHOT TOO HIGH!
HOLD IT AS FIRM AS YOU CAN AND AIM FOR THE CHEST IN-STEAD!
HOLD IT FIRM ...

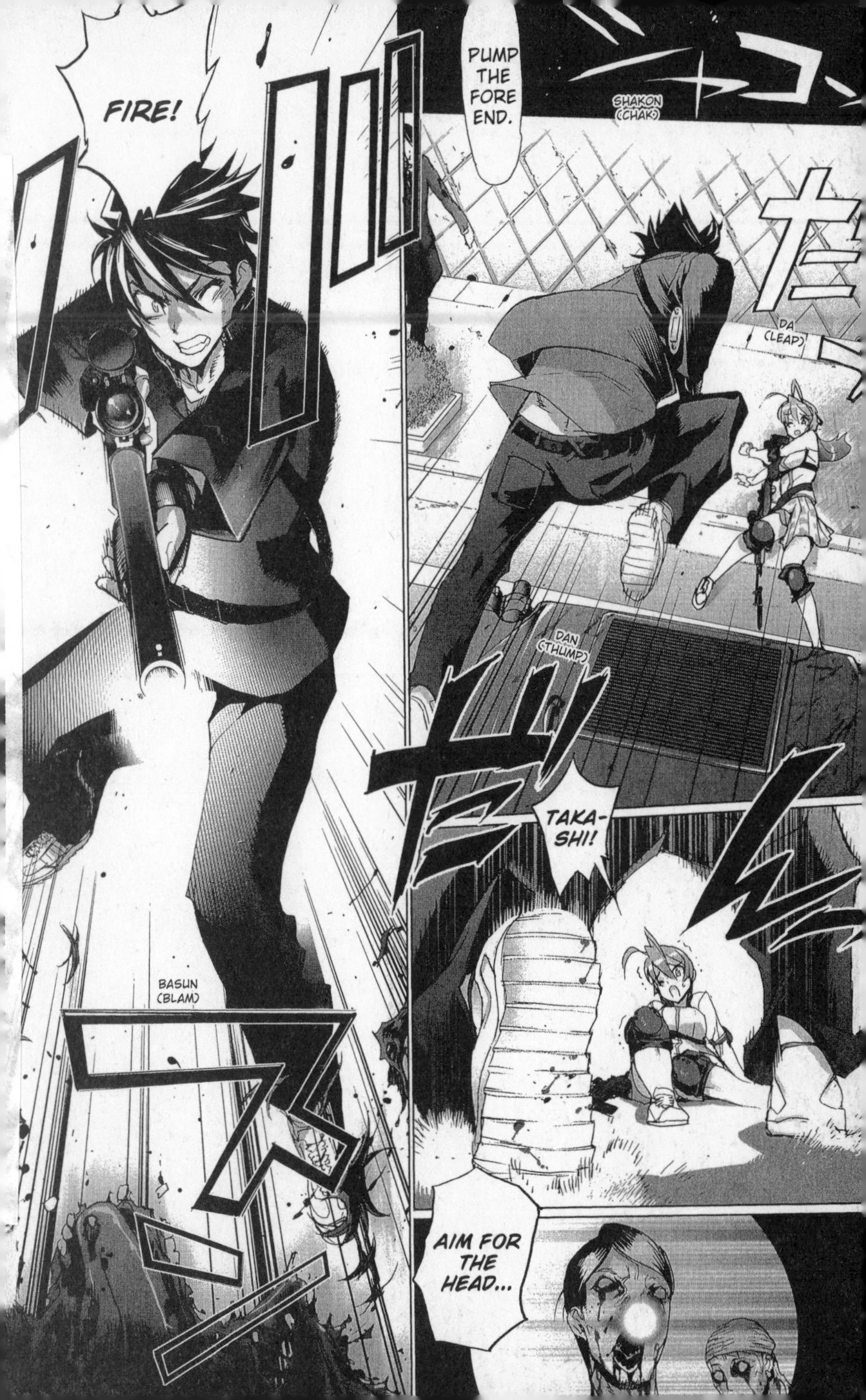
PUMP THE FORE END.
SHAKON (CHAK)
DA (LEAP)
DAN (THUMP)
TAKA-SHI!
AIM FOR THE HEAD...
FIRE!
BASUN (BLAM)

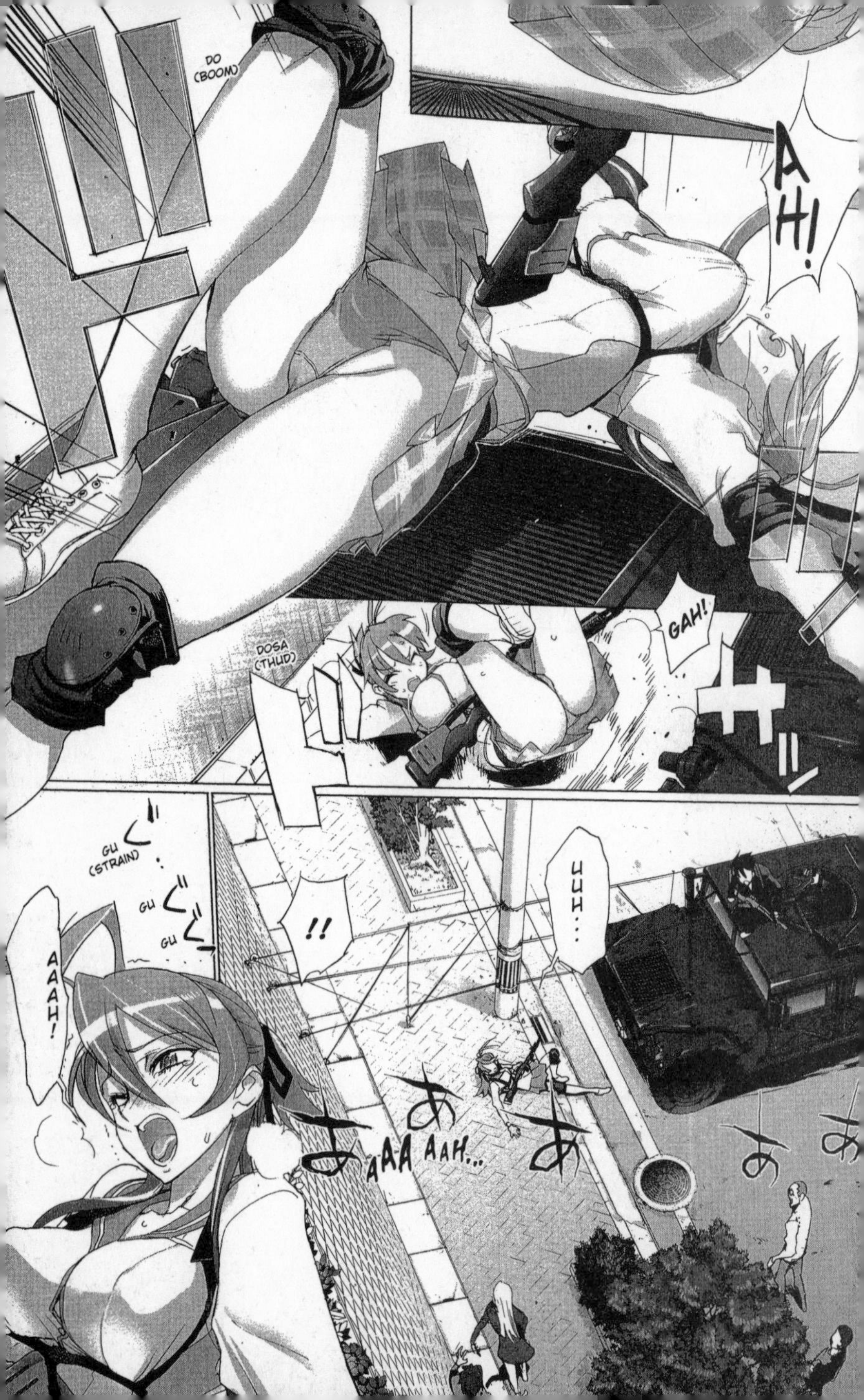
AH!
DO (BOOM)
GAH!
DOSA (THUD)
UUH...
!!
AAAA AAH...
GU (STRAIN)
GU
GU
AAAH!

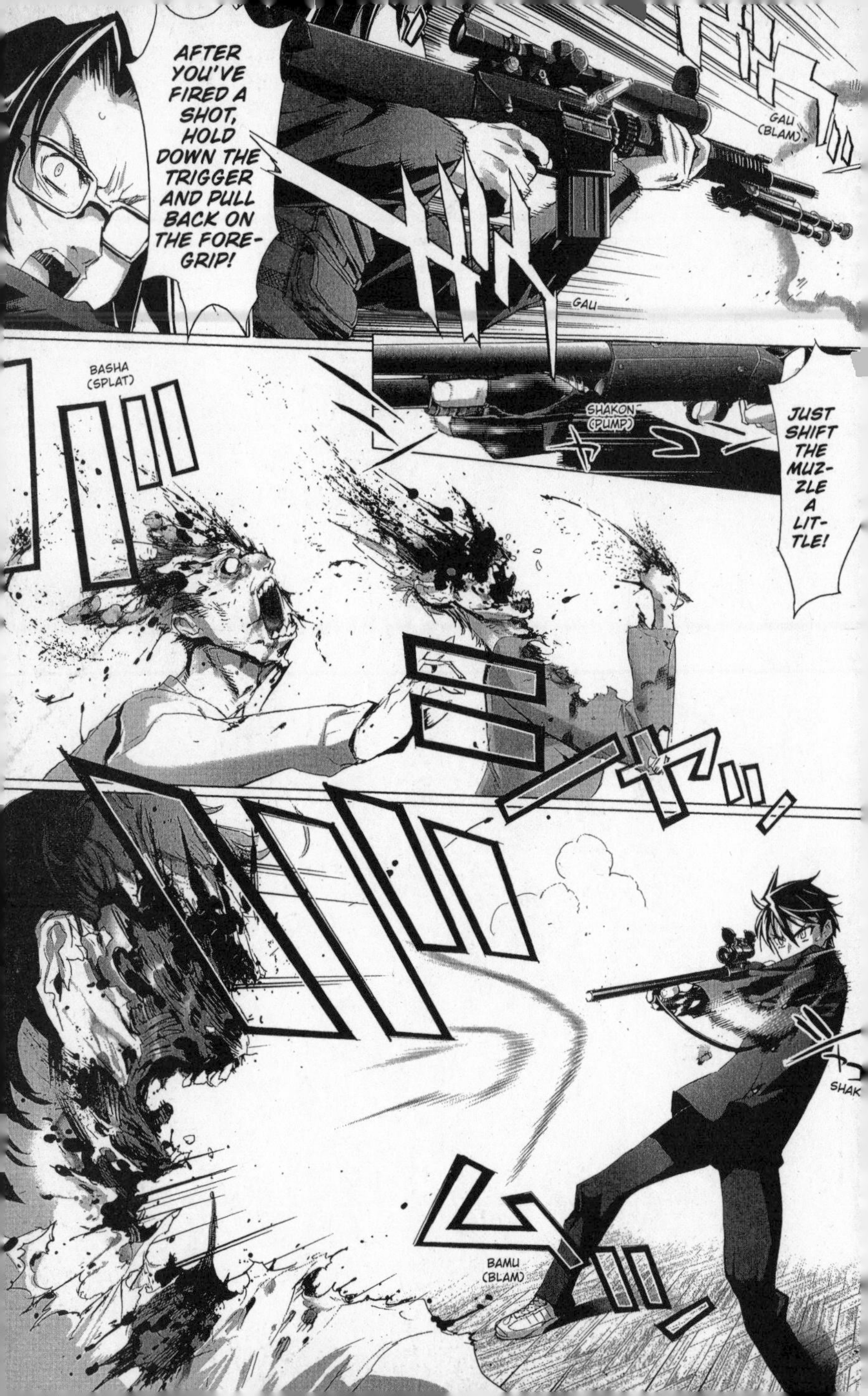
GAU (BLAM)
AFTER YOU'VE FIRED A SHOT, HOLD DOWN THE TRIGGER AND PULL BACK ON THE FORE-GRIP!
GAU
JUST SHIFT THE MUZ-ZLE A LIT-TLE!
SHAKON (PUMP)
BASHA (SPLAT)
SHAK
BAMU (BLAM)

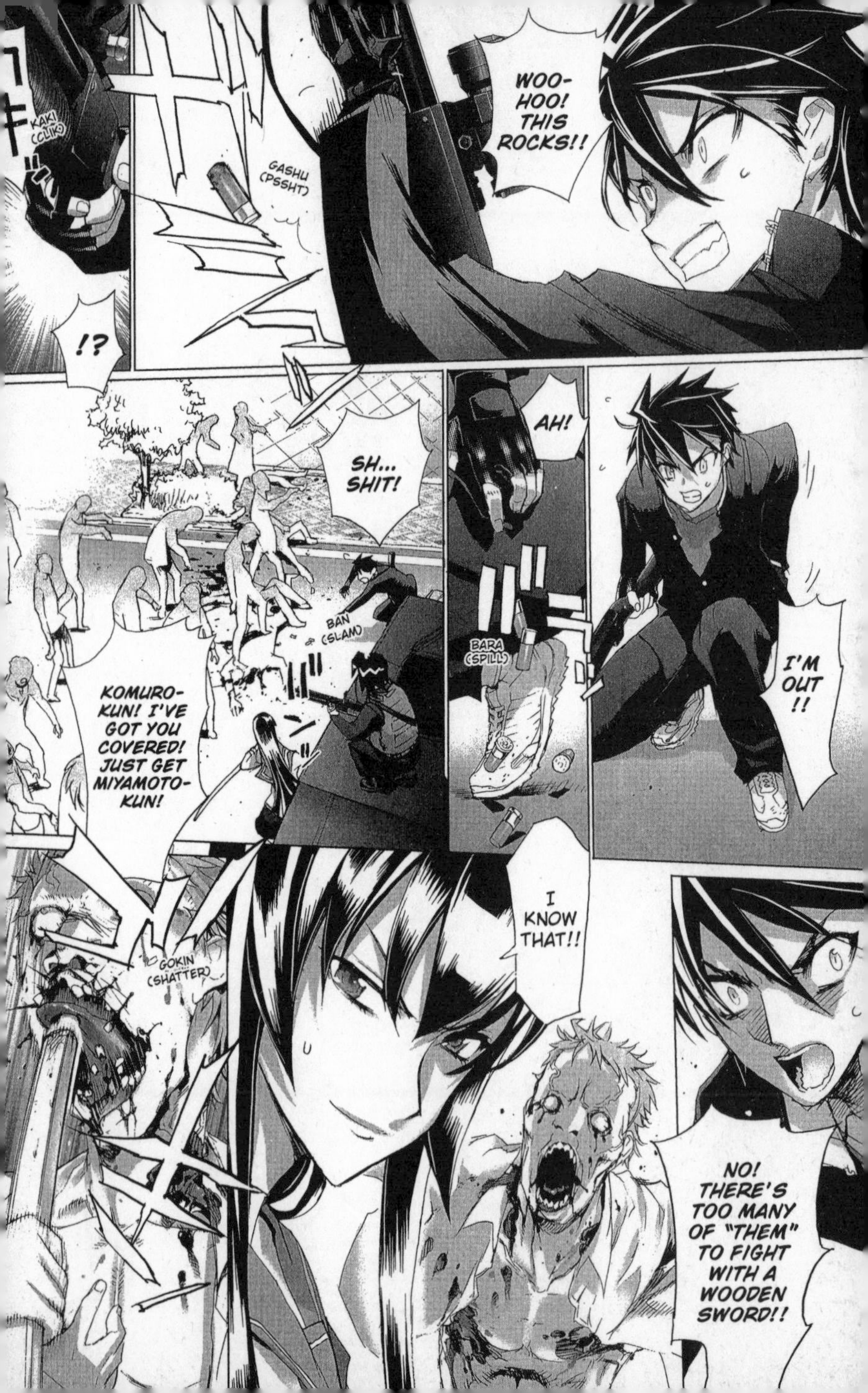
WOO-HOO! THIS ROCKS!!
GASHU (PSSHT)
KAKI (CLIK)
!?
I'M OUT!!
AH!
BARA (SPILL)
SH... SHIT!
BAN (SLAM)
KOMURO-KUN! I'VE GOT YOU COVERED! JUST GET MIYAMOTO-KUN!
NO! THERE'S TOO MANY OF "THEM" TO FIGHT WITH A WOODEN SWORD!!
I KNOW THAT!!
GOKIN (SHATTER)

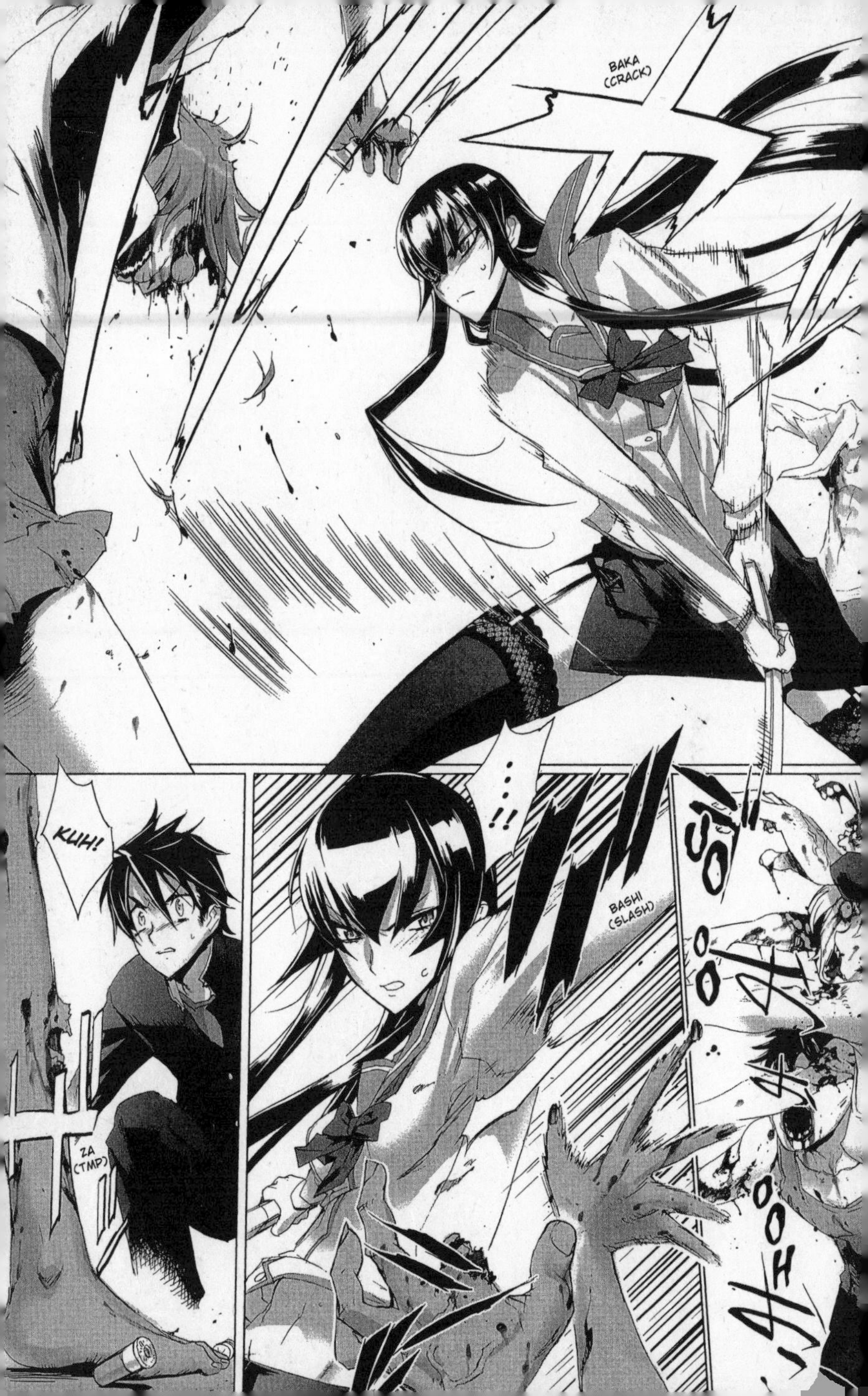
BAKA
(CRACK)
...!!
BASHI
(SLASH)
KUH!
ZA
(TMP)

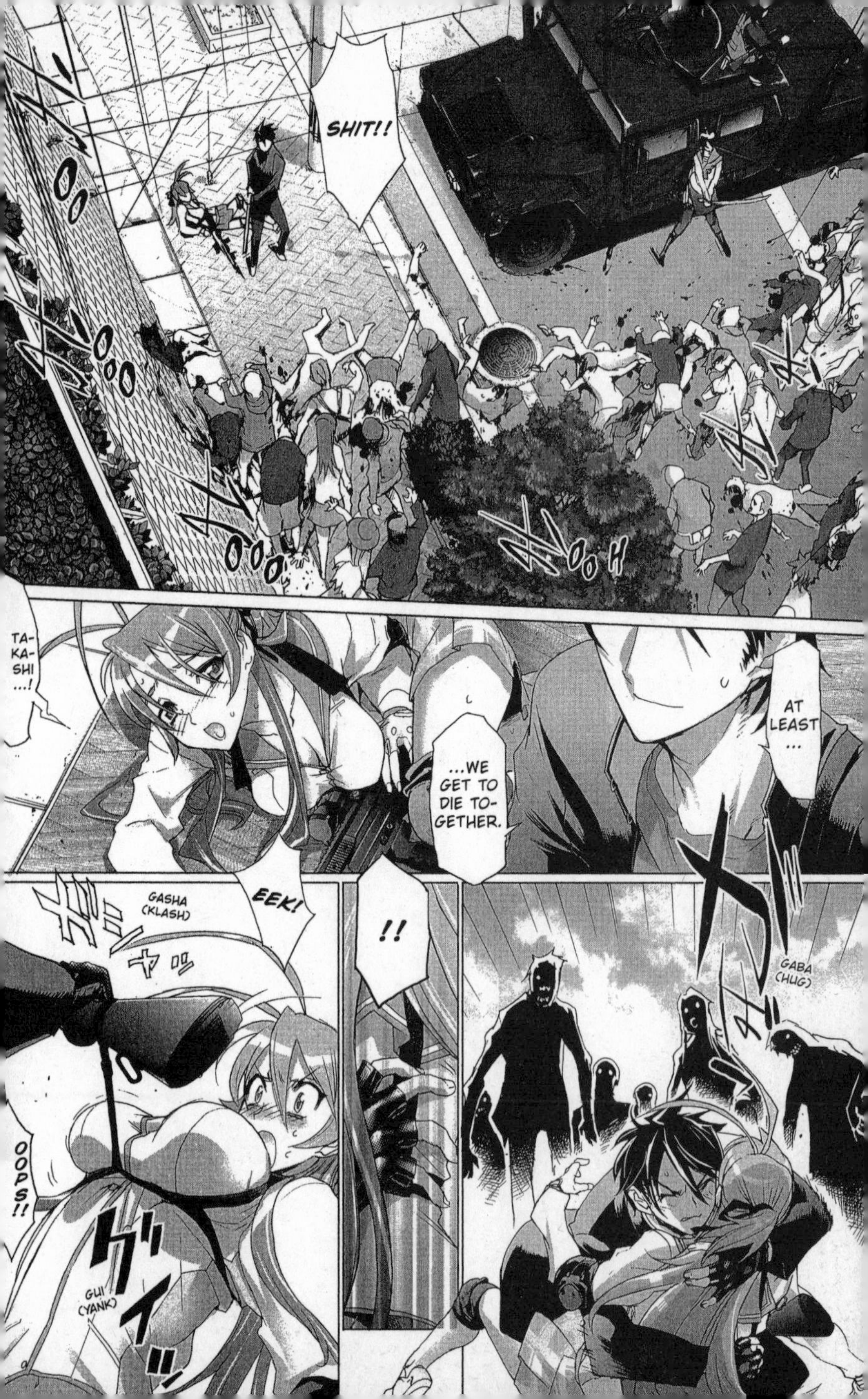
SHIT!!
AT LEAST ...
...WE GET TO DIE TO-GETHER.
TA-KA-SHI ...!
GABA (HUG)
!!
EEK!
GASHA (KLASH)
OOPS!!
GUI (YANK)

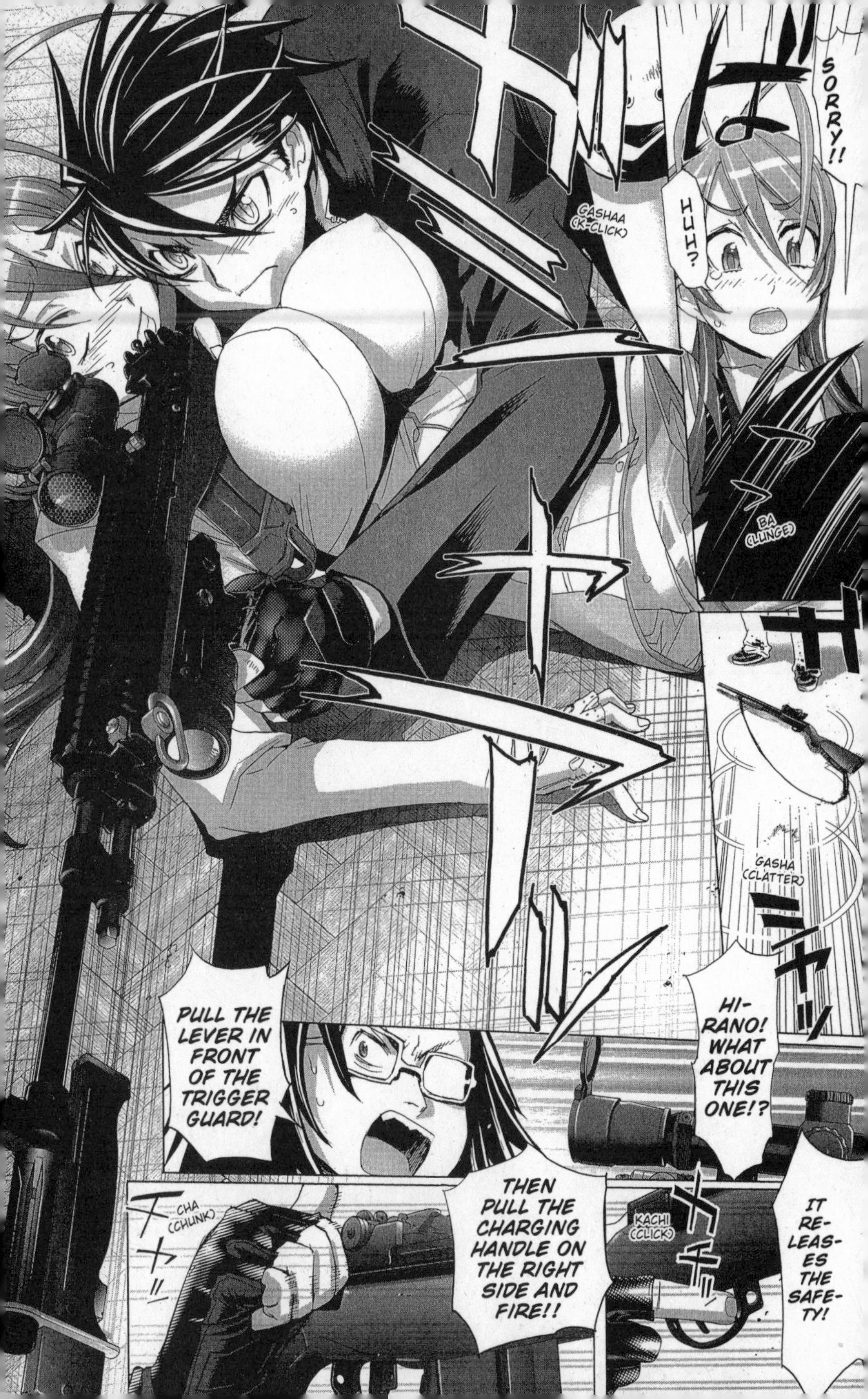
SORRY!!
HUH?
BA (LUNGE)
GASHAA (K-CLICK)
GASHA (CLATTER)
HI-RANO! WHAT ABOUT THIS ONE!?
PULL THE LEVER IN FRONT OF THE TRIGGER GUARD!
IT RE-LEAS-ES THE SAFE-TY!
KACHI (CLICK)
THEN PULL THE CHARGING HANDLE ON THE RIGHT SIDE AND FIRE!!
CHA (CHUNK)

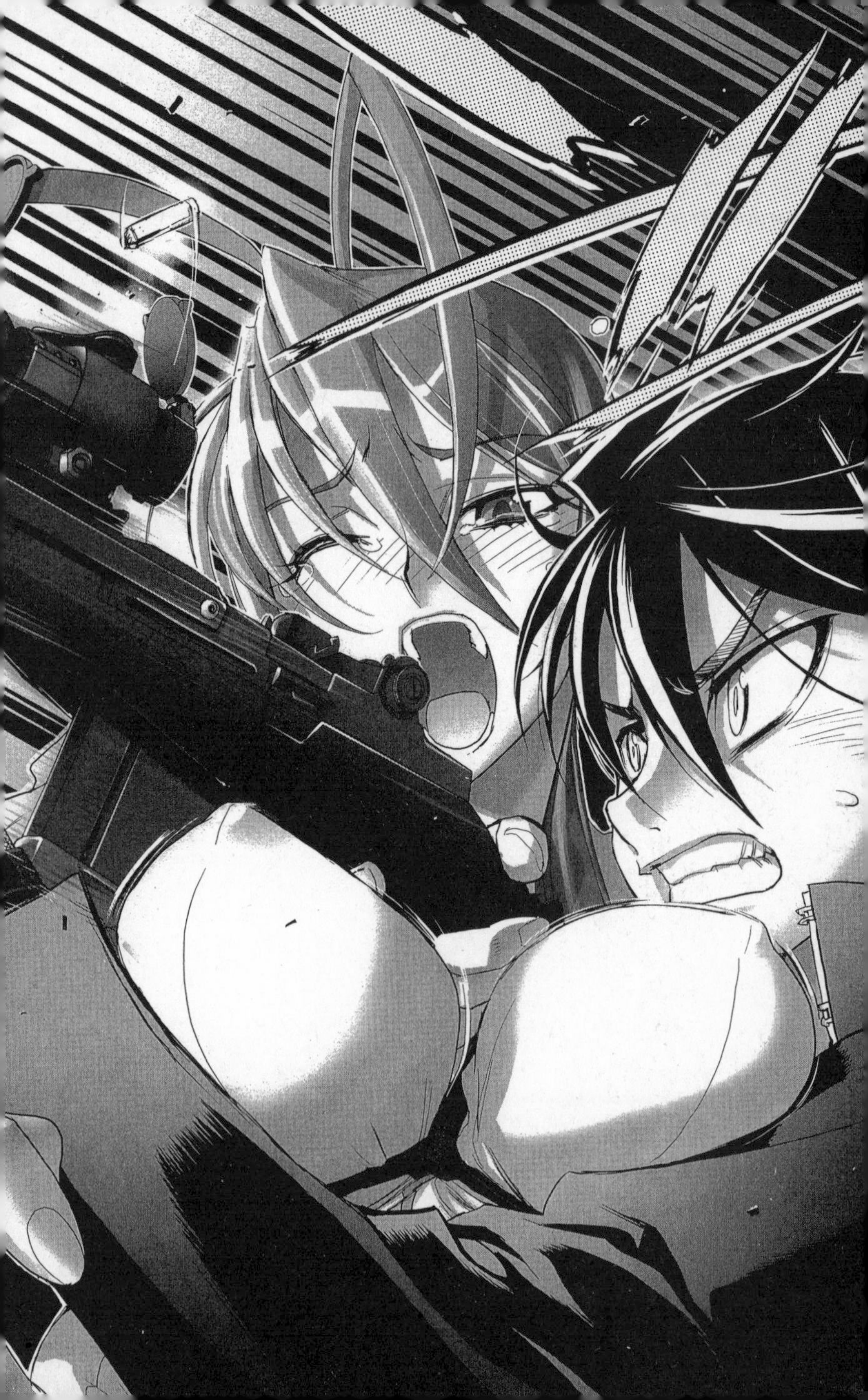

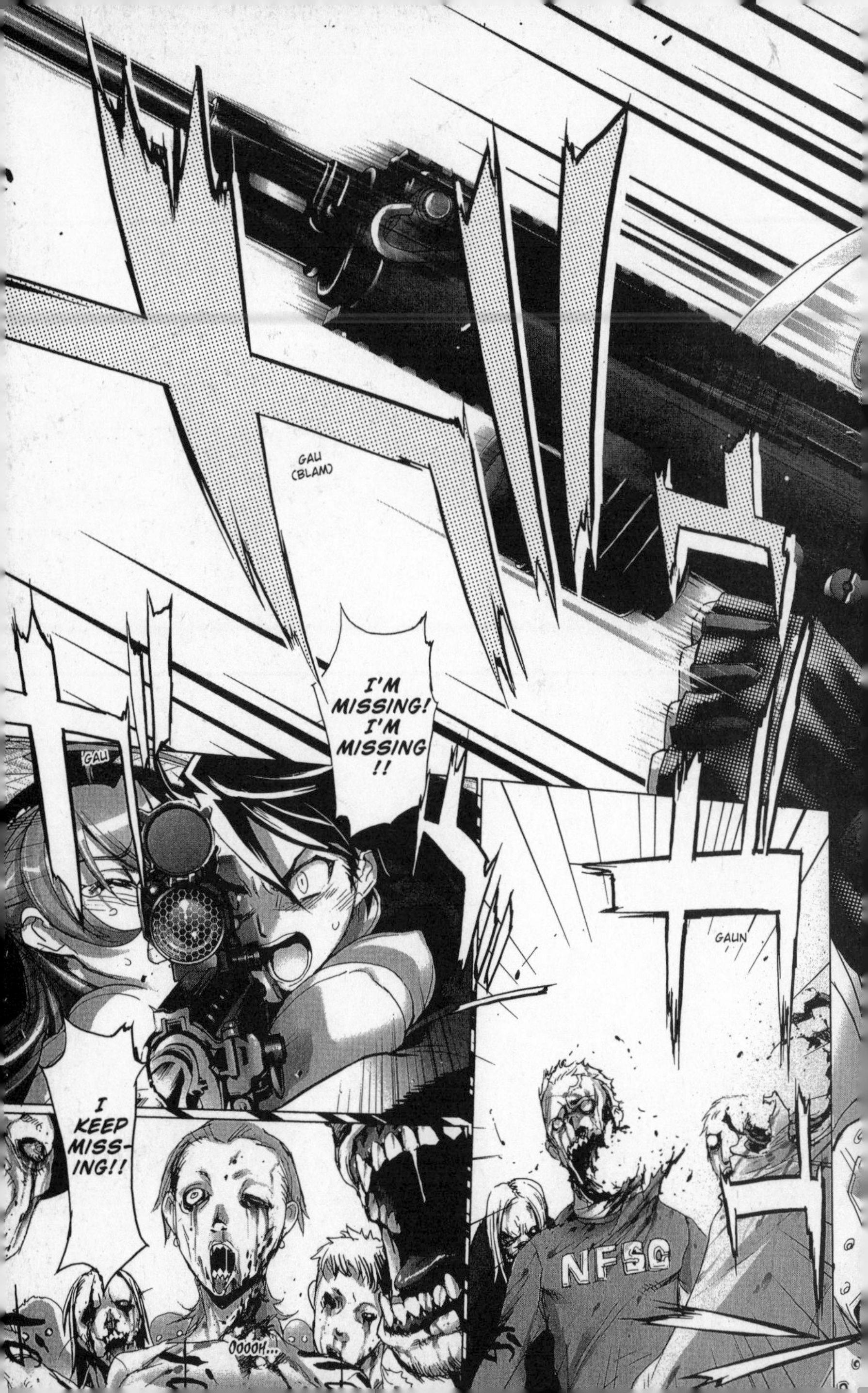
GAU
(BLAM)
I'M MISSING! I'M MISSING !!
GAU
GAUN
I KEEP MISS-ING!!
OOOOH...
NFSG

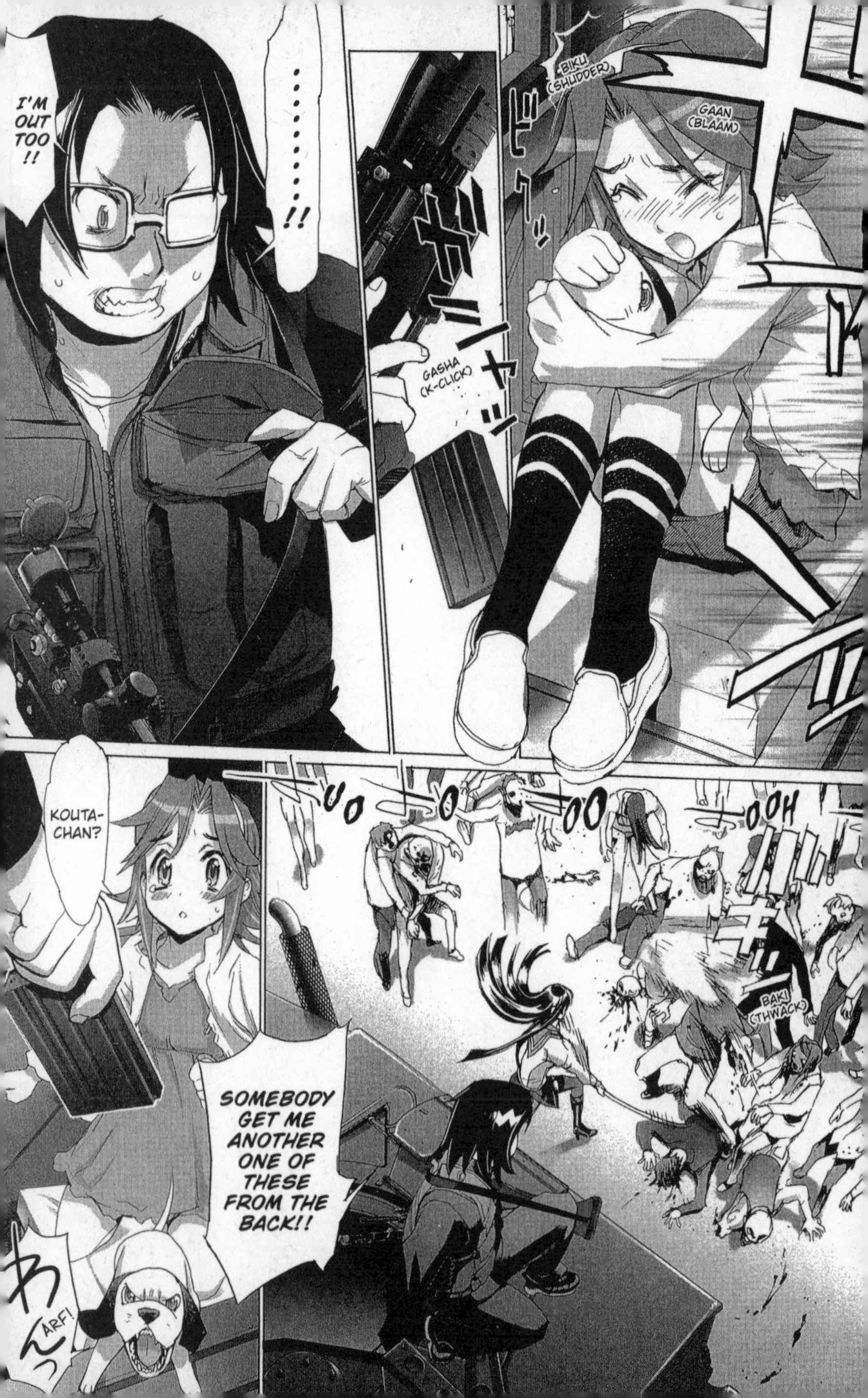
BIKU (SHUDDER)
GAAN (BLAAM)
GASHA (K-CLICK)
......!!
I'M OUT TOO!!
UO OO OOH
BAKI (THWACK)
SOMEBODY GET ME ANOTHER ONE OF THESE FROM THE BACK!!
KOUTA-CHAN?
ARF!

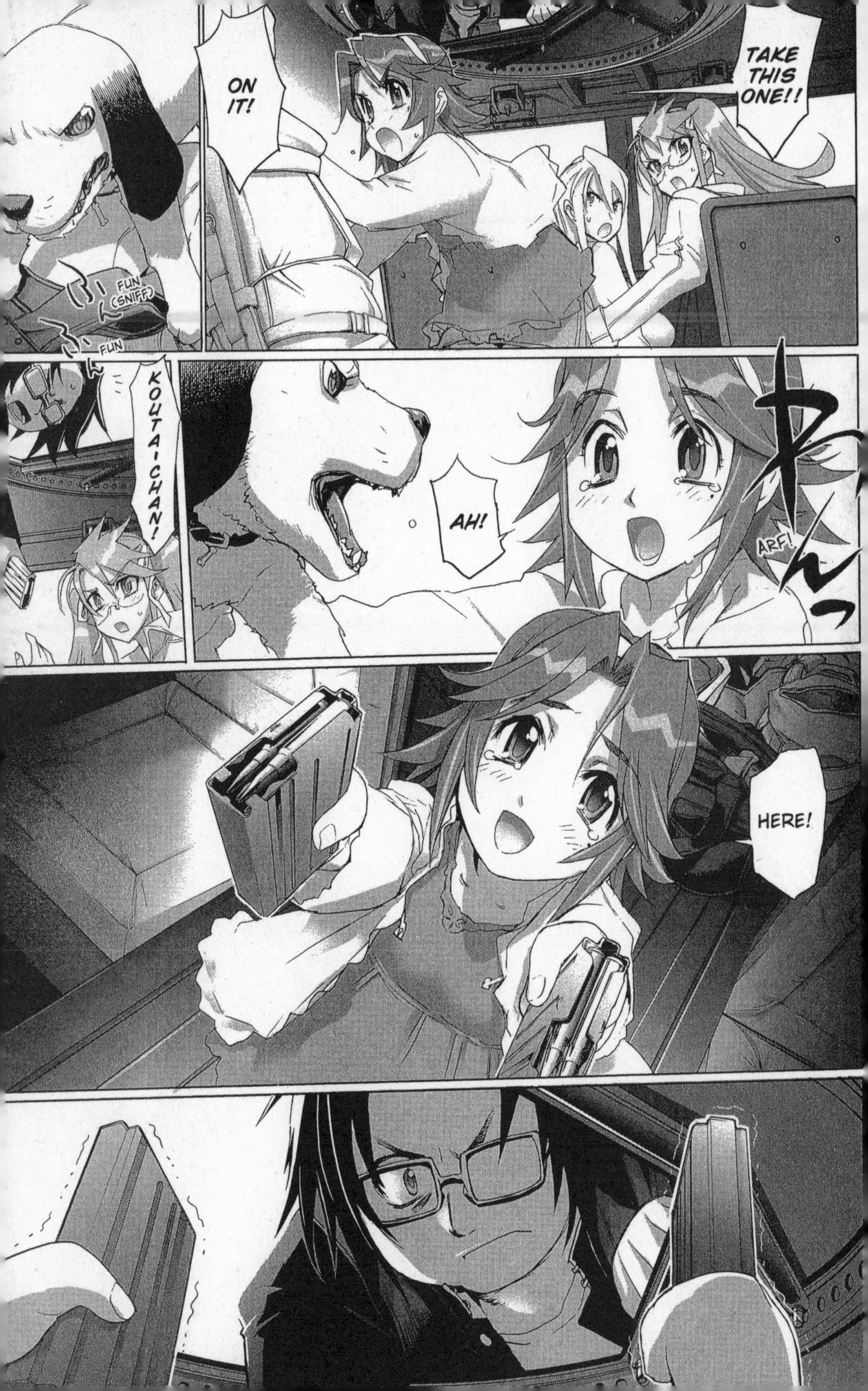

TAKE THIS ONE!!
ON IT!
FUN (SNIFF)
FUN
ARF!
AH!
KOUTAI-CHAN!
HERE!

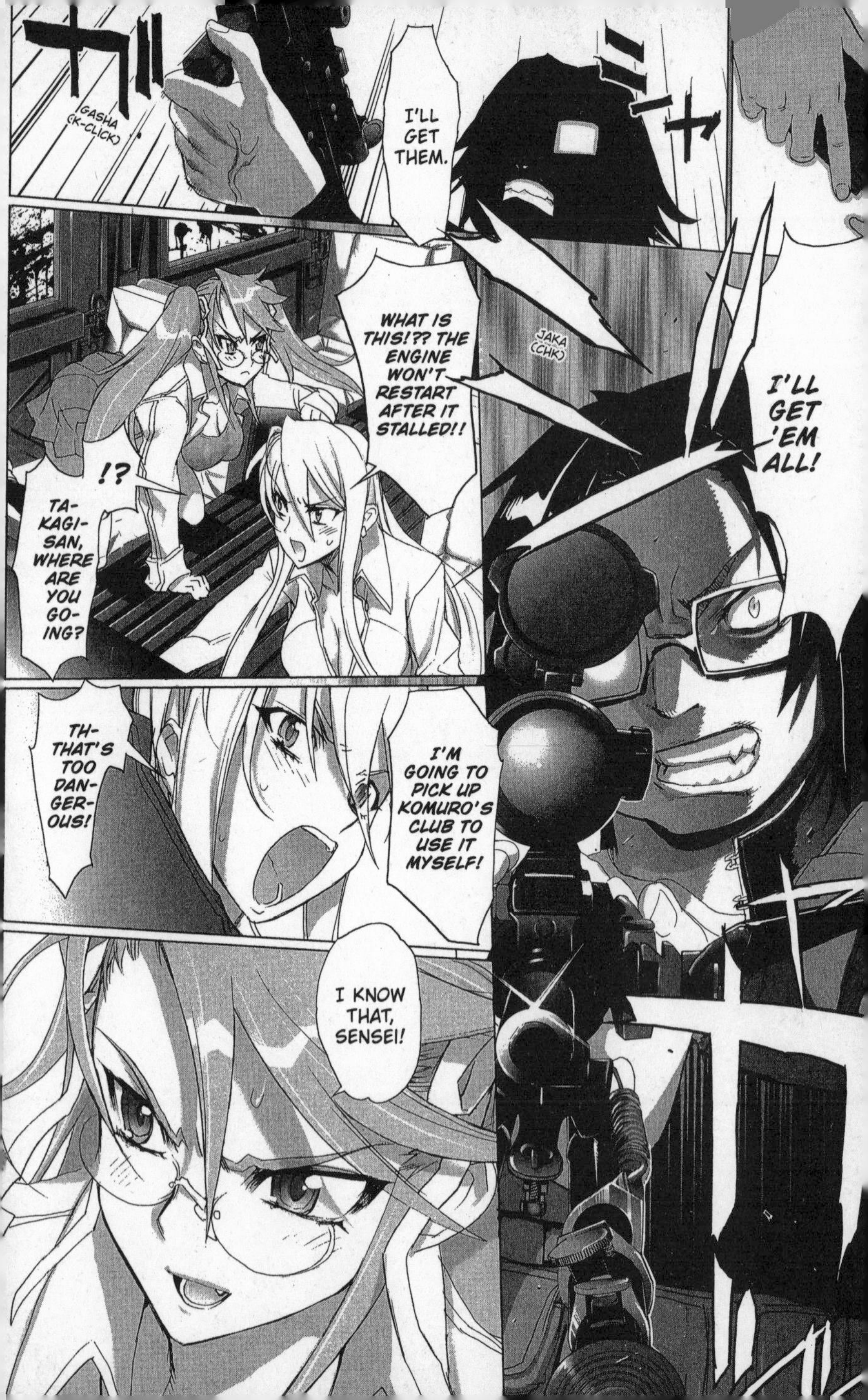
I'LL GET THEM.
GASHA (K-CLICK)
JAKA (CHK)
I'LL GET 'EM ALL!
WHAT IS THIS!?? THE ENGINE WON'T RESTART AFTER IT STALLED!!
!?
TA-KAGI-SAN, WHERE ARE YOU GO-ING?
I'M GOING TO PICK UP KOMURO'S CLUB TO USE IT MYSELF!
TH-THAT'S TOO DAN-GER-OUS!
I KNOW THAT, SENSEI!

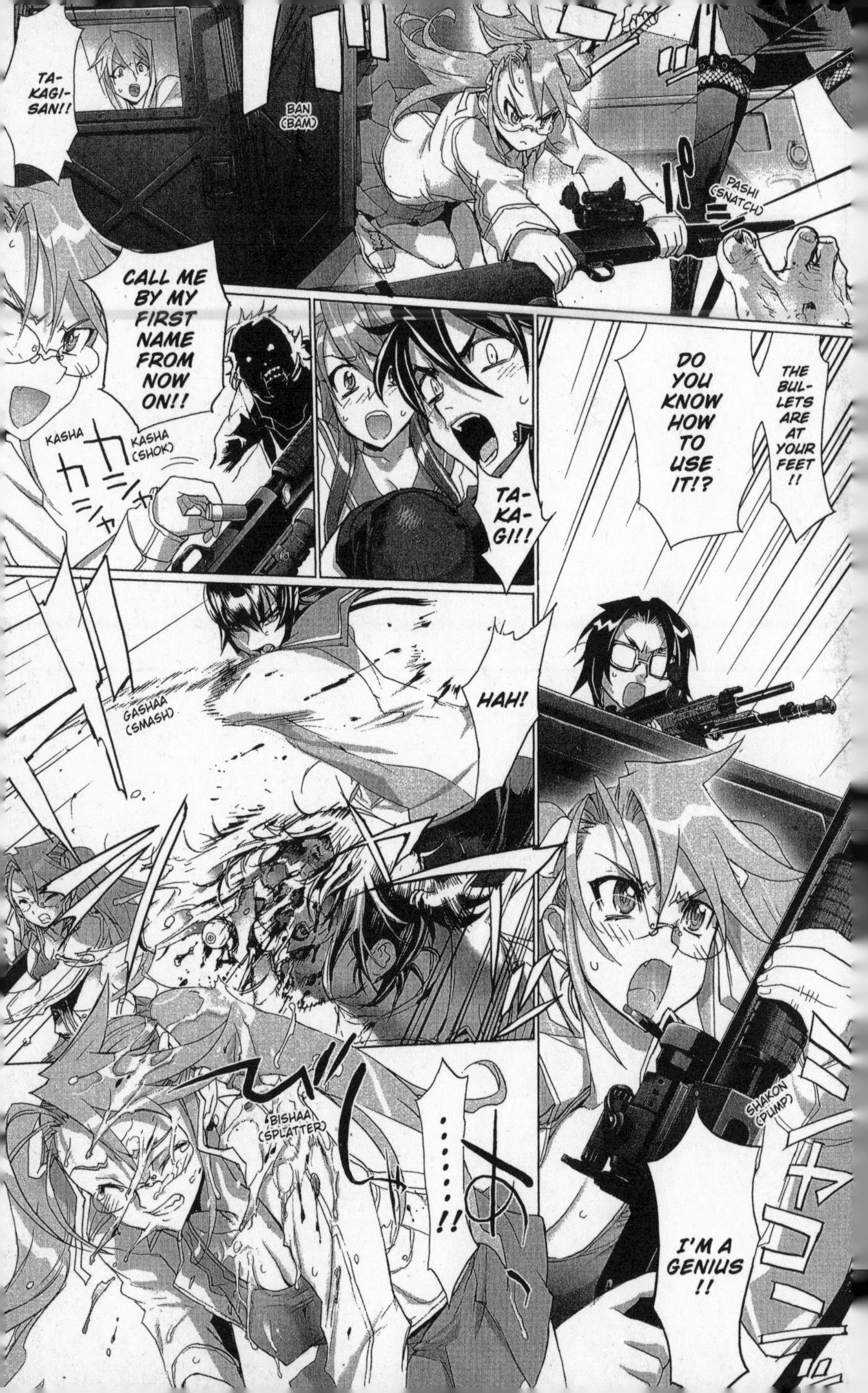
BAN (BAM)
PASHI (SNATCH)
TA-KAGI-SAN!!
THE BUL-LETS ARE AT YOUR FEET!!
DO YOU KNOW HOW TO USE IT!?
TA-KA-GI!!
CALL ME BY MY FIRST NAME FROM NOW ON!!
KASHA KASHA (SHOK)
SHAKON (PUMP)
I'M A GENIUS!!
HAH!
GASHAA (SMASH)
BISHAA (SPLATTER)
......!!

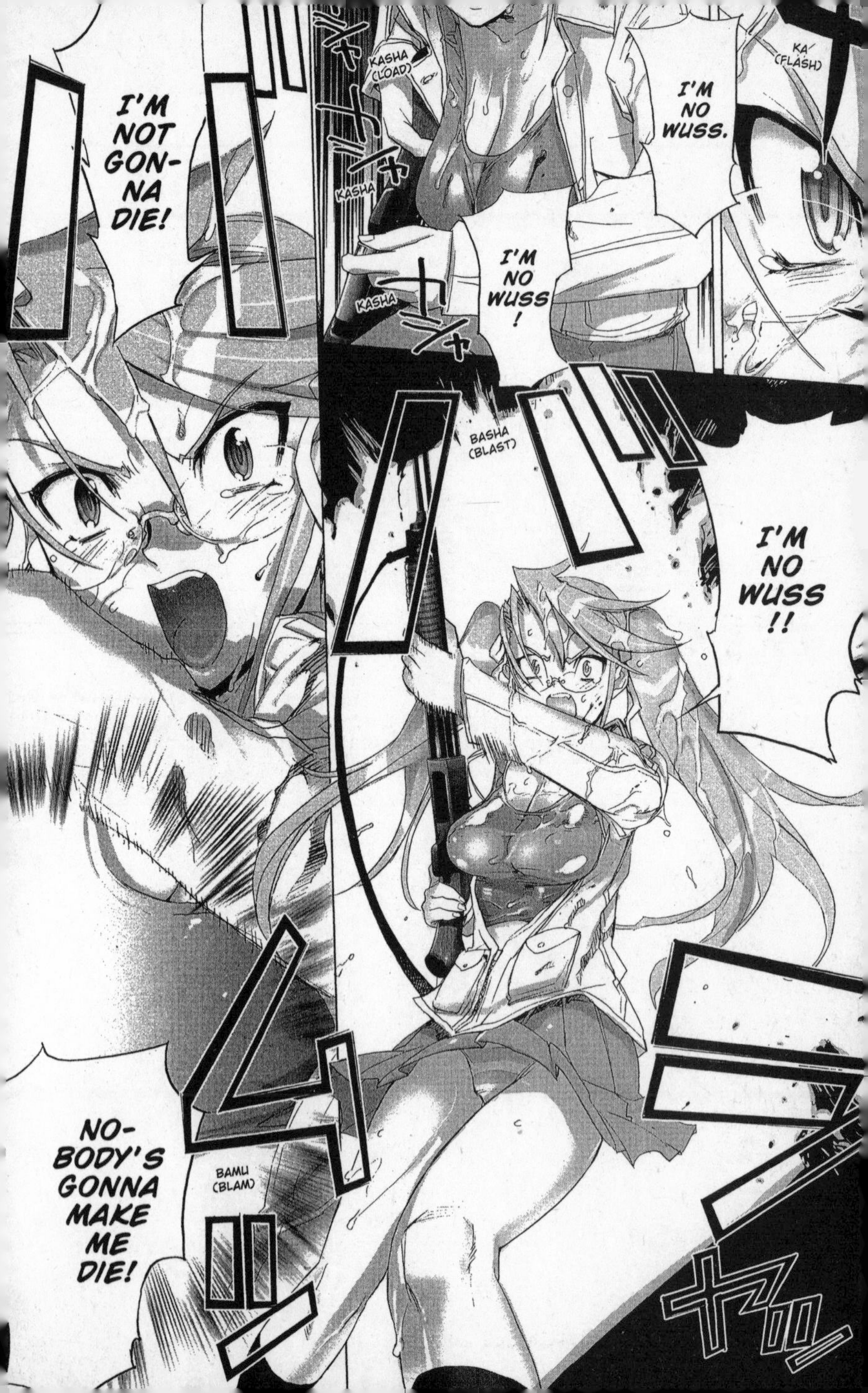
KA (FLASH)
I'M NO WUSS.
KASHA (LOAD)
KASHA
I'M NO WUSS!
KASHA
BASHA (BLAST)
I'M NO WUSS!!
I'M NOT GON-NA DIE!
BAMU (BLAM)
NO-BODY'S GONNA MAKE ME DIE!

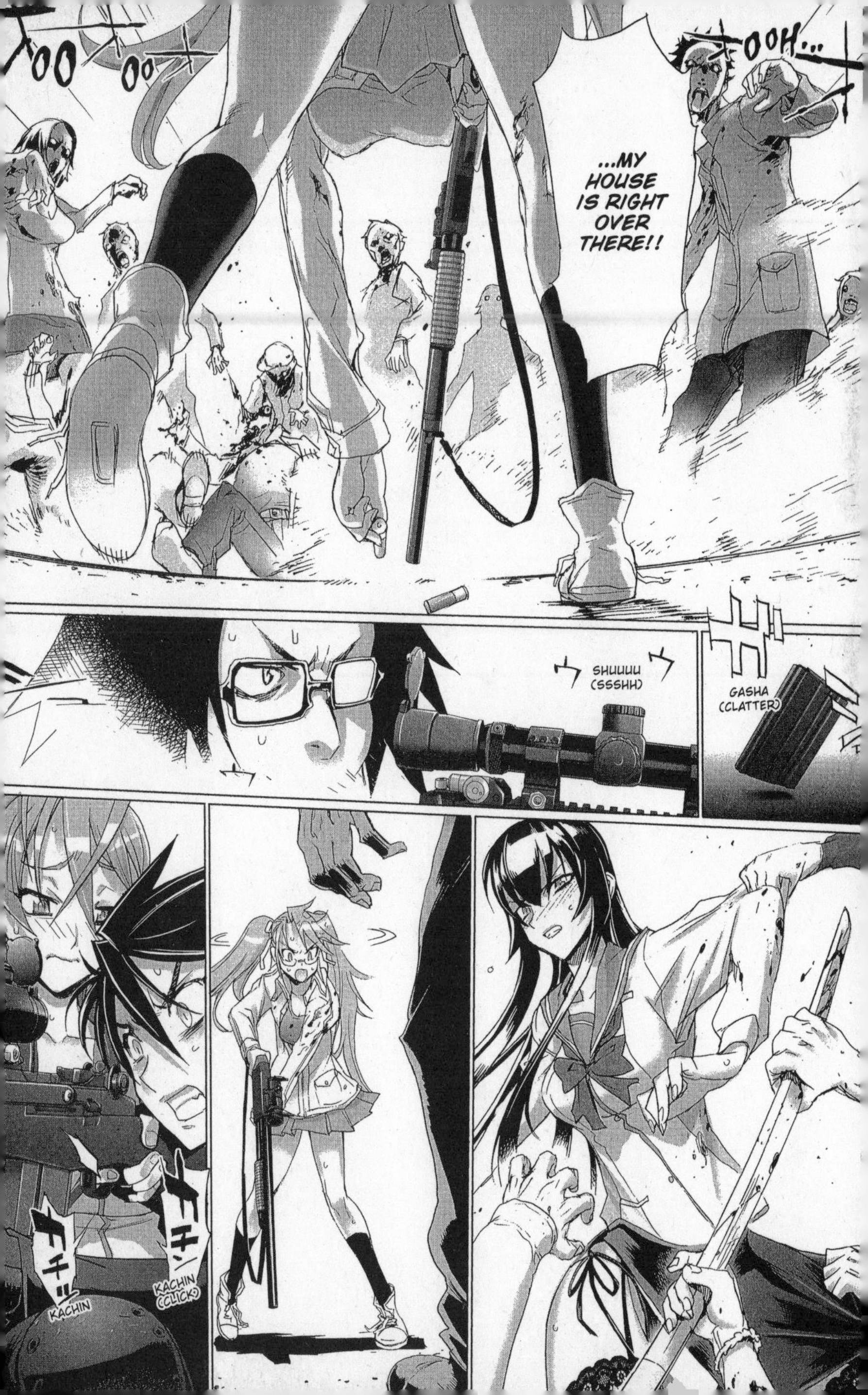
OOH...
...MY HOUSE IS RIGHT OVER THERE!!
GASHA (CLATTER)
SHUUUU (SSSHH)
KACHIN (CLICK)
KACHIN

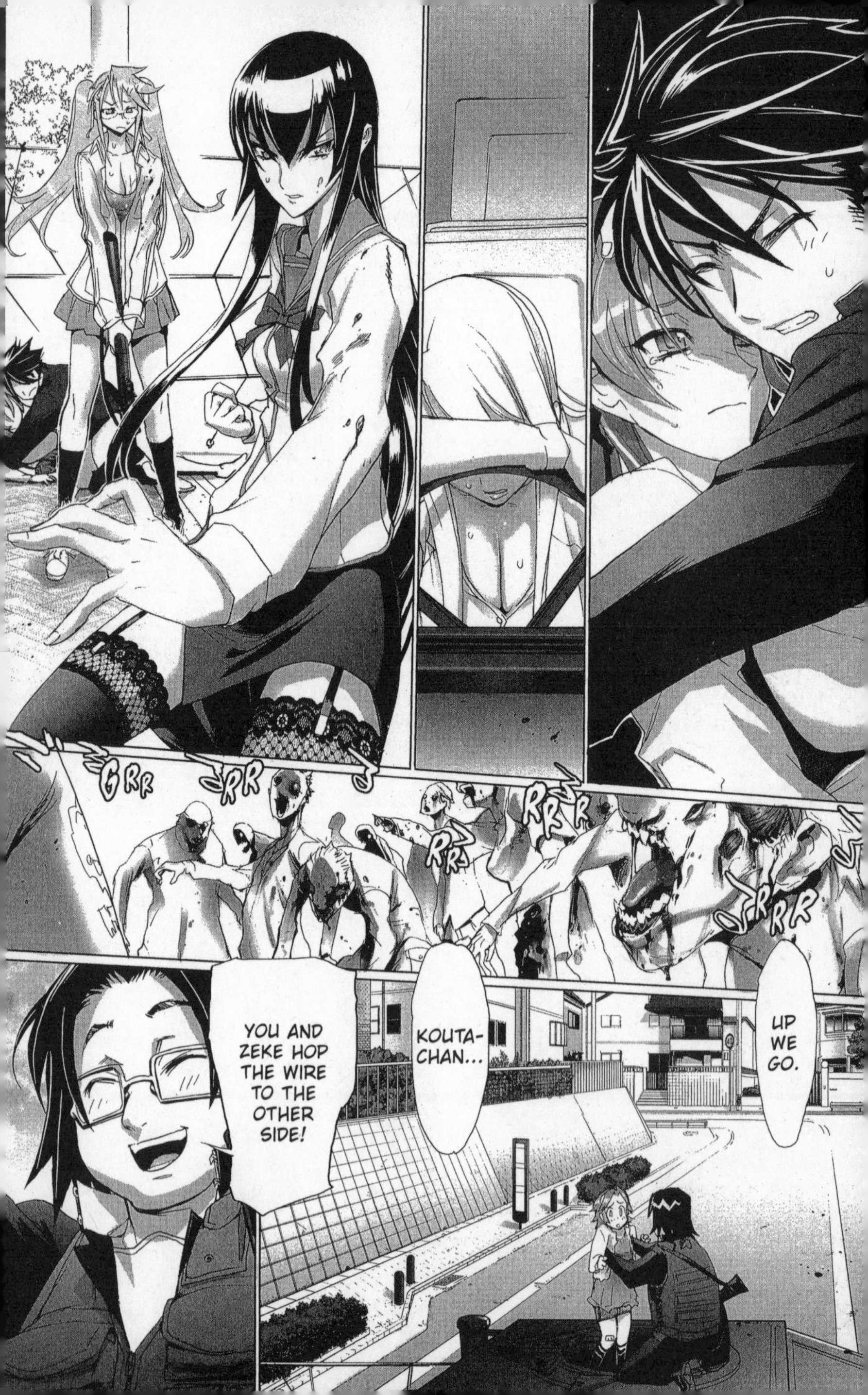
RRR
RRR
RR
RR
GRR
UP WE GO.
KOUTA-CHAN...
YOU AND ZEKE HOP THE WIRE TO THE OTHER SIDE!

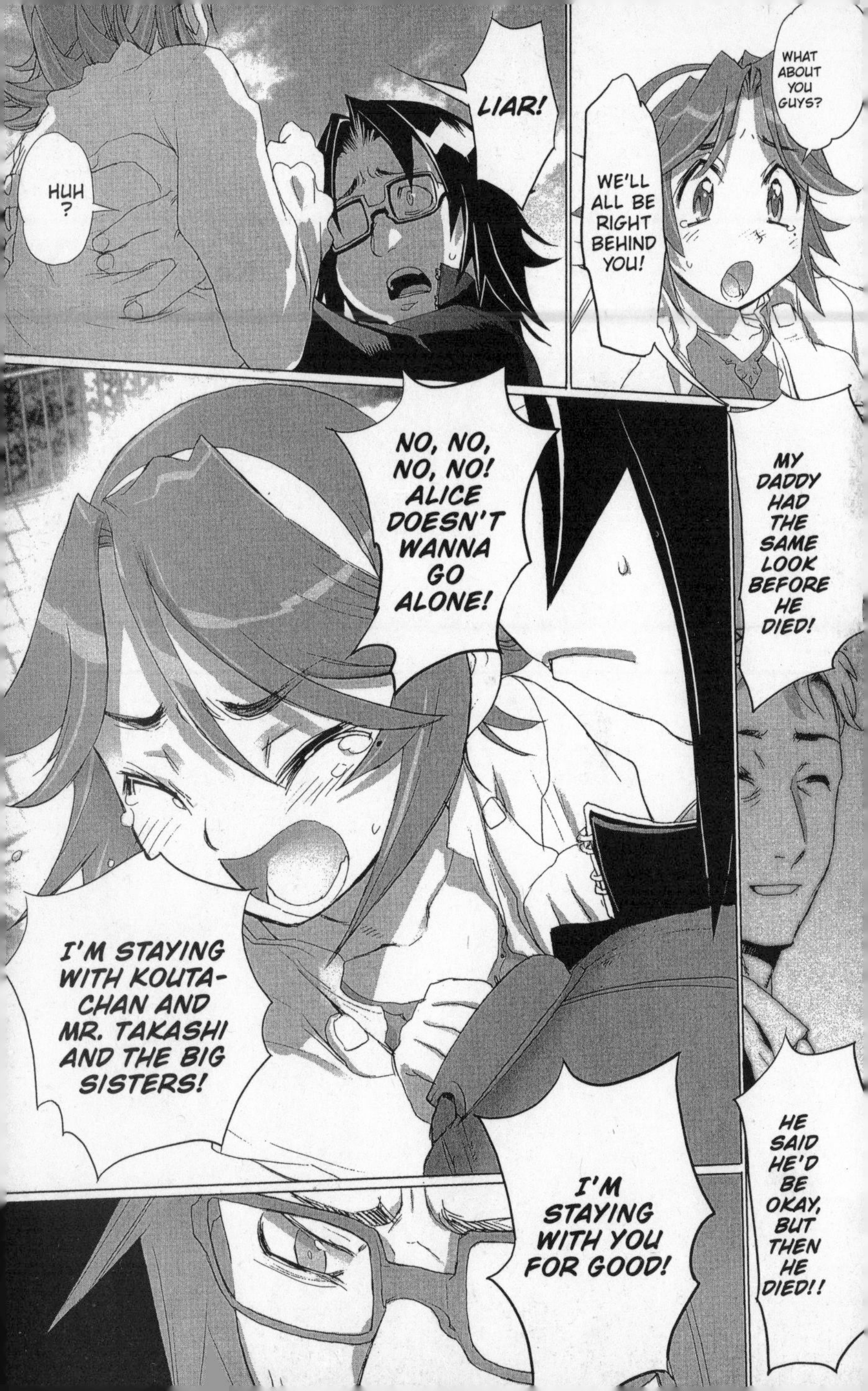
WHAT ABOUT YOU GUYS?
WE'LL ALL BE RIGHT BEHIND YOU!
LIAR!
HUH?
MY DADDY HAD THE SAME LOOK BEFORE HE DIED!
HE SAID HE'D BE OKAY, BUT THEN HE DIED!!
NO, NO, NO, NO! ALICE DOESN'T WANNA GO ALONE!
I'M STAYING WITH KOUTA-CHAN AND MR. TAKASHI AND THE BIG SISTERS!
I'M STAYING WITH YOU FOR GOOD!

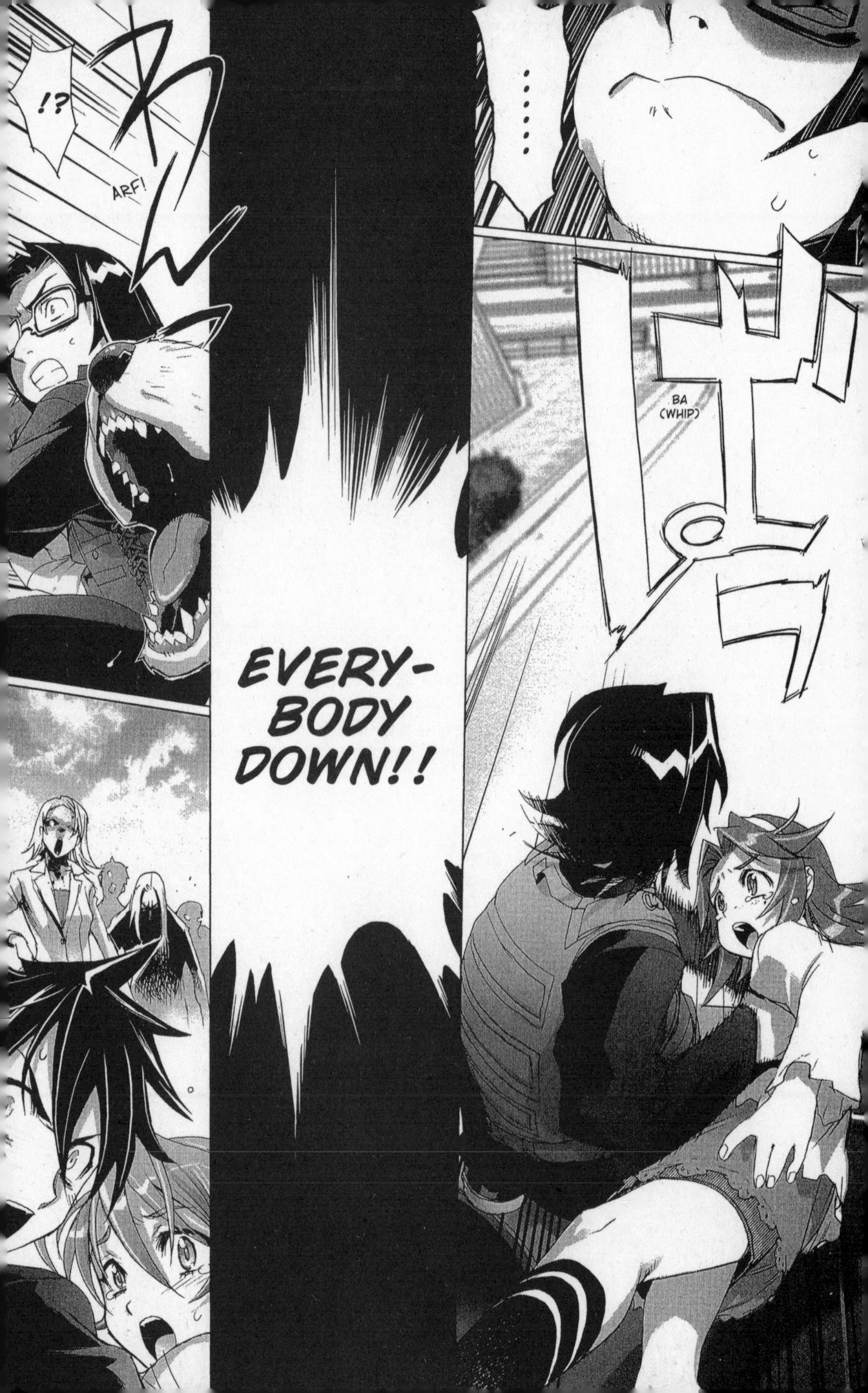
......
BA (WHIP)
EVERY-BODY DOWN!!
!?
ARF!

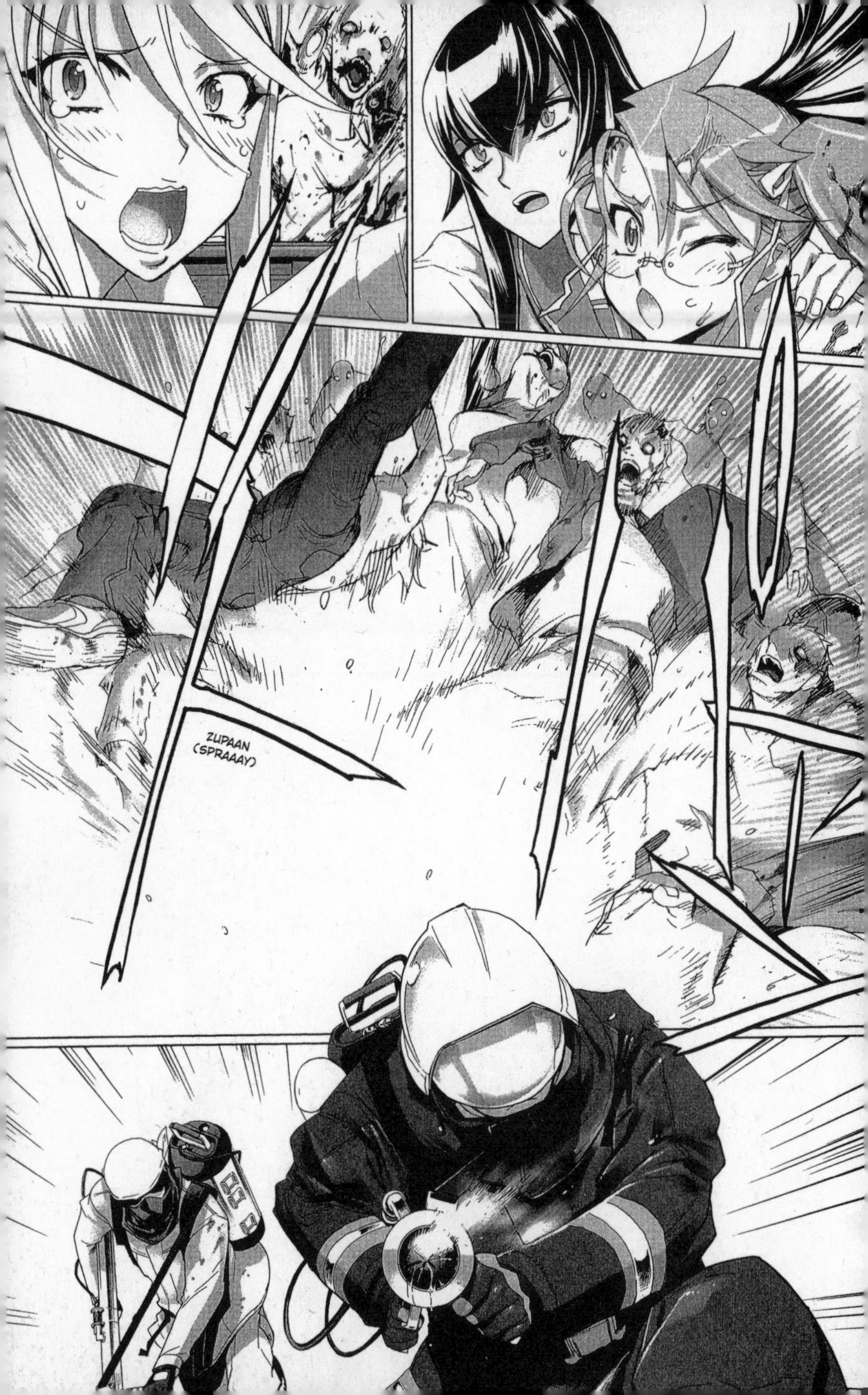
ZUPAAN
(SPRAAAY)

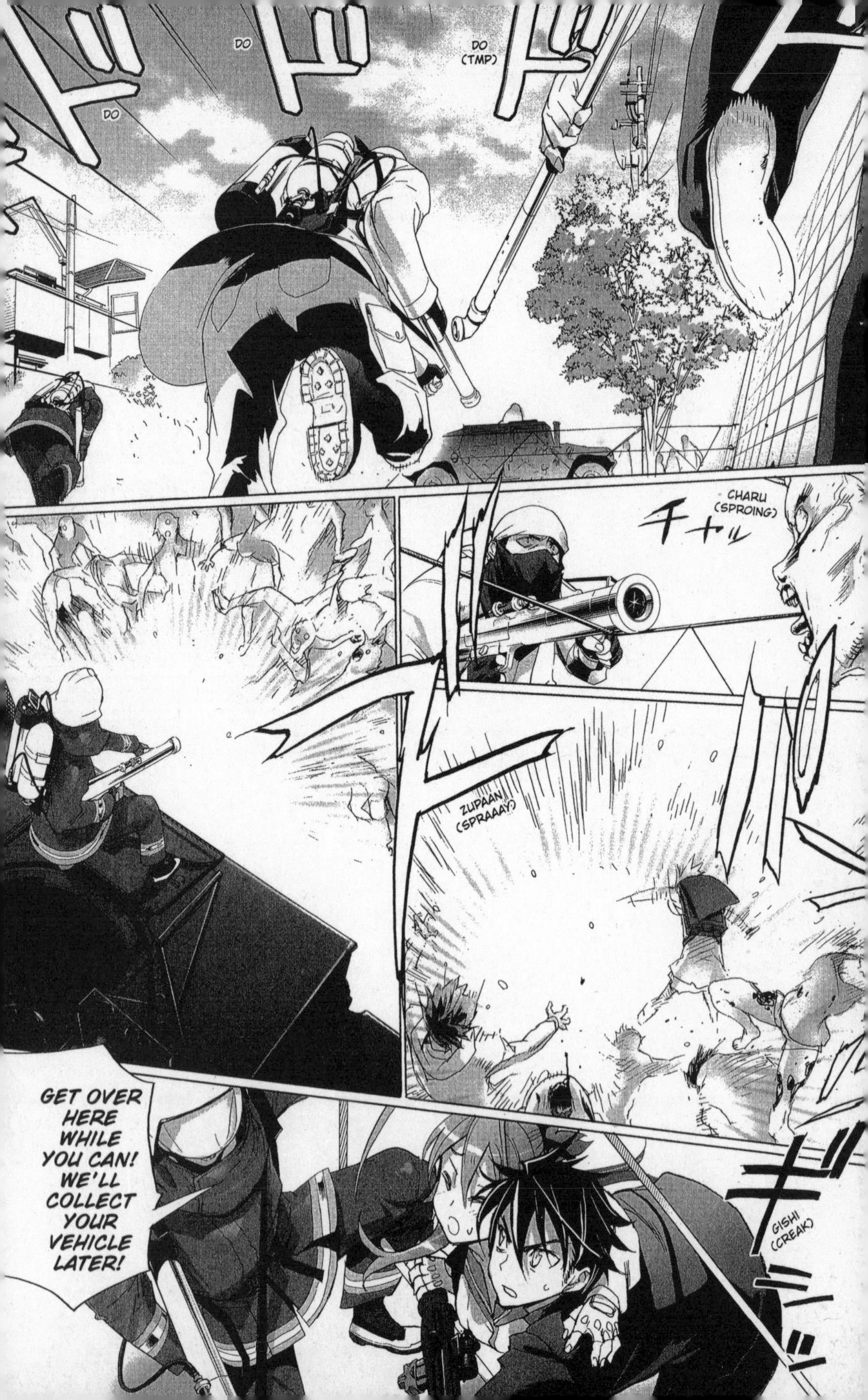
DO
(TMP)
DO
DO
CHARU
(SPROING)
ZUPAAN
(SPRAAAY)
GISHI
(CREAK)
GET OVER HERE WHILE YOU CAN! WE'LL COLLECT YOUR VEHICLE LATER!

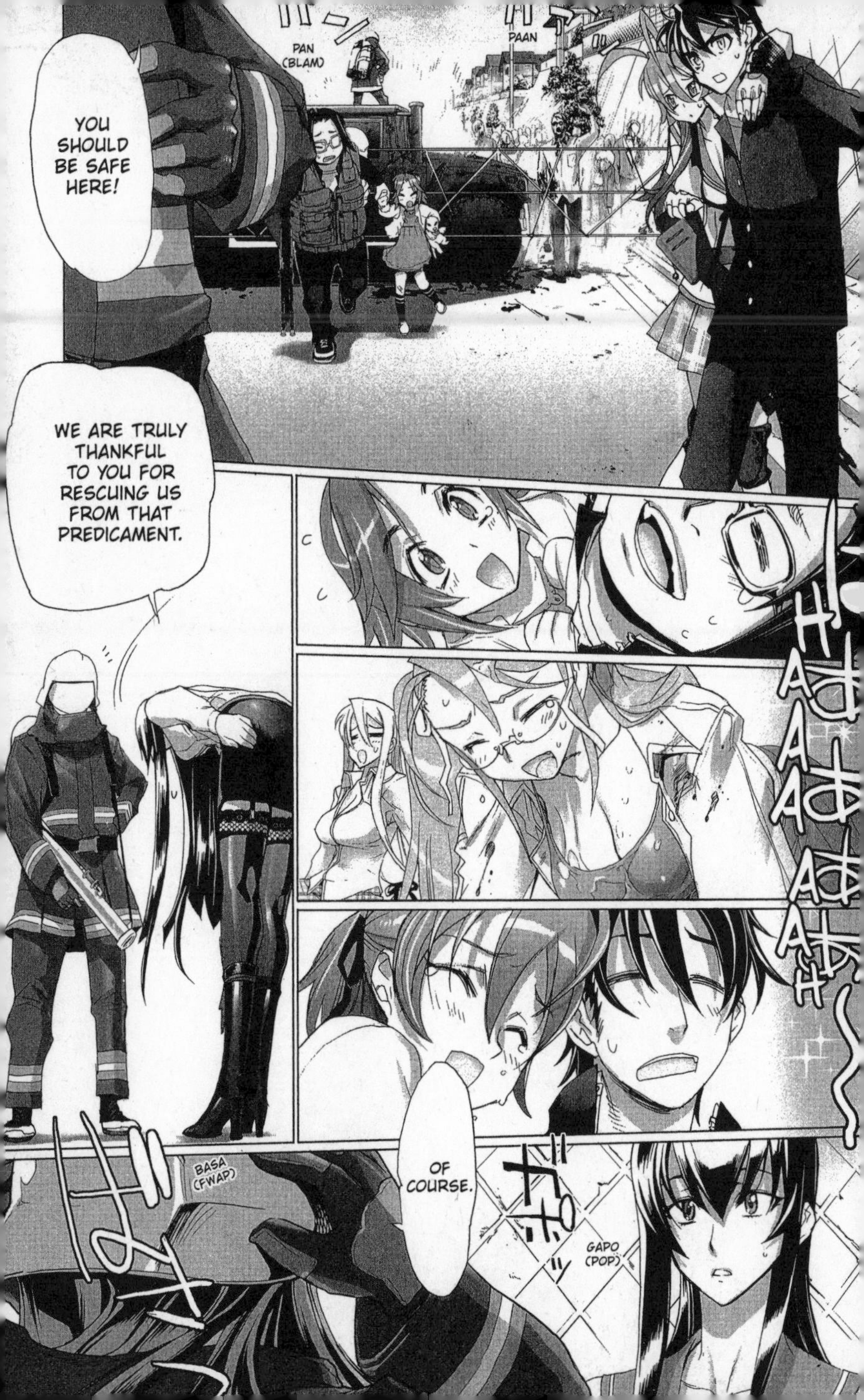
PAAN
PAN (BLAM)
YOU SHOULD BE SAFE HERE!
HAAAAAAH
WE ARE TRULY THANKFUL TO YOU FOR RESCUING US FROM THAT PREDICAMENT.
GAPO (POP)
OF COURSE.
BASA (FWAP)

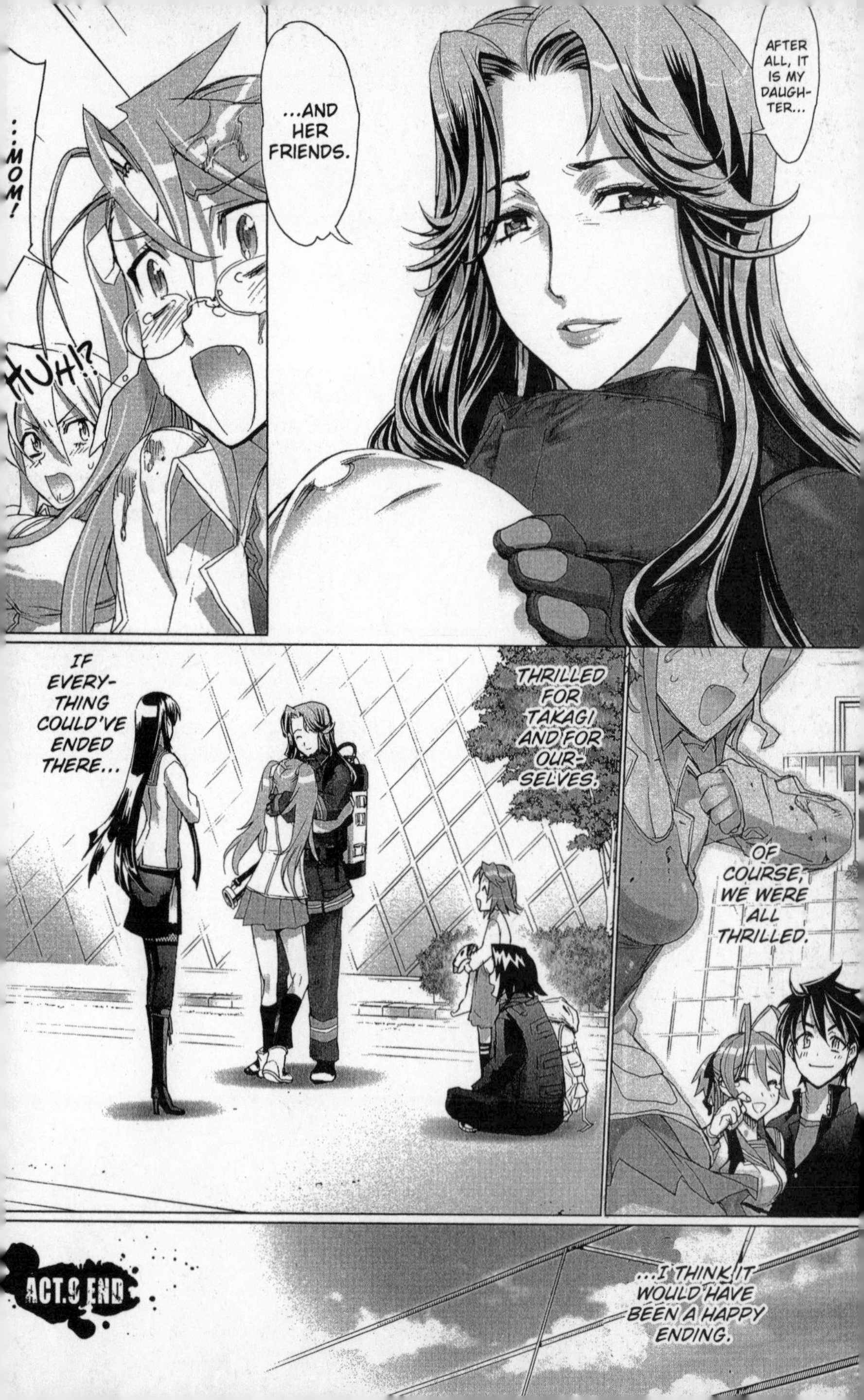
AFTER ALL, IT IS MY DAUGHTER...
...AND HER FRIENDS.
...MOM!
HUH!?
OF COURSE, WE WERE ALL THRILLED.
THRILLED FOR TAKAGI AND FOR OURSELVES.
IF EVERYTHING COULD'VE ENDED THERE...
...I THINK IT WOULD HAVE BEEN A HAPPY ENDING.
ACT.9 END

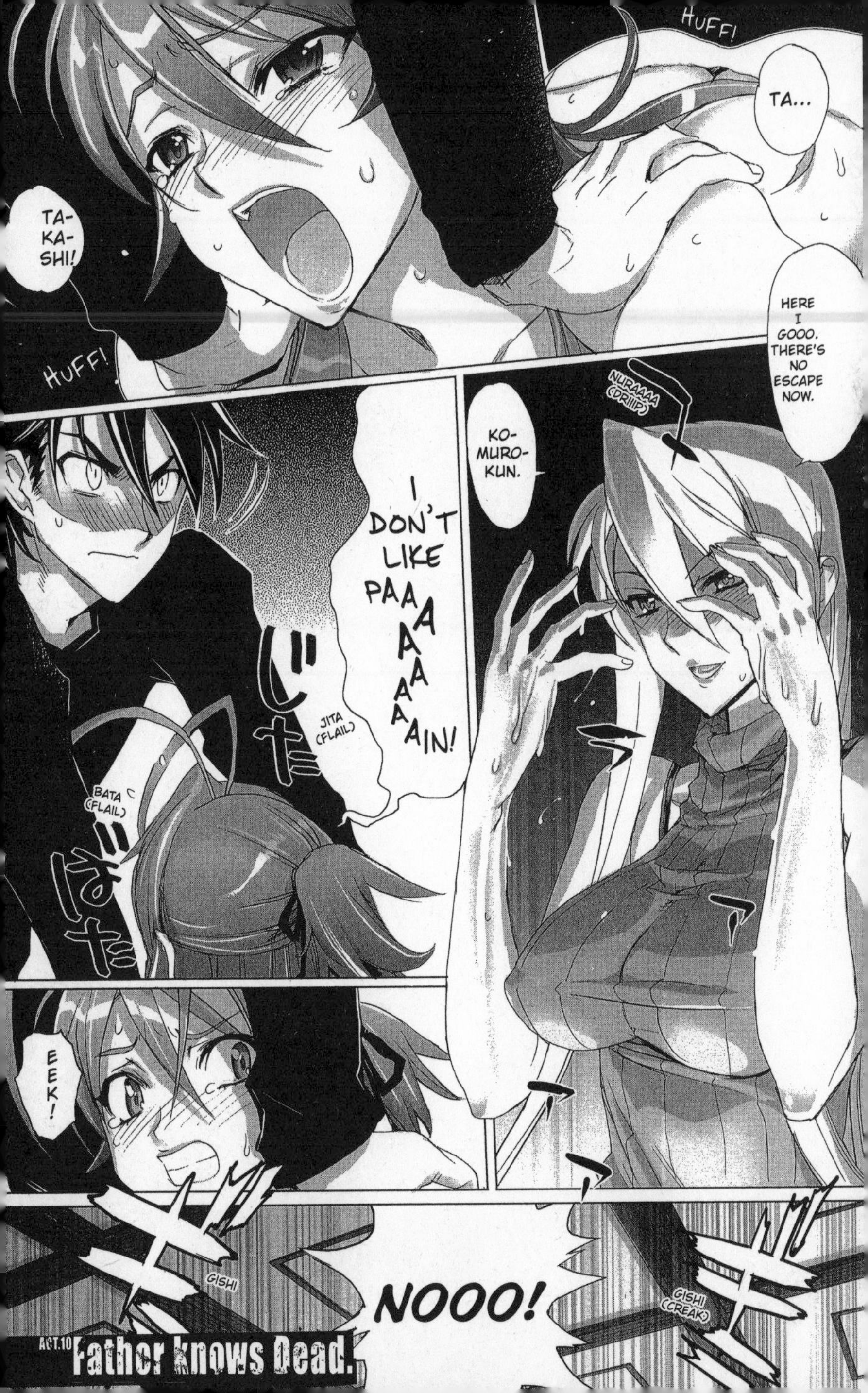
HUFF!
TA...
TA-KA-SHI!
HUFF!
HERE I GOOO. THERE'S NO ESCAPE NOW.
NURAAAA (DRIIIP)
KO-MURO-KUN.
I, DON'T LIKE PAAAAAAAIN!
JITA (FLAIL)
BATA (FLAIL)
EEK!
GISHI (CREAK)
NOOO!
GISHI
ACT.10 Father knows Dead.

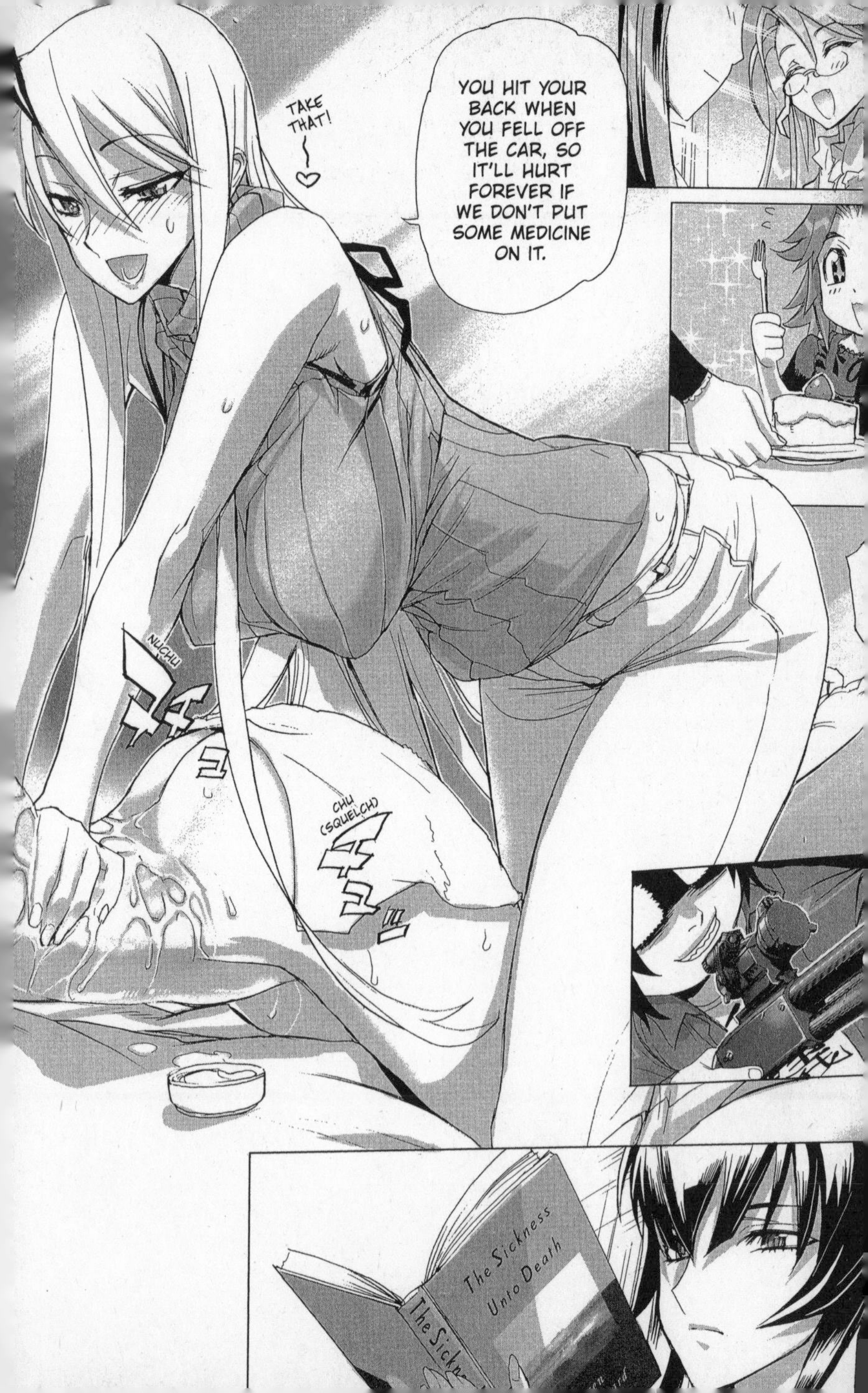
YOU HIT YOUR BACK WHEN YOU FELL OFF THE CAR, SO IT'LL HURT FOREVER IF WE DON'T PUT SOME MEDICINE ON IT.
TAKE THAT! ♡
NUCHU
CHU (SQUELCH)
The Sickness Unto Death

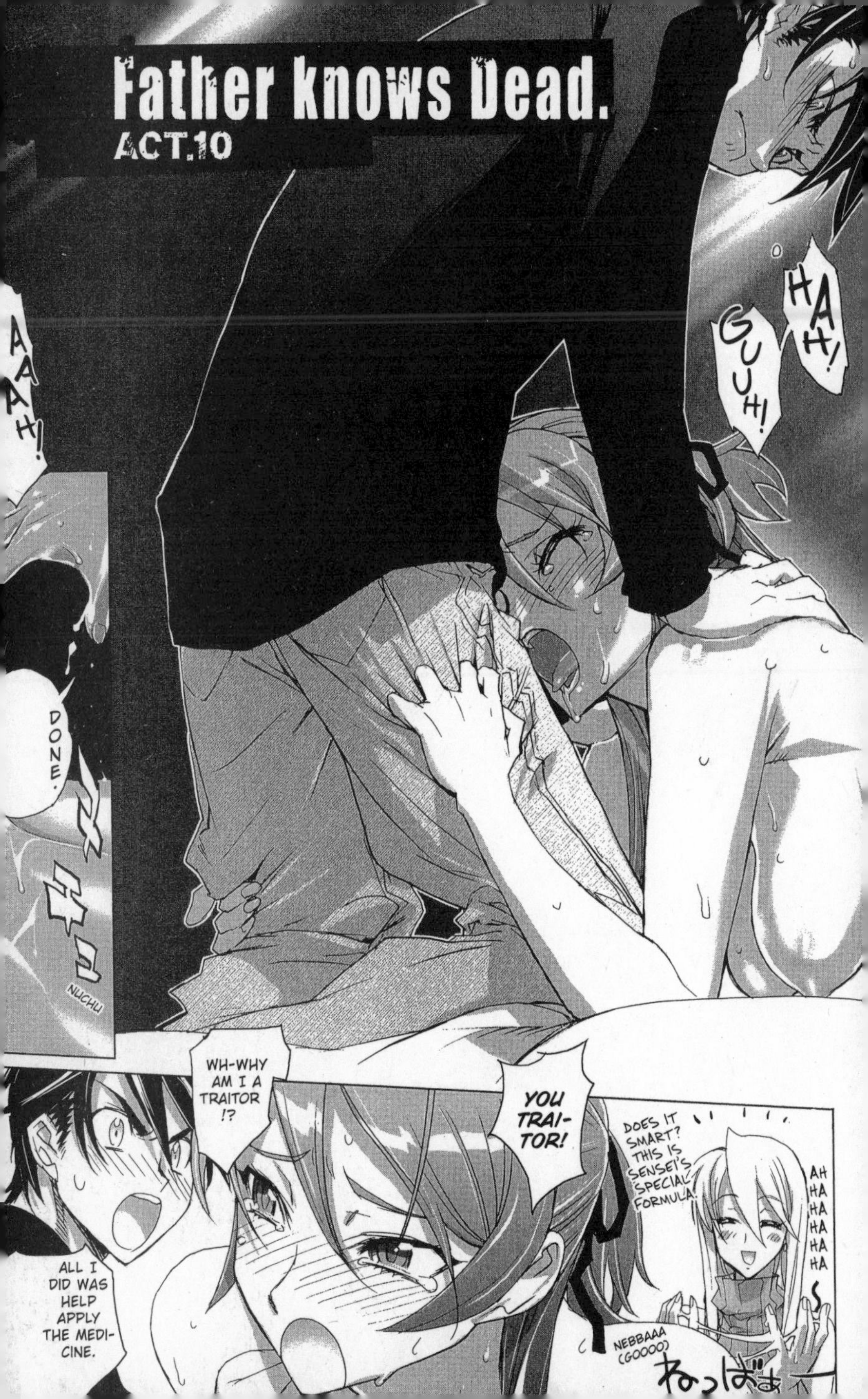
Father knows Dead.
ACT.10
HAH!
GUUH!
AAAAH!
DONE.
ヌチュ
NUCHU
DOES IT SMART? THIS IS SENSEI'S SPECIAL FORMULA!
AH HA HA HA HA HA HA
NEBBAAA (GOOOO)
ねっばぁー
YOU TRAITOR!
WH-WHY AM I A TRAITOR!?
ALL I DID WAS HELP APPLY THE MEDICINE.

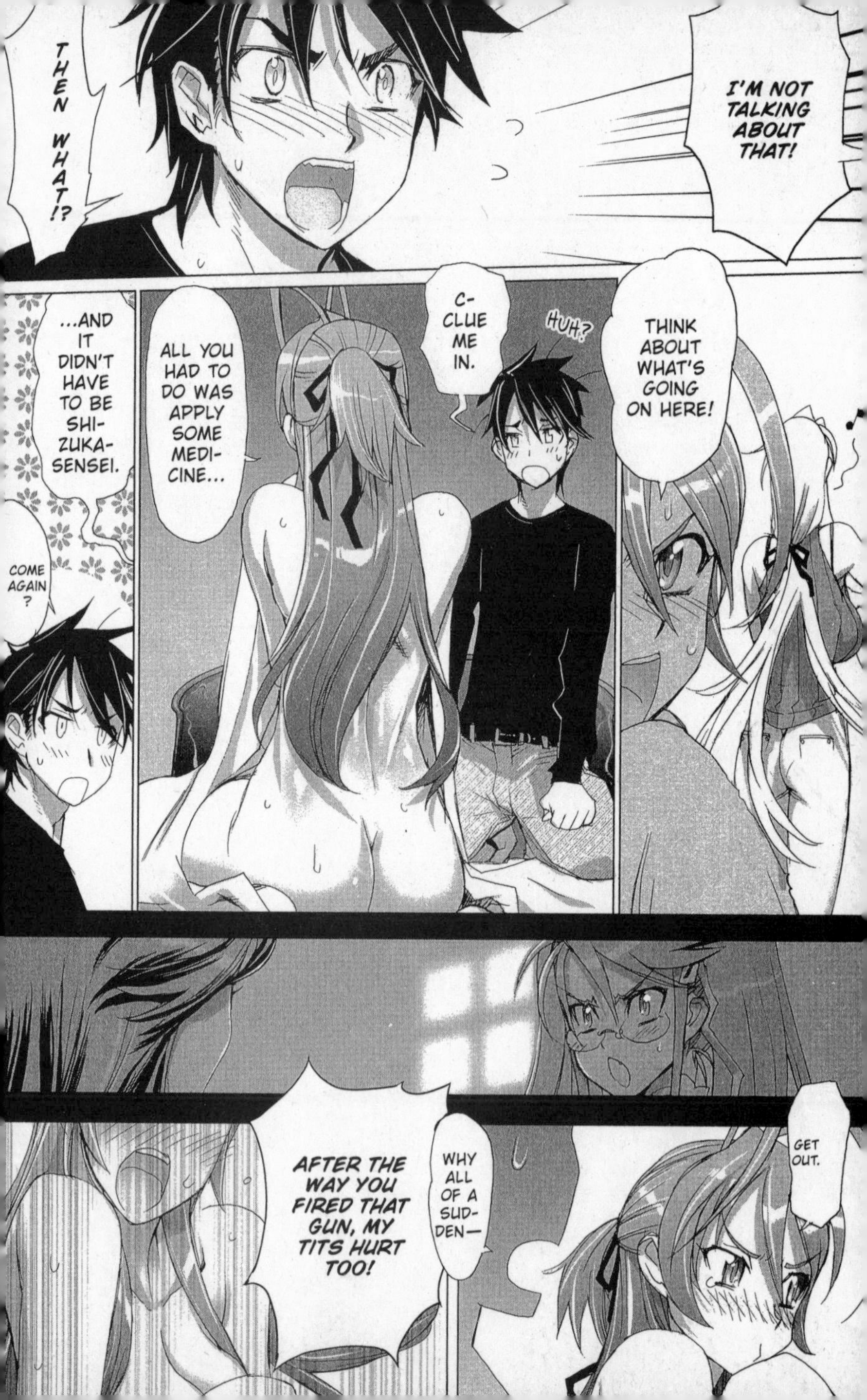
I'M NOT TALKING ABOUT THAT!
THEN WHAT!?
THINK ABOUT WHAT'S GOING ON HERE!
HUH?
C-CLUE ME IN.
ALL YOU HAD TO DO WAS APPLY SOME MEDI-CINE...
...AND IT DIDN'T HAVE TO BE SHI-ZUKA-SENSEI.
COME AGAIN?
GET OUT.
WHY ALL OF A SUD-DEN—
AFTER THE WAY YOU FIRED THAT GUN, MY TITS HURT TOO!

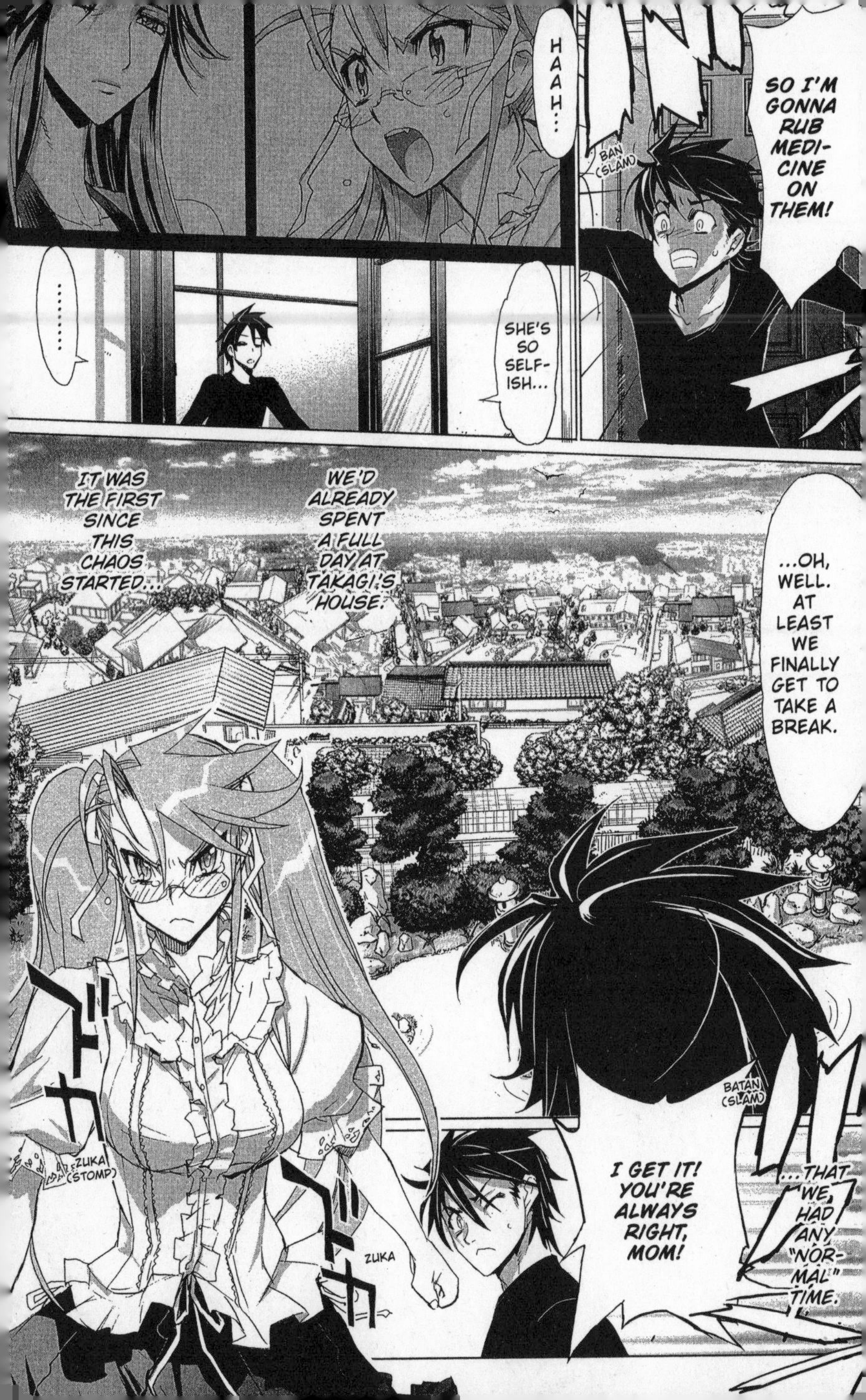
SO I'M GONNA RUB MEDICINE ON THEM!
BAN (SLAM)
HAAH...
SHE'S SO SELFISH...
......
...OH, WELL. AT LEAST WE FINALLY GET TO TAKE A BREAK.
WE'D ALREADY SPENT A FULL DAY AT TAKAGI'S HOUSE.
IT WAS THE FIRST SINCE THIS CHAOS STARTED...
BATAN (SLAM)
...THAT WE HAD ANY "NORMAL" TIME.
I GET IT! YOU'RE ALWAYS RIGHT, MOM!
ZUKA (STOMP)
ZUKA

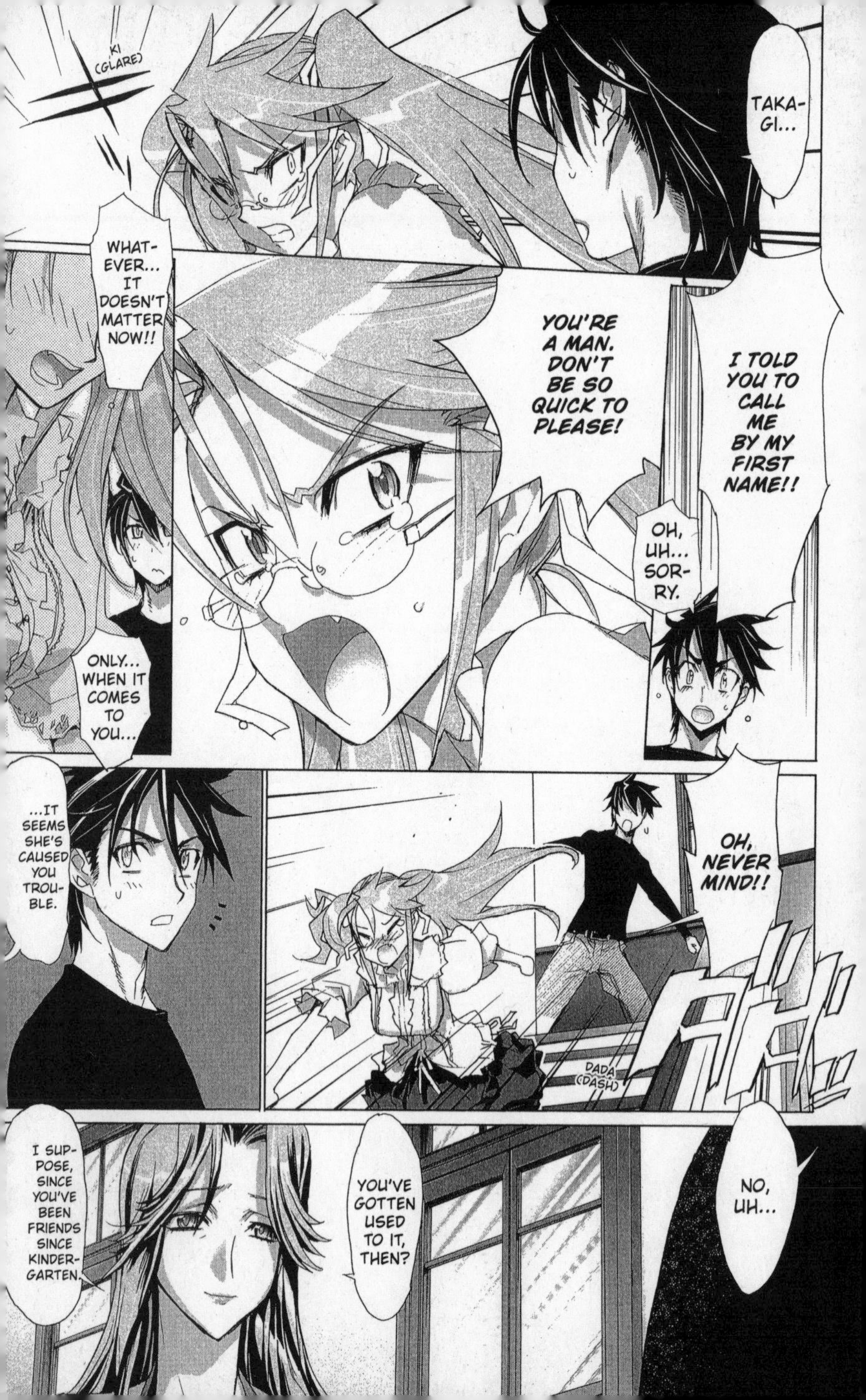
TAKAGI...
KI (GLARE)
WHATEVER... IT DOESN'T MATTER NOW!!
I TOLD YOU TO CALL ME BY MY FIRST NAME!!
YOU'RE A MAN. DON'T BE SO QUICK TO PLEASE!
OH, UH... SORRY.
ONLY... WHEN IT COMES TO YOU...
OH, NEVER MIND!!
DADA (DASH)
...IT SEEMS SHE'S CAUSED YOU TROUBLE.
NO, UH...
YOU'VE GOTTEN USED TO IT, THEN?
I SUPPOSE, SINCE YOU'VE BEEN FRIENDS SINCE KINDERGARTEN.

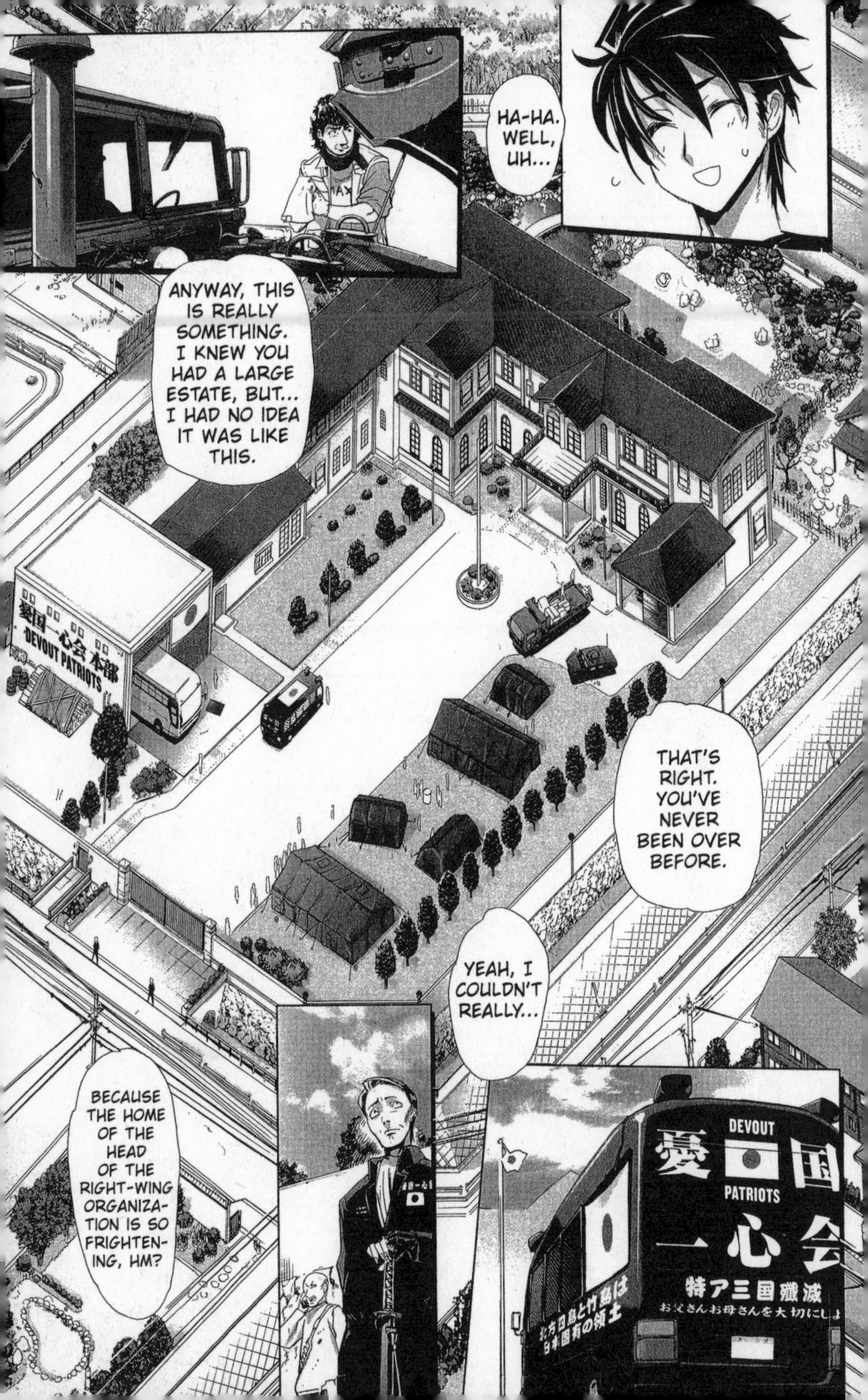
HA-HA. WELL, UH...
ANYWAY, THIS IS REALLY SOMETHING. I KNEW YOU HAD A LARGE ESTATE, BUT... I HAD NO IDEA IT WAS LIKE THIS.
憂国一心会 本部
DEVOUT PATRIOTS
THAT'S RIGHT. YOU'VE NEVER BEEN OVER BEFORE.
YEAH, I COULDN'T REALLY...
DEVOUT
憂国
PATRIOTS
一心会
特ア三国殲滅
お父さんお母さんを大切にしよ
北方四島と竹島は
日本国有の領土
BECAUSE THE HOME OF THE HEAD OF THE RIGHT-WING ORGANIZATION IS SO FRIGHTENING, HM?

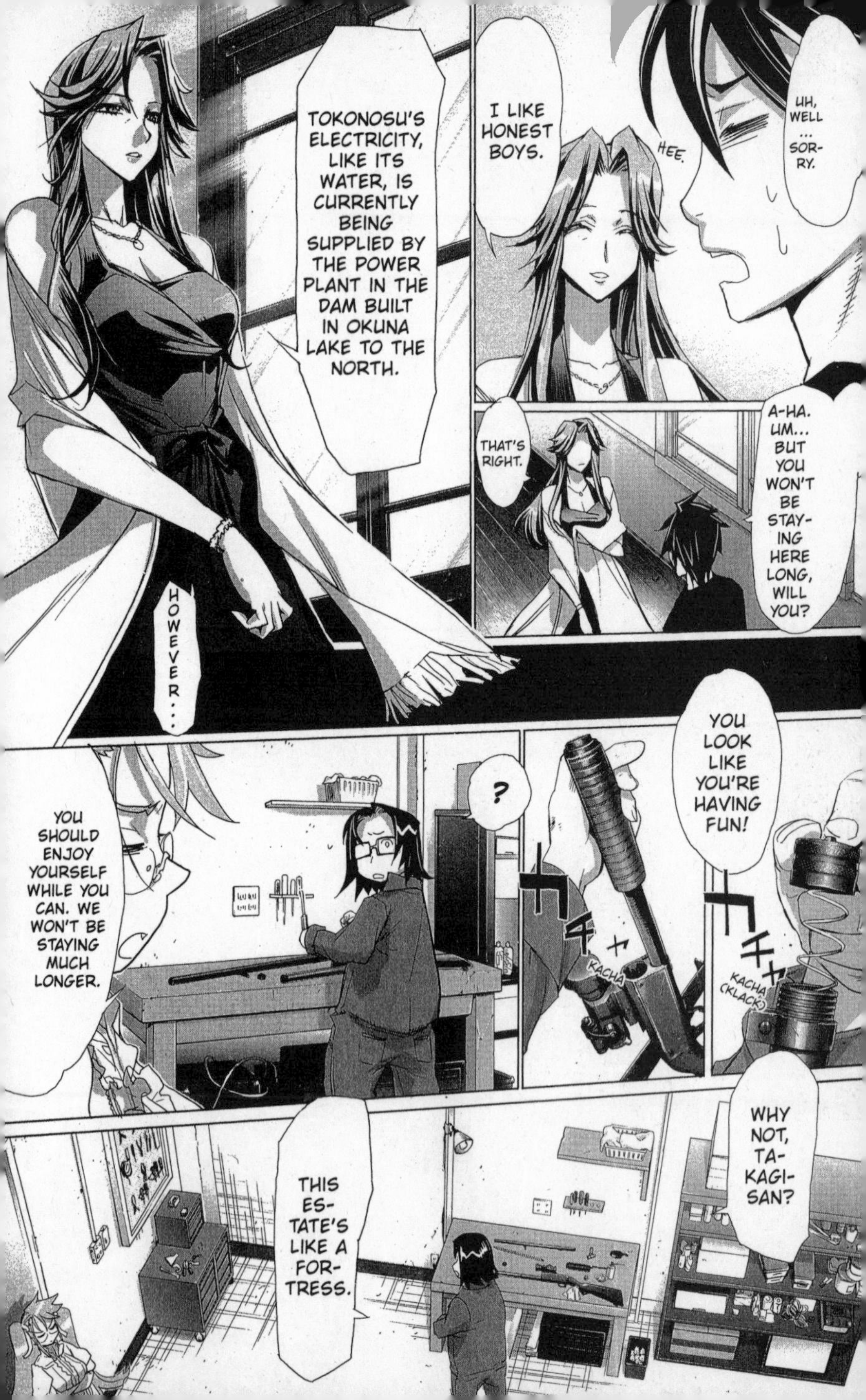
UH, WELL ... SORRY.
HEE.
I LIKE HONEST BOYS.
A-HA. UM... BUT YOU WON'T BE STAYING HERE LONG, WILL YOU?
THAT'S RIGHT.
TOKONOSU'S ELECTRICITY, LIKE ITS WATER, IS CURRENTLY BEING SUPPLIED BY THE POWER PLANT IN THE DAM BUILT IN OKUNA LAKE TO THE NORTH.
HOWEVER...
YOU LOOK LIKE YOU'RE HAVING FUN!
KACHA (KLACK)
KACHA
?
YOU SHOULD ENJOY YOURSELF WHILE YOU CAN. WE WON'T BE STAYING MUCH LONGER.
WHY NOT, TAKAGI-SAN?
THIS ESTATE'S LIKE A FORTRESS.

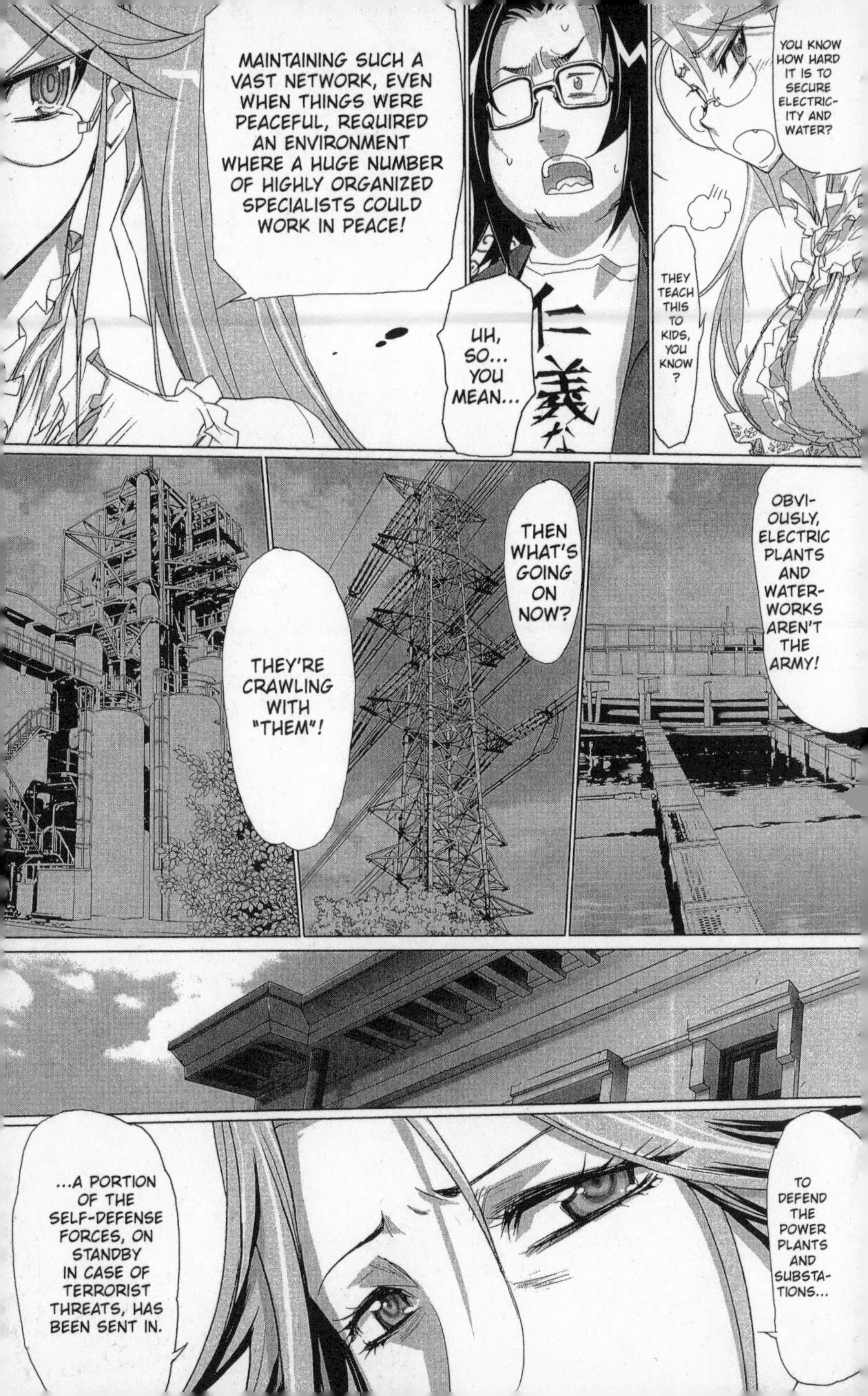
YOU KNOW HOW HARD IT IS TO SECURE ELECTRICITY AND WATER?
THEY TEACH THIS TO KIDS, YOU KNOW?
UH, SO... YOU MEAN...
MAINTAINING SUCH A VAST NETWORK, EVEN WHEN THINGS WERE PEACEFUL, REQUIRED AN ENVIRONMENT WHERE A HUGE NUMBER OF HIGHLY ORGANIZED SPECIALISTS COULD WORK IN PEACE!
OBVIOUSLY, ELECTRIC PLANTS AND WATERWORKS AREN'T THE ARMY!
THEN WHAT'S GOING ON NOW?
THEY'RE CRAWLING WITH "THEM"!
TO DEFEND THE POWER PLANTS AND SUBSTATIONS...
...A PORTION OF THE SELF-DEFENSE FORCES, ON STANDBY IN CASE OF TERRORIST THREATS, HAS BEEN SENT IN.

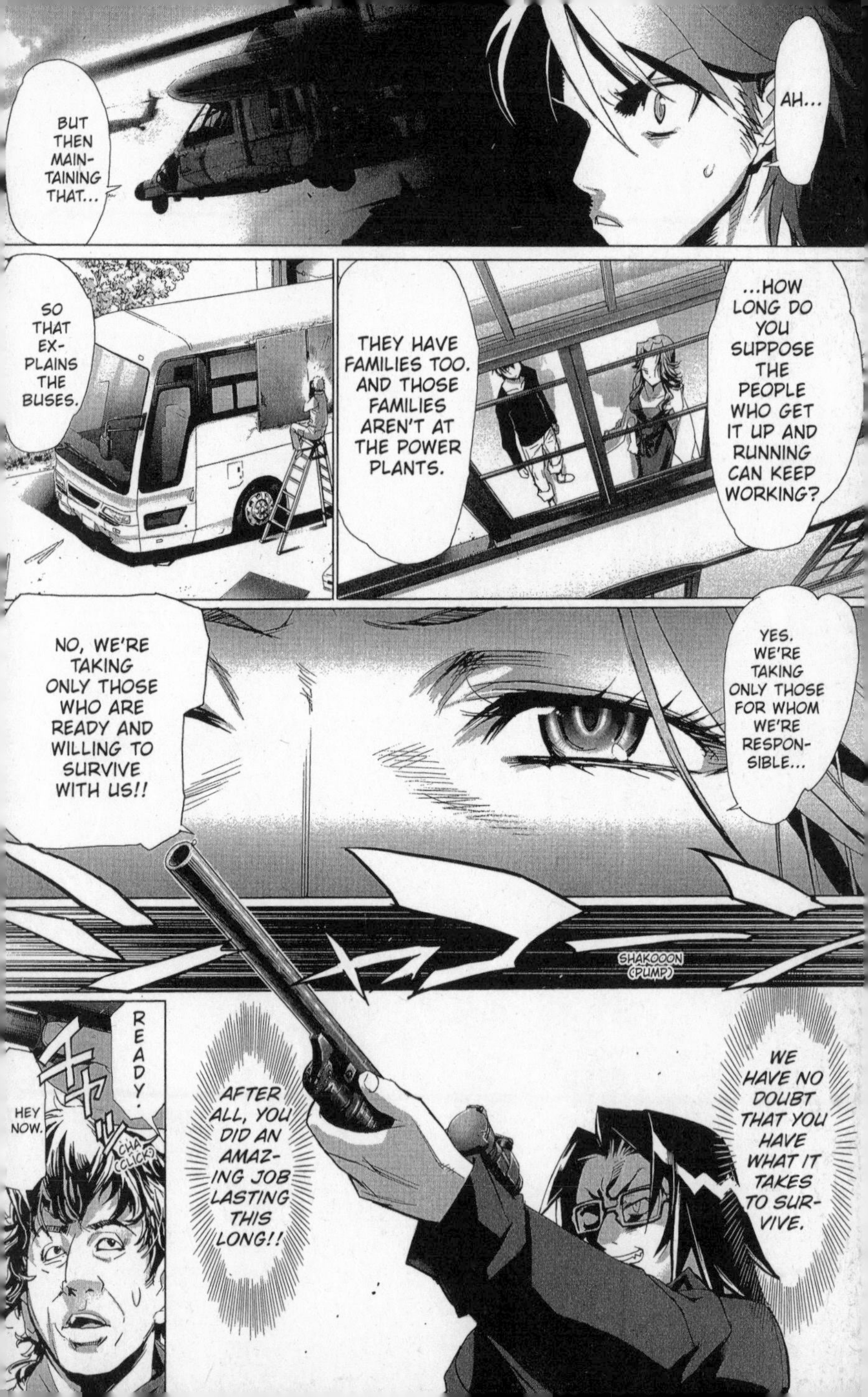
AH...
BUT THEN MAINTAINING THAT...
...HOW LONG DO YOU SUPPOSE THE PEOPLE WHO GET IT UP AND RUNNING CAN KEEP WORKING?
THEY HAVE FAMILIES TOO. AND THOSE FAMILIES AREN'T AT THE POWER PLANTS.
SO THAT EXPLAINS THE BUSES.
YES. WE'RE TAKING ONLY THOSE FOR WHOM WE'RE RESPONSIBLE...
NO, WE'RE TAKING ONLY THOSE WHO ARE READY AND WILLING TO SURVIVE WITH US!!
SHAKOOON (PUMP)
WE HAVE NO DOUBT THAT YOU HAVE WHAT IT TAKES TO SURVIVE.
AFTER ALL, YOU DID AN AMAZING JOB LASTING THIS LONG!!
READY.
CHA (CLICK)
HEY NOW.

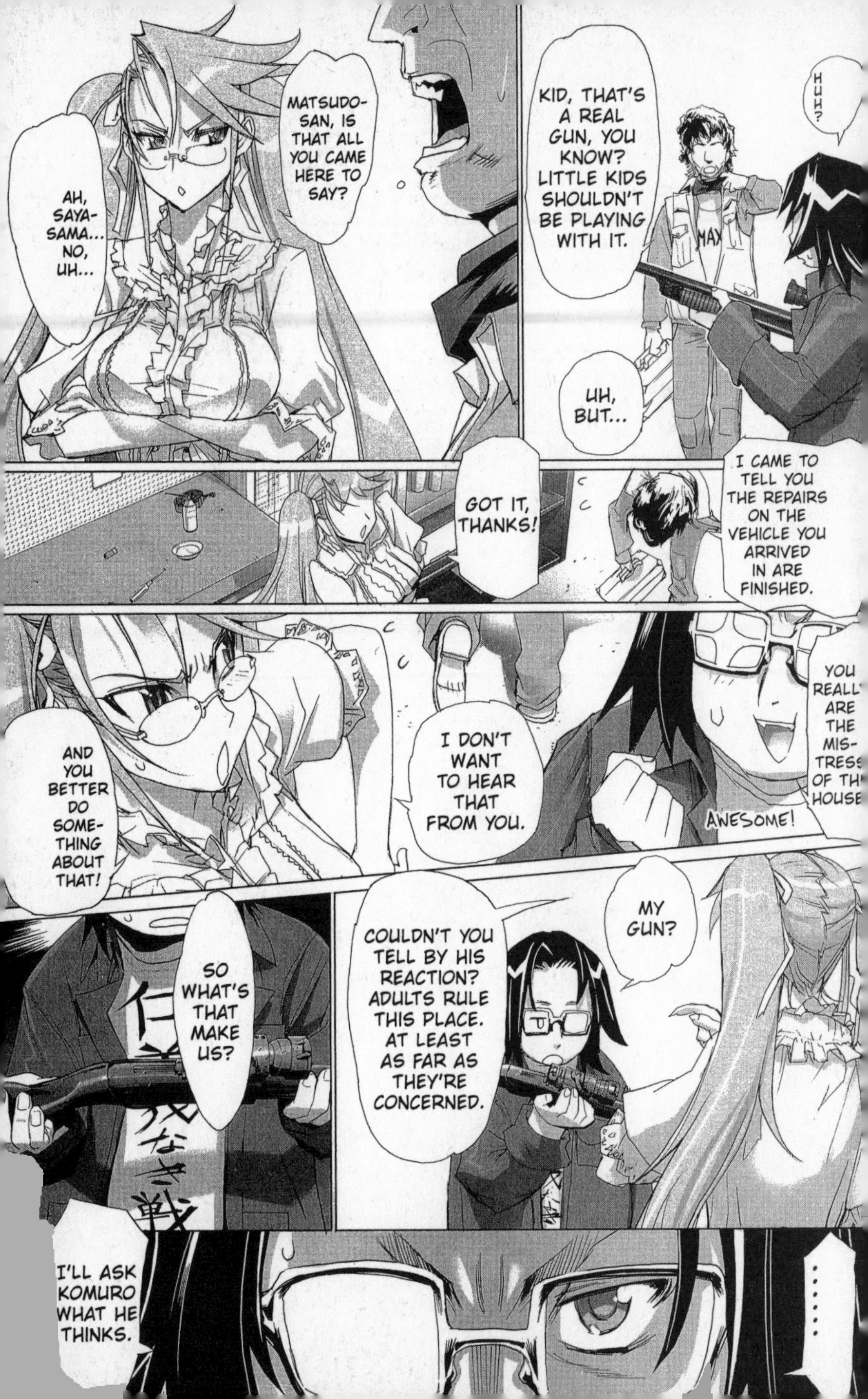
HUH?
KID, THAT'S A REAL GUN, YOU KNOW? LITTLE KIDS SHOULDN'T BE PLAYING WITH IT.
UH, BUT...
MATSUDO-SAN, IS THAT ALL YOU CAME HERE TO SAY?
AH, SAYA-SAMA... NO, UH...
I CAME TO TELL YOU THE REPAIRS ON THE VEHICLE YOU ARRIVED IN ARE FINISHED.
GOT IT, THANKS!
YOU REALL ARE THE MIS- TRES OF TH HOUSE
AWESOME!
I DON'T WANT TO HEAR THAT FROM YOU.
AND YOU BETTER DO SOME- THING ABOUT THAT!
MY GUN?
COULDN'T YOU TELL BY HIS REACTION? ADULTS RULE THIS PLACE. AT LEAST AS FAR AS THEY'RE CONCERNED.
SO WHAT'S THAT MAKE US?
......
I'LL ASK KOMURO WHAT HE THINKS.

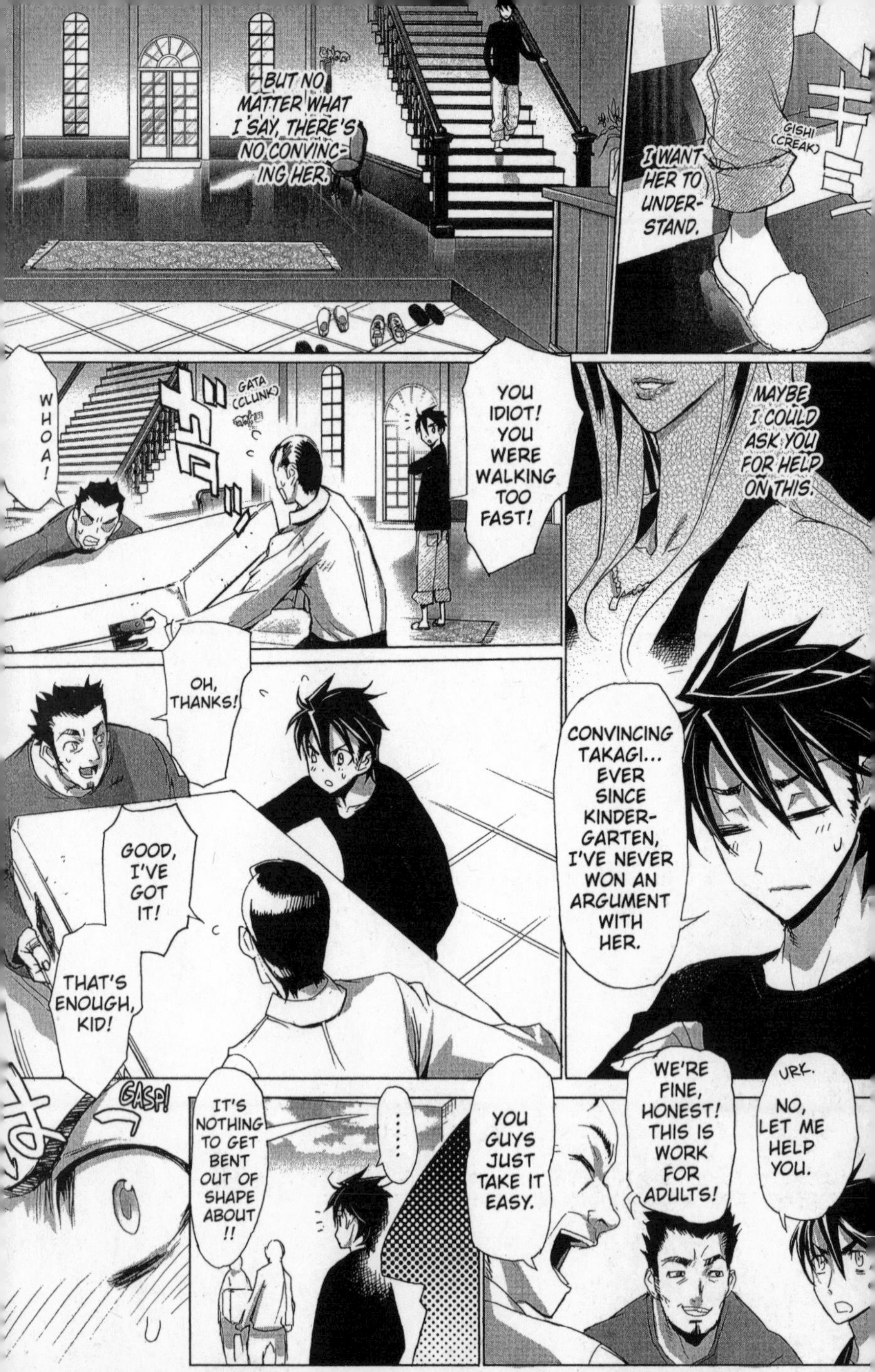

GISHI (CREAK)
I WANT HER TO UNDERSTAND.
BUT NO MATTER WHAT I SAY, THERE'S NO CONVINCING HER.
MAYBE I COULD ASK YOU FOR HELP ON THIS.
CONVINCING TAKAGI... EVER SINCE KINDERGARTEN, I'VE NEVER WON AN ARGUMENT WITH HER.
YOU IDIOT! YOU WERE WALKING TOO FAST!
GATA (CLUNK)
WHOA!
OH, THANKS!
GOOD, I'VE GOT IT!
THAT'S ENOUGH, KID!
URK.
NO, LET ME HELP YOU.
WE'RE FINE, HONEST! THIS IS WORK FOR ADULTS!
YOU GUYS JUST TAKE IT EASY.
......
IT'S NOTHING TO GET BENT OUT OF SHAPE ABOUT!!
GASP!

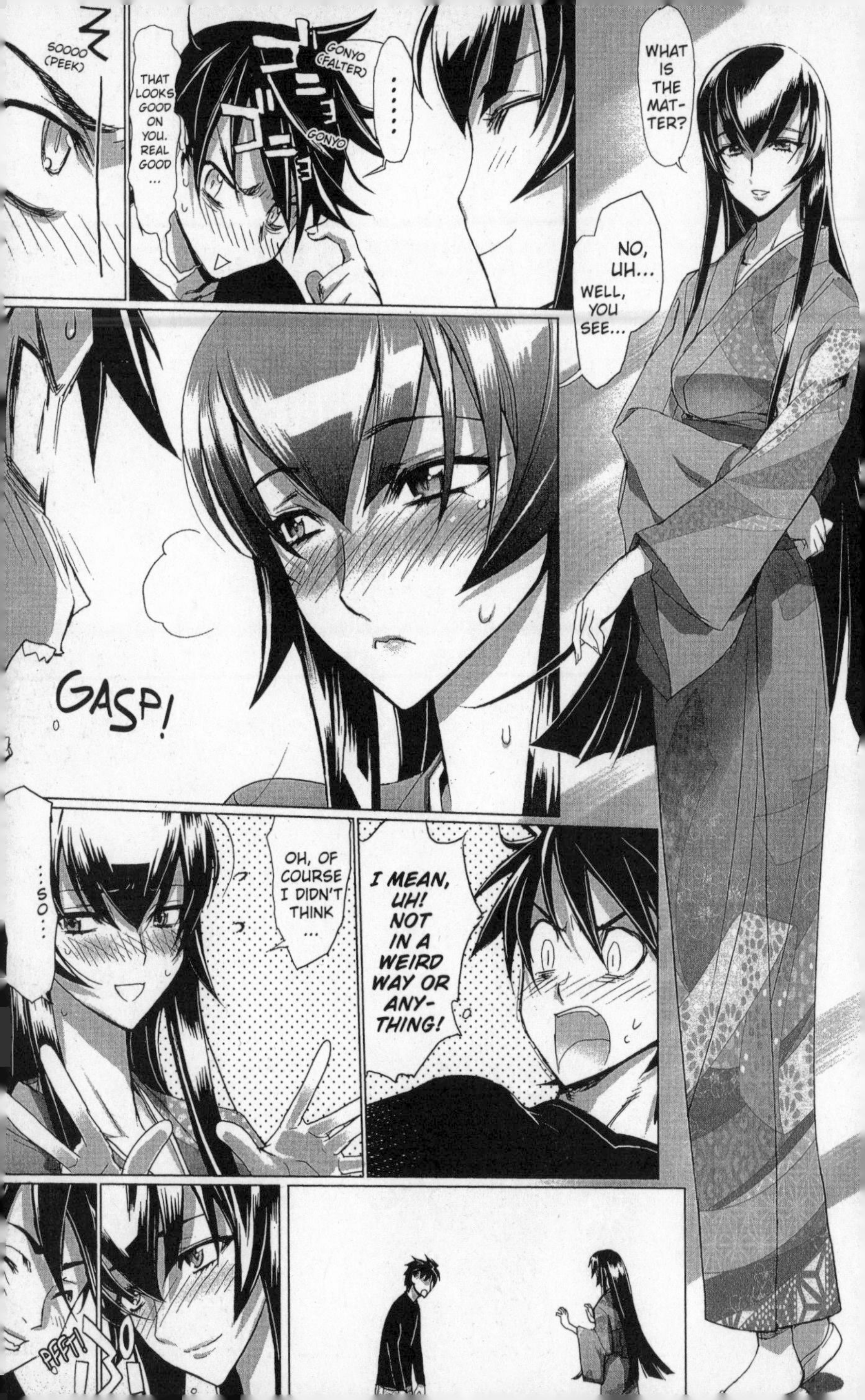
WHAT IS THE MAT-TER?
NO, UH... WELL, YOU SEE...
......
GONYO (FALTER)
THAT LOOKS GOOD ON YOU. REAL GOOD ...
GONYO
SOOOO (PEEK)
GASP!
I MEAN, UH! NOT IN A WEIRD WAY OR ANY-THING!
OH, OF COURSE I DIDN'T THINK ...
...SO...
PFFT!

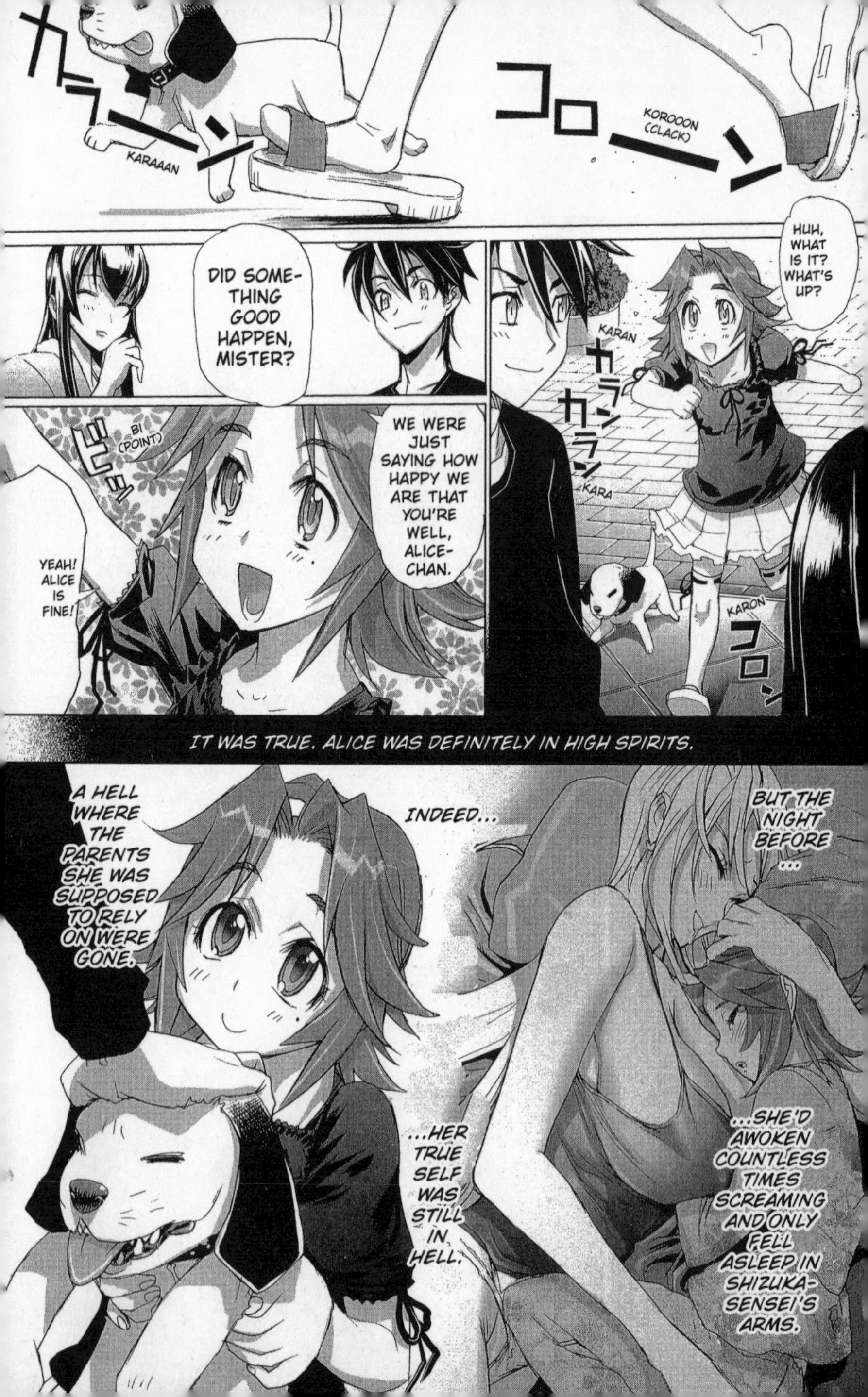

コローン
KOROOON (CLACK)
カラーン
KARAAAN
HUH, WHAT IS IT? WHAT'S UP?
カラン
KARAN
カラン
KARA
コロン
KARON
DID SOME-THING GOOD HAPPEN, MISTER?
WE WERE JUST SAYING HOW HAPPY WE ARE THAT YOU'RE WELL, ALICE-CHAN.
BI (POINT)
YEAH! ALICE IS FINE!
IT WAS TRUE. ALICE WAS DEFINITELY IN HIGH SPIRITS.
BUT THE NIGHT BEFORE...
...SHE'D AWOKEN COUNTLESS TIMES SCREAMING AND ONLY FELL ASLEEP IN SHIZUKA-SENSEI'S ARMS.
INDEED...
...HER TRUE SELF WAS STILL IN HELL.
A HELL WHERE THE PARENTS SHE WAS SUPPOSED TO RELY ON WERE GONE.

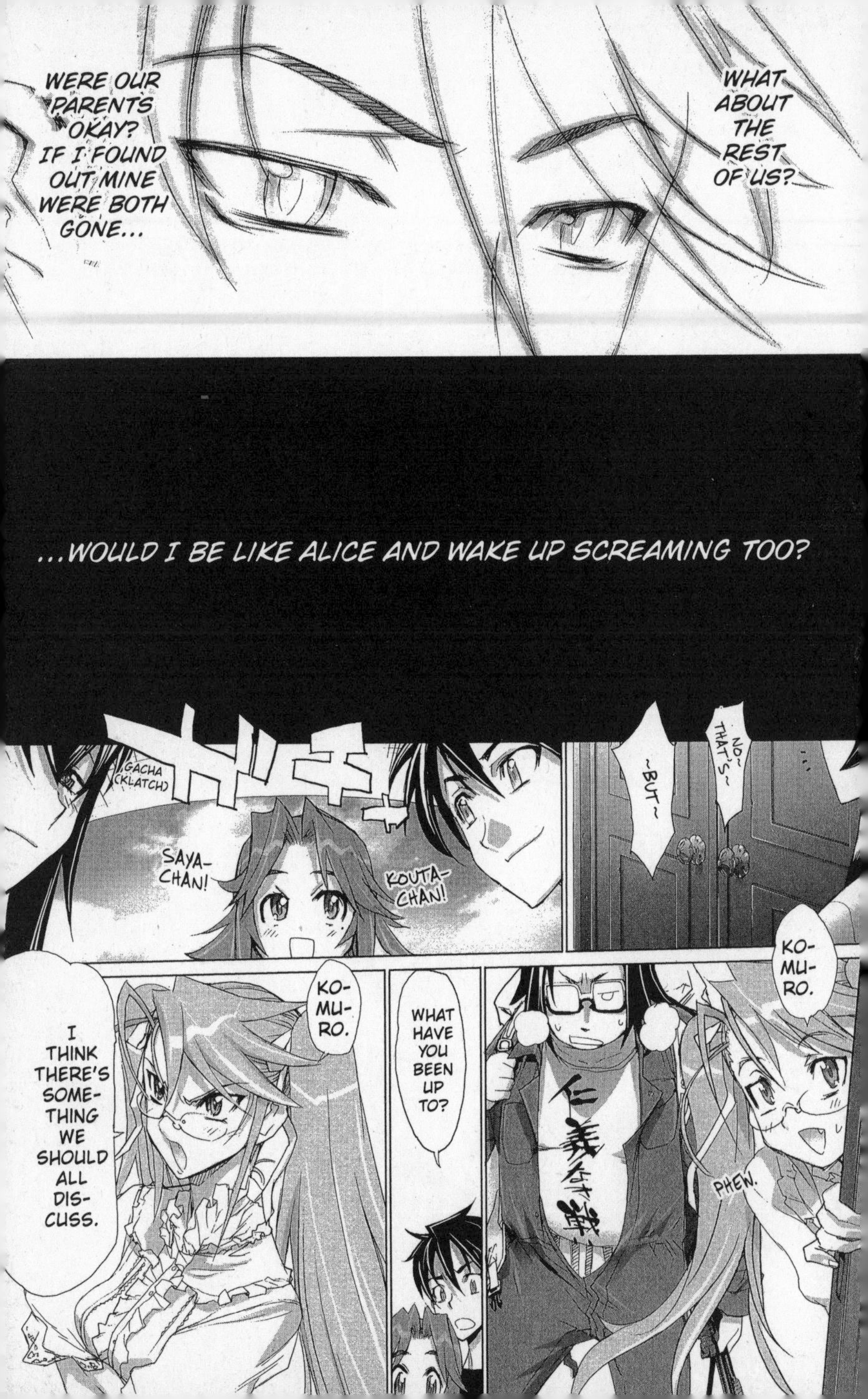
WHAT ABOUT THE REST OF US?
WERE OUR PARENTS OKAY? IF I FOUND OUT MINE WERE BOTH GONE...
...WOULD I BE LIKE ALICE AND WAKE UP SCREAMING TOO?
NO~ THAT'S~
~BUT~
KOUTA-CHAN!
SAYA-CHAN!
GACHA (KLATCH)
KO-MU-RO.
PHEW.
WHAT HAVE YOU BEEN UP TO?
KO-MU-RO.
I THINK THERE'S SOME-THING WE SHOULD ALL DIS-CUSS.

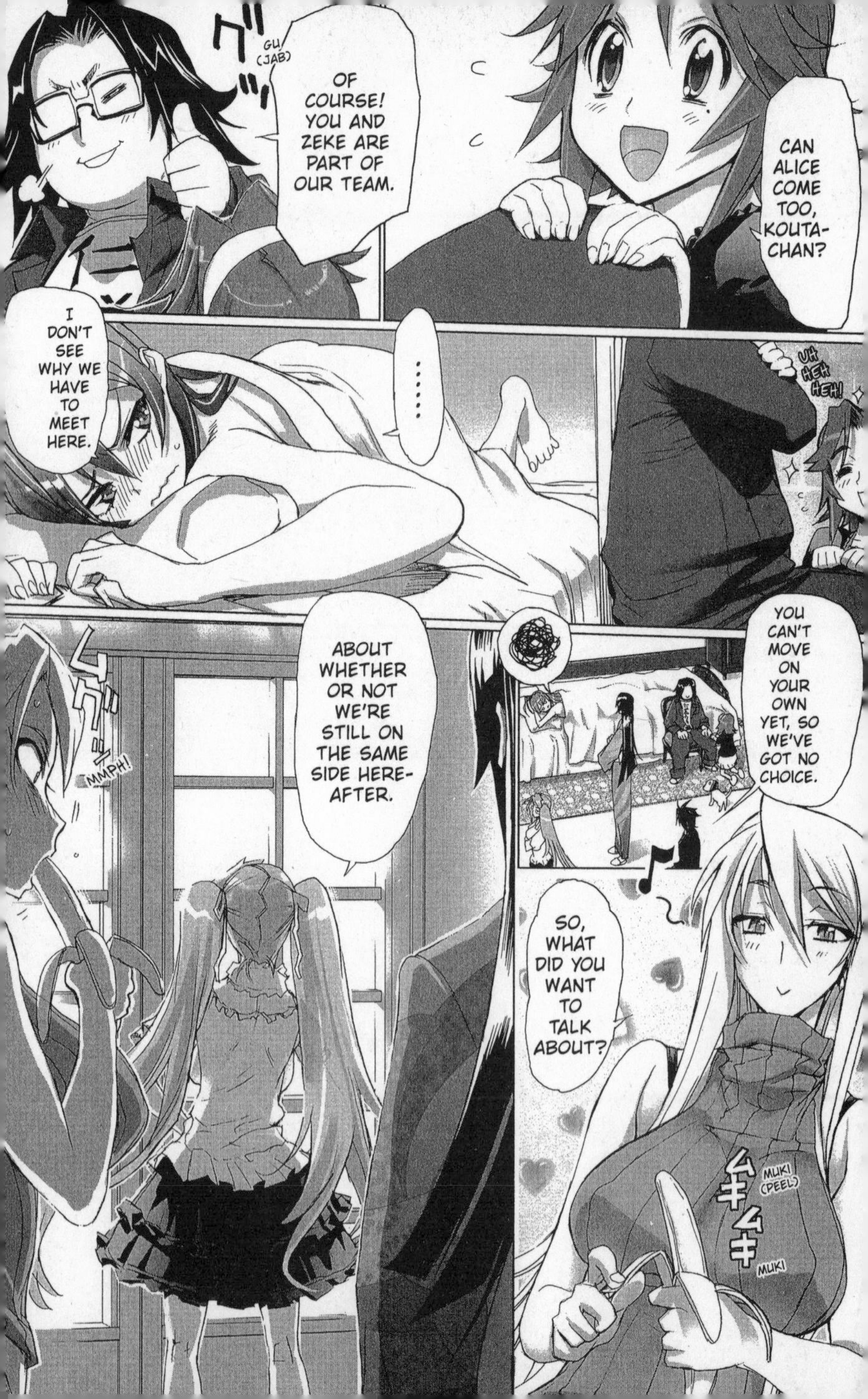
CAN ALICE COME TOO, KOUTA-CHAN?
GU (JAB)
OF COURSE! YOU AND ZEKE ARE PART OF OUR TEAM.
UH HEH HEH!
......
I DON'T SEE WHY WE HAVE TO MEET HERE.
YOU CAN'T MOVE ON YOUR OWN YET, SO WE'VE GOT NO CHOICE.
SO, WHAT DID YOU WANT TO TALK ABOUT?
MUKI (PEEL)
MUKI
ABOUT WHETHER OR NOT WE'RE STILL ON THE SAME SIDE HERE-AFTER.
MMPH!

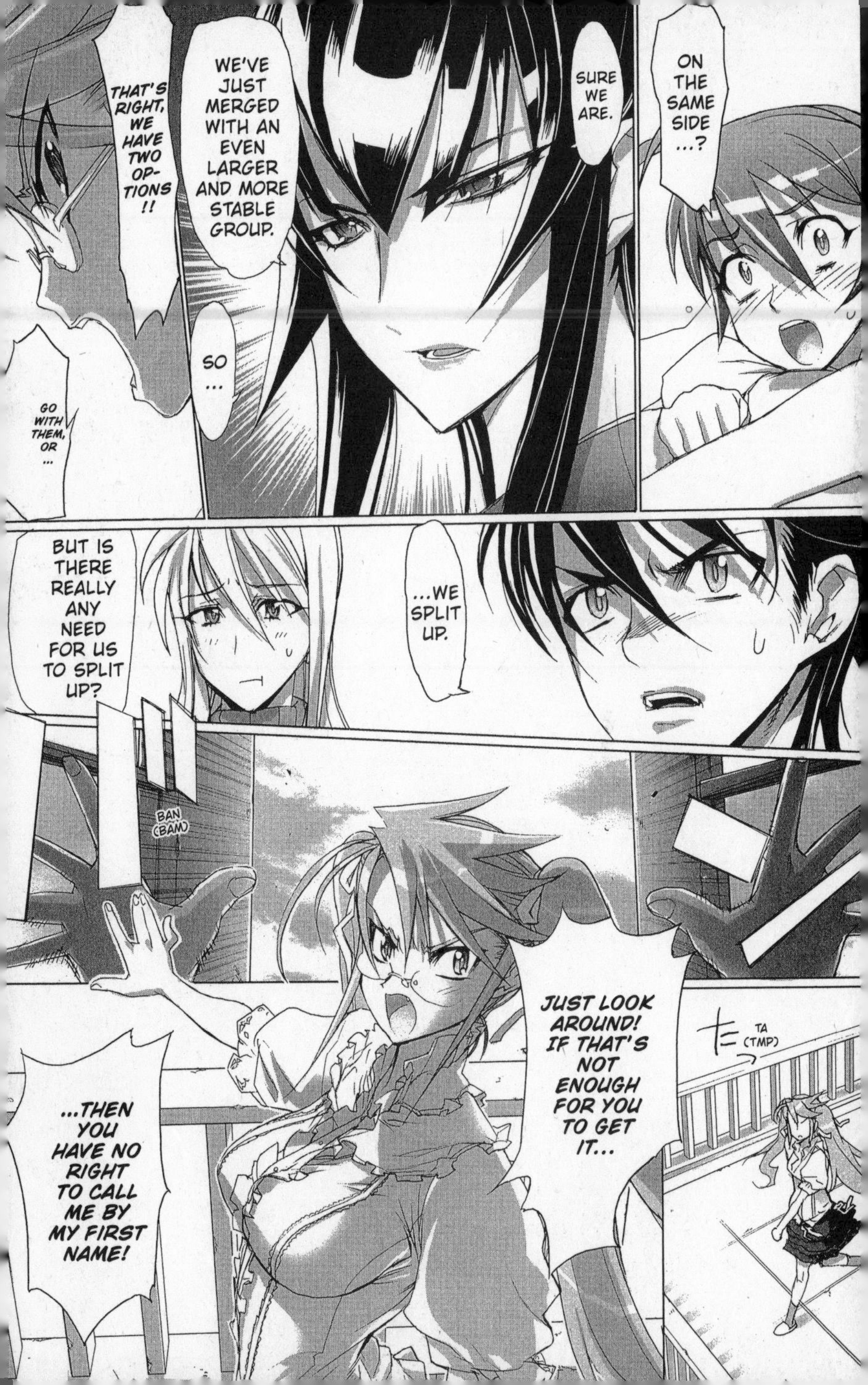
ON THE SAME SIDE ...?
SURE WE ARE.
WE'VE JUST MERGED WITH AN EVEN LARGER AND MORE STABLE GROUP.
SO ...
THAT'S RIGHT, WE HAVE TWO OP-TIONS!!
GO WITH THEM, OR ...
...WE SPLIT UP.
BUT IS THERE REALLY ANY NEED FOR US TO SPLIT UP?
BAN (BAM)
TA (TMP)
JUST LOOK AROUND! IF THAT'S NOT ENOUGH FOR YOU TO GET IT...
...THEN YOU HAVE NO RIGHT TO CALL ME BY MY FIRST NAME!

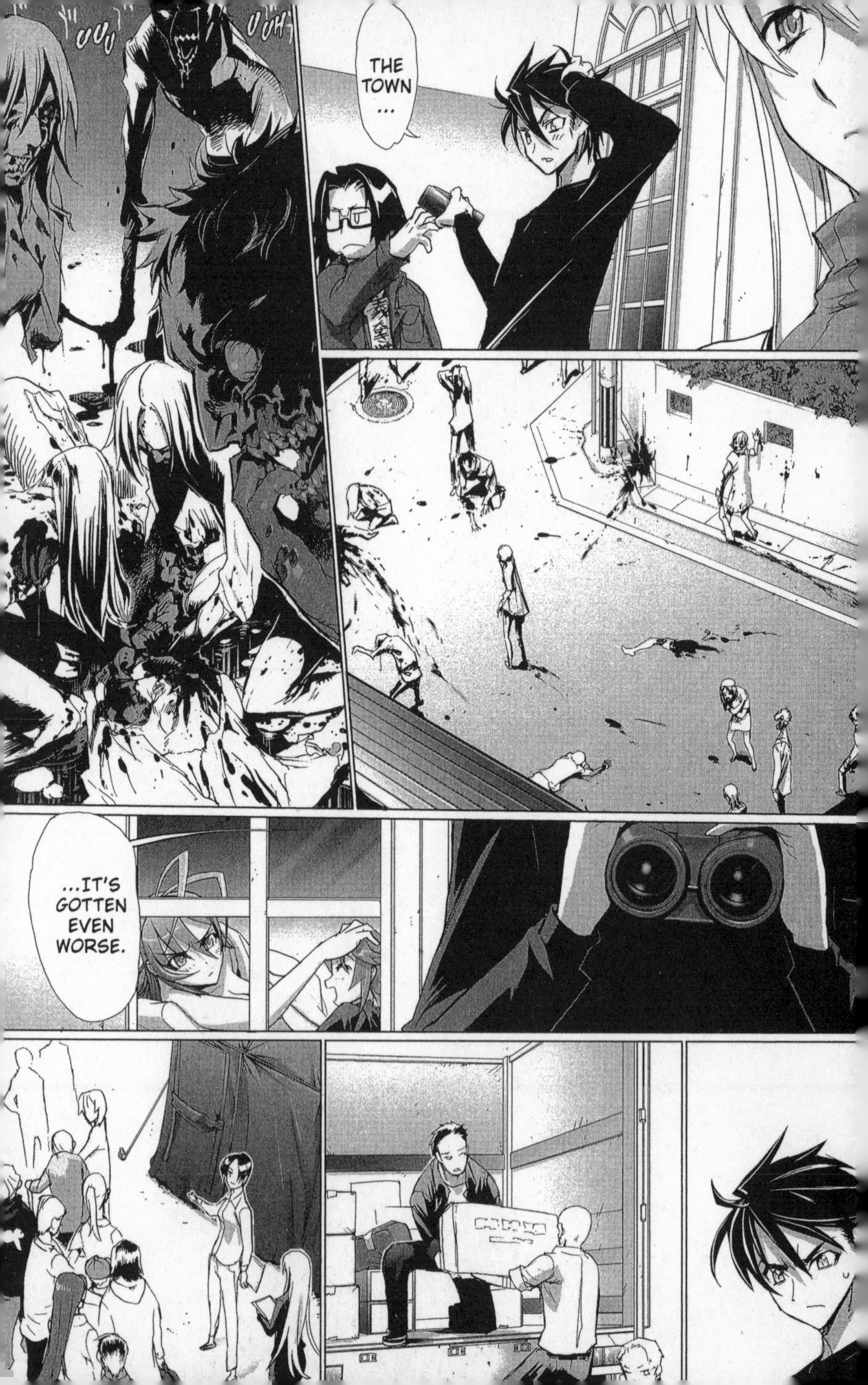
THE TOWN ...
UUU
UUH
...IT'S GOTTEN EVEN WORSE.

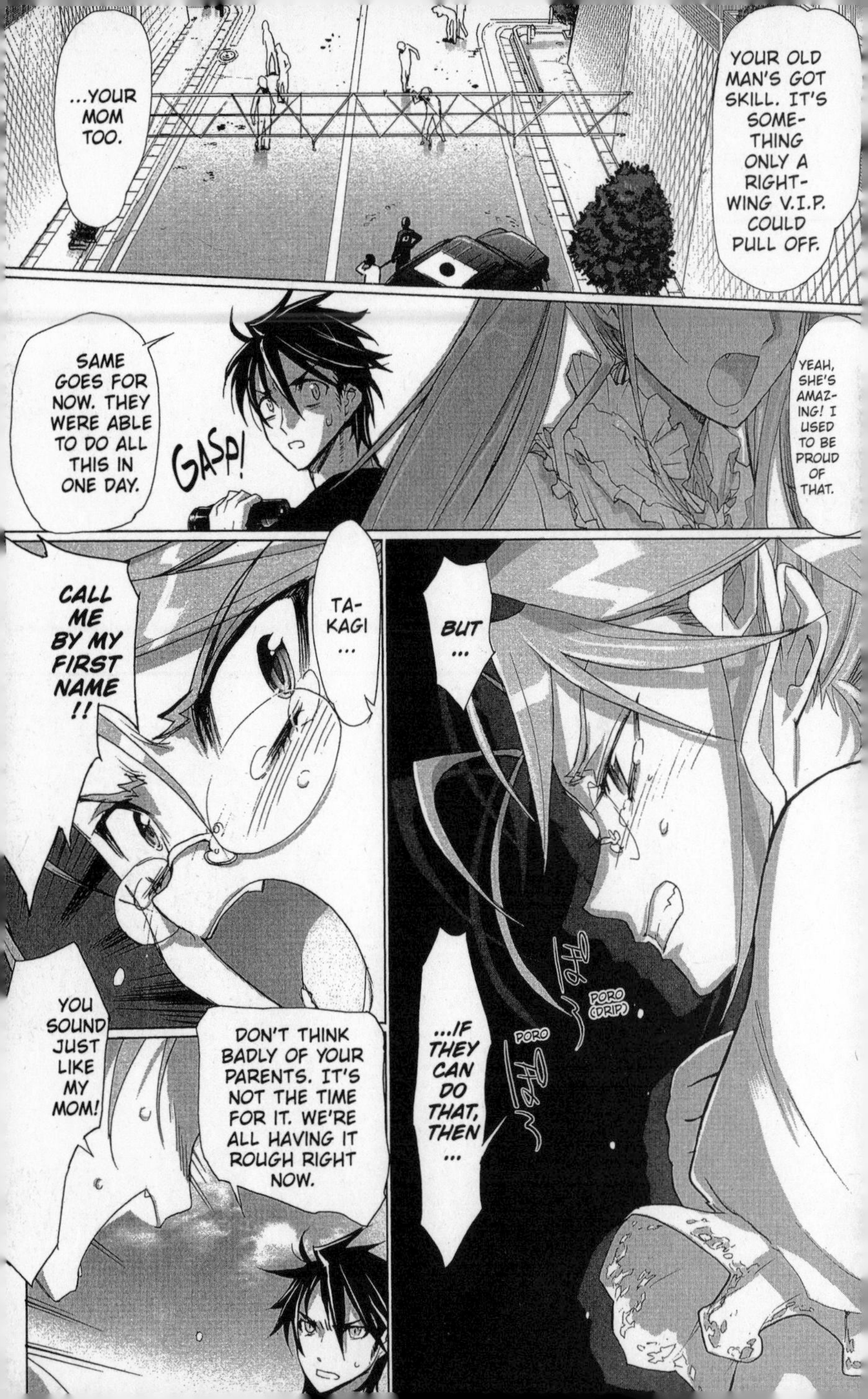
YOUR OLD MAN'S GOT SKILL. IT'S SOME-THING ONLY A RIGHT-WING V.I.P. COULD PULL OFF.
...YOUR MOM TOO.
YEAH, SHE'S AMAZ-ING! I USED TO BE PROUD OF THAT.
SAME GOES FOR NOW. THEY WERE ABLE TO DO ALL THIS IN ONE DAY.
GASP!
BUT...
...IF THEY CAN DO THAT, THEN...
PORO (DRIP)
PORO
TA-KAGI...
CALL ME BY MY FIRST NAME!!
DON'T THINK BADLY OF YOUR PARENTS. IT'S NOT THE TIME FOR IT. WE'RE ALL HAVING IT ROUGH RIGHT NOW.
YOU SOUND JUST LIKE MY MOM!

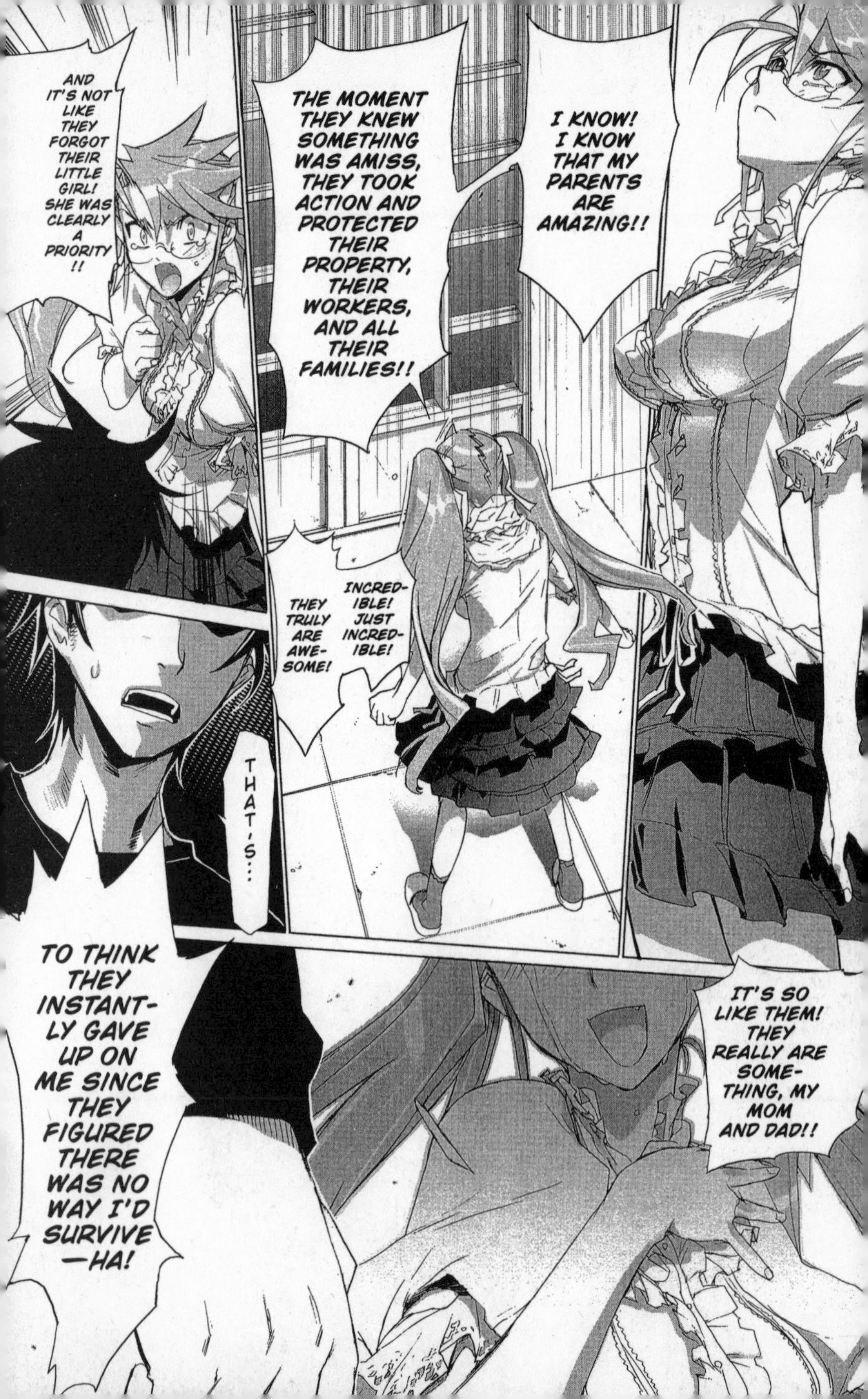
I KNOW! I KNOW THAT MY PARENTS ARE AMAZING!!
THE MOMENT THEY KNEW SOMETHING WAS AMISS, THEY TOOK ACTION AND PROTECTED THEIR PROPERTY, THEIR WORKERS, AND ALL THEIR FAMILIES!!
INCRED-IBLE! JUST INCRED-IBLE!
THEY TRULY ARE AWE-SOME!
AND IT'S NOT LIKE THEY FORGOT THEIR LITTLE GIRL! SHE WAS CLEARLY A PRIORITY!!
THAT'S...
IT'S SO LIKE THEM! THEY REALLY ARE SOME-THING, MY MOM AND DAD!!
TO THINK THEY INSTANT-LY GAVE UP ON ME SINCE THEY FIGURED THERE WAS NO WAY I'D SURVIVE—HA!

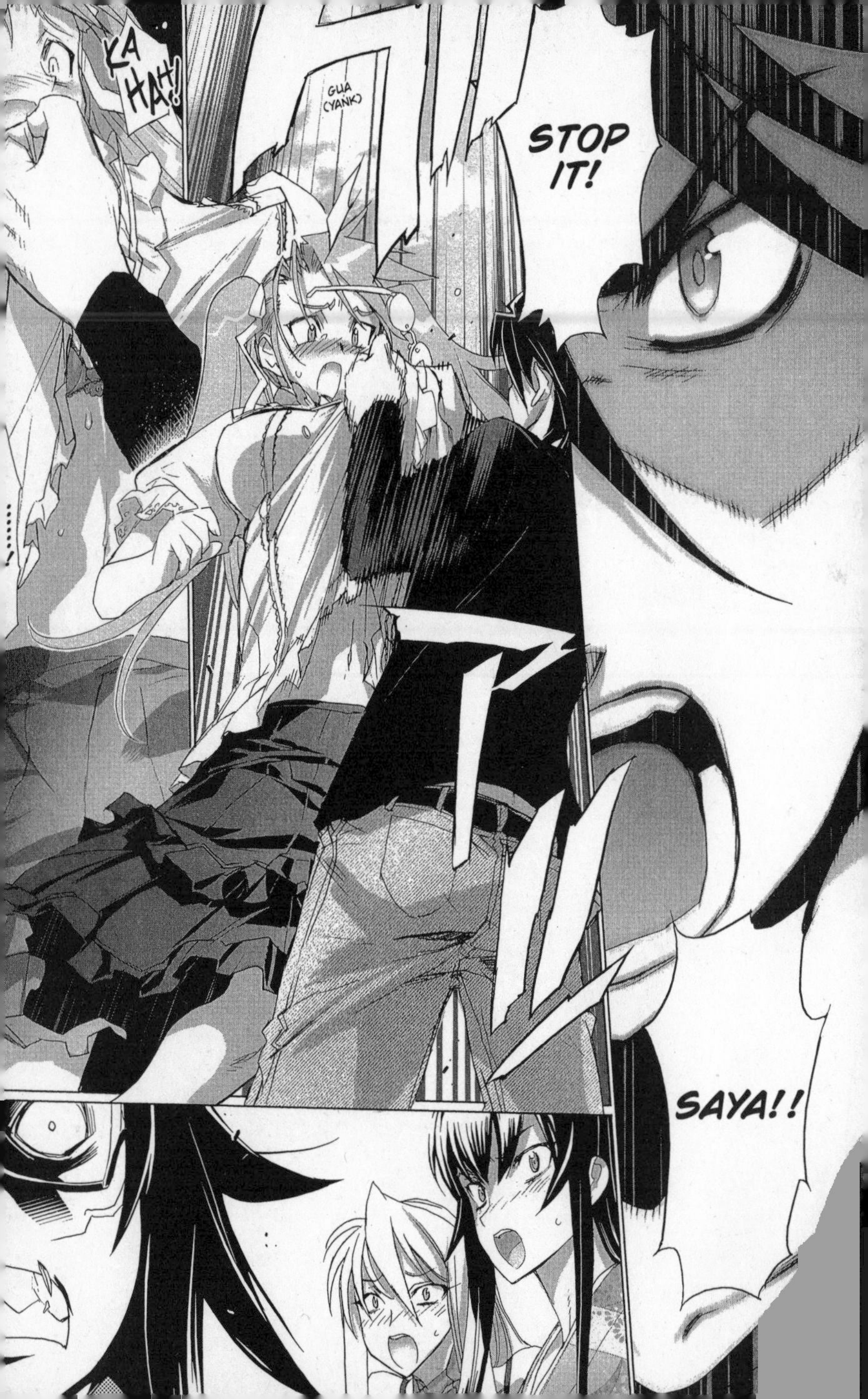
STOP IT!
KA HAH!
GUA (YANK)
......!
SAYA!!

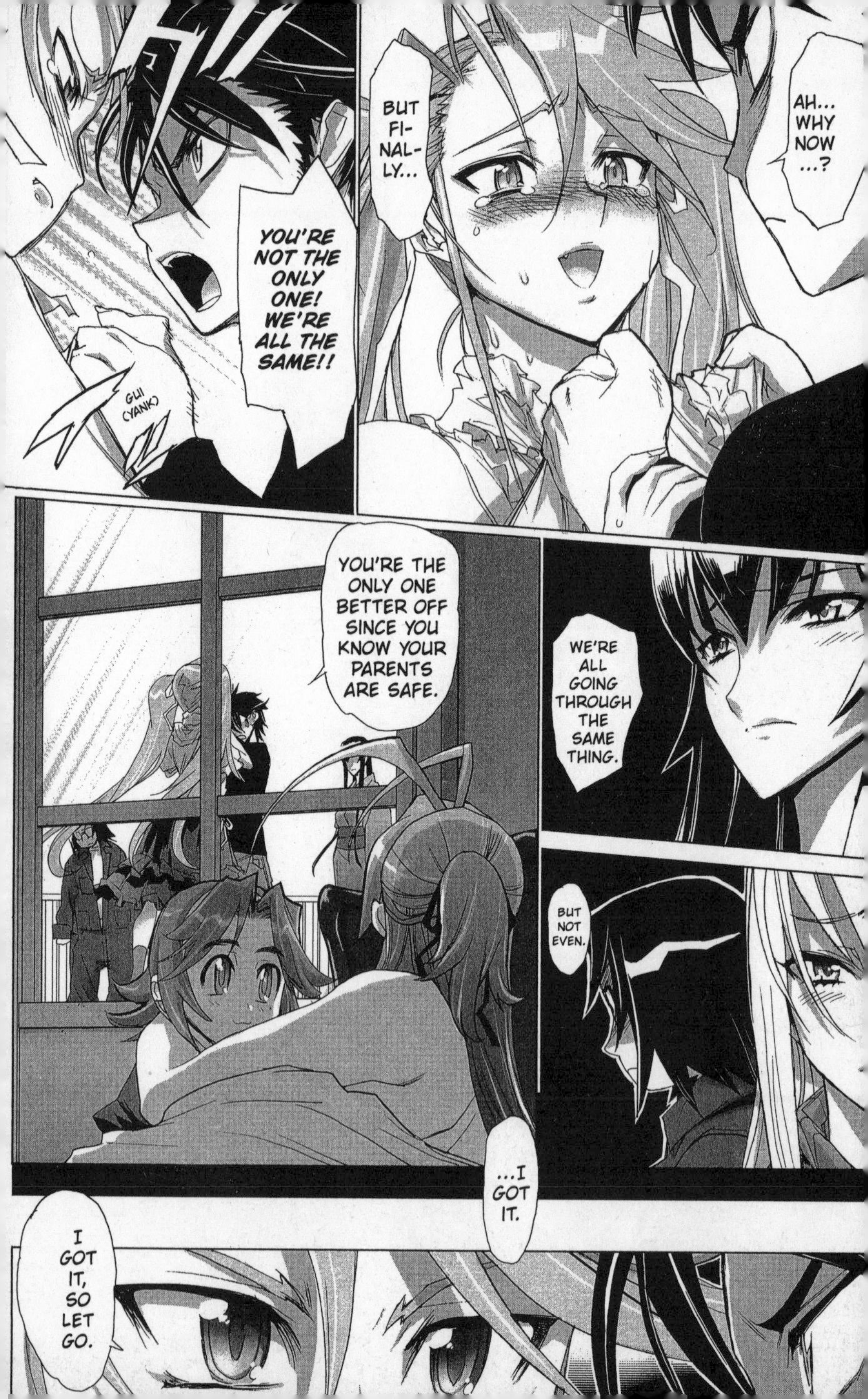
AH... WHY NOW ...?
BUT FI-NAL-LY...
YOU'RE NOT THE ONLY ONE! WE'RE ALL THE SAME!!
GUI (YANK)
WE'RE ALL GOING THROUGH THE SAME THING.
BUT NOT EVEN.
YOU'RE THE ONLY ONE BETTER OFF SINCE YOU KNOW YOUR PARENTS ARE SAFE.
...I GOT IT.
I GOT IT, SO LET GO.

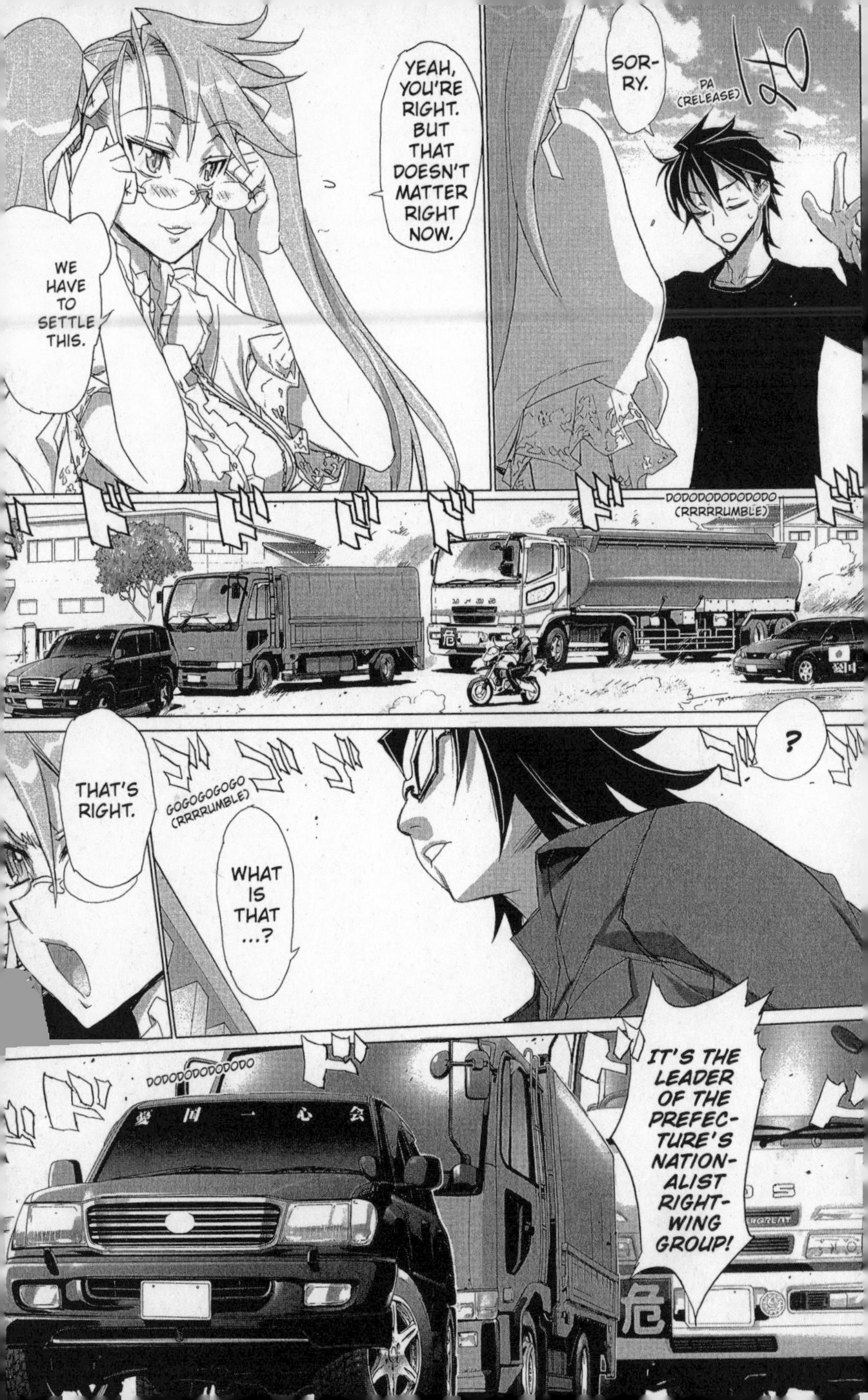
SOR-RY.
PA (RELEASE)
YEAH, YOU'RE RIGHT. BUT THAT DOESN'T MATTER RIGHT NOW.
WE HAVE TO SETTLE THIS.
DODODODODODODO (RRRRRUMBLE)
?
WHAT IS THAT ...?
GOGOGOGOGO (RRRRUMBLE)
THAT'S RIGHT.
IT'S THE LEADER OF THE PREFEC-TURE'S NATION-ALIST RIGHT-WING GROUP!
DODODODODODODO
愛国一心会

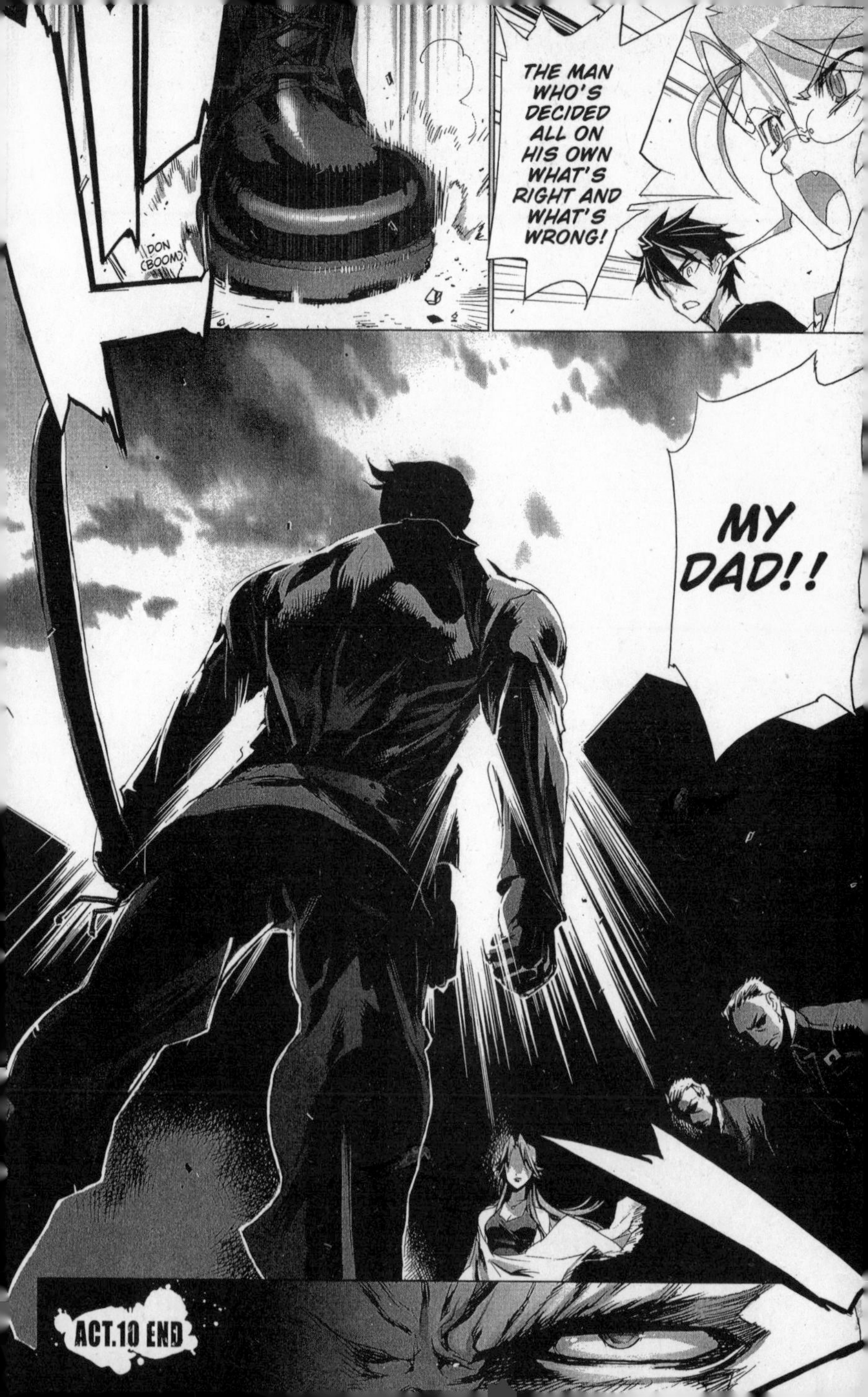
THE MAN WHO'S DECIDED ALL ON HIS OWN WHAT'S RIGHT AND WHAT'S WRONG!
DON (BOOM)
MY DAD!!
ACT.10 END

ACT.11
The Dead's house rules.

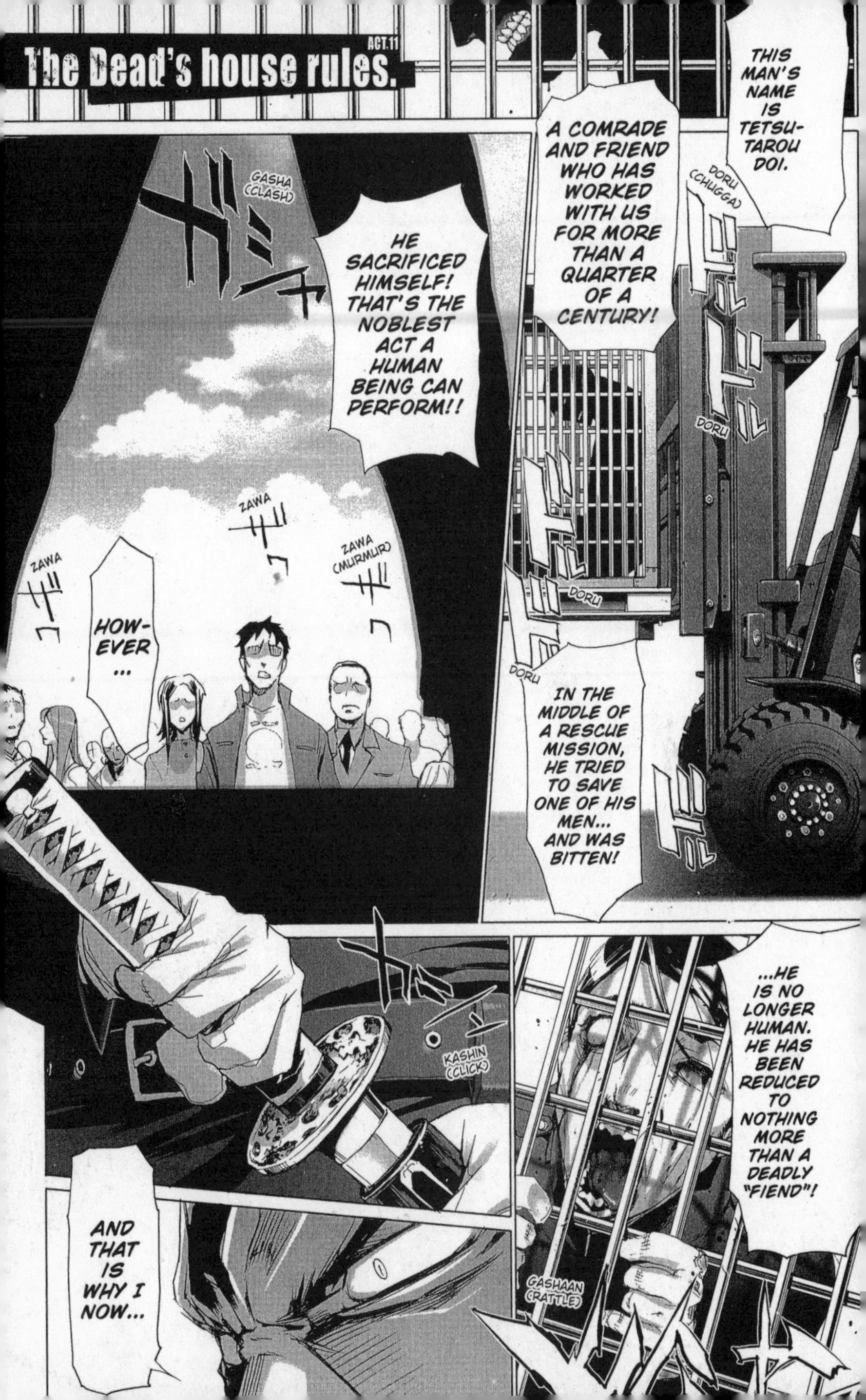
THIS MAN'S NAME IS TETSU-TAROU DOI.
A COMRADE AND FRIEND WHO HAS WORKED WITH US FOR MORE THAN A QUARTER OF A CENTURY!
DORU (CHUGGA)
DORU
DORU
DORU
IN THE MIDDLE OF A RESCUE MISSION, HE TRIED TO SAVE ONE OF HIS MEN... AND WAS BITTEN!
GASHA (CLASH)
HE SACRIFICED HIMSELF! THAT'S THE NOBLEST ACT A HUMAN BEING CAN PERFORM!!
ZAWA
ZAWA (MURMUR)
ZAWA
HOW-EVER...
...HE IS NO LONGER HUMAN. HE HAS BEEN REDUCED TO NOTHING MORE THAN A DEADLY "FIEND"!
GASHAAN (RATTLE)
KASHIN (CLICK)
AND THAT IS WHY I NOW...

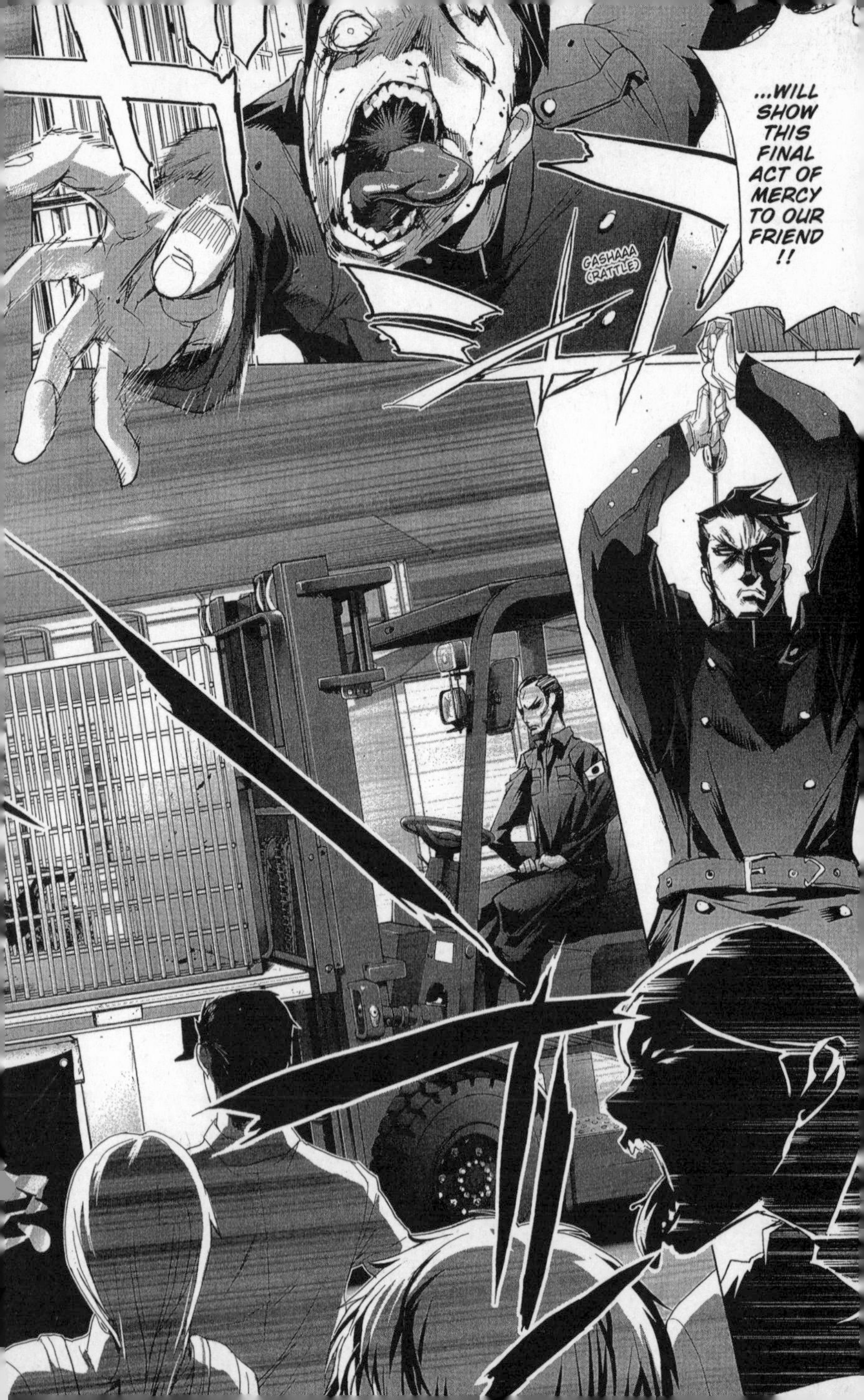
...WILL SHOW THIS FINAL ACT OF MERCY TO OUR FRIEND !!
GASHAAA (RATTLE)

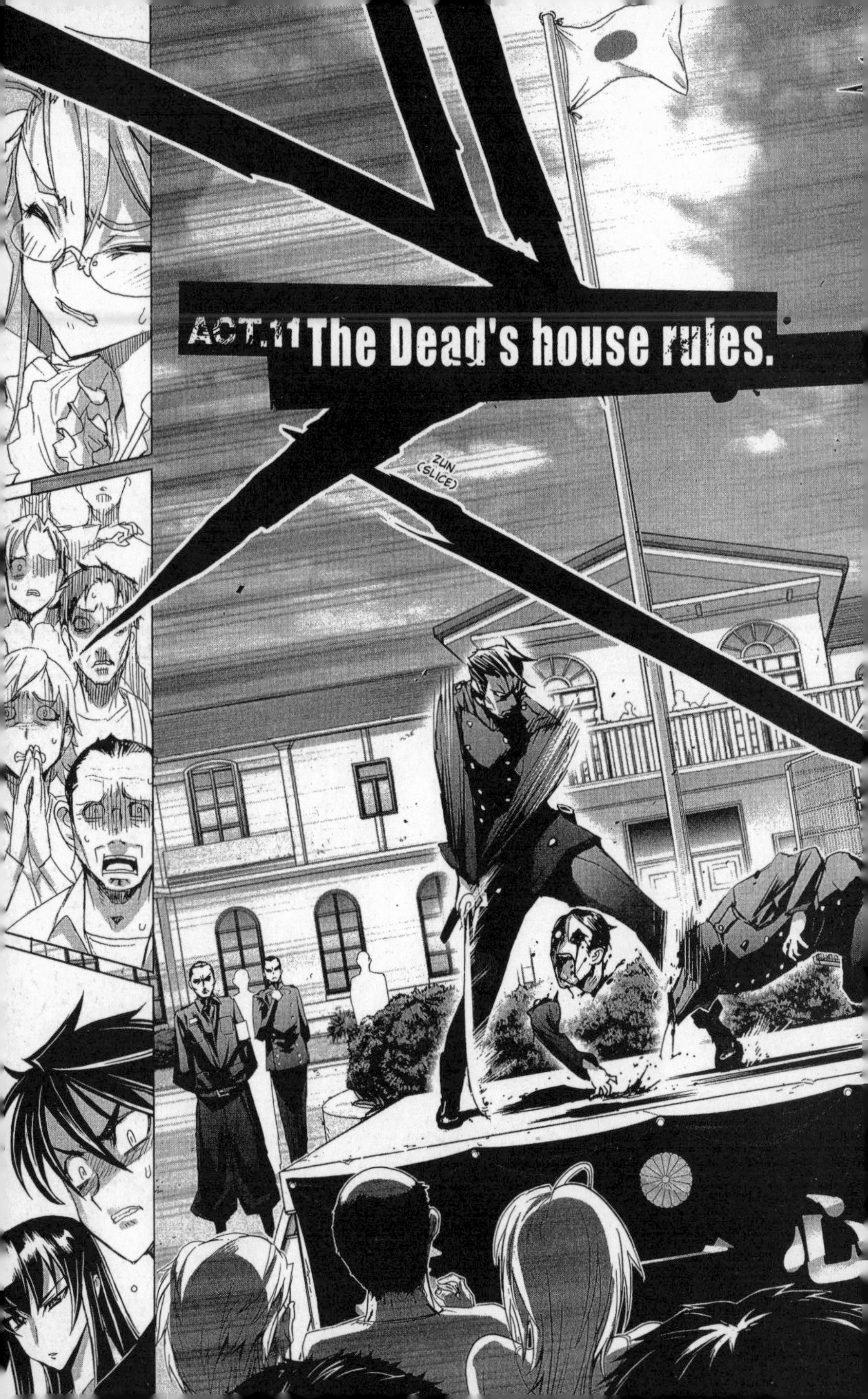
ACT.11 The Dead's house rules.
ZLIN (SLICE)

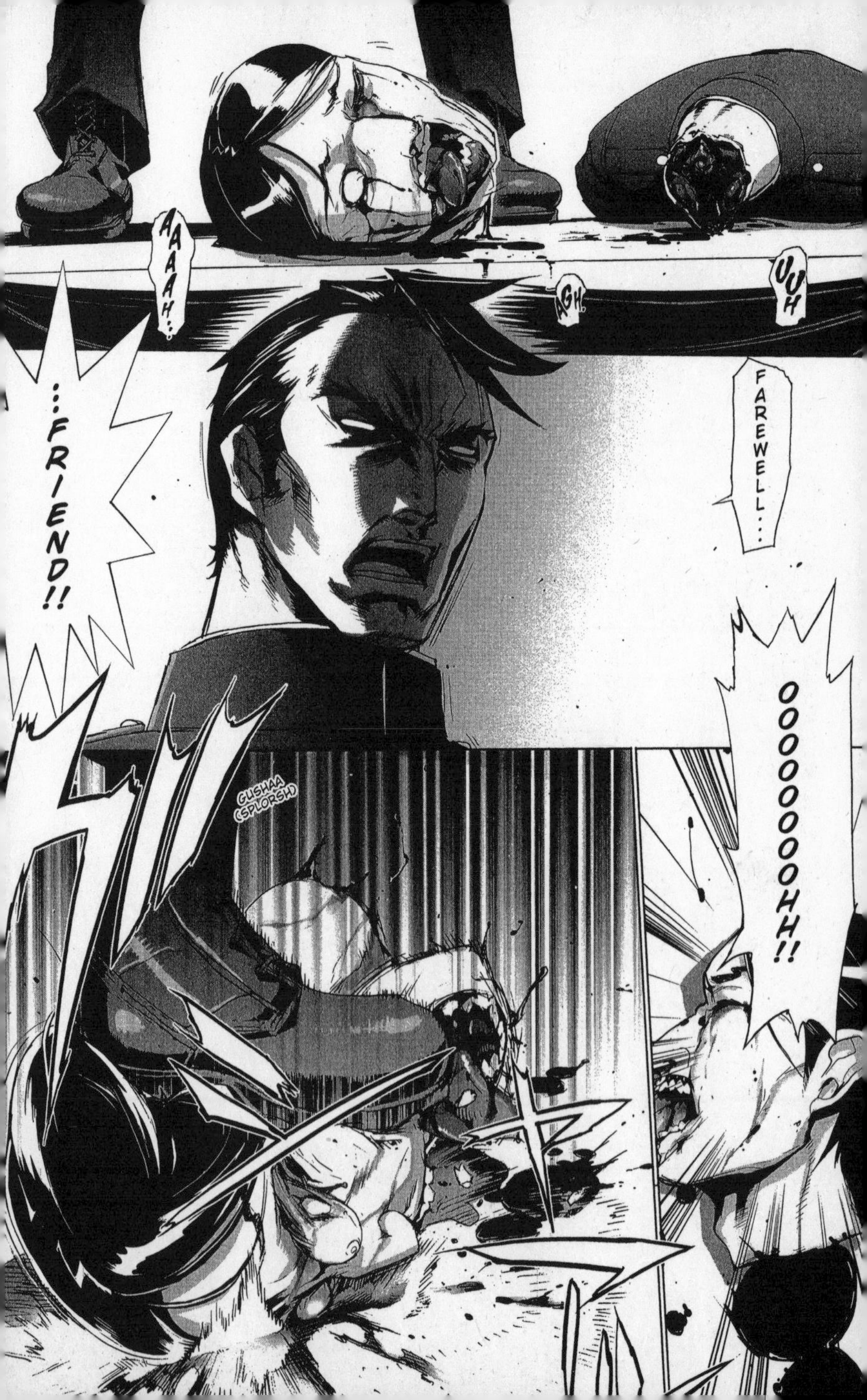
UUH
AGH
AAAAH...
FAREWELL...
...FRIEND!!
OOOOOOOOHH!!
GUSHAA (SPLORSH)

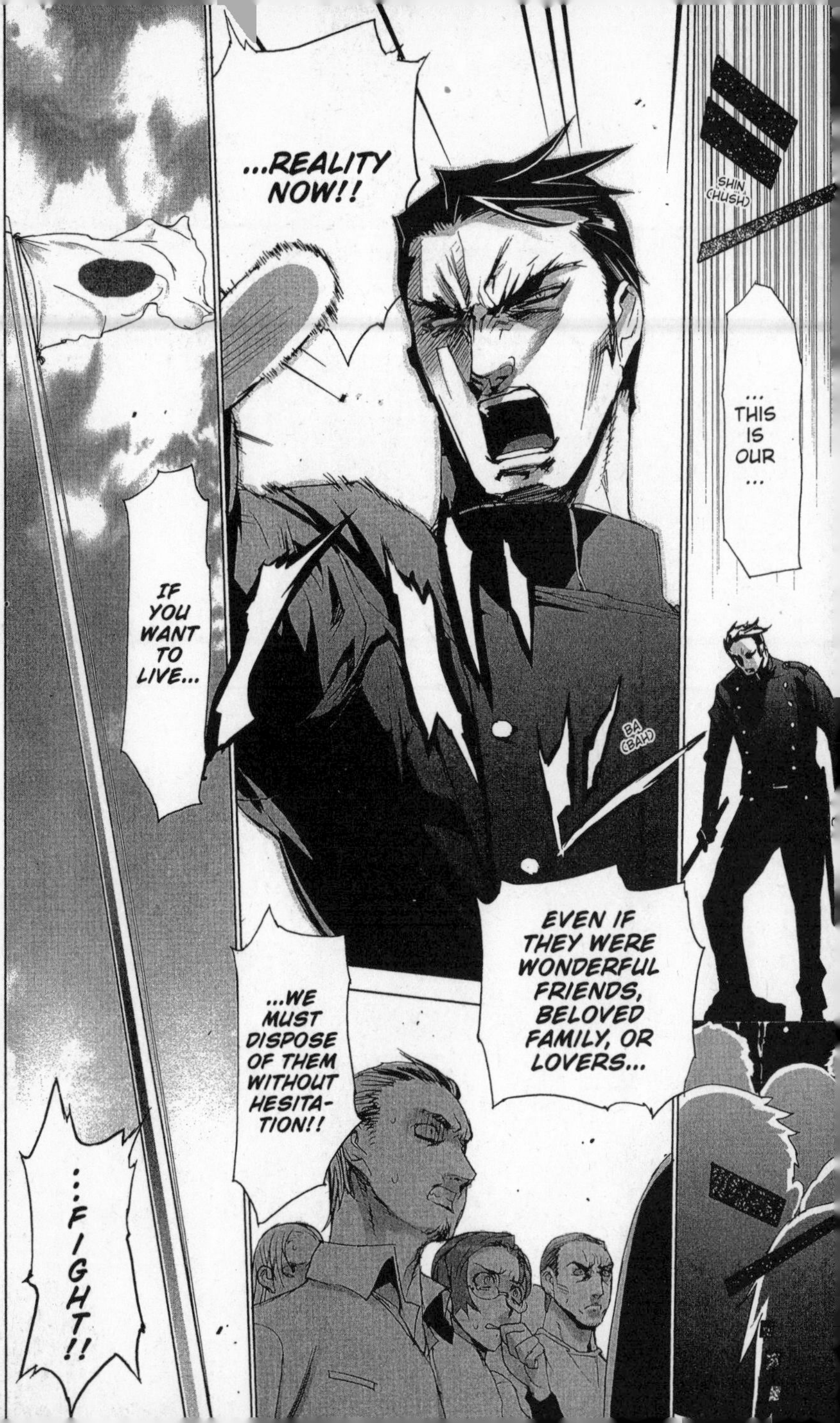
SHIN (HUSH)
... THIS IS OUR ...
...REALITY NOW!!
BA (BAH)
EVEN IF THEY WERE WONDERFUL FRIENDS, BELOVED FAMILY, OR LOVERS...
...WE MUST DISPOSE OF THEM WITHOUT HESITATION!!
IF YOU WANT TO LIVE...
...FIGHT!!

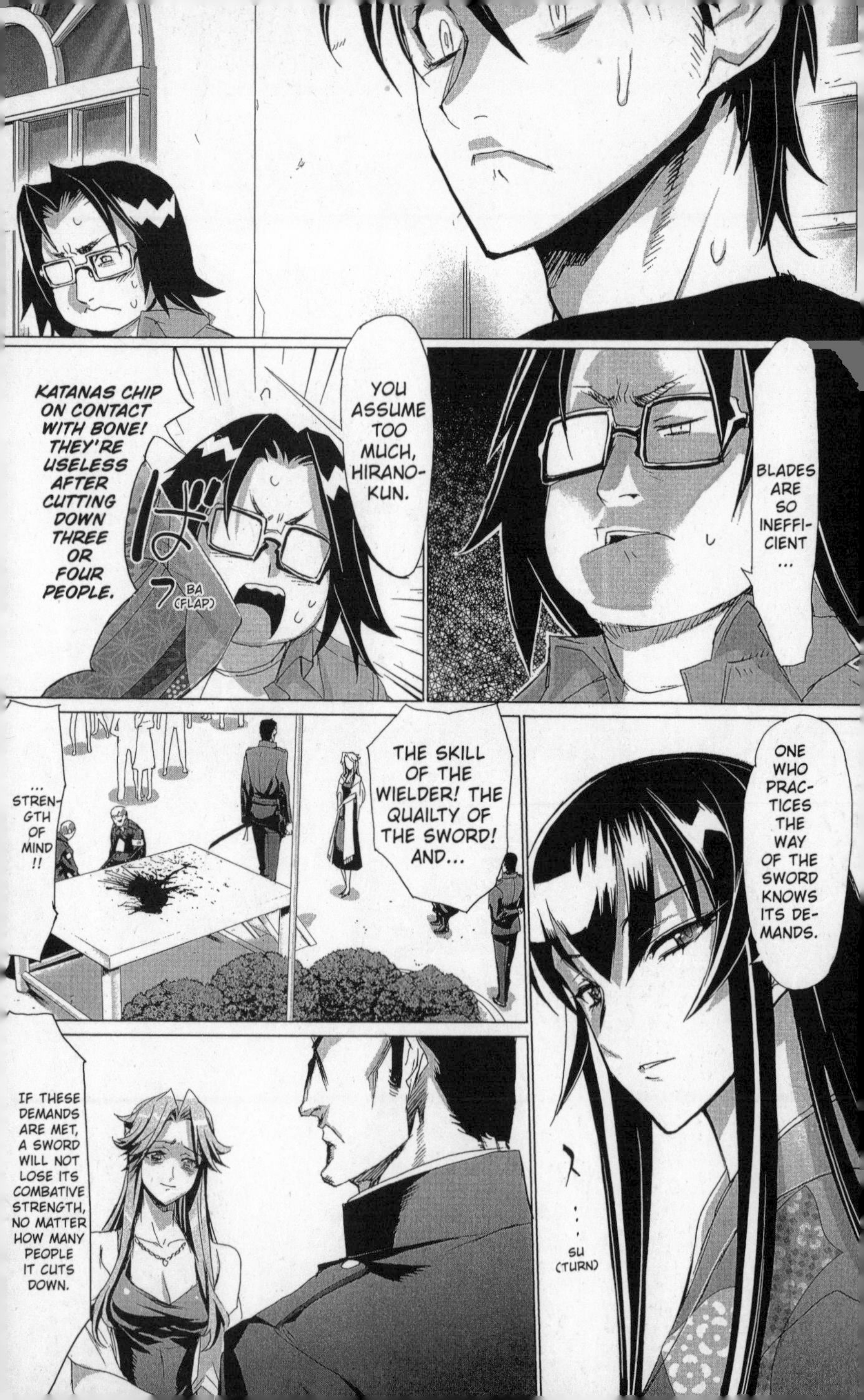

BLADES ARE SO INEFFICIENT...
YOU ASSUME TOO MUCH, HIRANO-KUN.
KATANAS CHIP ON CONTACT WITH BONE! THEY'RE USELESS AFTER CUTTING DOWN THREE OR FOUR PEOPLE.
BA (FLAP)
ONE WHO PRACTICES THE WAY OF THE SWORD KNOWS ITS DEMANDS.
...
SU (TURN)
THE SKILL OF THE WIELDER! THE QUAILTY OF THE SWORD! AND...
...STRENGTH OF MIND!!
IF THESE DEMANDS ARE MET, A SWORD WILL NOT LOSE ITS COMBATIVE STRENGTH, NO MATTER HOW MANY PEOPLE IT CUTS DOWN.

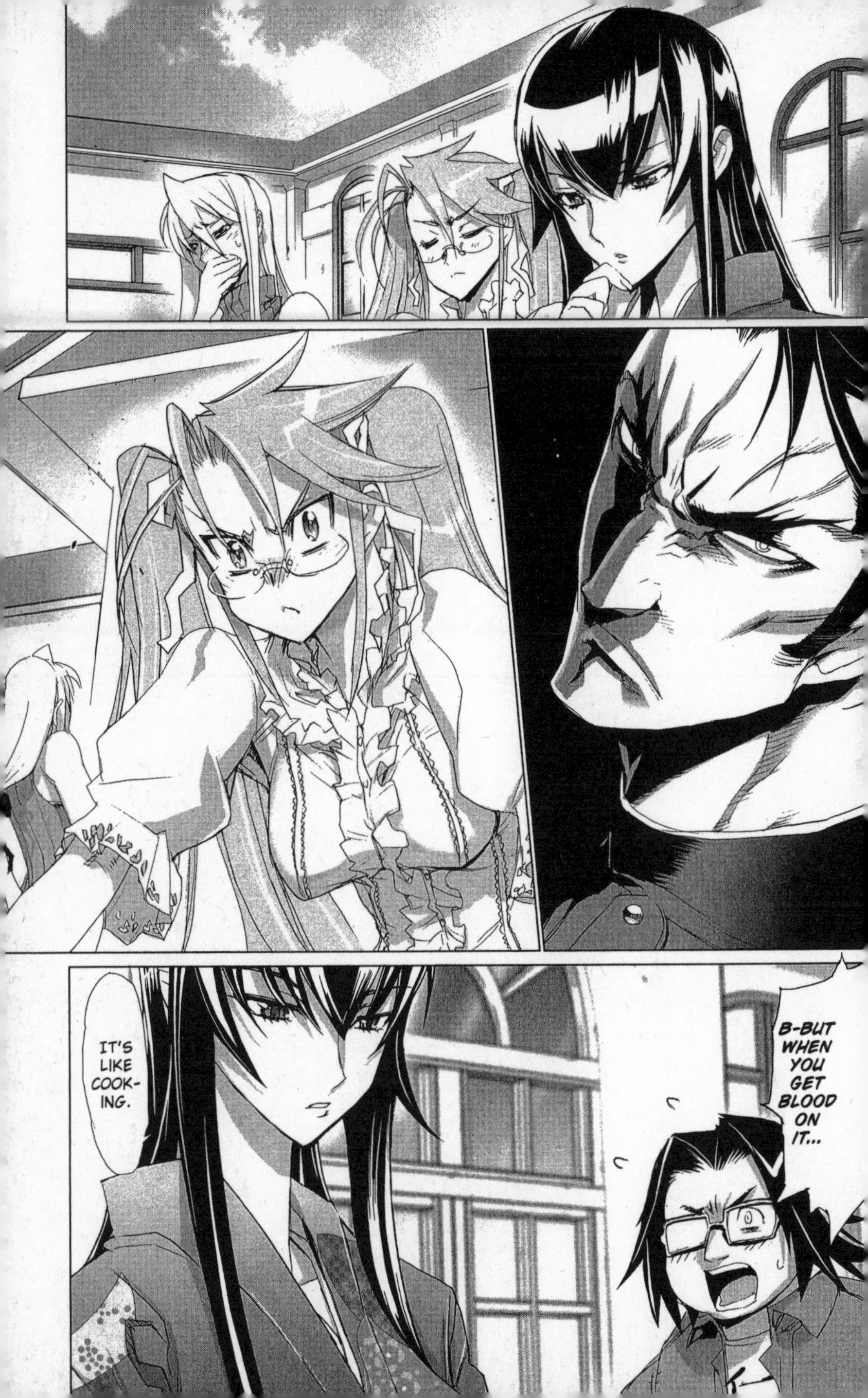
B-BUT WHEN YOU GET BLOOD ON IT...
IT'S LIKE COOK-ING.

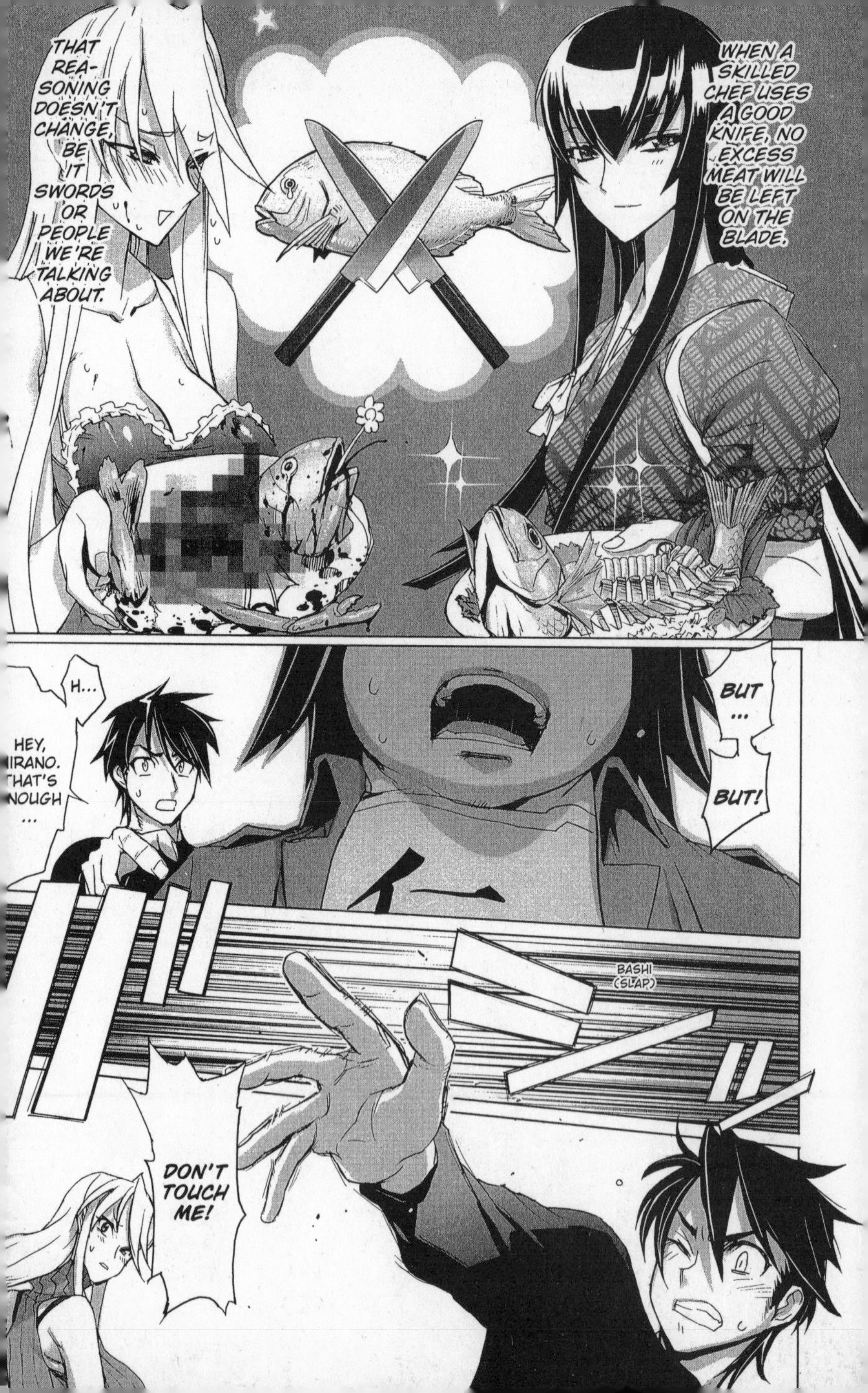
WHEN A SKILLED CHEF USES A GOOD KNIFE, NO EXCESS MEAT WILL BE LEFT ON THE BLADE.
THAT REASONING DOESN'T CHANGE, BE IT SWORDS OR PEOPLE WE'RE TALKING ABOUT.
BUT ...
BUT!
H...
HEY, IRANO. THAT'S NOUGH ...
BASHI (SLAP)
DON'T TOUCH ME!

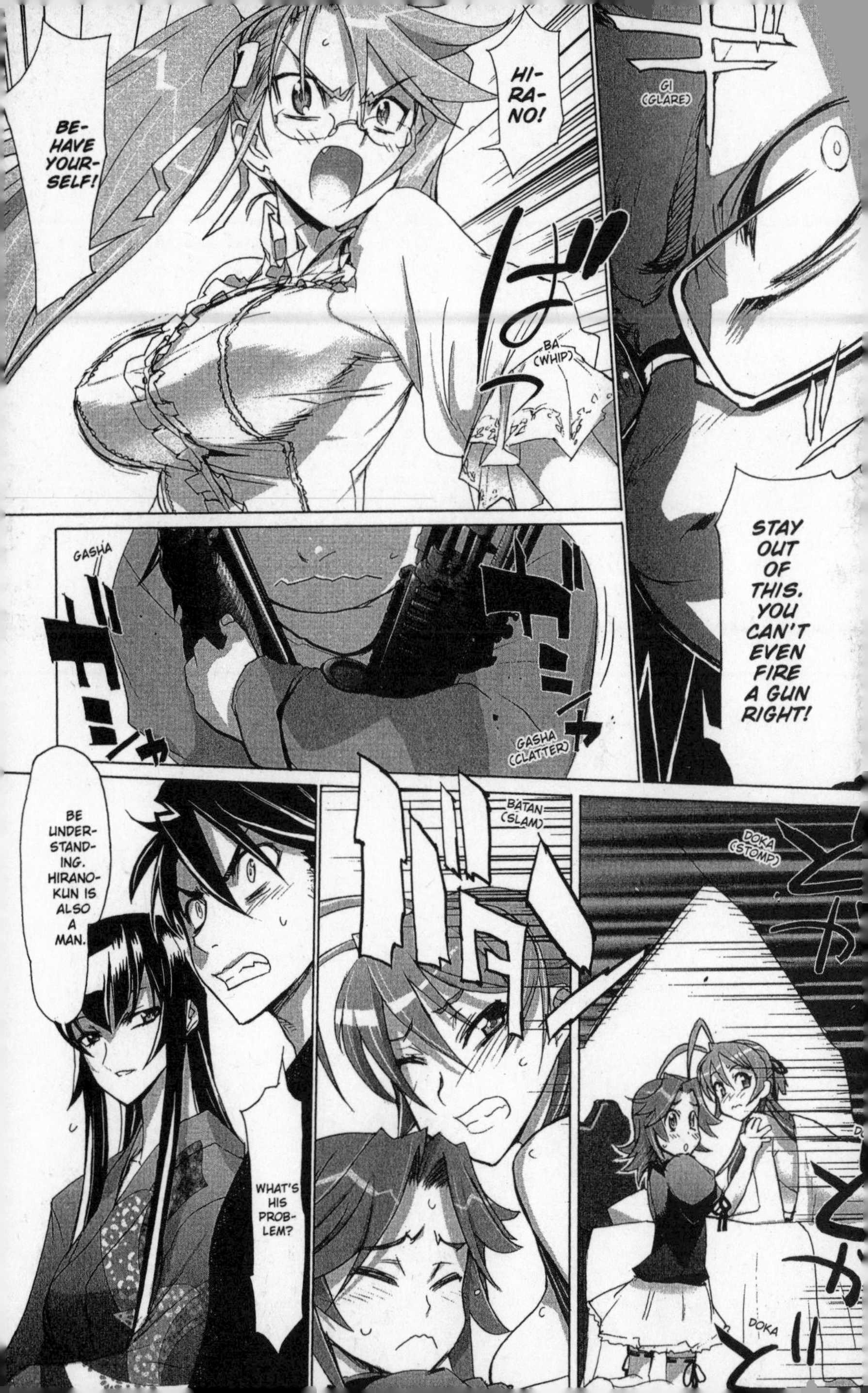
GI (GLARE)
STAY OUT OF THIS. YOU CAN'T EVEN FIRE A GUN RIGHT!
HI-RA-NO!
BE-HAVE YOUR-SELF!
BA (WHIP)
GASHA
GASHA (CLATTER)
DOKA (STOMP)
DOKA
BATAN (SLAM)
WHAT'S HIS PROB-LEM?
BE UNDER-STAND-ING. HIRANO-KUN IS ALSO A MAN.

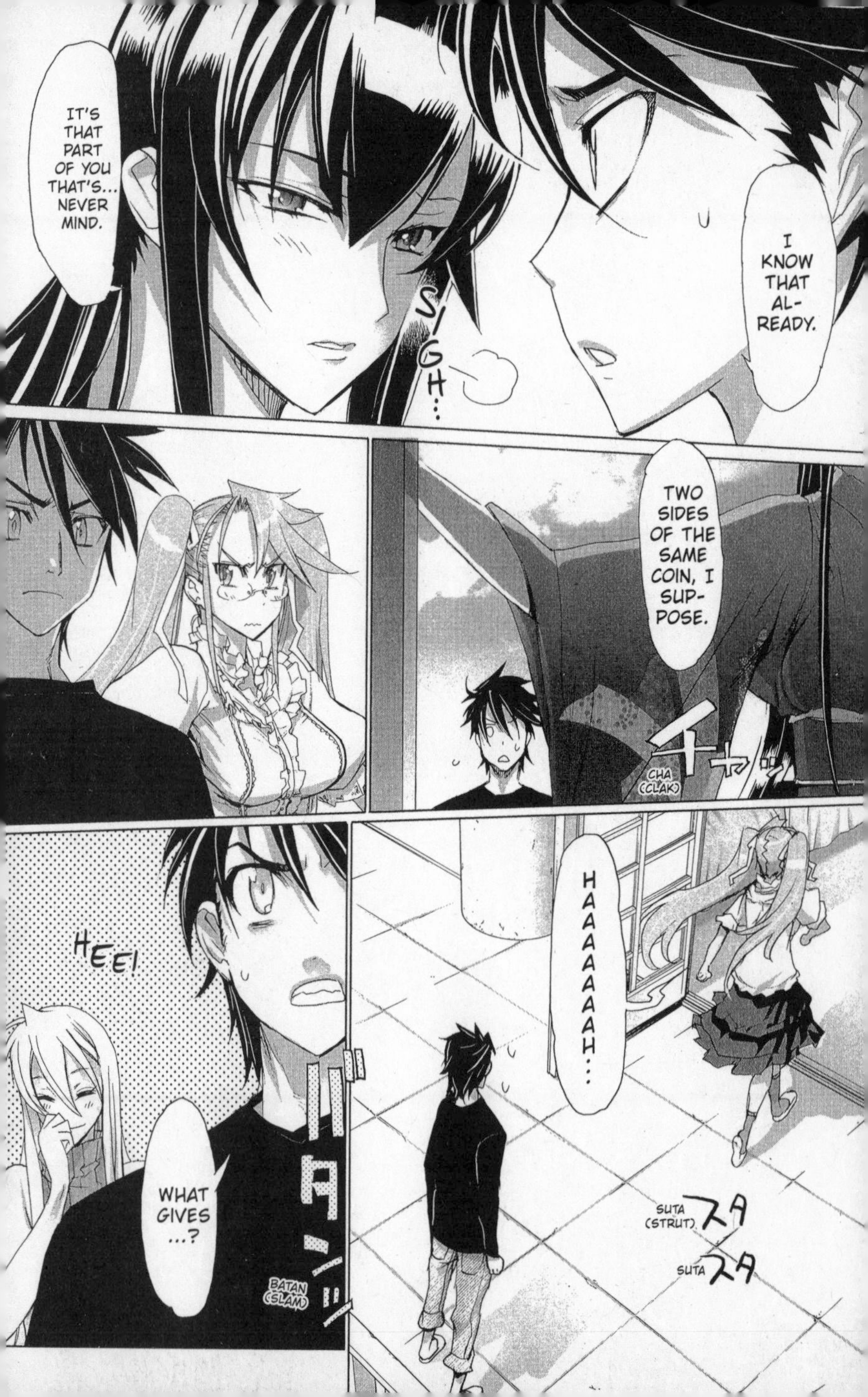
I KNOW THAT AL-READY.
SIGH...
IT'S THAT PART OF YOU THAT'S... NEVER MIND.
TWO SIDES OF THE SAME COIN, I SUPPOSE.
CHA (CLAK)
HAAAAAAAAH...
SUTA (STRUT)
SUTA
BATAN (SLAM)
WHAT GIVES ...?
HEEI

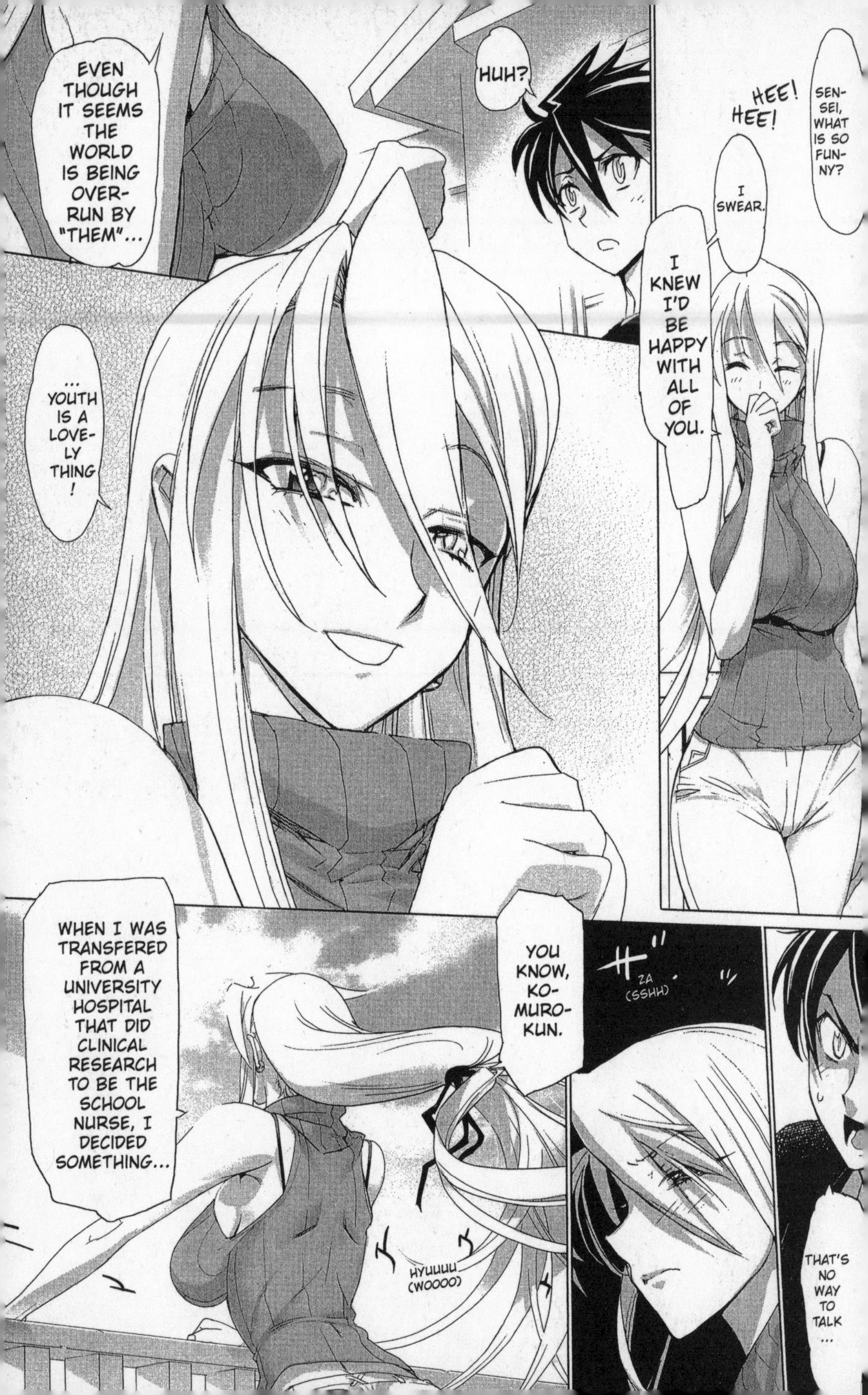
SEN-SEI, WHAT IS SO FUN-NY?
HEE! HEE!
I SWEAR.
I KNEW I'D BE HAPPY WITH ALL OF YOU.
HUH?
EVEN THOUGH IT SEEMS THE WORLD IS BEING OVER-RUN BY "THEM"...
... YOUTH IS A LOVE-LY THING!
THAT'S NO WAY TO TALK...
ZA (SSHH)
YOU KNOW, KO-MURO-KUN.
WHEN I WAS TRANSFERED FROM A UNIVERSITY HOSPITAL THAT DID CLINICAL RESEARCH TO BE THE SCHOOL NURSE, I DECIDED SOMETHING...
HYUUUU (WOOOO)

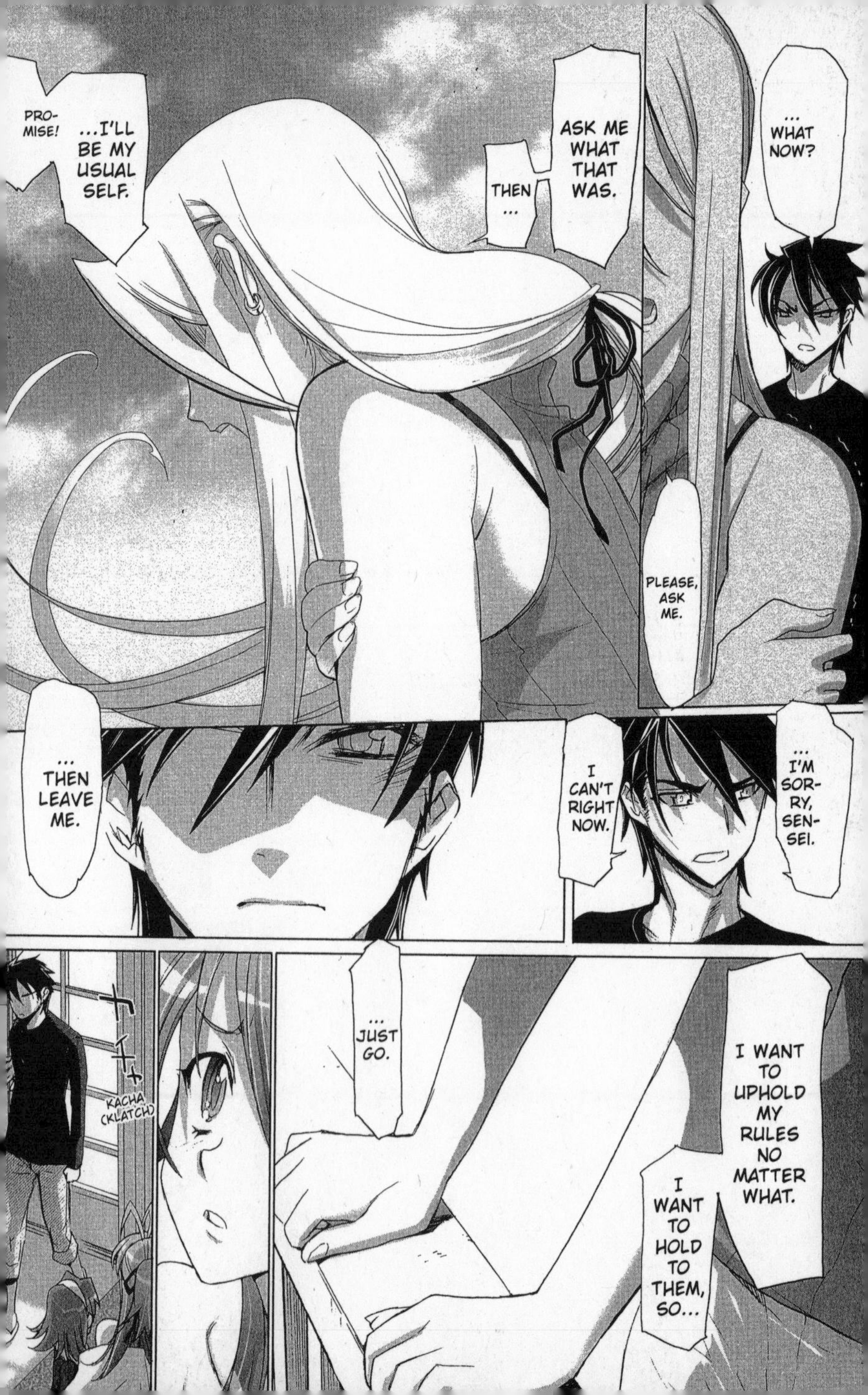
...WHAT NOW?
PLEASE, ASK ME.
ASK ME WHAT THAT WAS.
THEN ...
...I'LL BE MY USUAL SELF.
PRO-MISE!
...I'M SOR-RY, SEN-SEI.
I CAN'T RIGHT NOW.
...THEN LEAVE ME.
I WANT TO UPHOLD MY RULES NO MATTER WHAT.
I WANT TO HOLD TO THEM, SO...
...JUST GO.
KACHA (KLATCH)

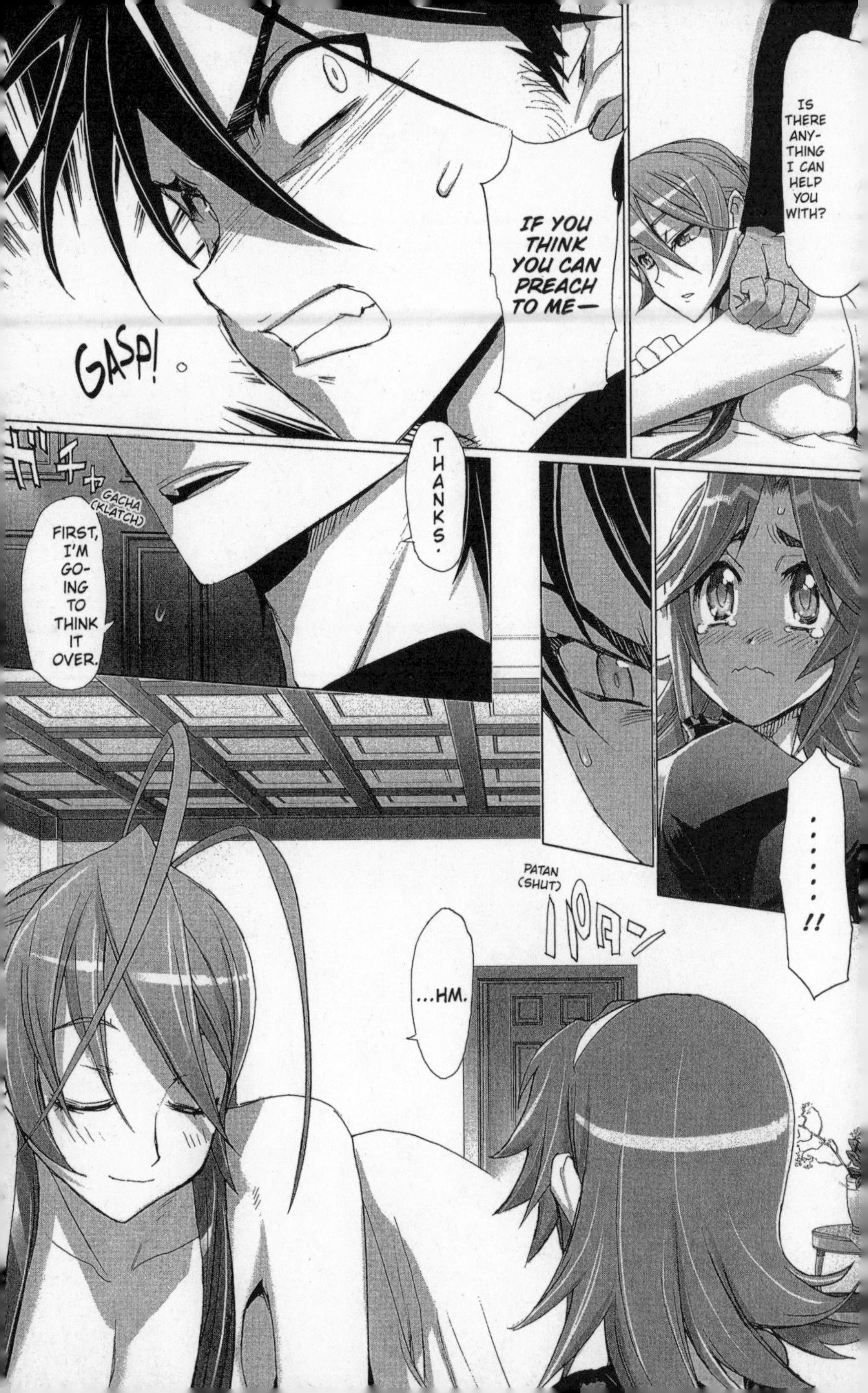
IS THERE ANYTHING I CAN HELP YOU WITH?
IF YOU THINK YOU CAN PREACH TO ME—
GASP!
......!!
THANKS.
GACHA (KLATCH)
FIRST, I'M GOING TO THINK IT OVER.
PATAN (SHUT)
...HM.

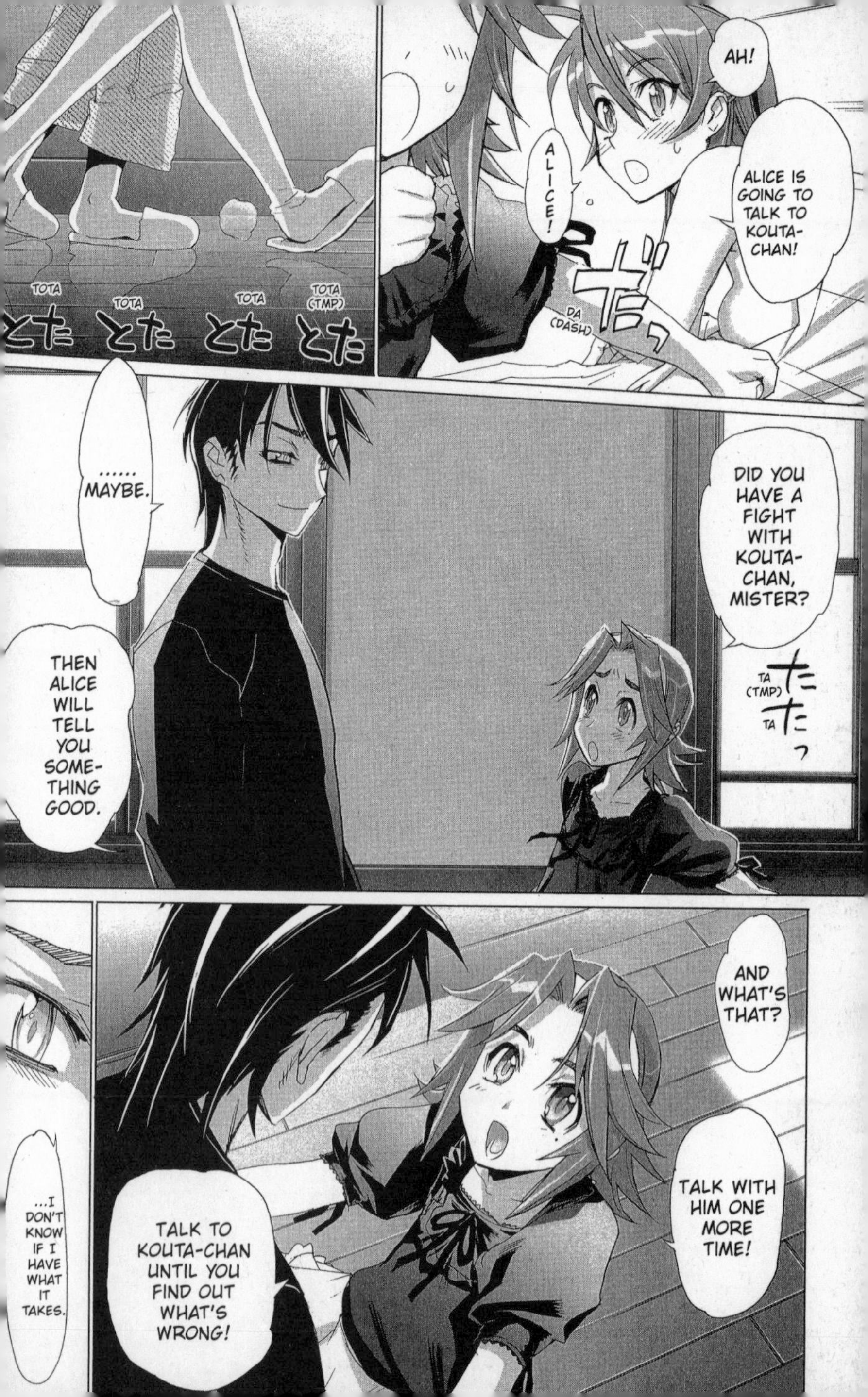
AH!
ALICE IS GOING TO TALK TO KOUTA-CHAN!
ALICE!
ダッ
DA (DASH)
とた
TOTA (TMP)
とた
TOTA
とた
TOTA
とた
TOTA
DID YOU HAVE A FIGHT WITH KOUTA-CHAN, MISTER?
たたっ
TA (TMP)
TA
...... MAYBE.
THEN ALICE WILL TELL YOU SOMETHING GOOD.
AND WHAT'S THAT?
TALK WITH HIM ONE MORE TIME!
TALK TO KOUTA-CHAN UNTIL YOU FIND OUT WHAT'S WRONG!
...I DON'T KNOW IF I HAVE WHAT IT TAKES.

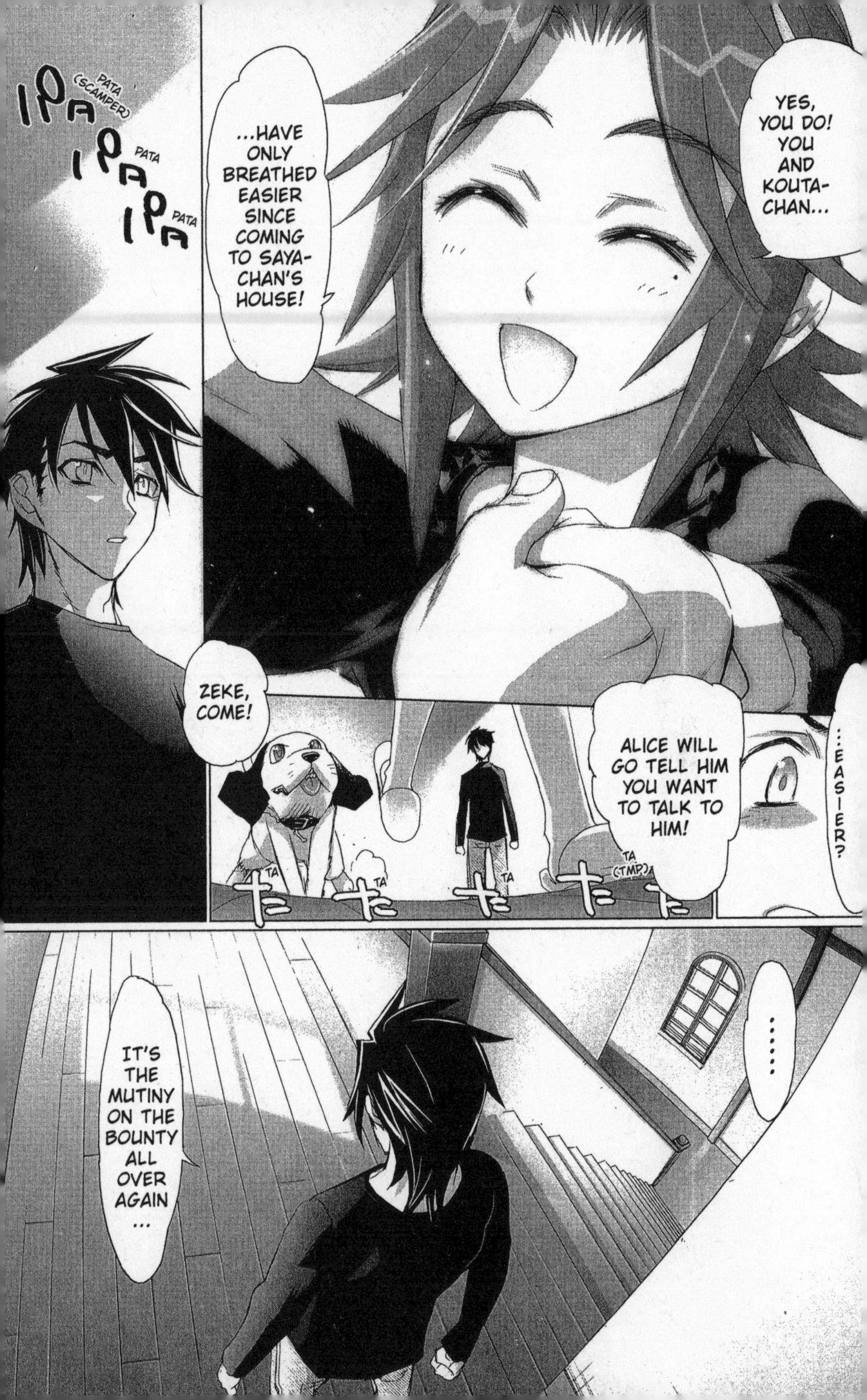

YES, YOU DO! YOU AND KOUTA-CHAN...
...HAVE ONLY BREATHED EASIER SINCE COMING TO SAYA-CHAN'S HOUSE!
...EASIER?
ALICE WILL GO TELL HIM YOU WANT TO TALK TO HIM!
TA (TMP)
TA
TA
TA
ZEKE, COME!
PATA (SCAMPER)
PATA
PATA
......
IT'S THE MUTINY ON THE BOUNTY ALL OVER AGAIN...

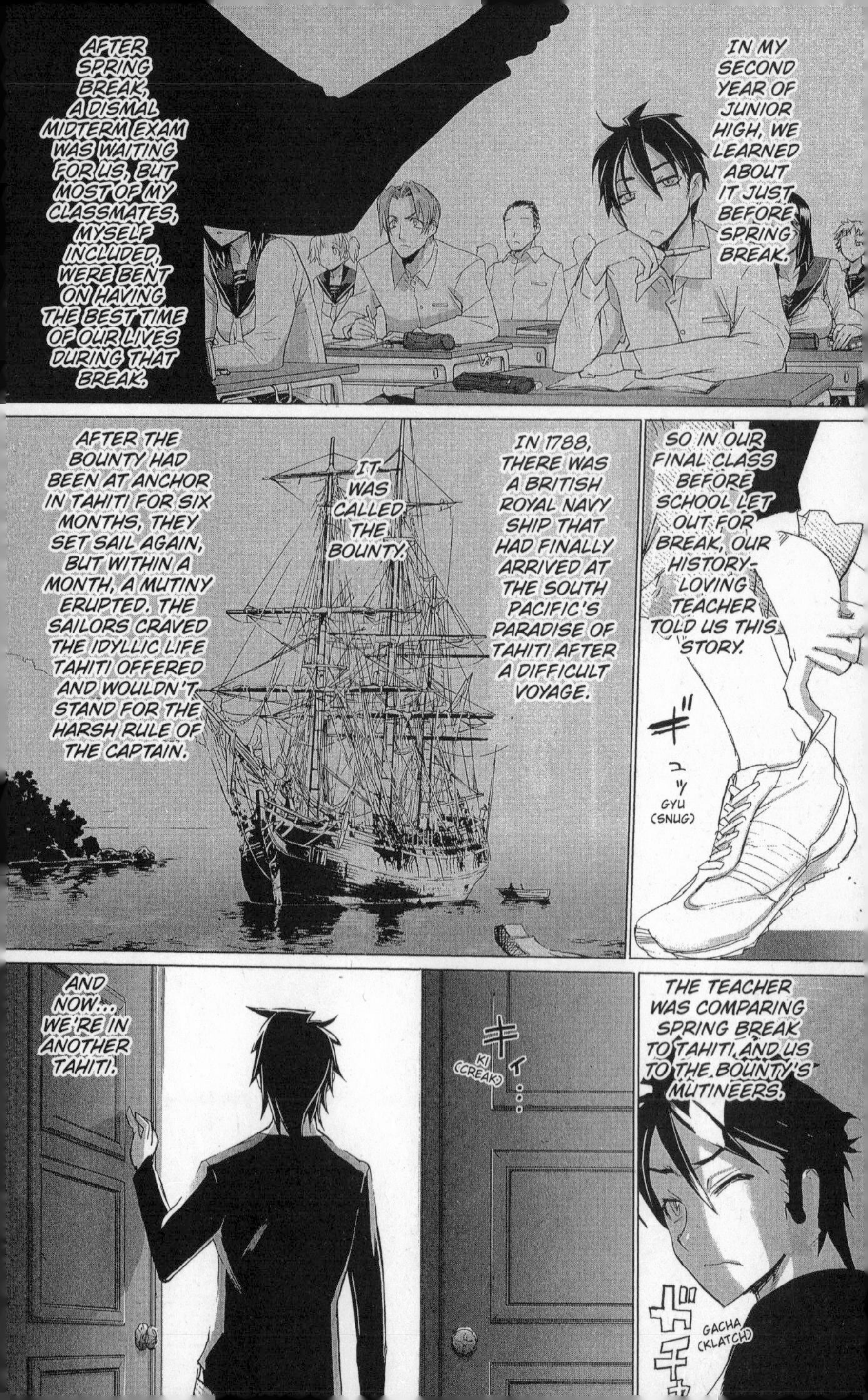

IN MY SECOND YEAR OF JUNIOR HIGH, WE LEARNED ABOUT IT JUST BEFORE SPRING BREAK.
AFTER SPRING BREAK, A DISMAL MIDTERM EXAM WAS WAITING FOR US, BUT MOST OF MY CLASSMATES, MYSELF INCLUDED, WERE BENT ON HAVING THE BEST TIME OF OUR LIVES DURING THAT BREAK.
SO IN OUR FINAL CLASS BEFORE SCHOOL LET OUT FOR BREAK, OUR HISTORY-LOVING TEACHER TOLD US THIS STORY.
ギュッ
GYU (SNUG)
IN 1788, THERE WAS A BRITISH ROYAL NAVY SHIP THAT HAD FINALLY ARRIVED AT THE SOUTH PACIFIC'S PARADISE OF TAHITI AFTER A DIFFICULT VOYAGE.
IT WAS CALLED THE BOUNTY.
AFTER THE BOUNTY HAD BEEN AT ANCHOR IN TAHITI FOR SIX MONTHS, THEY SET SAIL AGAIN, BUT WITHIN A MONTH, A MUTINY ERUPTED. THE SAILORS CRAVED THE IDYLLIC LIFE TAHITI OFFERED AND WOULDN'T STAND FOR THE HARSH RULE OF THE CAPTAIN.
THE TEACHER WAS COMPARING SPRING BREAK TO TAHITI, AND US TO THE BOUNTY'S MUTINEERS.
ガチャ
GACHA (KLATCH)
キィ…
KI (CREAK)
AND NOW... WE'RE IN ANOTHER TAHITI.

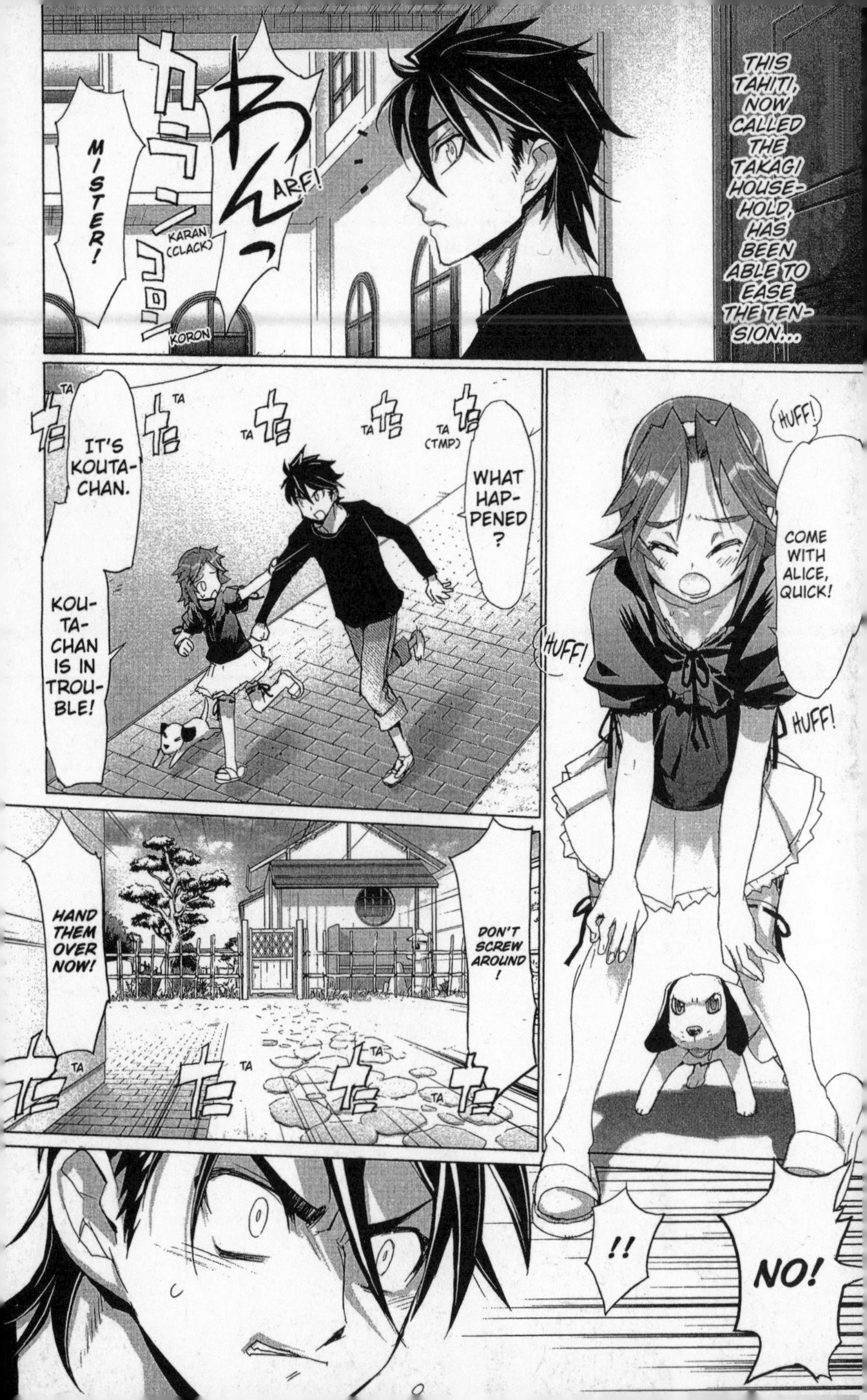

THIS TAHITI, NOW CALLED THE TAKAGI HOUSEHOLD, HAS BEEN ABLE TO EASE THE TENSION...
ARF!
KARAN (CLACK)
KORON
MISTER!
HUFF!
COME WITH ALICE, QUICK!
HUFF!
HUFF!
TA (TMP)
TA
TA
TA
TA
WHAT HAPPENED?
IT'S KOUTA-CHAN.
KOUTA-CHAN IS IN TROUBLE!
DON'T SCREW AROUND!
TA
TA
TA
TA
HAND THEM OVER NOW!
NO!
!!

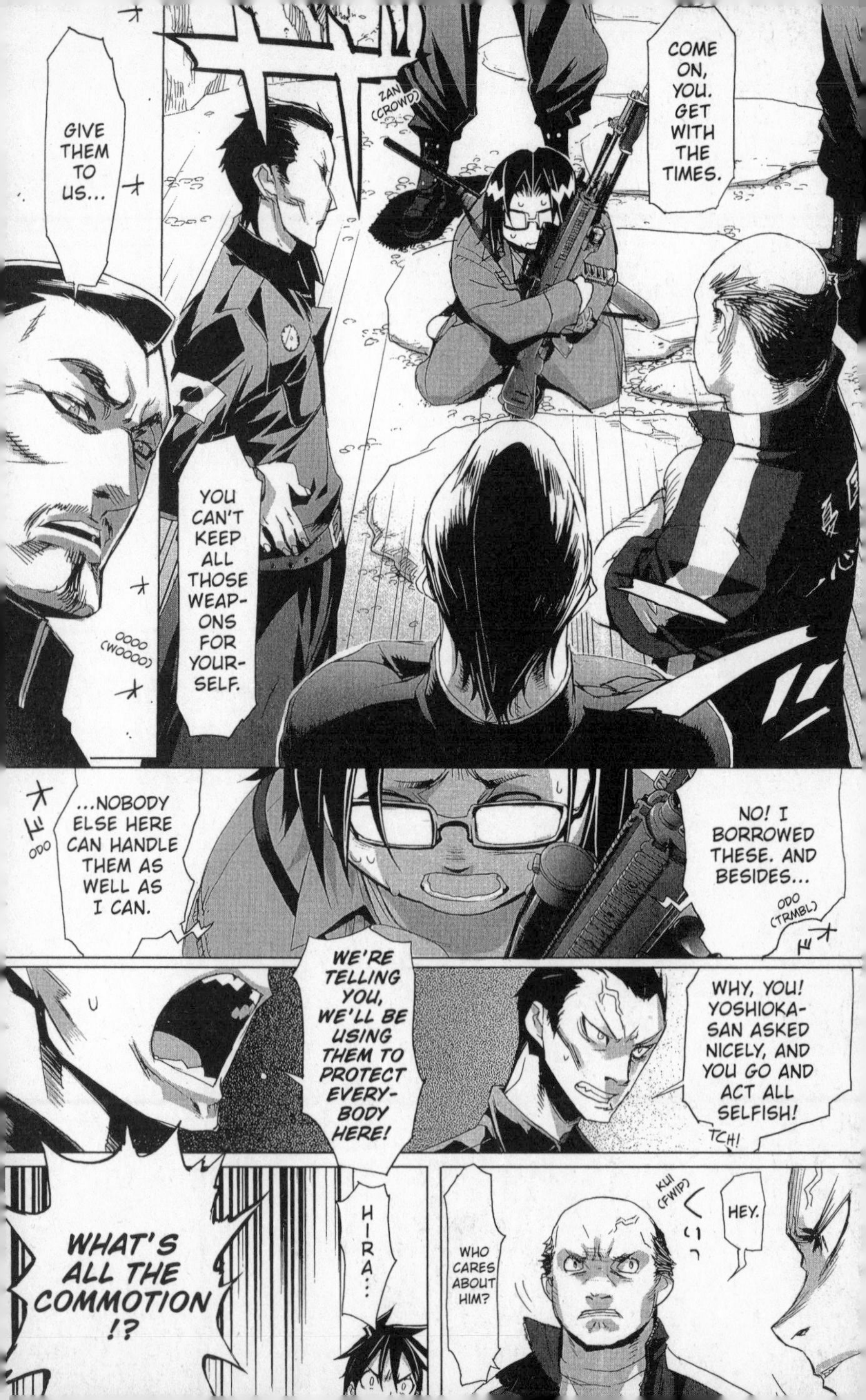
COME ON, YOU. GET WITH THE TIMES.
ZAN (CROWD)
GIVE THEM TO US...
YOU CAN'T KEEP ALL THOSE WEAPONS FOR YOURSELF.
OOOO (WOOOO)
NO! I BORROWED THESE. AND BESIDES...
ODO (TRMBL)
...NOBODY ELSE HERE CAN HANDLE THEM AS WELL AS I CAN.
ODO
WHY, YOU! YOSHIOKA-SAN ASKED NICELY, AND YOU GO AND ACT ALL SELFISH!
TCH!
WE'RE TELLING YOU, WE'LL BE USING THEM TO PROTECT EVERYBODY HERE!
HEY.
KUI (FWIP)
WHO CARES ABOUT HIM?
HIRA...
WHAT'S ALL THE COMMOTION!?

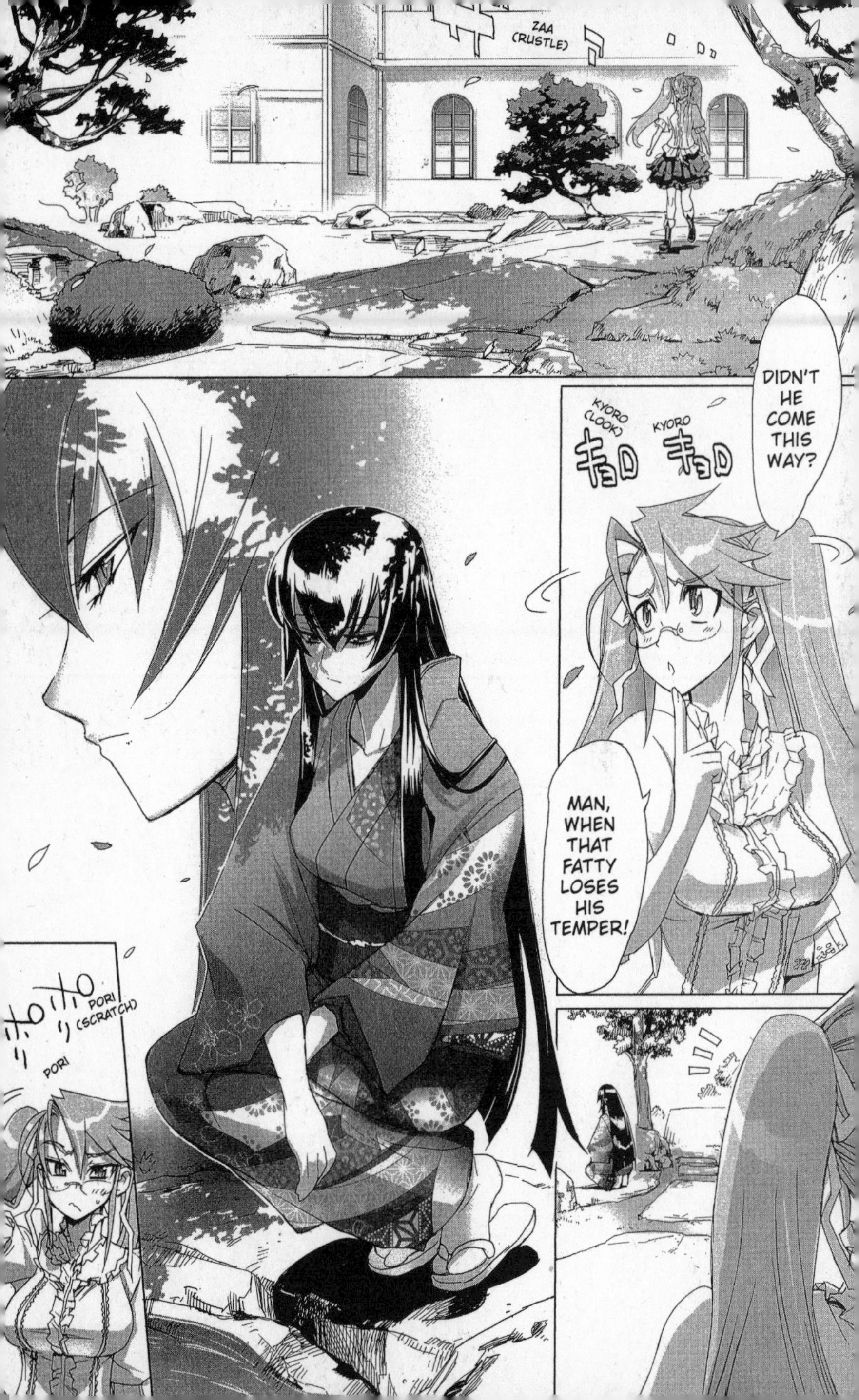
ZAA (RUSTLE)
DIDN'T HE COME THIS WAY?
KYORO (LOOK) KYORO
MAN, WHEN THAT FATTY LOSES HIS TEMPER!
PORI (SCRATCH) PORI

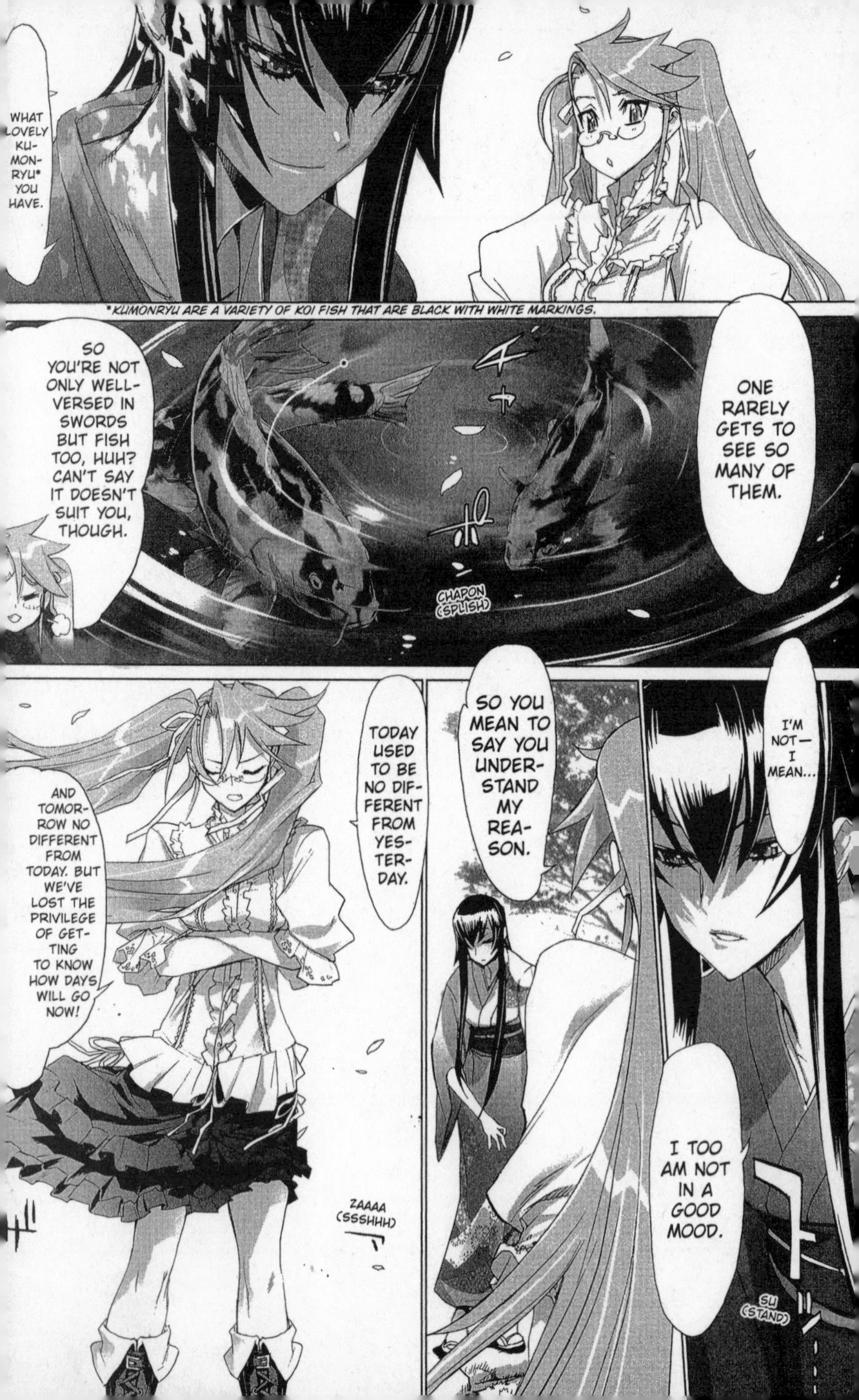
WHAT LOVELY KUMONRYU* YOU HAVE.
ONE RARELY GETS TO SEE SO MANY OF THEM.
CHAPON (SPLISH)
SO YOU'RE NOT ONLY WELL-VERSED IN SWORDS BUT FISH TOO, HUH? CAN'T SAY IT DOESN'T SUIT YOU, THOUGH.
I'M NOT— I MEAN...
SO YOU MEAN TO SAY YOU UNDERSTAND MY REASON.
I TOO AM NOT IN A GOOD MOOD.
SU (STAND)
TODAY USED TO BE NO DIFFERENT FROM YESTERDAY.
AND TOMORROW NO DIFFERENT FROM TODAY. BUT WE'VE LOST THE PRIVILEGE OF GETTING TO KNOW HOW DAYS WILL GO NOW!
ZAAAA (SSSHHH)

*KUMONRYU ARE A VARIETY OF KOI FISH THAT ARE BLACK WITH WHITE MARKINGS.

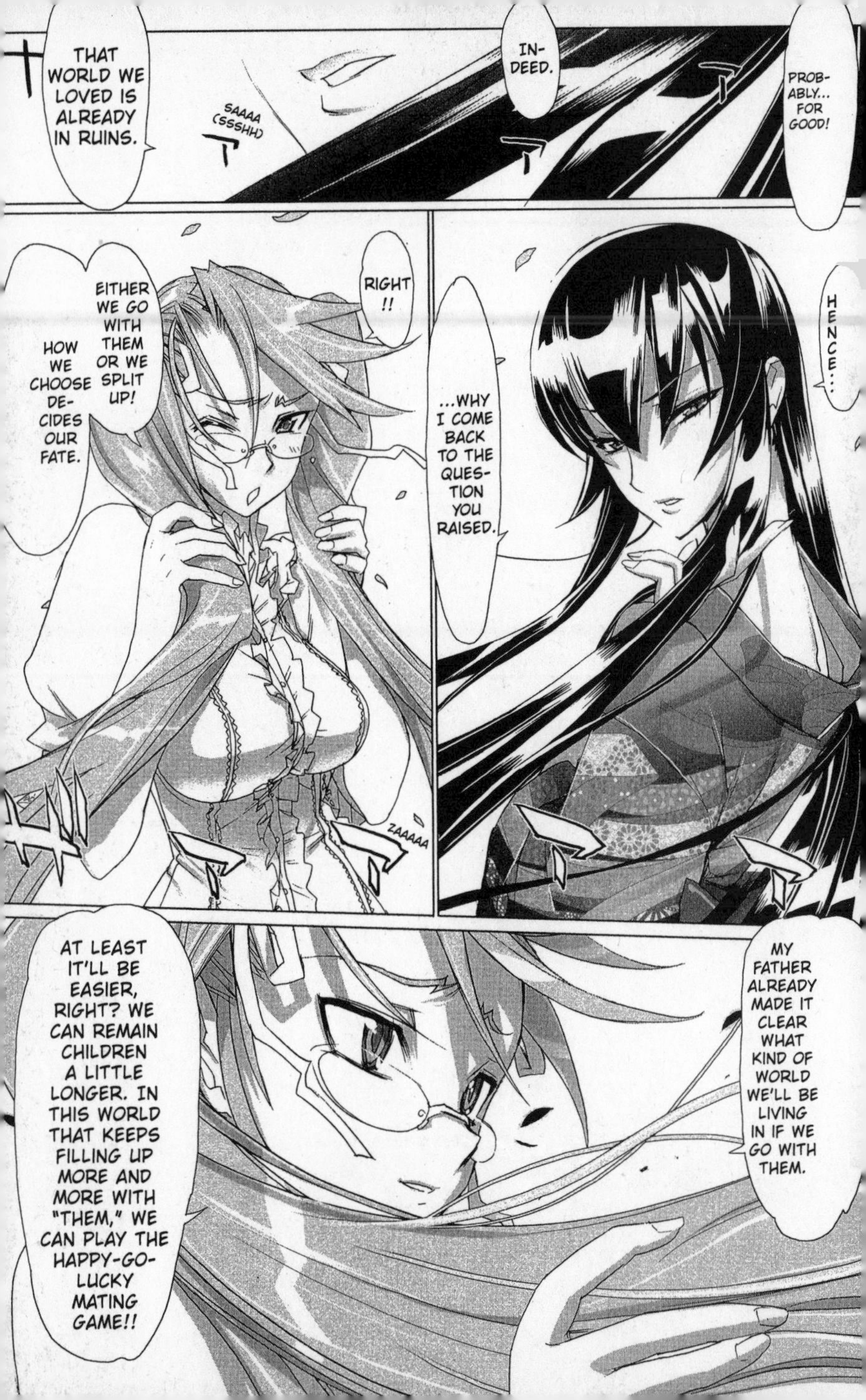
PROB-ABLY... FOR GOOD!
IN-DEED.
SAAAA (SSSHH)
THAT WORLD WE LOVED IS ALREADY IN RUINS.
HENCE...
...WHY I COME BACK TO THE QUES-TION YOU RAISED.
RIGHT!!
EITHER WE GO WITH THEM OR WE SPLIT UP!
HOW WE CHOOSE DE-CIDES OUR FATE.
ZAAAAA
MY FATHER ALREADY MADE IT CLEAR WHAT KIND OF WORLD WE'LL BE LIVING IN IF WE GO WITH THEM.
AT LEAST IT'LL BE EASIER, RIGHT? WE CAN REMAIN CHILDREN A LITTLE LONGER. IN THIS WORLD THAT KEEPS FILLING UP MORE AND MORE WITH "THEM," WE CAN PLAY THE HAPPY-GO-LUCKY MATING GAME!!

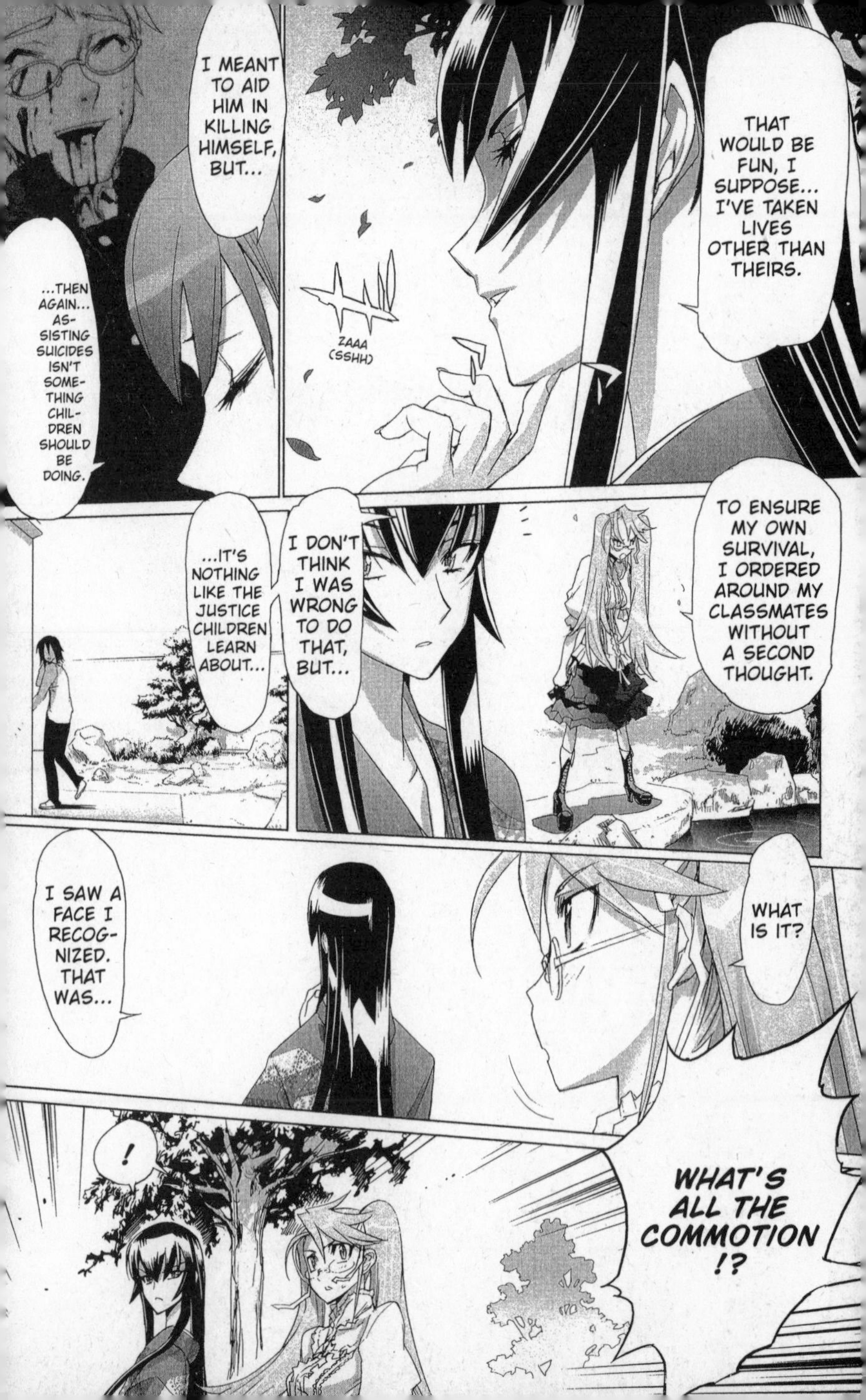
THAT WOULD BE FUN, I SUPPOSE... I'VE TAKEN LIVES OTHER THAN THEIRS.
ZAAA (SSHH)
I MEANT TO AID HIM IN KILLING HIMSELF, BUT...
...THEN AGAIN... ASSISTING SUICIDES ISN'T SOMETHING CHILDREN SHOULD BE DOING.
TO ENSURE MY OWN SURVIVAL, I ORDERED AROUND MY CLASSMATES WITHOUT A SECOND THOUGHT.
I DON'T THINK I WAS WRONG TO DO THAT, BUT...
...IT'S NOTHING LIKE THE JUSTICE CHILDREN LEARN ABOUT...
WHAT IS IT?
I SAW A FACE I RECOGNIZED. THAT WAS...
WHAT'S ALL THE COMMOTION!?
!

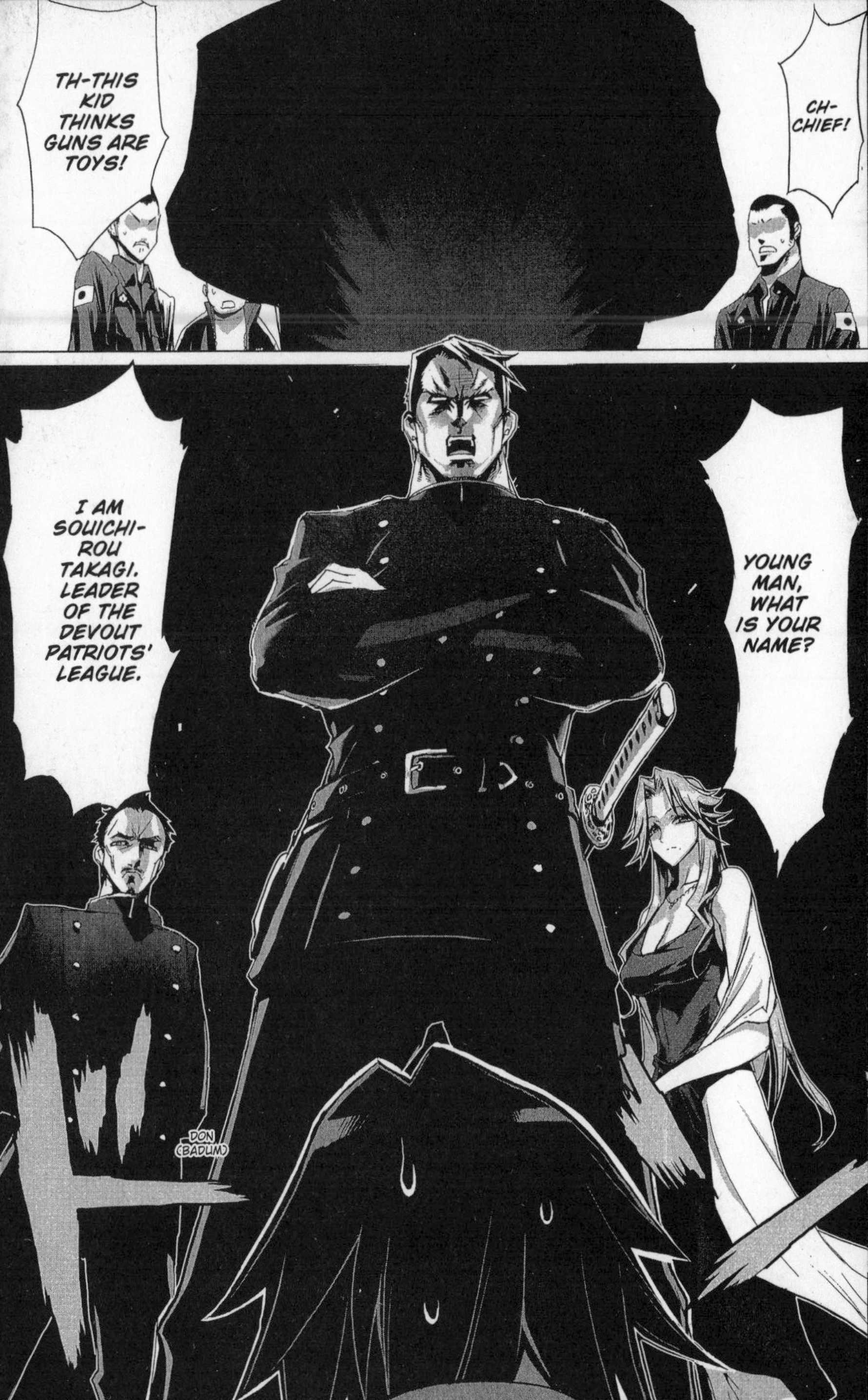
CH-CHIEF!
TH-THIS KID THINKS GUNS ARE TOYS!
I AM SOUICHI-ROU TAKAGI. LEADER OF THE DEVOUT PATRIOTS' LEAGUE.
YOUNG MAN, WHAT IS YOUR NAME?
DON (BADUM)

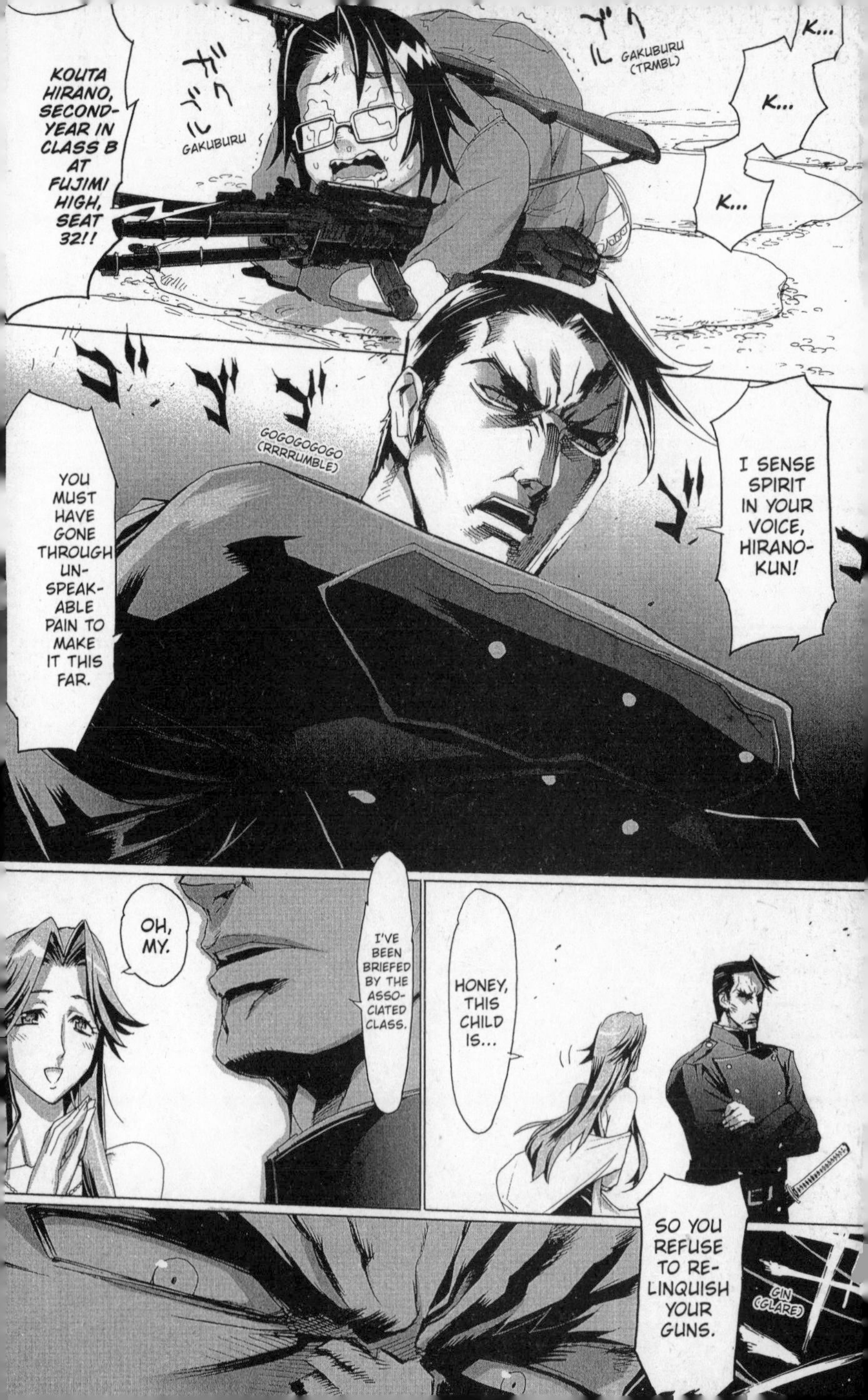
K...
K...
K...
GAKUBURU (TRMBL)
GAKUBURU
KOUTA HIRANO, SECOND-YEAR IN CLASS B AT FUJIMI HIGH, SEAT 32!!
I SENSE SPIRIT IN YOUR VOICE, HIRANO-KUN!
GOGOGOGOGO (RRRRUMBLE)
YOU MUST HAVE GONE THROUGH UNSPEAKABLE PAIN TO MAKE IT THIS FAR.
HONEY, THIS CHILD IS...
I'VE BEEN BRIEFED BY THE ASSOCIATED CLASS.
OH, MY.
SO YOU REFUSE TO RELINQUISH YOUR GUNS.
GIN (GLARE)

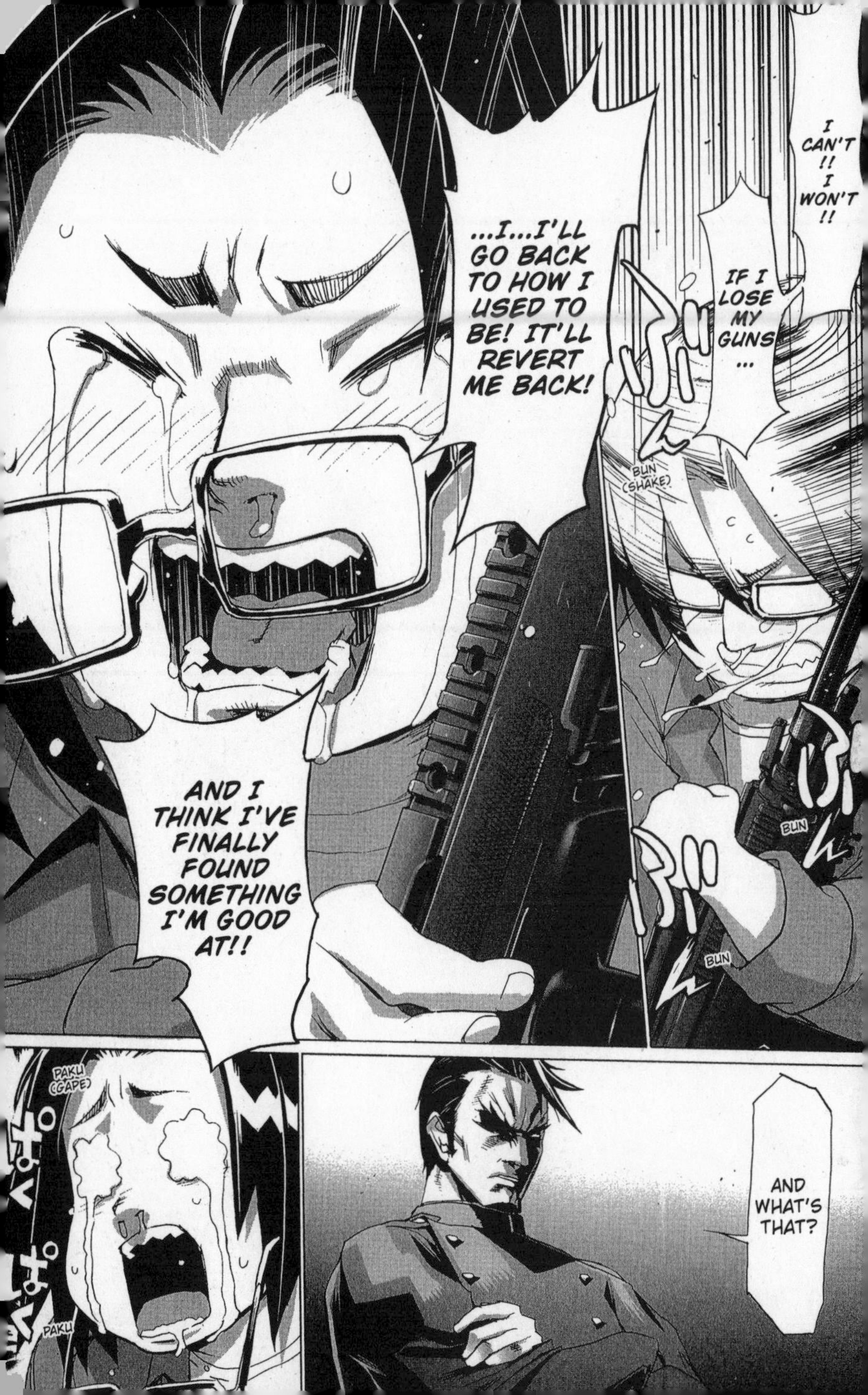
I CAN'T!! I WON'T!!
IF I LOSE MY GUNS...
...I...I'LL GO BACK TO HOW I USED TO BE! IT'LL REVERT ME BACK!
BUN (SHAKE)
BUN
BUN
AND I THINK I'VE FINALLY FOUND SOMETHING I'M GOOD AT!!
AND WHAT'S THAT?
PAKU (GAPE)
PAKU

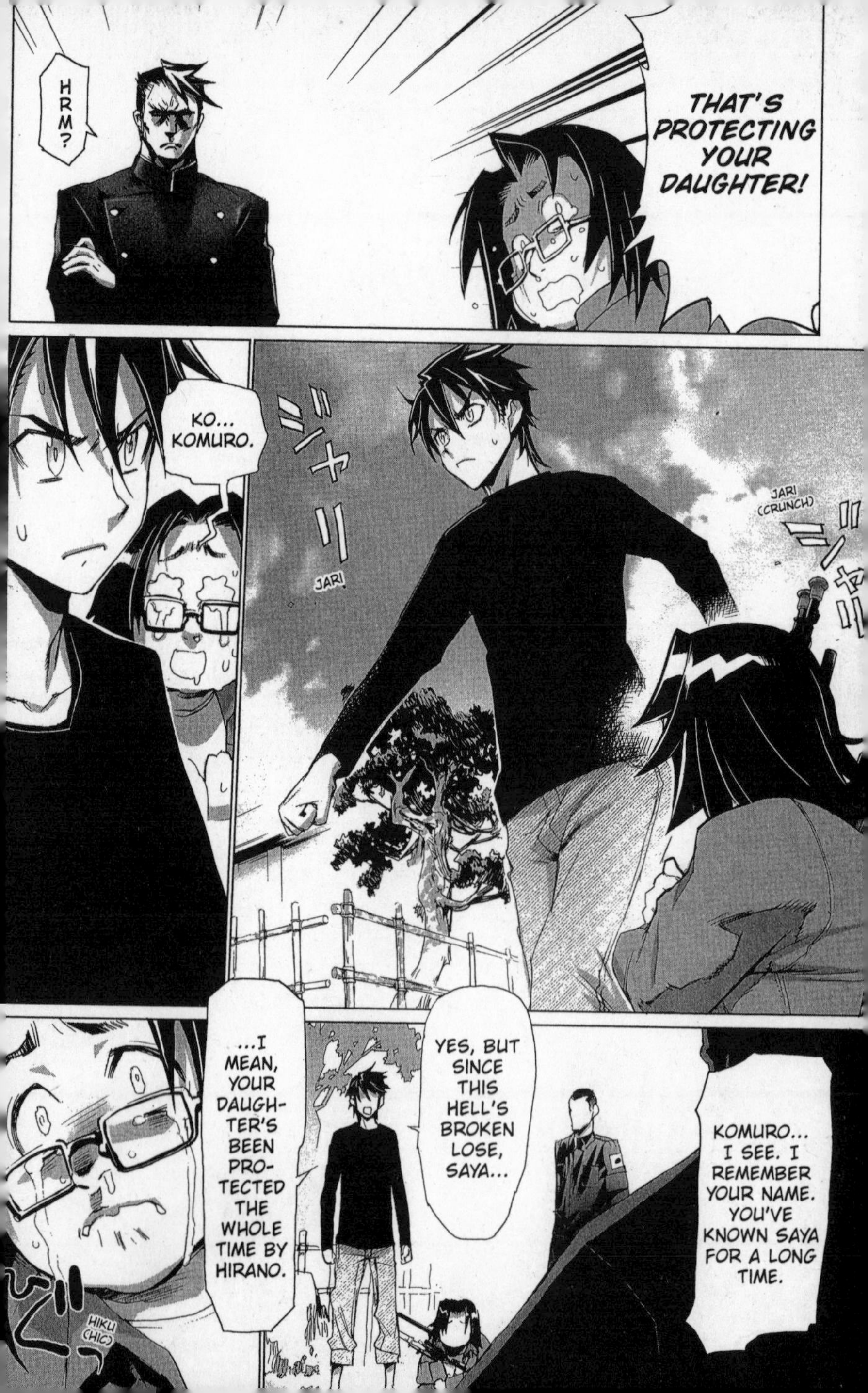
THAT'S PROTECTING YOUR DAUGHTER!
HRM?
ジャリ
JARI (CRUNCH)
ジャリ
JARI!
KO... KOMURO.
KOMURO... I SEE. I REMEMBER YOUR NAME. YOU'VE KNOWN SAYA FOR A LONG TIME.
YES, BUT SINCE THIS HELL'S BROKEN LOSE, SAYA...
...I MEAN, YOUR DAUGHTER'S BEEN PROTECTED THE WHOLE TIME BY HIRANO.
HIKU (HIC)

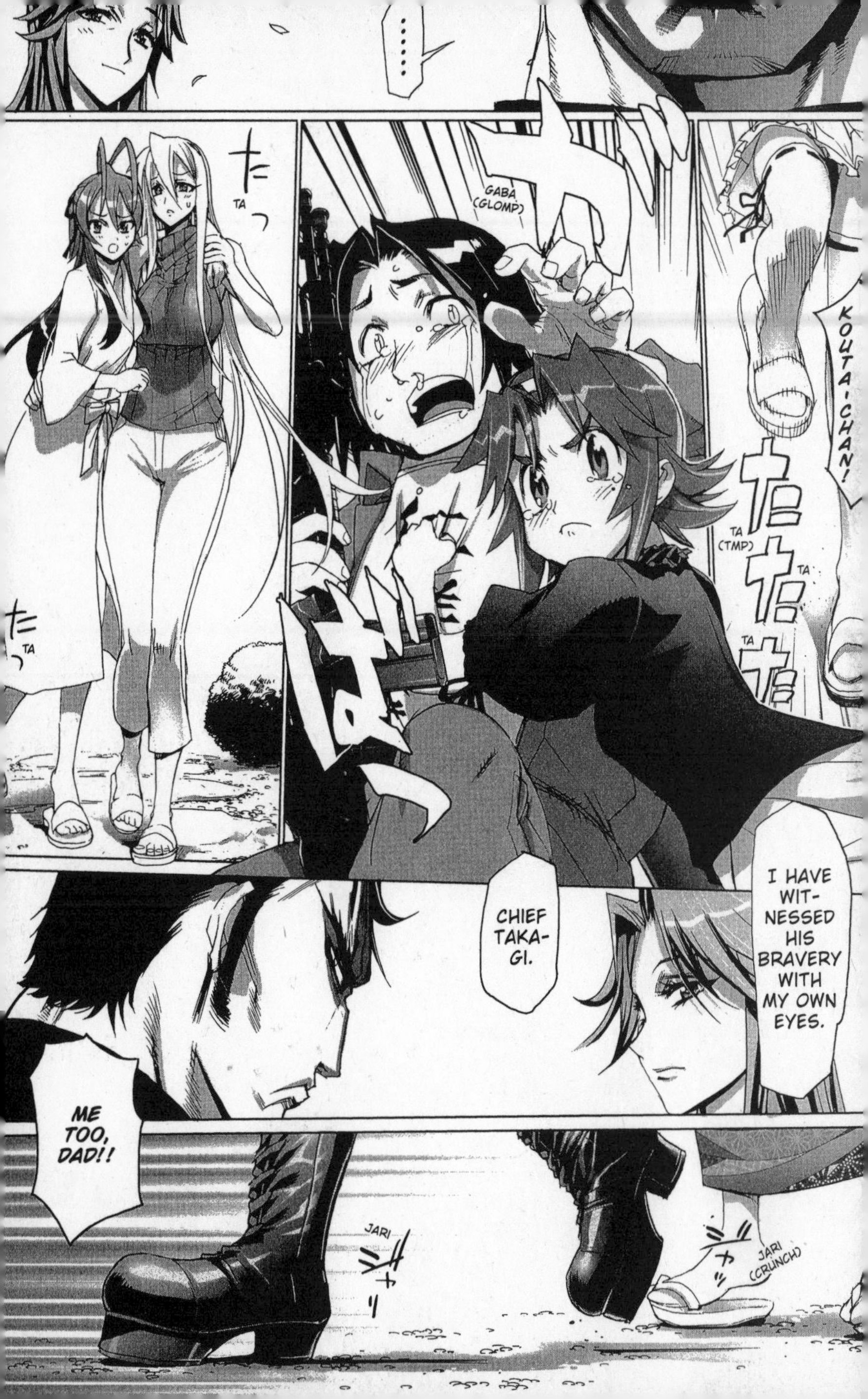
......
KOUTA-CHAN!
TA (TMP)
TA
TA
GABA (GLOMP)
TA
TA
I HAVE WIT-NESSED HIS BRAVERY WITH MY OWN EYES.
CHIEF TAKA-GI.
ME TOO, DAD!!
JARI (CRUNCH)
JARI

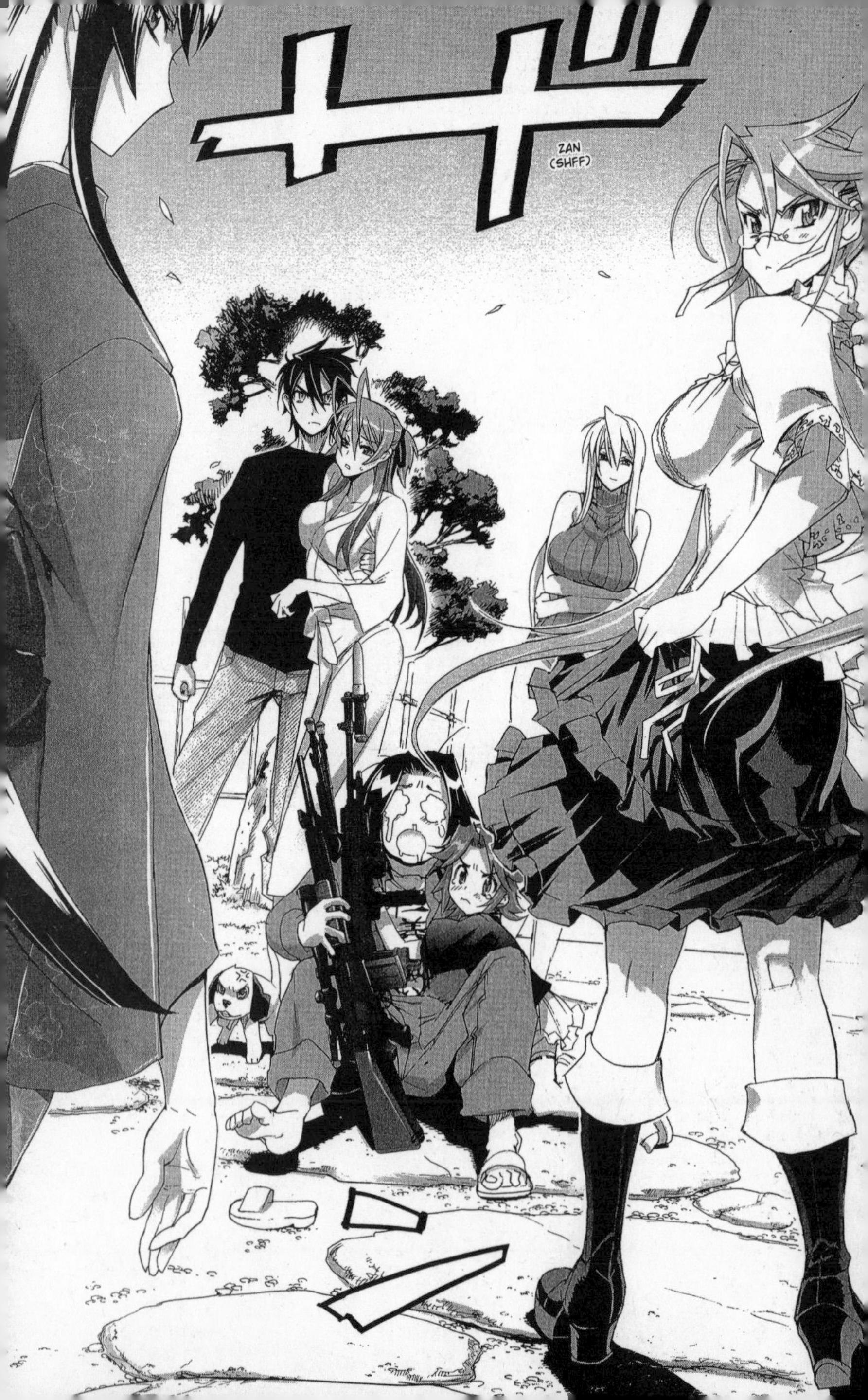
ZAN
(SHFF)

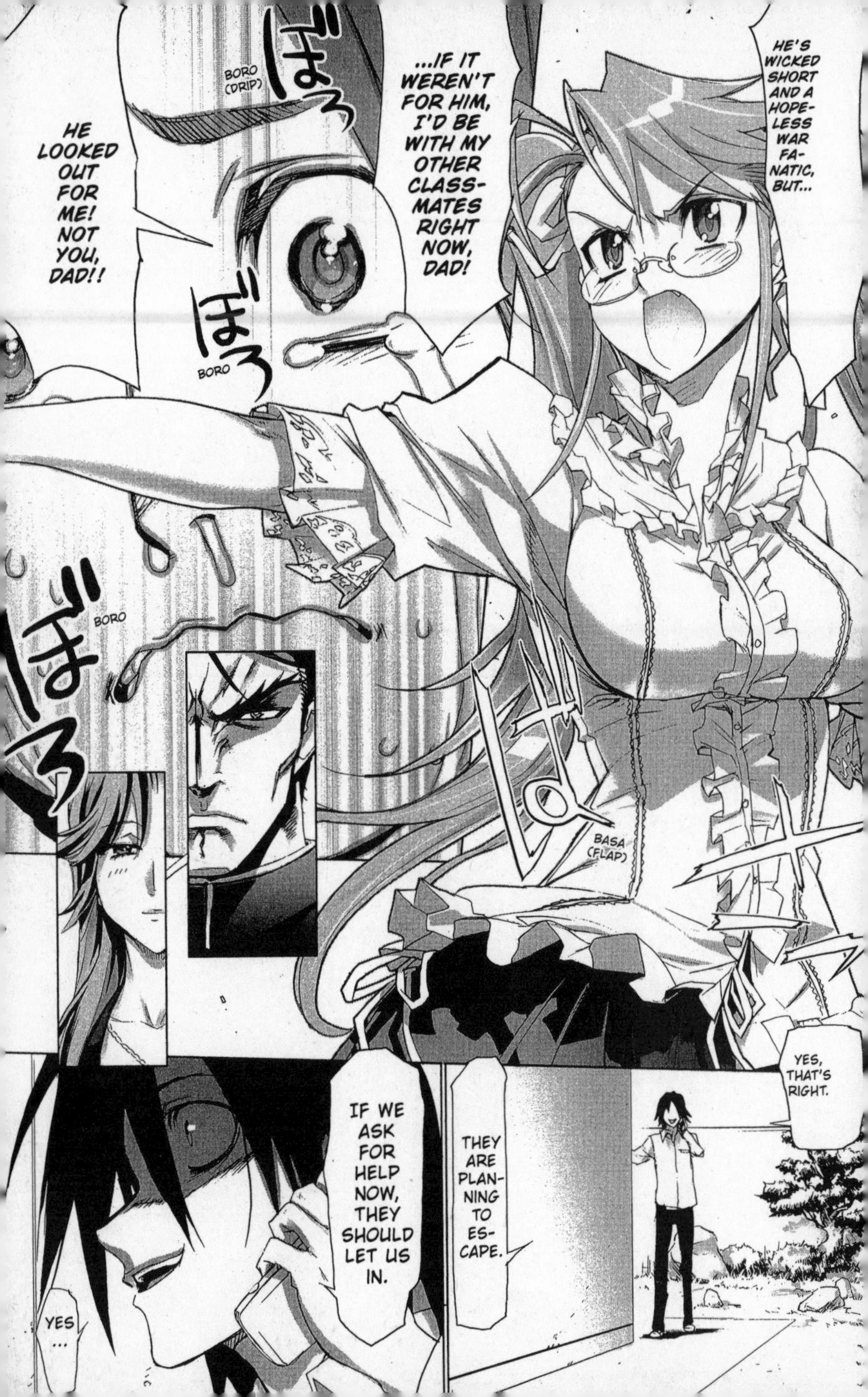
HE'S WICKED SHORT AND A HOPE-LESS WAR FA-NATIC, BUT...
...IF IT WEREN'T FOR HIM, I'D BE WITH MY OTHER CLASS-MATES RIGHT NOW, DAD!
ぼろ
BORO (DRIP)
HE LOOKED OUT FOR ME! NOT YOU, DAD!!
ぼろ
BORO
ぼろ
BORO
BASA (FLAP)
YES, THAT'S RIGHT.
THEY ARE PLAN-NING TO ES-CAPE.
IF WE ASK FOR HELP NOW, THEY SHOULD LET US IN.
YES...

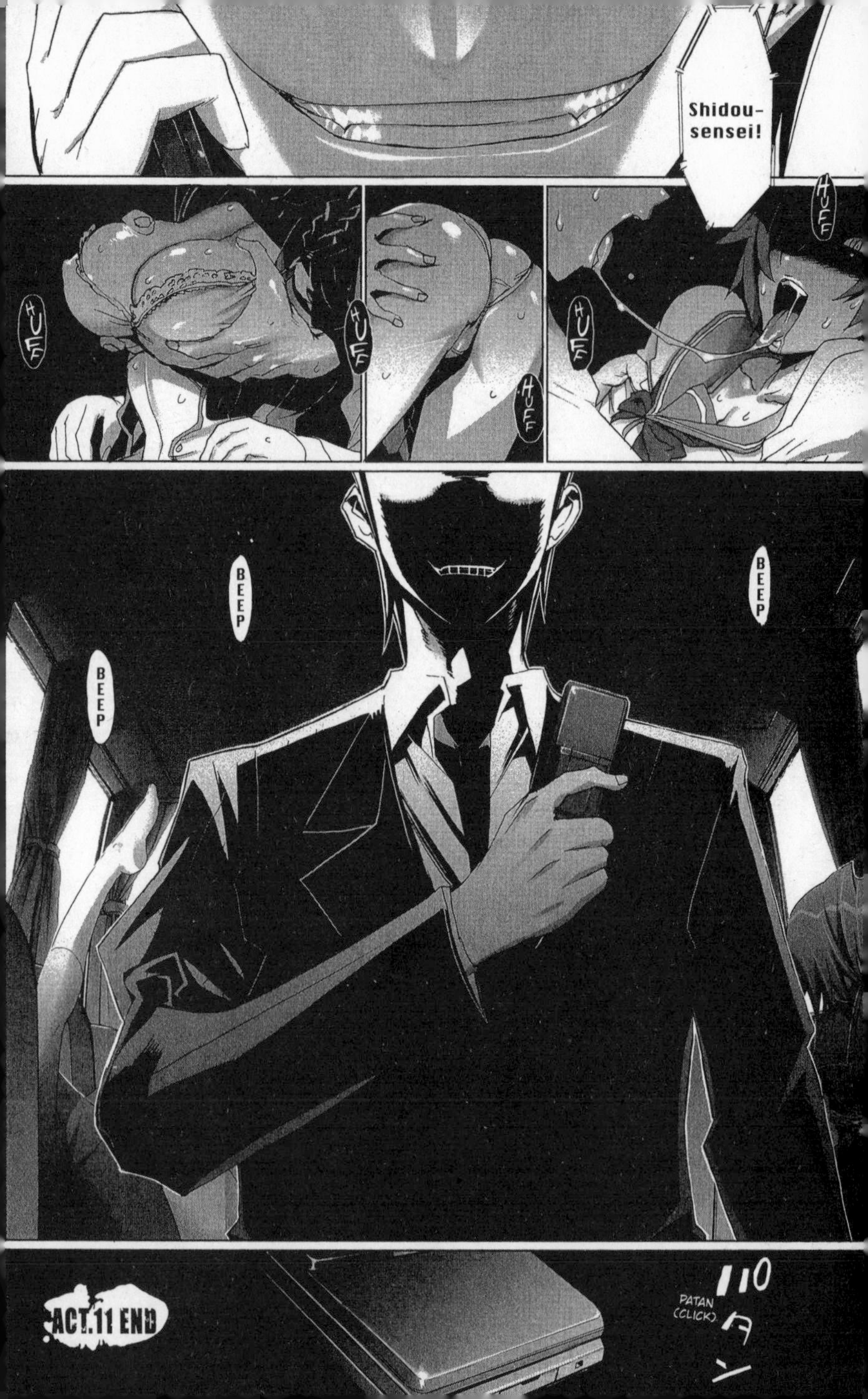
Shidou-sensei!
HUFF
HUFF
HUFF
HUFF
HUFF
BEEP
BEEP
BEEP
PATAN (CLICK)
ACT.11 END

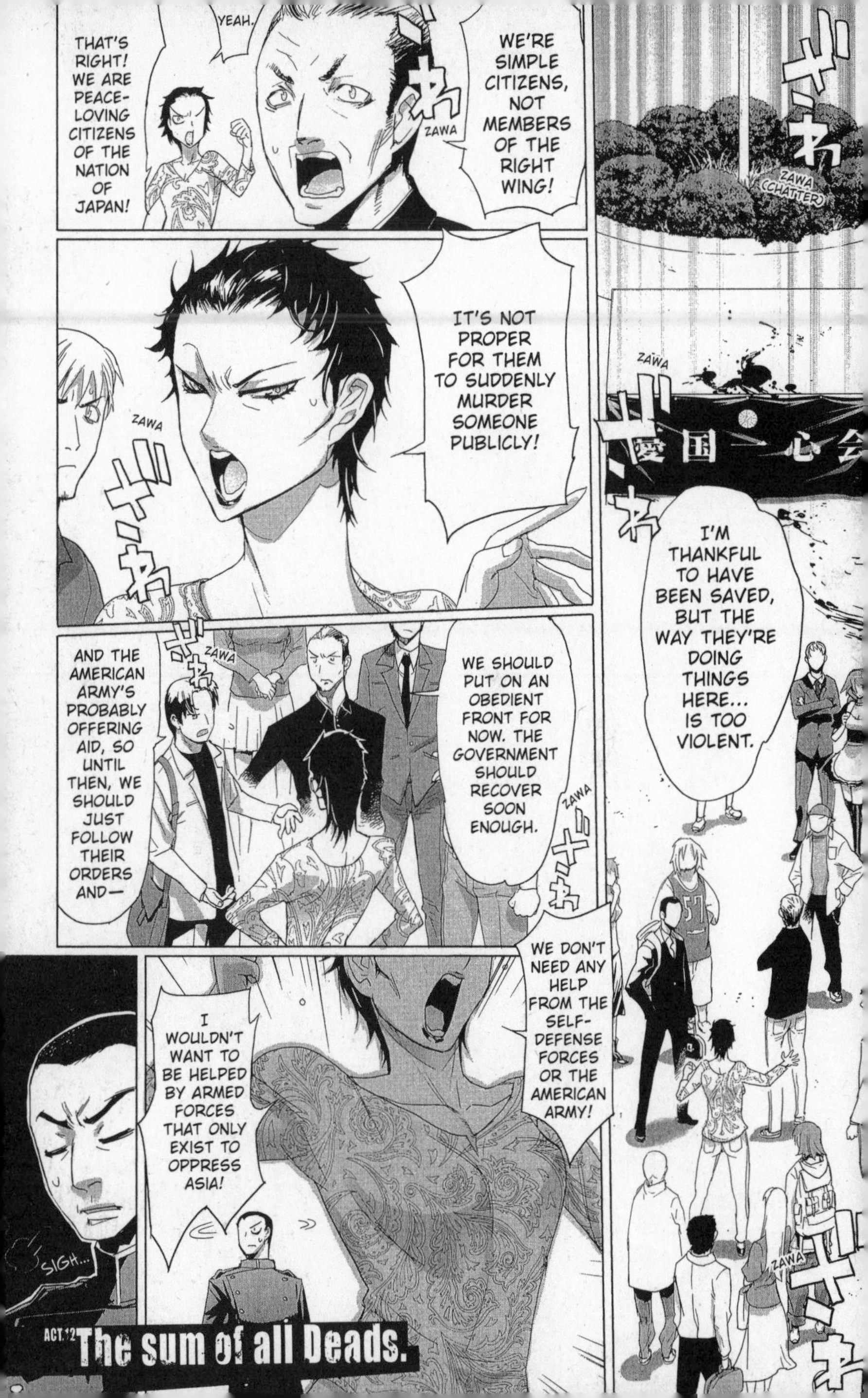
ZAWA (CHATTER)
ZAWA
I'M THANKFUL TO HAVE BEEN SAVED, BUT THE WAY THEY'RE DOING THINGS HERE... IS TOO VIOLENT.
ZAWA
WE'RE SIMPLE CITIZENS, NOT MEMBERS OF THE RIGHT WING!
ZAWA
YEAH.
THAT'S RIGHT! WE ARE PEACE-LOVING CITIZENS OF THE NATION OF JAPAN!
IT'S NOT PROPER FOR THEM TO SUDDENLY MURDER SOMEONE PUBLICLY!
ZAWA
WE SHOULD PUT ON AN OBEDIENT FRONT FOR NOW. THE GOVERNMENT SHOULD RECOVER SOON ENOUGH.
ZAWA
ZAWA
AND THE AMERICAN ARMY'S PROBABLY OFFERING AID, SO UNTIL THEN, WE SHOULD JUST FOLLOW THEIR ORDERS AND—
WE DON'T NEED ANY HELP FROM THE SELF-DEFENSE FORCES OR THE AMERICAN ARMY!
I WOULDN'T WANT TO BE HELPED BY ARMED FORCES THAT ONLY EXIST TO OPPRESS ASIA!
SIGH...
ACT.12 The sum of all Deads.

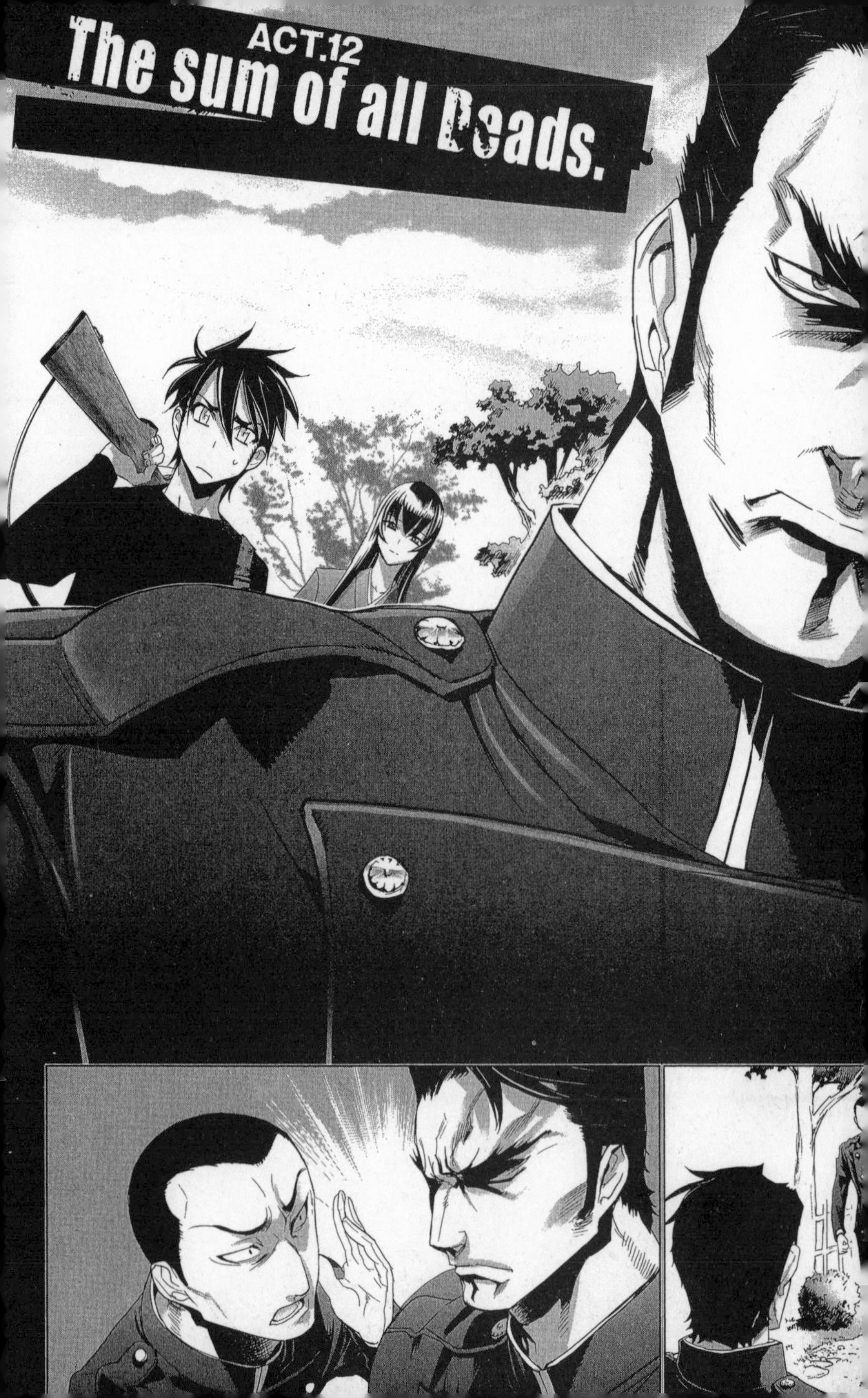
ACT.12
The sum of all Deads.

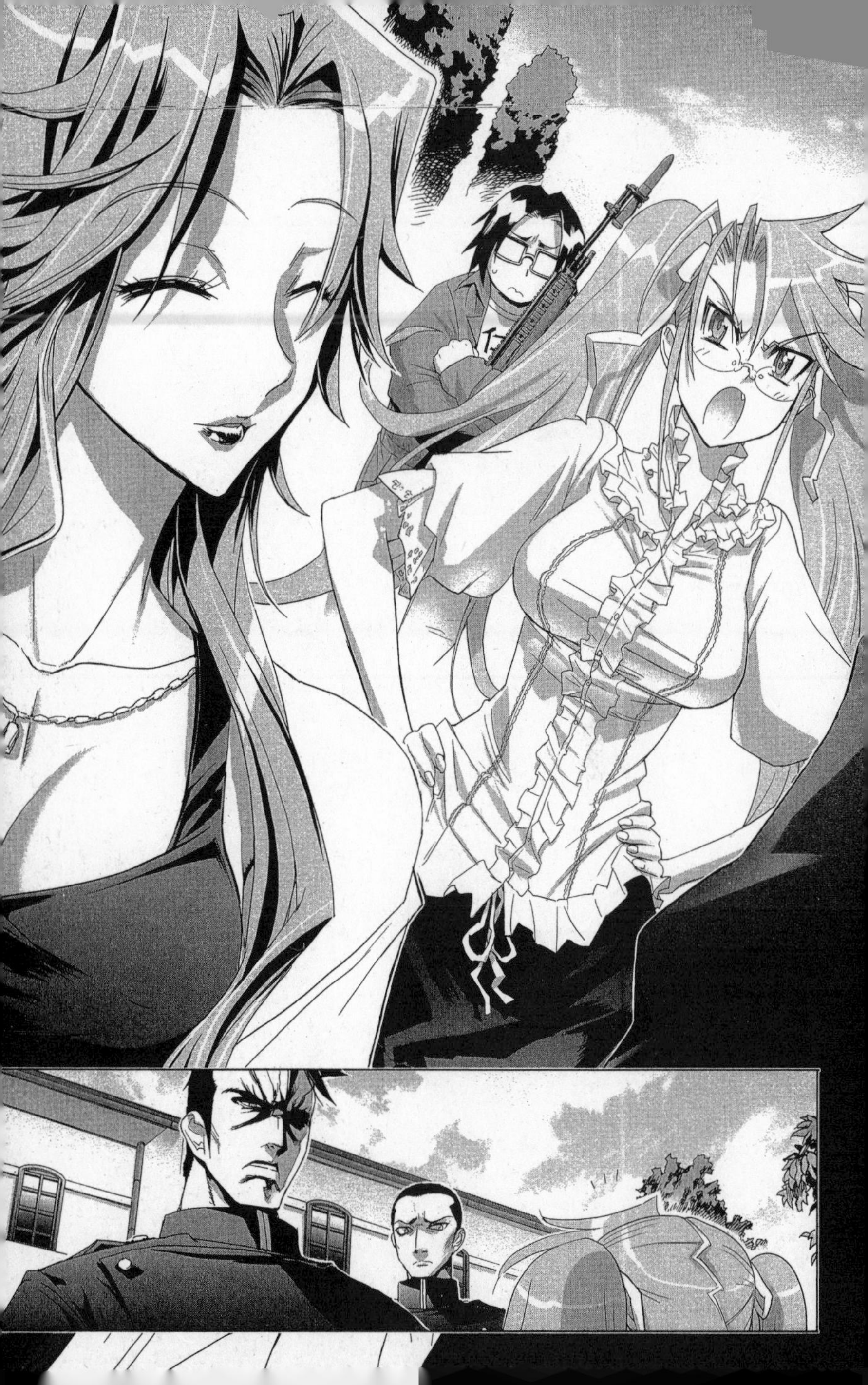

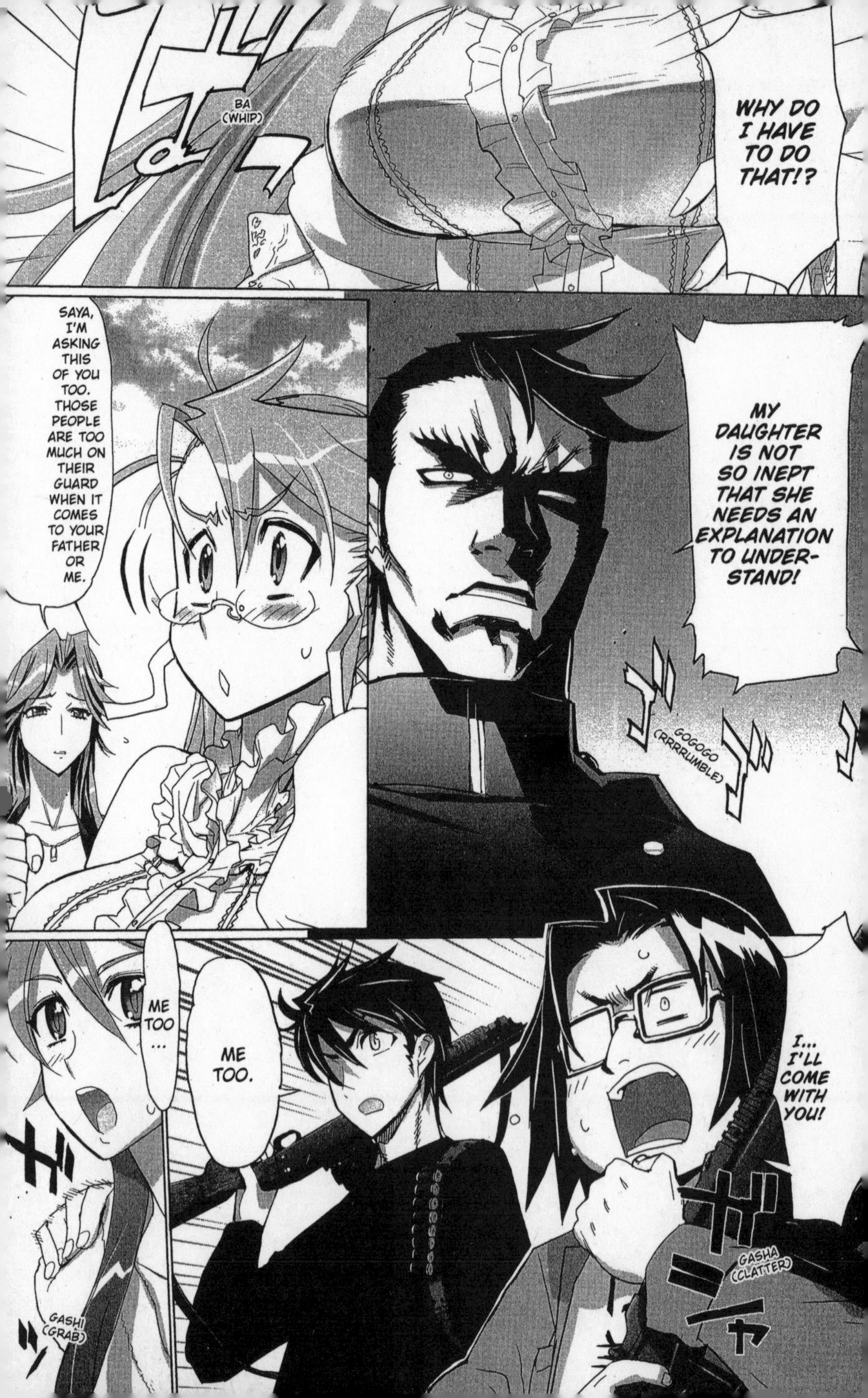
WHY DO I HAVE TO DO THAT!?
BA (WHIP)
MY DAUGHTER IS NOT SO INEPT THAT SHE NEEDS AN EXPLANATION TO UNDER-STAND!
GOGOGO (RRRRUMBLE)
SAYA, I'M ASKING THIS OF YOU TOO. THOSE PEOPLE ARE TOO MUCH ON THEIR GUARD WHEN IT COMES TO YOUR FATHER OR ME.
I... I'LL COME WITH YOU!
GASHA (CLATTER)
ME TOO.
ME TOO...
GASHI (GRAB)

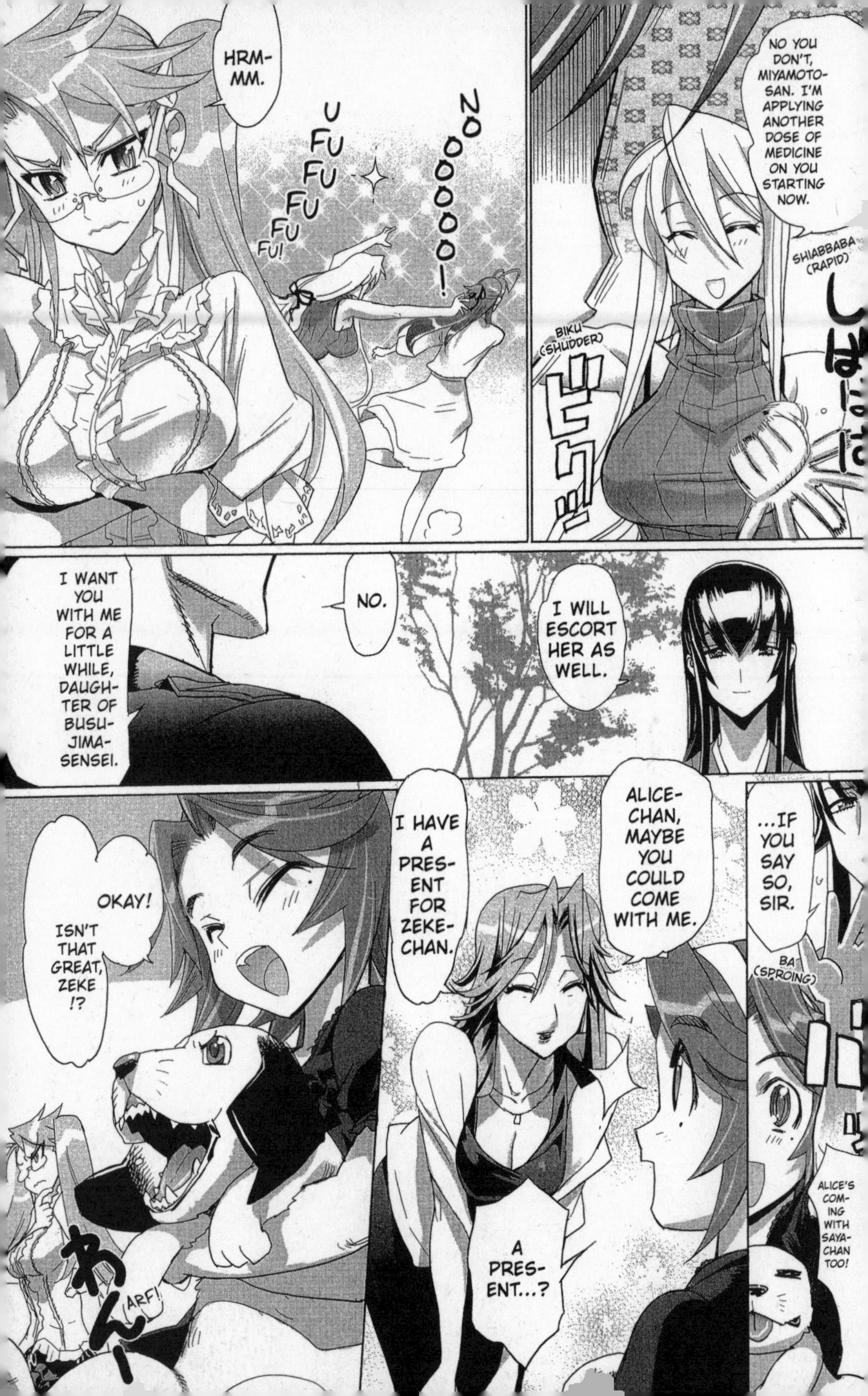
NO YOU DON'T, MIYAMOTO-SAN. I'M APPLYING ANOTHER DOSE OF MEDICINE ON YOU STARTING NOW.
SHIABBABA (RAPID)
BIKU (SHUDDER)
NOOOOOOOO!
UFUFUFUFUFUFU!
HRM-MM.
I WILL ESCORT HER AS WELL.
NO.
I WANT YOU WITH ME FOR A LITTLE WHILE, DAUGHTER OF BUSUJIMA-SENSEI.
...IF YOU SAY SO, SIR.
BA (SPROING)
ALICE'S COMING WITH SAYA-CHAN TOO!
ALICE-CHAN, MAYBE YOU COULD COME WITH ME.
I HAVE A PRESENT FOR ZEKE-CHAN.
A PRESENT...?
OKAY!
ISN'T THAT GREAT, ZEKE!?
ARF!

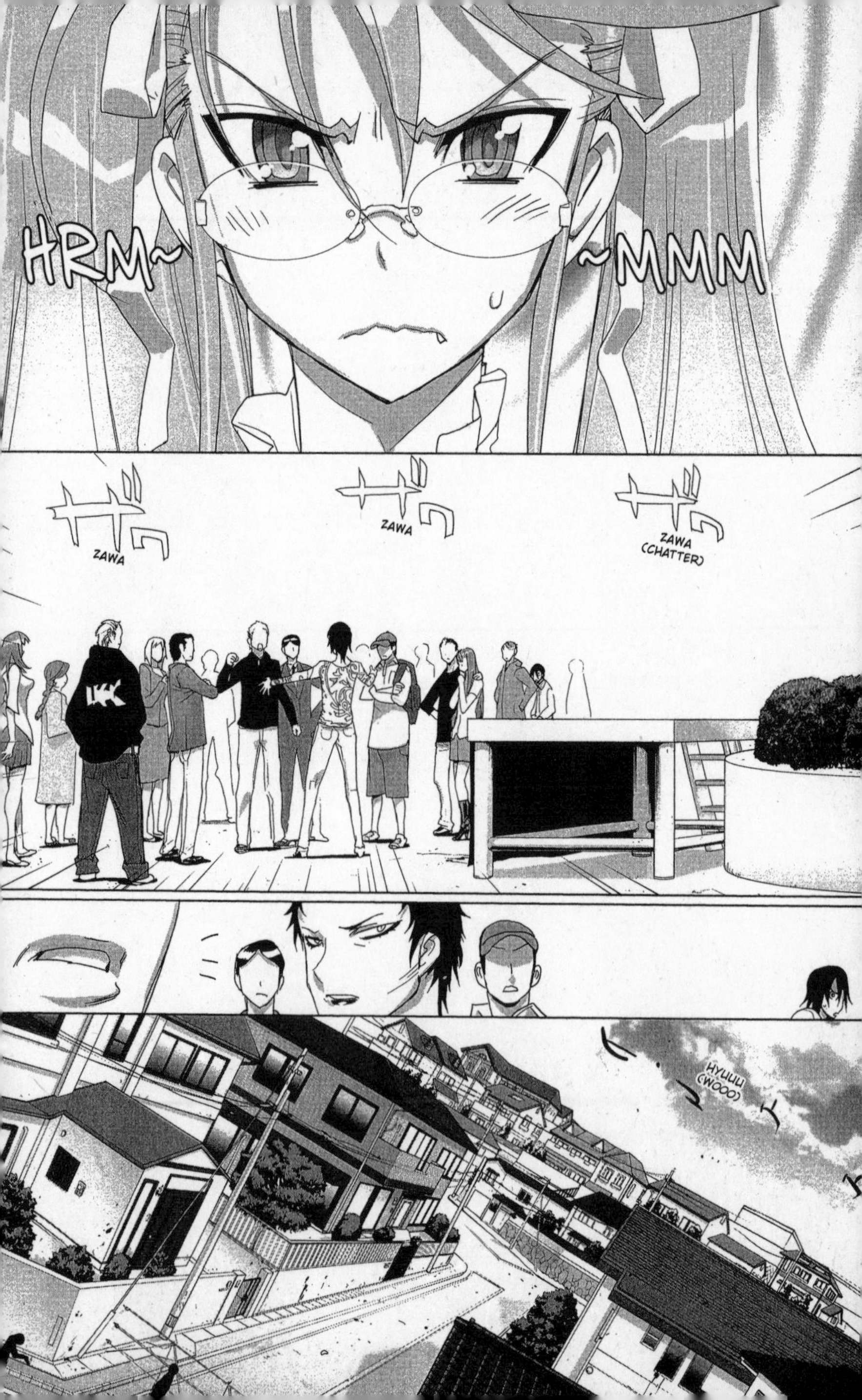
HRM~
~MMM
ザワ
ZAWA (CHATTER)
ザワ
ZAWA
ザワ
ZAWA
HYUUU (WOOO)

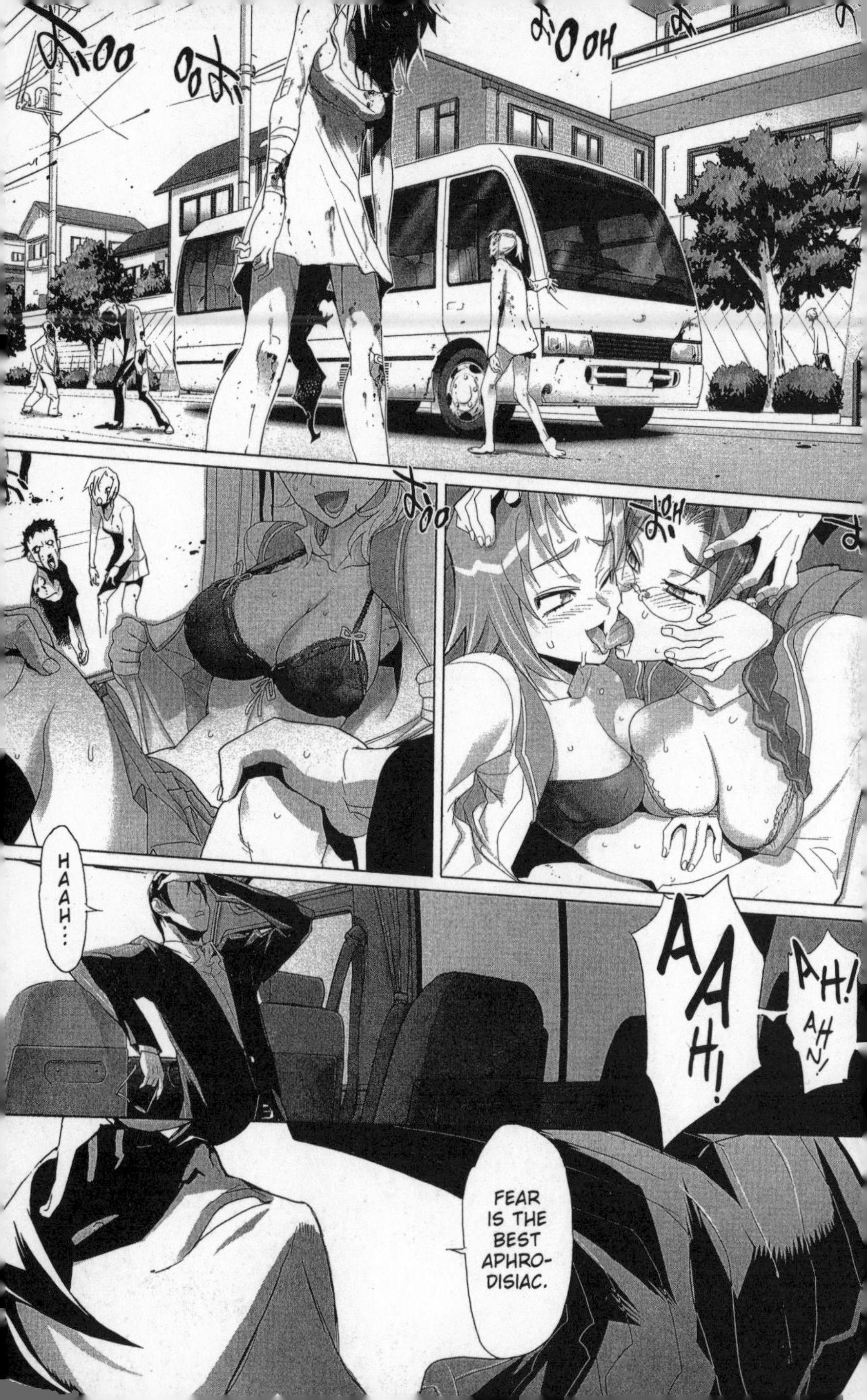
おOOH
おOO
おOO
おOH
おOO
AAAH!
AH! AHN!
HAAAH...
FEAR IS THE BEST APHRO-DISIAC.

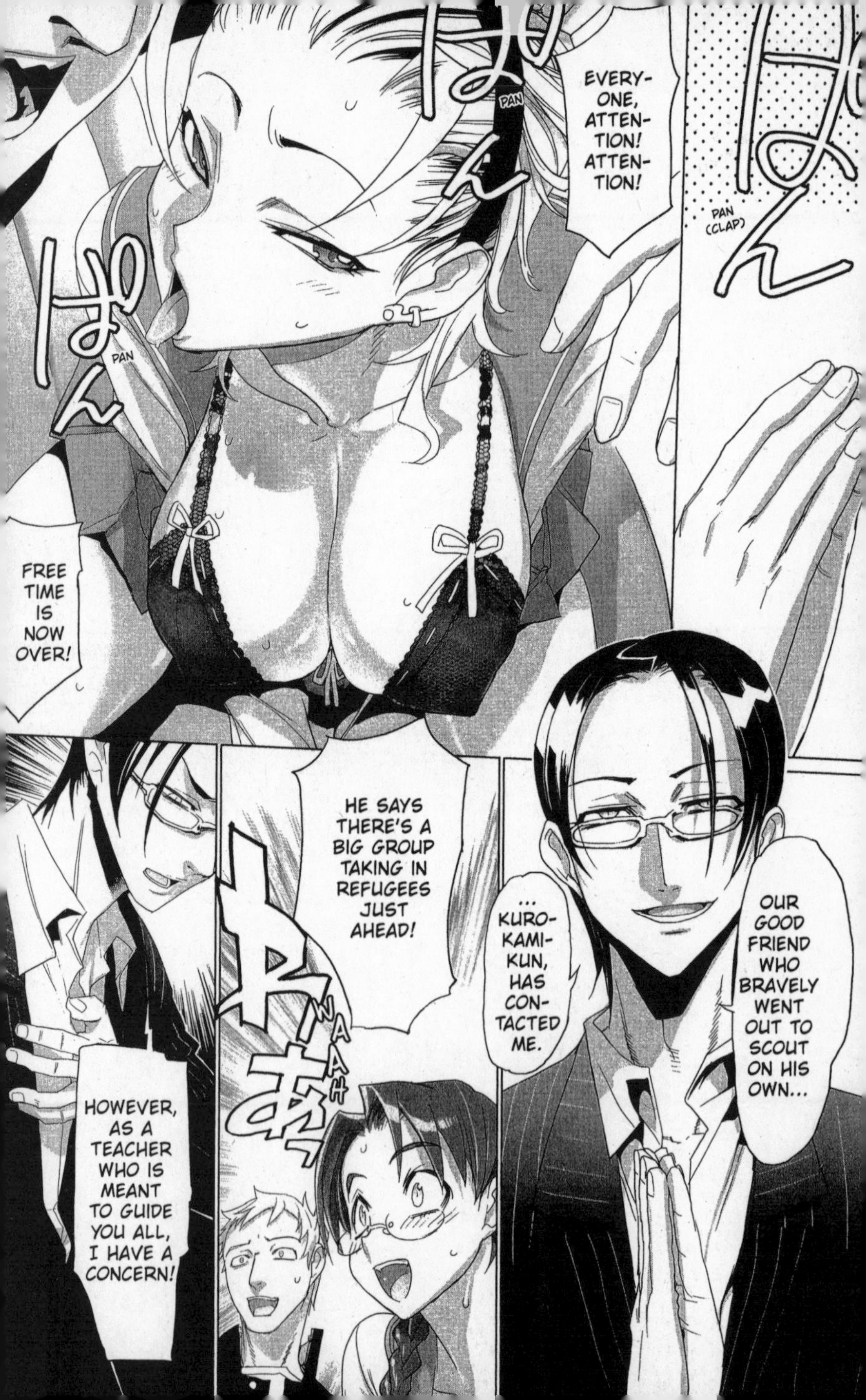
はん
PAN (CLAP)
EVERY-ONE, ATTENTION! ATTENTION!
ぱん
PAN
ぱん
PAN
FREE TIME IS NOW OVER!
OUR GOOD FRIEND WHO BRAVELY WENT OUT TO SCOUT ON HIS OWN...
...KURO-KAMI-KUN, HAS CON-TACTED ME.
HE SAYS THERE'S A BIG GROUP TAKING IN REFUGEES JUST AHEAD!
WAAH
HOWEVER, AS A TEACHER WHO IS MEANT TO GUIDE YOU ALL, I HAVE A CONCERN!

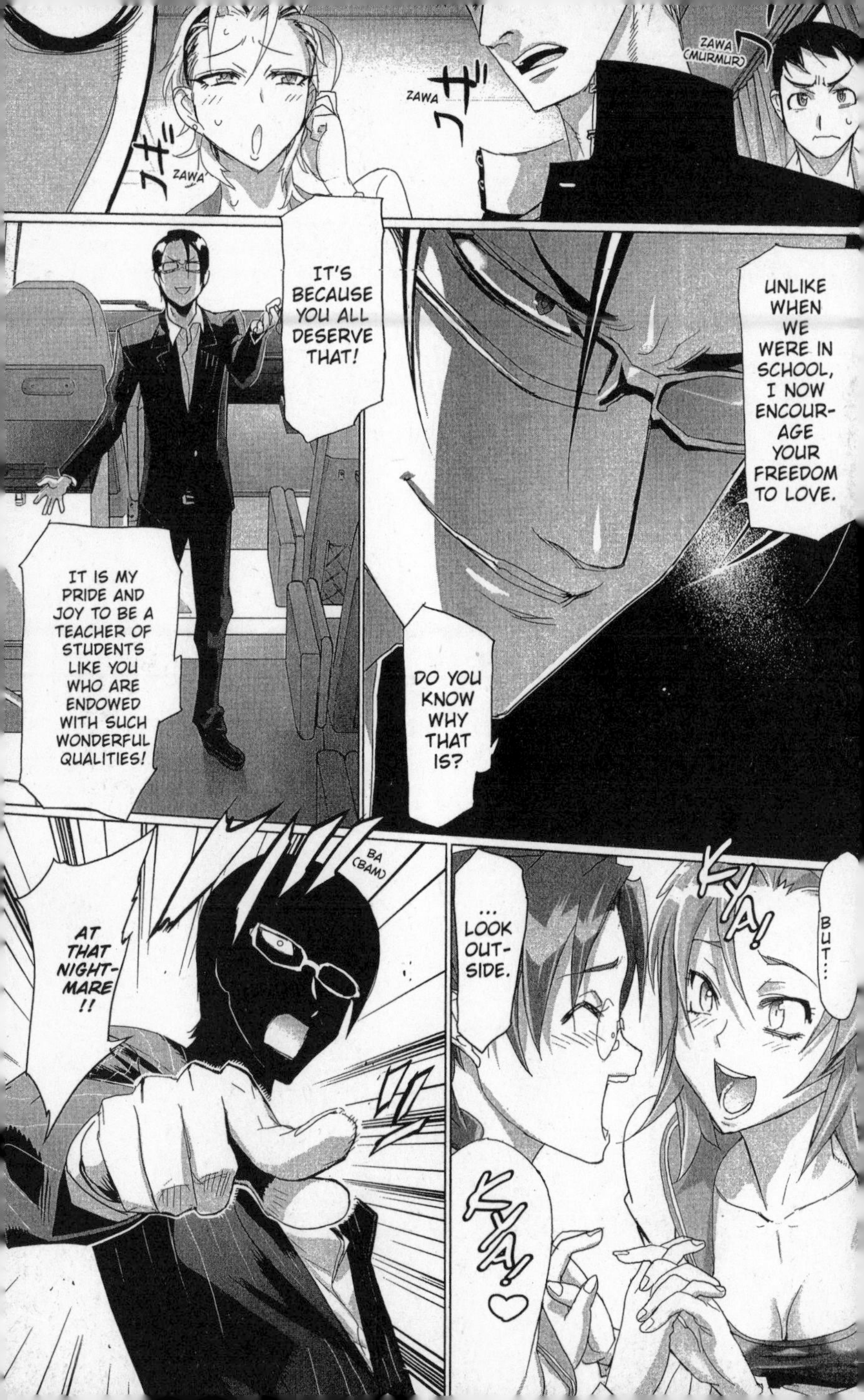
ZAWA (MURMUR)
ZAWA
ZAWA
UNLIKE WHEN WE WERE IN SCHOOL, I NOW ENCOURAGE YOUR FREEDOM TO LOVE.
DO YOU KNOW WHY THAT IS?
IT'S BECAUSE YOU ALL DESERVE THAT!
IT IS MY PRIDE AND JOY TO BE A TEACHER OF STUDENTS LIKE YOU WHO ARE ENDOWED WITH SUCH WONDERFUL QUALITIES!
BUT...
KYA!
...LOOK OUTSIDE.
KYA! ♡
BA (BAM)
AT THAT NIGHTMARE!!

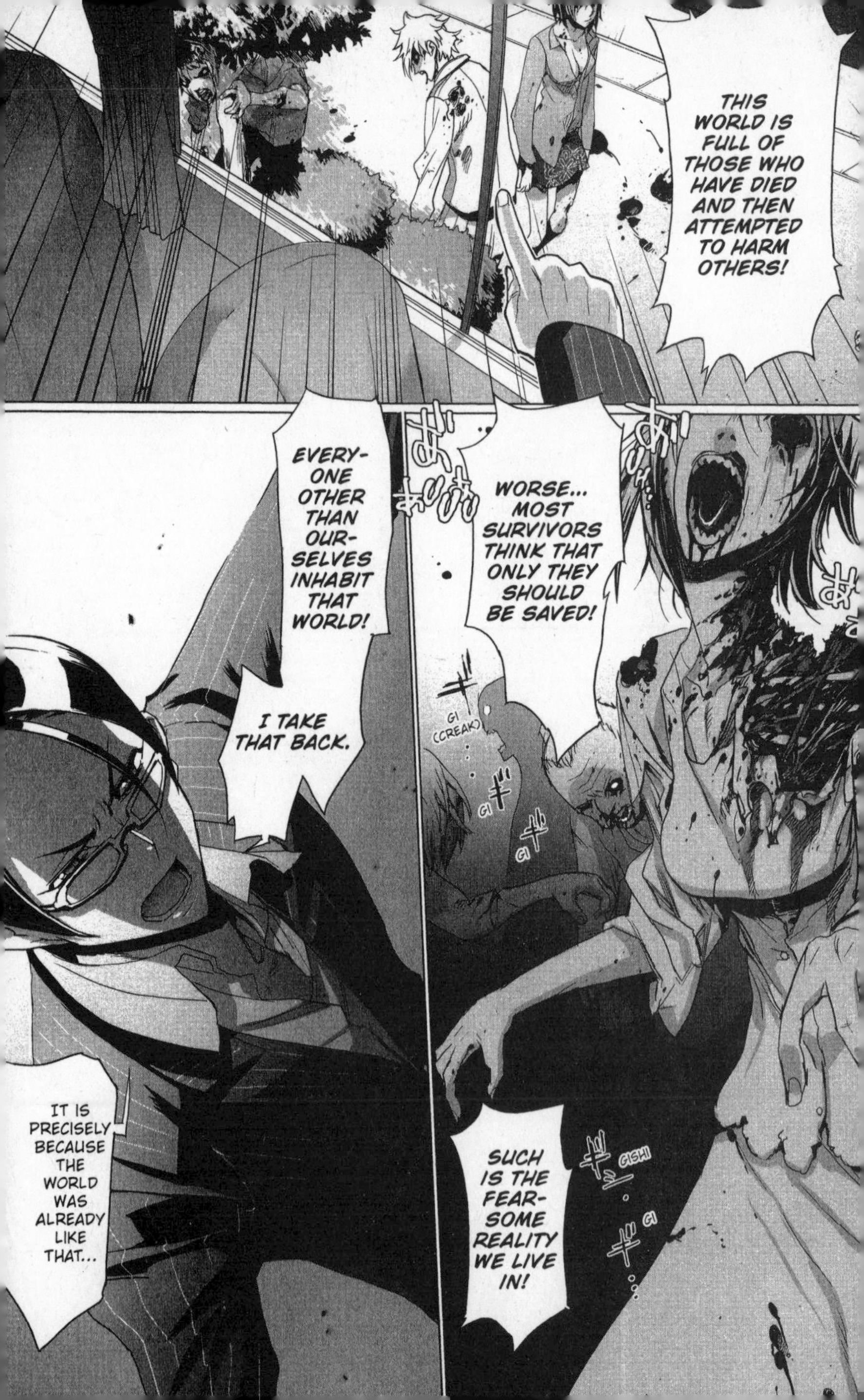
THIS WORLD IS FULL OF THOSE WHO HAVE DIED AND THEN ATTEMPTED TO HARM OTHERS!
WORSE... MOST SURVIVORS THINK THAT ONLY THEY SHOULD BE SAVED!
GI (CREAK)
GI
GI
SUCH IS THE FEAR-SOME REALITY WE LIVE IN!
GISHI
GI
EVERY-ONE OTHER THAN OUR-SELVES INHABIT THAT WORLD!
I TAKE THAT BACK.
IT IS PRECISELY BECAUSE THE WORLD WAS ALREADY LIKE THAT...

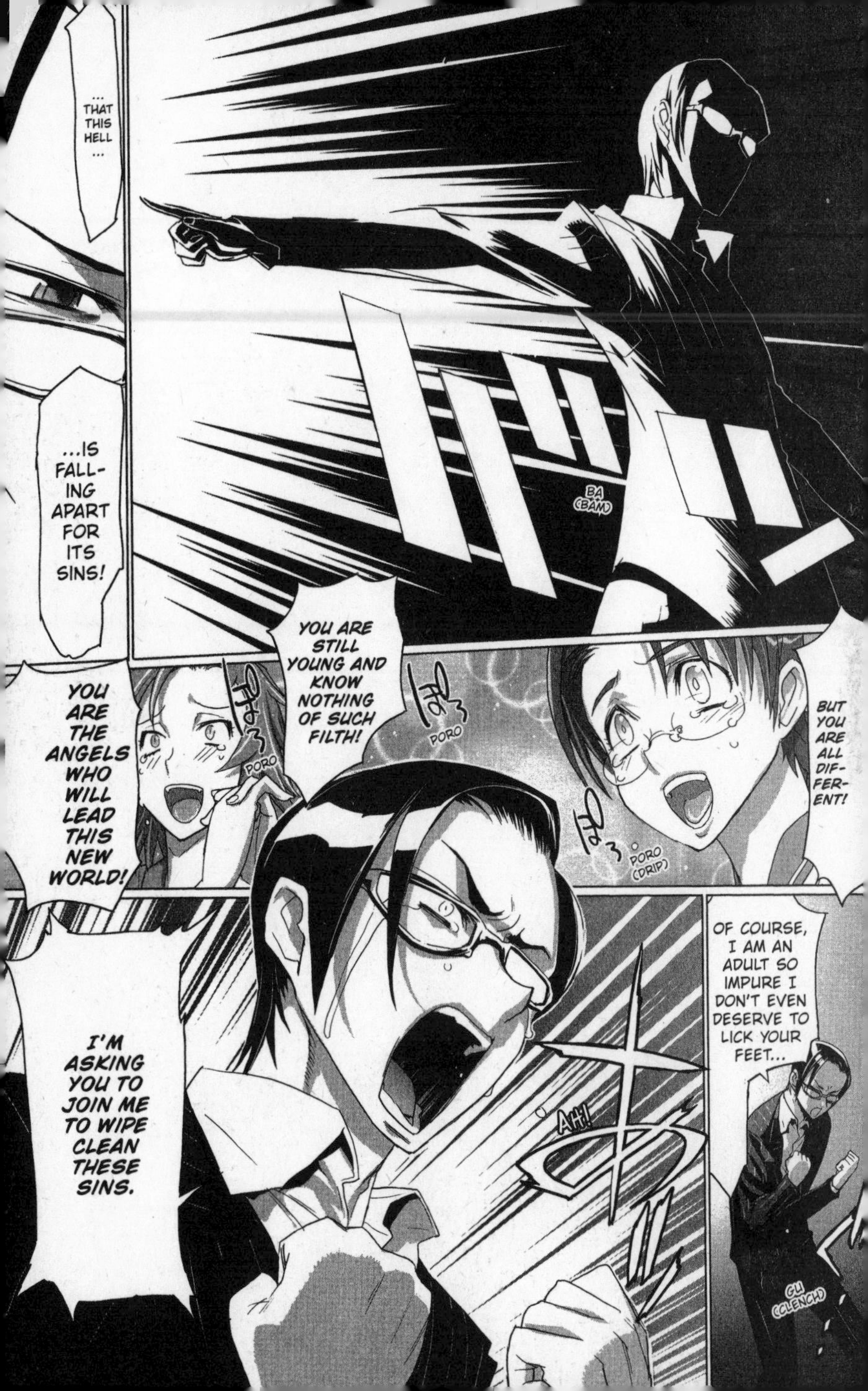

BA (BAM)
...THAT THIS HELL...
...IS FALLING APART FOR ITS SINS!
BUT YOU ARE ALL DIFFERENT!
YOU ARE STILL YOUNG AND KNOW NOTHING OF SUCH FILTH!
PORO
PORO (DRIP)
YOU ARE THE ANGELS WHO WILL LEAD THIS NEW WORLD!
PORO
OF COURSE, I AM AN ADULT SO IMPURE I DON'T EVEN DESERVE TO LICK YOUR FEET...
GU (CLENCH)
AH!
I'M ASKING YOU TO JOIN ME TO WIPE CLEAN THESE SINS.

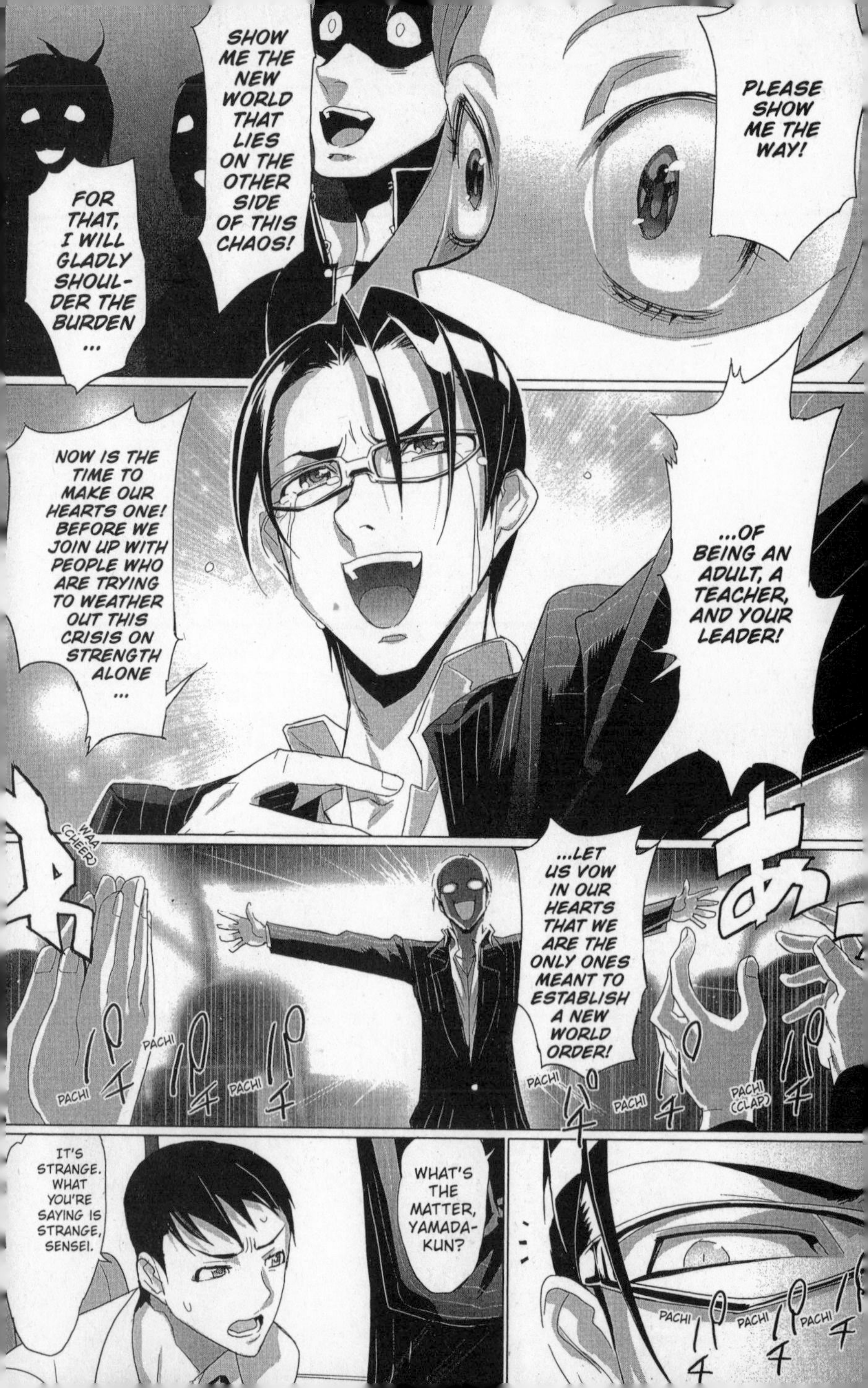
PLEASE SHOW ME THE WAY!
SHOW ME THE NEW WORLD THAT LIES ON THE OTHER SIDE OF THIS CHAOS!
FOR THAT, I WILL GLADLY SHOULDER THE BURDEN...
...OF BEING AN ADULT, A TEACHER, AND YOUR LEADER!
NOW IS THE TIME TO MAKE OUR HEARTS ONE! BEFORE WE JOIN UP WITH PEOPLE WHO ARE TRYING TO WEATHER OUT THIS CRISIS ON STRENGTH ALONE...
...LET US VOW IN OUR HEARTS THAT WE ARE THE ONLY ONES MEANT TO ESTABLISH A NEW WORLD ORDER!
PACHI (CLAP)
PACHI
PACHI
PACHI
PACHI
PACHI
WAA (CHEER)
...
PACHI
PACHI
PACHI
WHAT'S THE MATTER, YAMADA-KUN?
IT'S STRANGE. WHAT YOU'RE SAYING IS STRANGE, SENSEI.

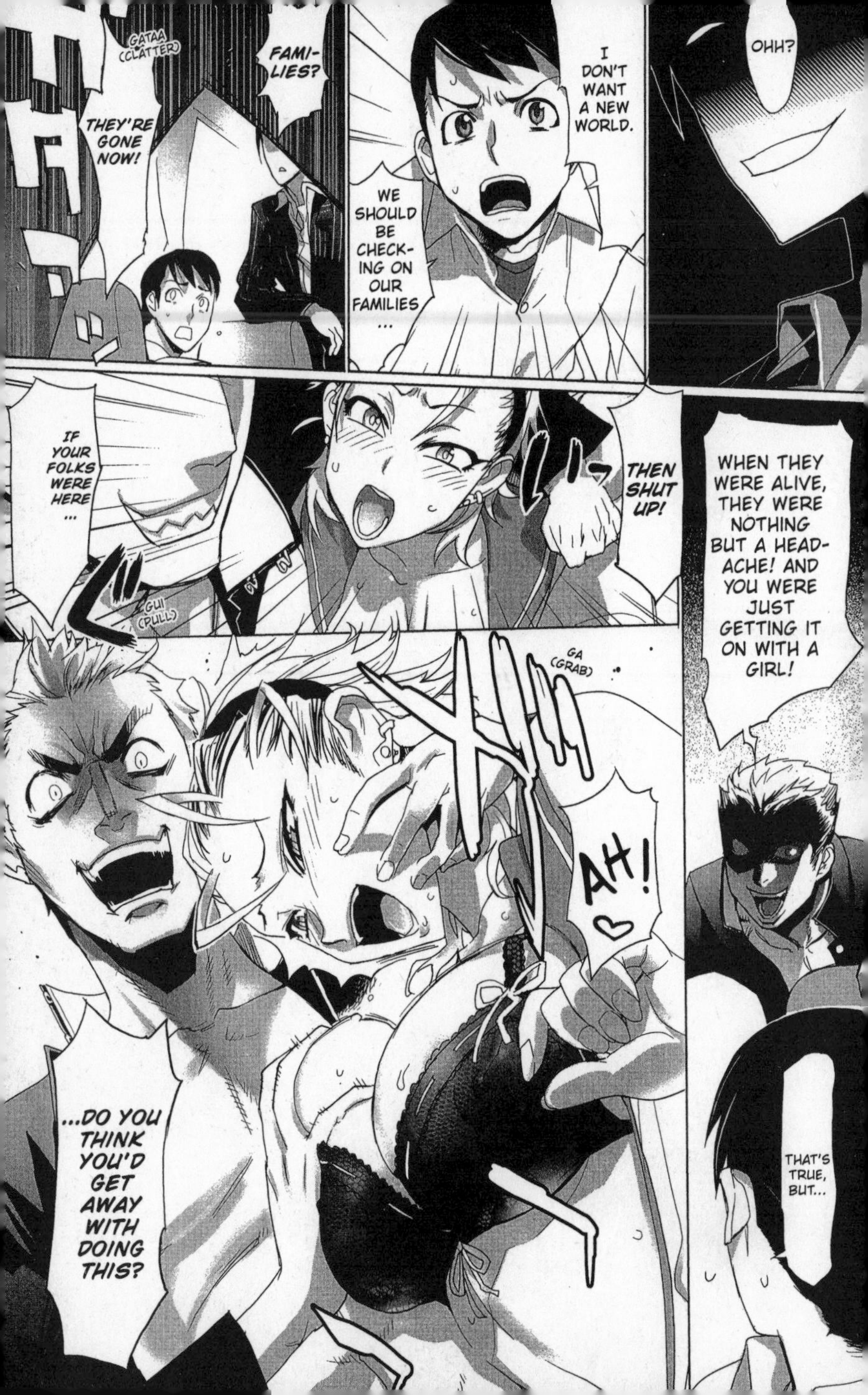
OHH?
I DON'T WANT A NEW WORLD.
WE SHOULD BE CHECKING ON OUR FAMILIES...
FAMILIES?
GATAA (CLATTER)
THEY'RE GONE NOW!
WHEN THEY WERE ALIVE, THEY WERE NOTHING BUT A HEADACHE! AND YOU WERE JUST GETTING IT ON WITH A GIRL!
THAT'S TRUE, BUT...
THEN SHUT UP!
IF YOUR FOLKS WERE HERE...
GUI (PULL)
GA (GRAB)
AH! ♥
...DO YOU THINK YOU'D GET AWAY WITH DOING THIS?

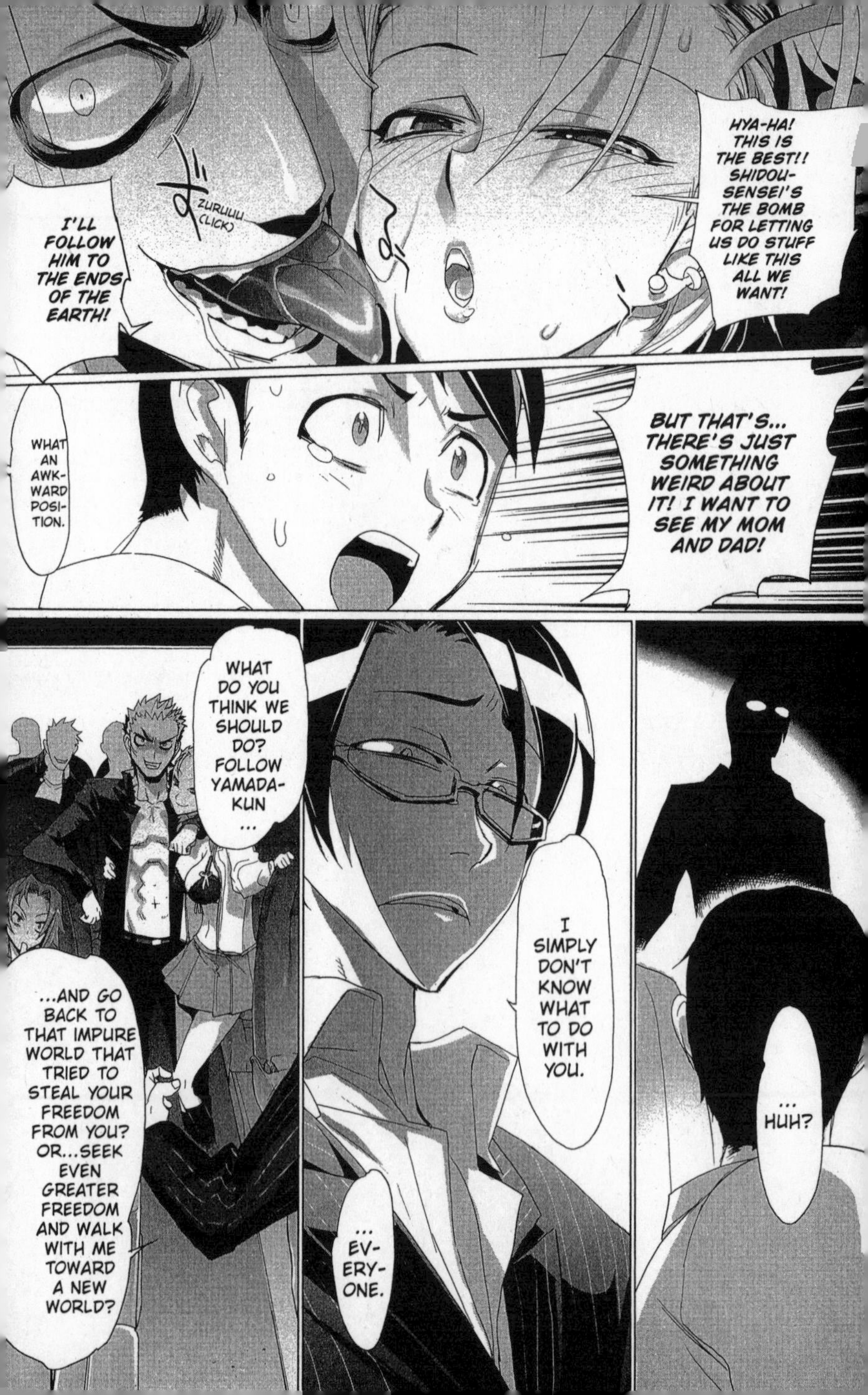
HYA-HA! THIS IS THE BEST!! SHIDOU-SENSEI'S THE BOMB FOR LETTING US DO STUFF LIKE THIS ALL WE WANT!
ZURUUU (LICK)
I'LL FOLLOW HIM TO THE ENDS OF THE EARTH!
BUT THAT'S... THERE'S JUST SOMETHING WEIRD ABOUT IT! I WANT TO SEE MY MOM AND DAD!
WHAT AN AWK-WARD POSI-TION.
... HUH?
I SIMPLY DON'T KNOW WHAT TO DO WITH YOU.
... EV-ERY-ONE.
WHAT DO YOU THINK WE SHOULD DO? FOLLOW YAMADA-KUN ...
...AND GO BACK TO THAT IMPURE WORLD THAT TRIED TO STEAL YOUR FREEDOM FROM YOU? OR...SEEK EVEN GREATER FREEDOM AND WALK WITH ME TOWARD A NEW WORLD?

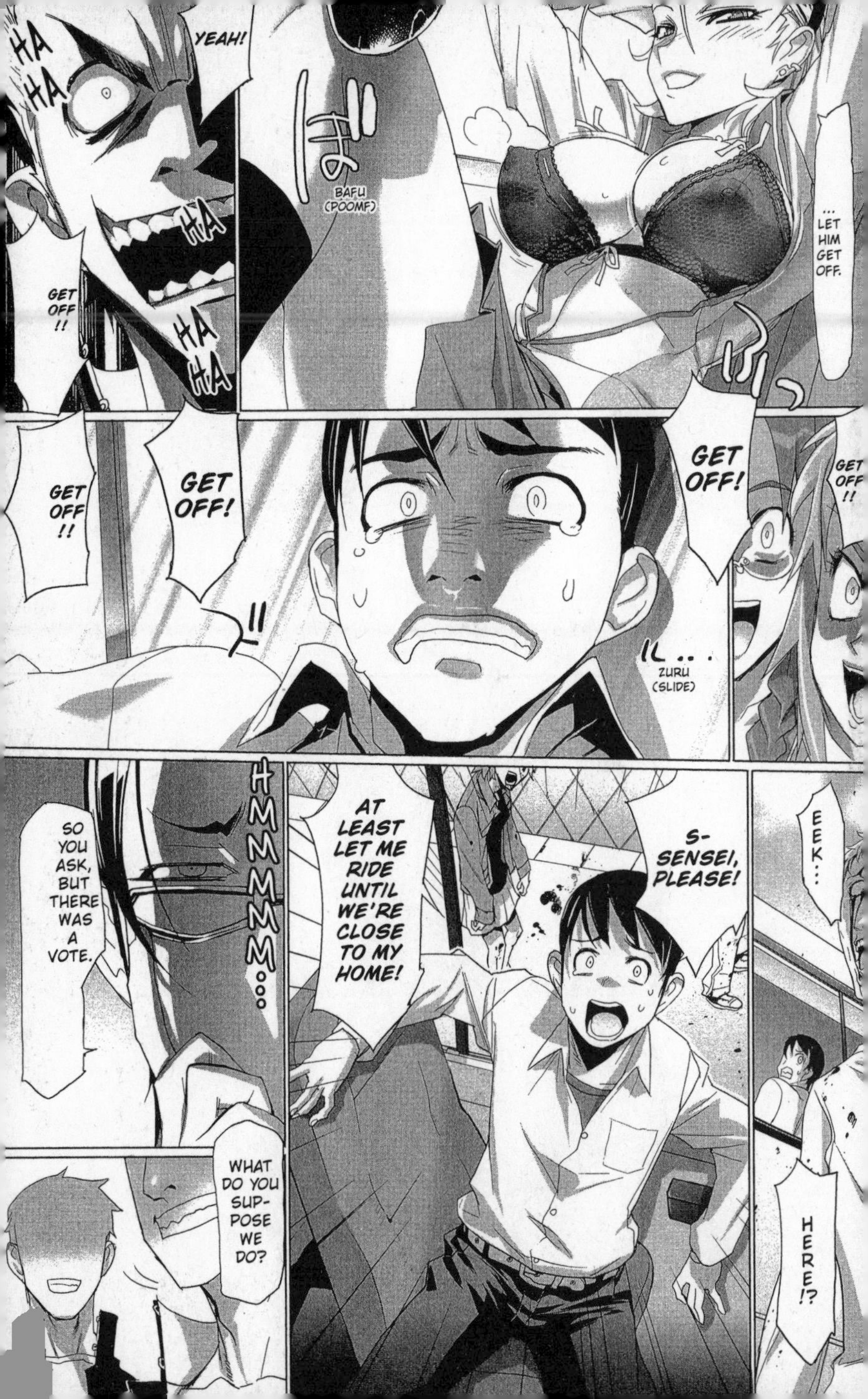
...LET HIM GET OFF.
BAFU (POOMF)
YEAH!
HA HA
HA
HA HA
GET OFF!!
GET OFF!!
GET OFF!
ZURU (SLIDE)
GET OFF!
GET OFF!!
EEK...
HERE!?
S-SENSEI, PLEASE!
AT LEAST LET ME RIDE UNTIL WE'RE CLOSE TO MY HOME!
HMMMMM...
SO YOU ASK, BUT THERE WAS A VOTE.
WHAT DO YOU SUPPOSE WE DO?

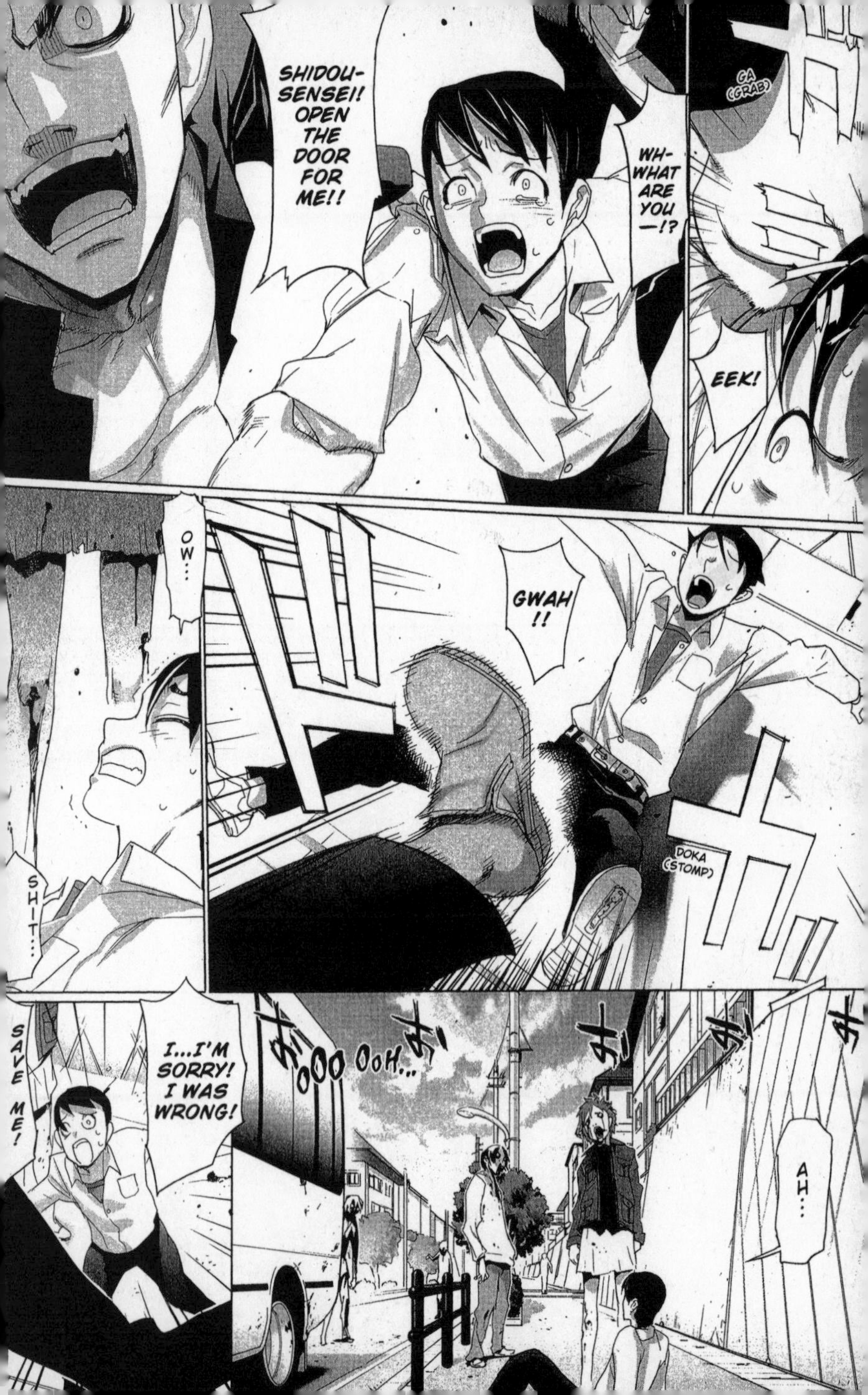
GA (GRAB)
EEK!
SHIDOU-SENSEI!! OPEN THE DOOR FOR ME!!
WH-WHAT ARE YOU—!?
GWAH!!
DOKA (STOMP)
OW...
SHIT...
AH...
OOO OOH...
I...I'M SORRY! I WAS WRONG!
SAVE ME!

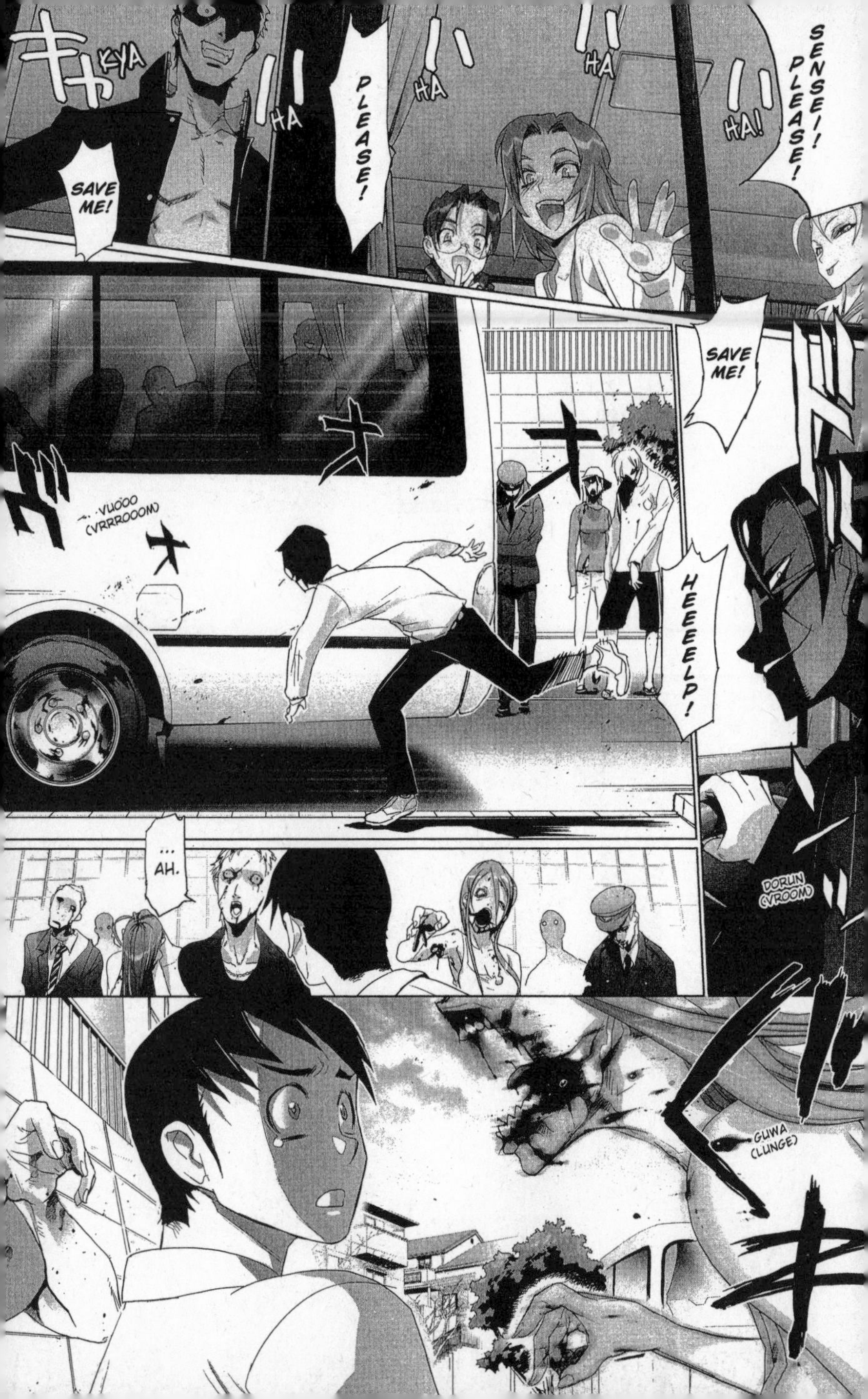
SENSEI! PLEASE!
HA!
HA
HA
PLEASE!
HA
KYA
SAVE ME!
SAVE ME!
HEEEEELP!
DORUN (VROOM)
...VUOOO (VRRROOOM)
... AH.
GUWA (LUNGE)

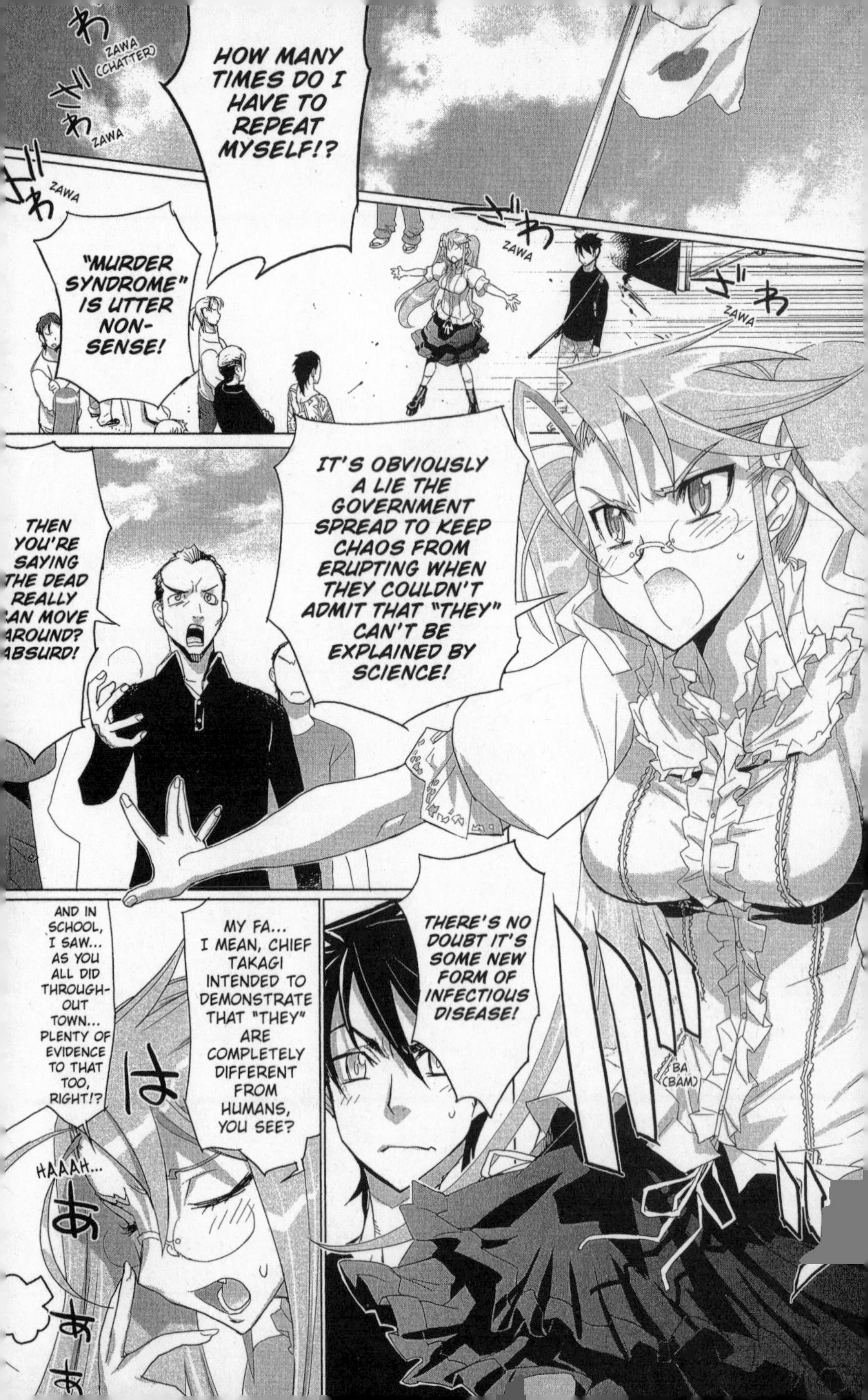
HOW MANY TIMES DO I HAVE TO REPEAT MYSELF!?
ZAWA (CHATTER)
ZAWA
ZAWA
ZAWA
ZAWA
"MURDER SYNDROME" IS UTTER NON-SENSE!
IT'S OBVIOUSLY A LIE THE GOVERNMENT SPREAD TO KEEP CHAOS FROM ERUPTING WHEN THEY COULDN'T ADMIT THAT "THEY" CAN'T BE EXPLAINED BY SCIENCE!
THEN YOU'RE SAYING THE DEAD REALLY CAN MOVE AROUND? ABSURD!
THERE'S NO DOUBT IT'S SOME NEW FORM OF INFECTIOUS DISEASE!
BA (BAM)
MY FA... I MEAN, CHIEF TAKAGI INTENDED TO DEMONSTRATE THAT "THEY" ARE COMPLETELY DIFFERENT FROM HUMANS, YOU SEE?
AND IN SCHOOL, I SAW... AS YOU ALL DID THROUGH-OUT TOWN... PLENTY OF EVIDENCE TO THAT TOO, RIGHT!?
HAAAH...

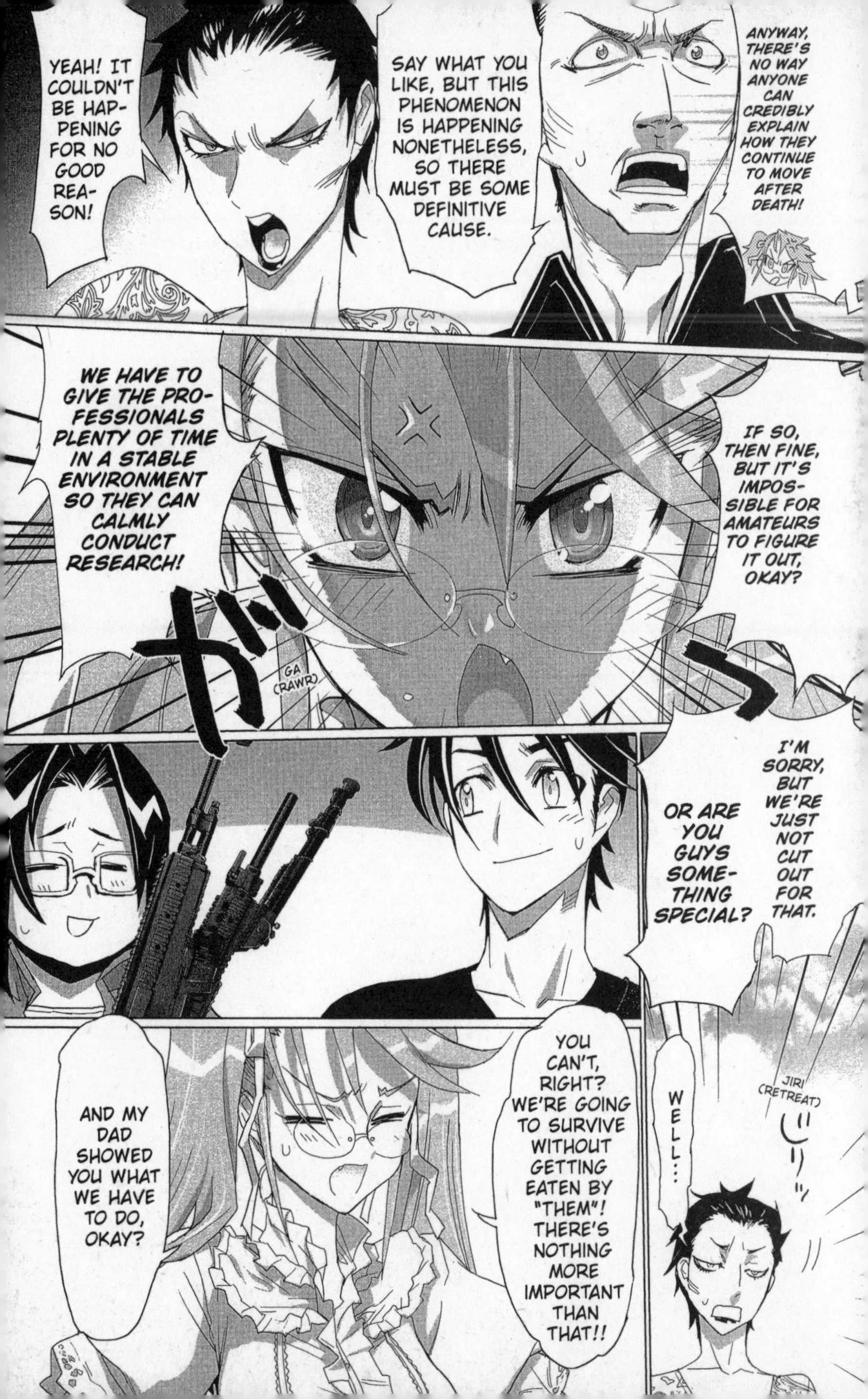
ANYWAY, THERE'S NO WAY ANYONE CAN CREDIBLY EXPLAIN HOW THEY CONTINUE TO MOVE AFTER DEATH!
SAY WHAT YOU LIKE, BUT THIS PHENOMENON IS HAPPENING NONETHELESS, SO THERE MUST BE SOME DEFINITIVE CAUSE.
YEAH! IT COULDN'T BE HAP-PENING FOR NO GOOD REA-SON!
IF SO, THEN FINE, BUT IT'S IMPOS-SIBLE FOR AMATEURS TO FIGURE IT OUT, OKAY?
WE HAVE TO GIVE THE PRO-FESSIONALS PLENTY OF TIME IN A STABLE ENVIRONMENT SO THEY CAN CALMLY CONDUCT RESEARCH!
ガッ
GA (RAWR)
I'M SORRY, BUT WE'RE JUST NOT CUT OUT FOR THAT.
OR ARE YOU GUYS SOME-THING SPECIAL?
JIRI (RETREAT)
WELL...
YOU CAN'T, RIGHT? WE'RE GOING TO SURVIVE WITHOUT GETTING EATEN BY "THEM"! THERE'S NOTHING MORE IMPORTANT THAN THAT!!
AND MY DAD SHOWED YOU WHAT WE HAVE TO DO, OKAY?

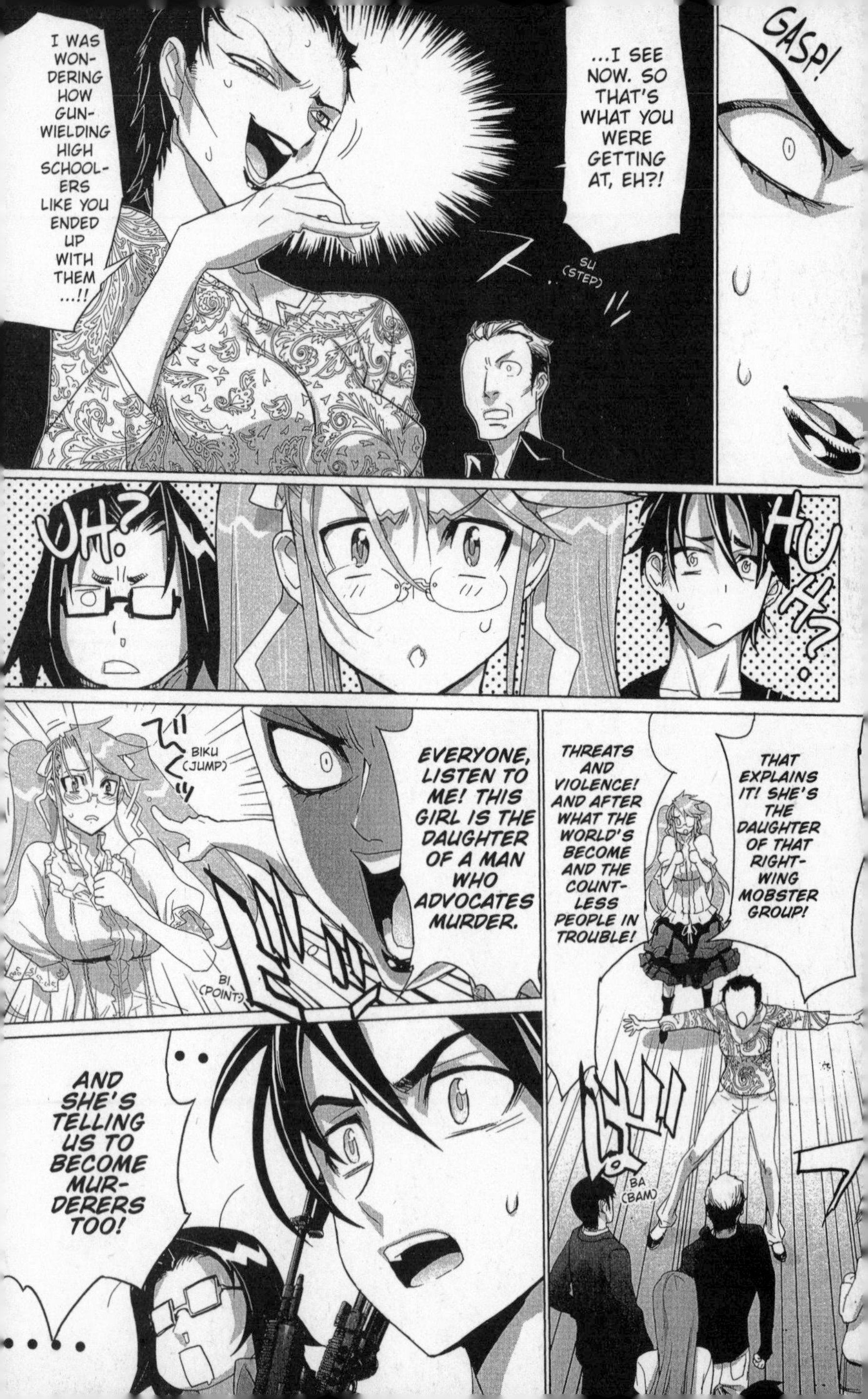
GASP!
...I SEE NOW. SO THAT'S WHAT YOU WERE GETTING AT, EH?!
SU (STEP)
I WAS WONDERING HOW GUN-WIELDING HIGH SCHOOLERS LIKE YOU ENDED UP WITH THEM ...!!
HUH?
UH?
THAT EXPLAINS IT! SHE'S THE DAUGHTER OF THAT RIGHT-WING MOBSTER GROUP!
THREATS AND VIOLENCE! AND AFTER WHAT THE WORLD'S BECOME AND THE COUNTLESS PEOPLE IN TROUBLE!
BA (BAM)
EVERYONE, LISTEN TO ME! THIS GIRL IS THE DAUGHTER OF A MAN WHO ADVOCATES MURDER.
BIKU (JUMP)
BI (POINT)
AND SHE'S TELLING US TO BECOME MURDERERS TOO!
...
....

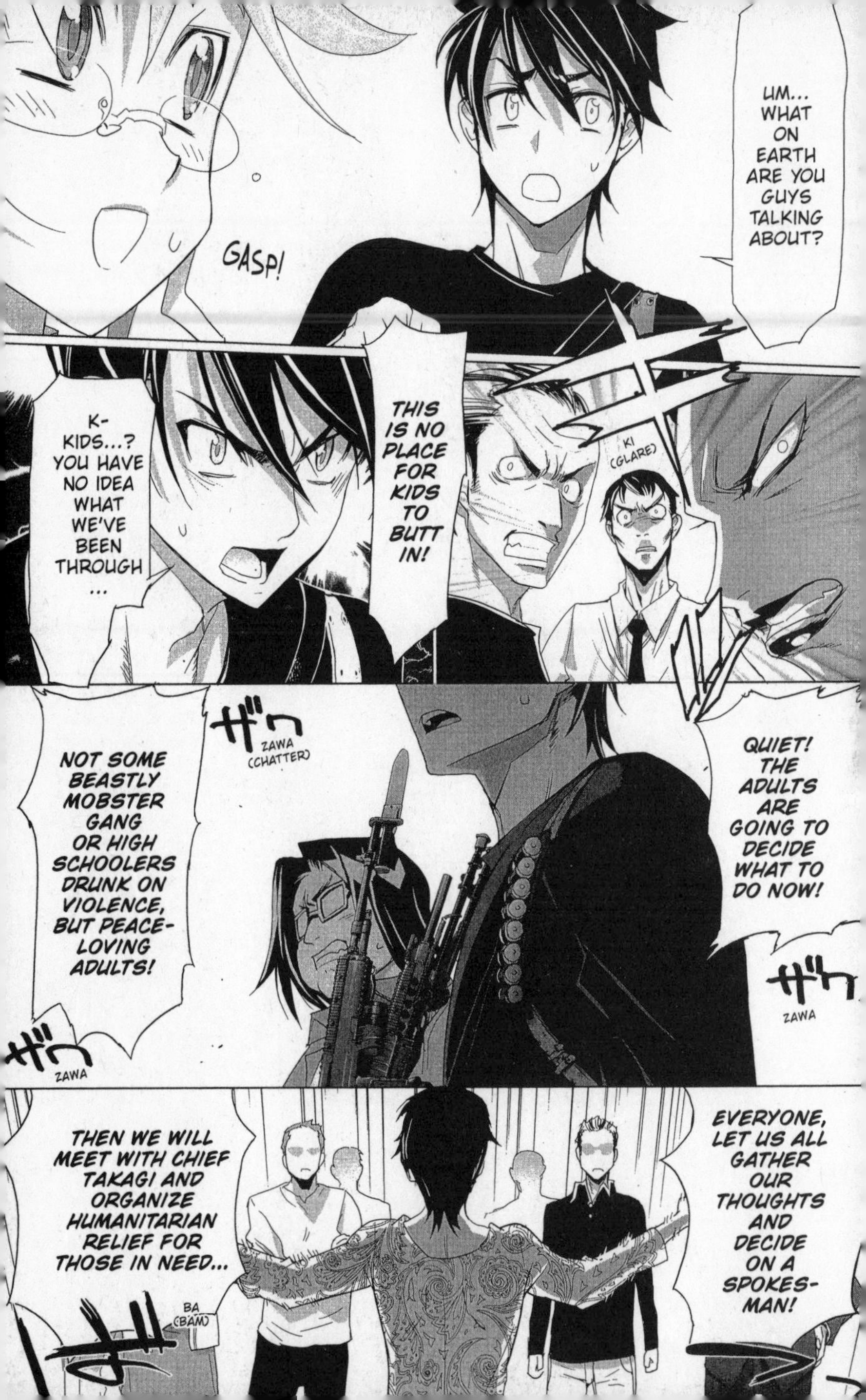
UM... WHAT ON EARTH ARE YOU GUYS TALKING ABOUT?
GASP!
KI (GLARE)
THIS IS NO PLACE FOR KIDS TO BUTT IN!
K-KIDS...? YOU HAVE NO IDEA WHAT WE'VE BEEN THROUGH...
QUIET! THE ADULTS ARE GOING TO DECIDE WHAT TO DO NOW!
ZAWA
ZAWA (CHATTER)
NOT SOME BEASTLY MOBSTER GANG OR HIGH SCHOOLERS DRUNK ON VIOLENCE, BUT PEACE-LOVING ADULTS!
ZAWA
EVERYONE, LET US ALL GATHER OUR THOUGHTS AND DECIDE ON A SPOKES-MAN!
THEN WE WILL MEET WITH CHIEF TAKAGI AND ORGANIZE HUMANITARIAN RELIEF FOR THOSE IN NEED...
BA (BAM)

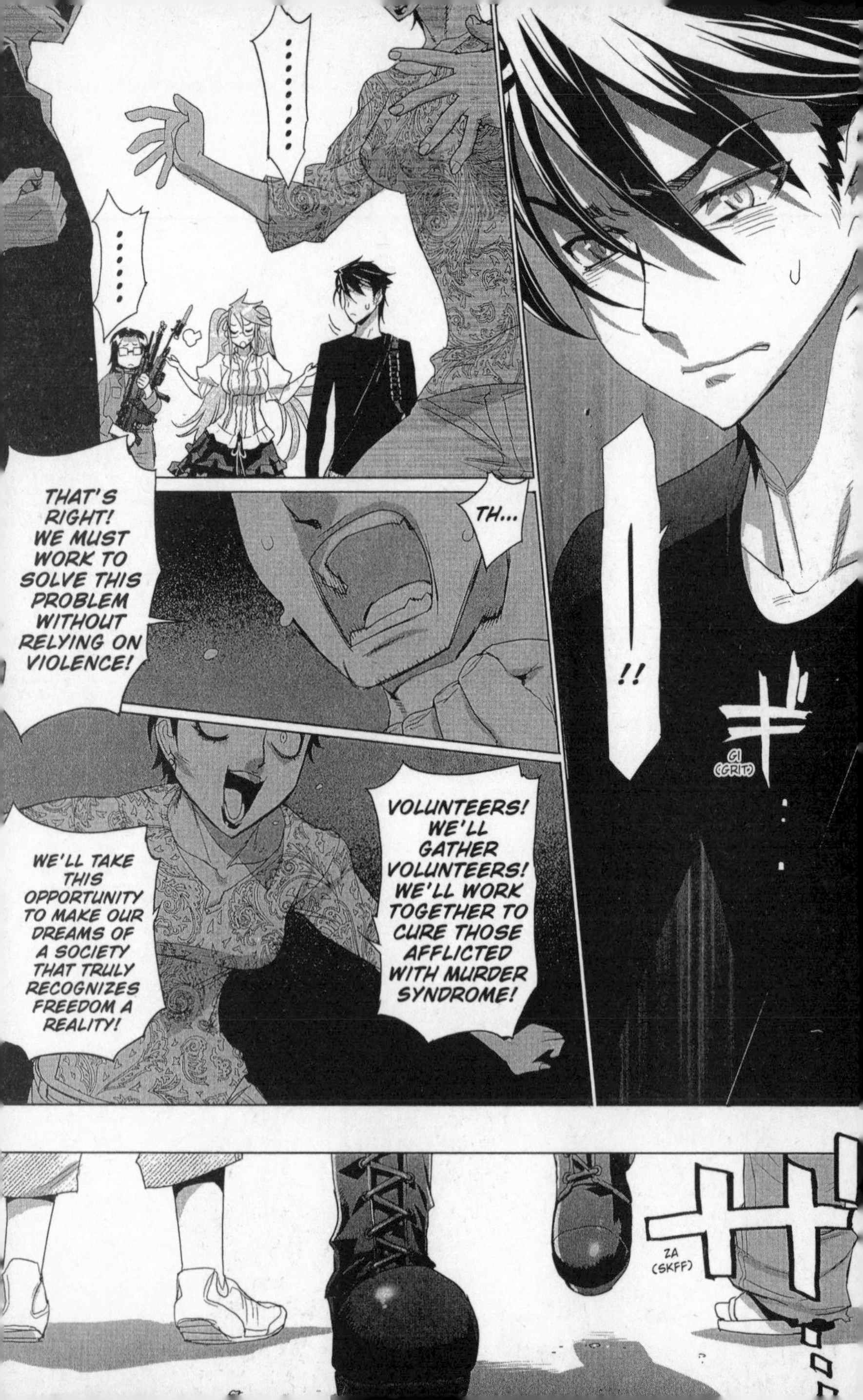
!!
GI (GRIT)
......
......
TH...
THAT'S RIGHT! WE MUST WORK TO SOLVE THIS PROBLEM WITHOUT RELYING ON VIOLENCE!
VOLUNTEERS! WE'LL GATHER VOLUNTEERS! WE'LL WORK TOGETHER TO CURE THOSE AFFLICTED WITH MURDER SYNDROME!
WE'LL TAKE THIS OPPORTUNITY TO MAKE OUR DREAMS OF A SOCIETY THAT TRULY RECOGNIZES FREEDOM A REALITY!
ZA (SKFF)

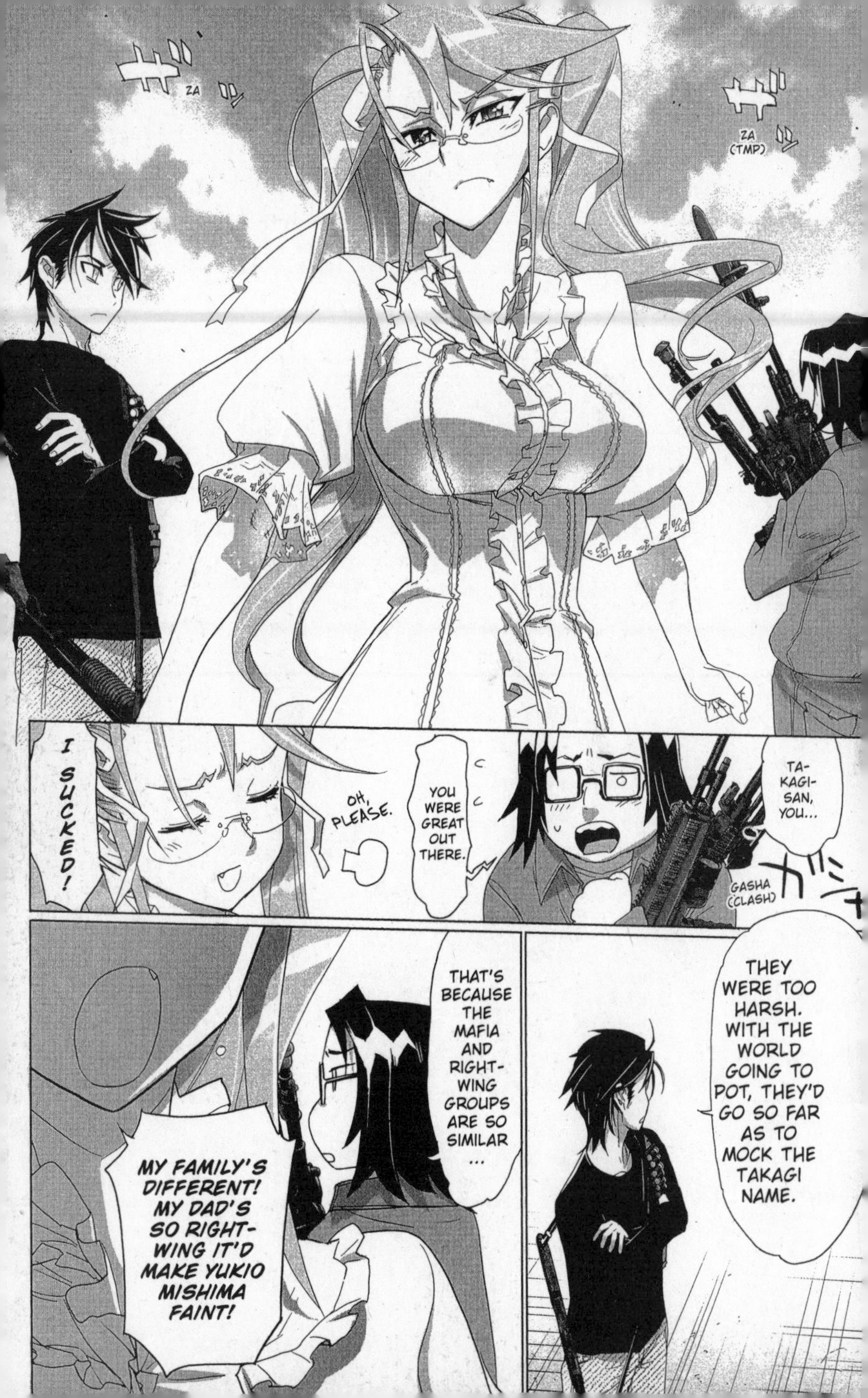
ZA (TMP)
ZA
TAKAGI-SAN, YOU...
GASHA (CLASH)
YOU WERE GREAT OUT THERE.
OH, PLEASE.
I SUCKED!
THEY WERE TOO HARSH. WITH THE WORLD GOING TO POT, THEY'D GO SO FAR AS TO MOCK THE TAKAGI NAME.
THAT'S BECAUSE THE MAFIA AND RIGHT-WING GROUPS ARE SO SIMILAR...
MY FAMILY'S DIFFERENT! MY DAD'S SO RIGHT-WING IT'D MAKE YUKIO MISHIMA FAINT!

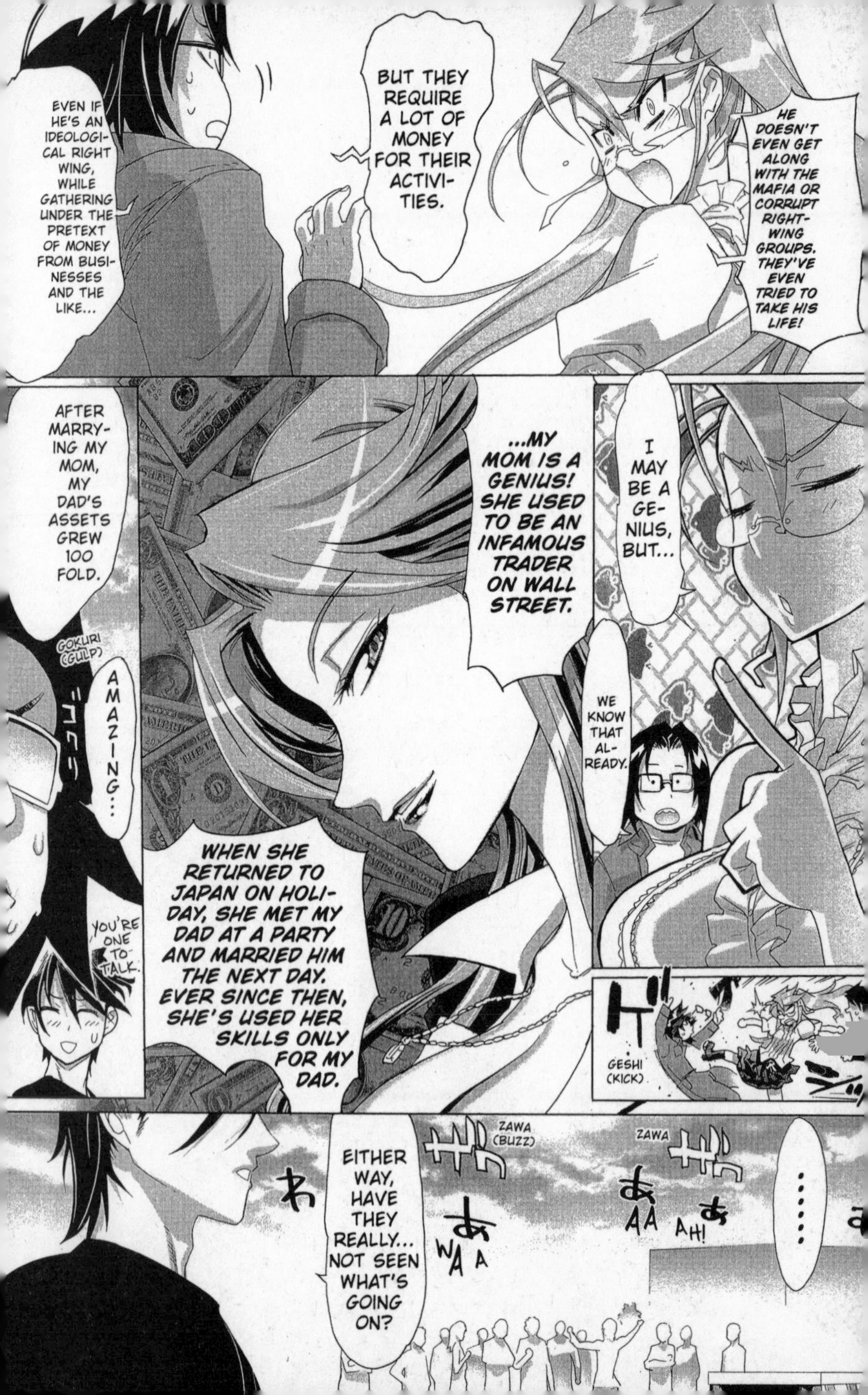
HE DOESN'T EVEN GET ALONG WITH THE MAFIA OR CORRUPT RIGHT-WING GROUPS. THEY'VE EVEN TRIED TO TAKE HIS LIFE!
BUT THEY REQUIRE A LOT OF MONEY FOR THEIR ACTIVITIES.
EVEN IF HE'S AN IDEOLOGICAL RIGHT WING, WHILE GATHERING UNDER THE PRETEXT OF MONEY FROM BUSINESSES AND THE LIKE...
I MAY BE A GENIUS, BUT...
WE KNOW THAT ALREADY.
GESHI (KICK)
...MY MOM IS A GENIUS! SHE USED TO BE AN INFAMOUS TRADER ON WALL STREET.
WHEN SHE RETURNED TO JAPAN ON HOLIDAY, SHE MET MY DAD AT A PARTY AND MARRIED HIM THE NEXT DAY. EVER SINCE THEN, SHE'S USED HER SKILLS ONLY FOR MY DAD.
AFTER MARRYING MY MOM, MY DAD'S ASSETS GREW 100 FOLD.
GOKURI (GULP)
AMAZING...
YOU'RE ONE TO TALK.
......
ZAWA
AH!
AA
ZAWA (BUZZ)
WAA
EITHER WAY, HAVE THEY REALLY... NOT SEEN WHAT'S GOING ON?

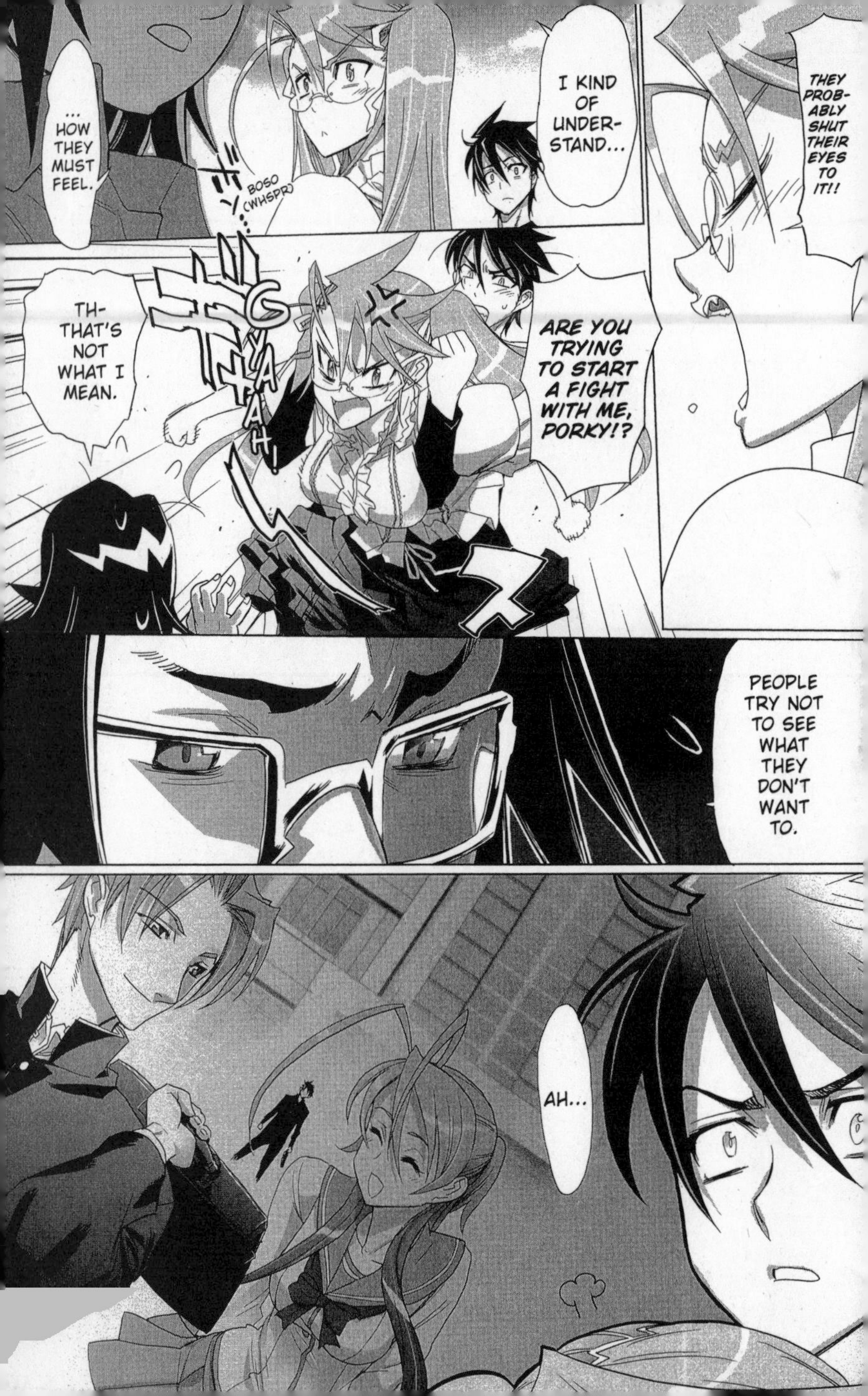
THEY PROBABLY SHUT THEIR EYES TO IT!!
I KIND OF UNDERSTAND...
... HOW THEY MUST FEEL.
BOSO (WHSPR)
ARE YOU TRYING TO START A FIGHT WITH ME, PORKY!?
GYAAAH!
TH-THAT'S NOT WHAT I MEAN.
PEOPLE TRY NOT TO SEE WHAT THEY DON'T WANT TO.
AH...

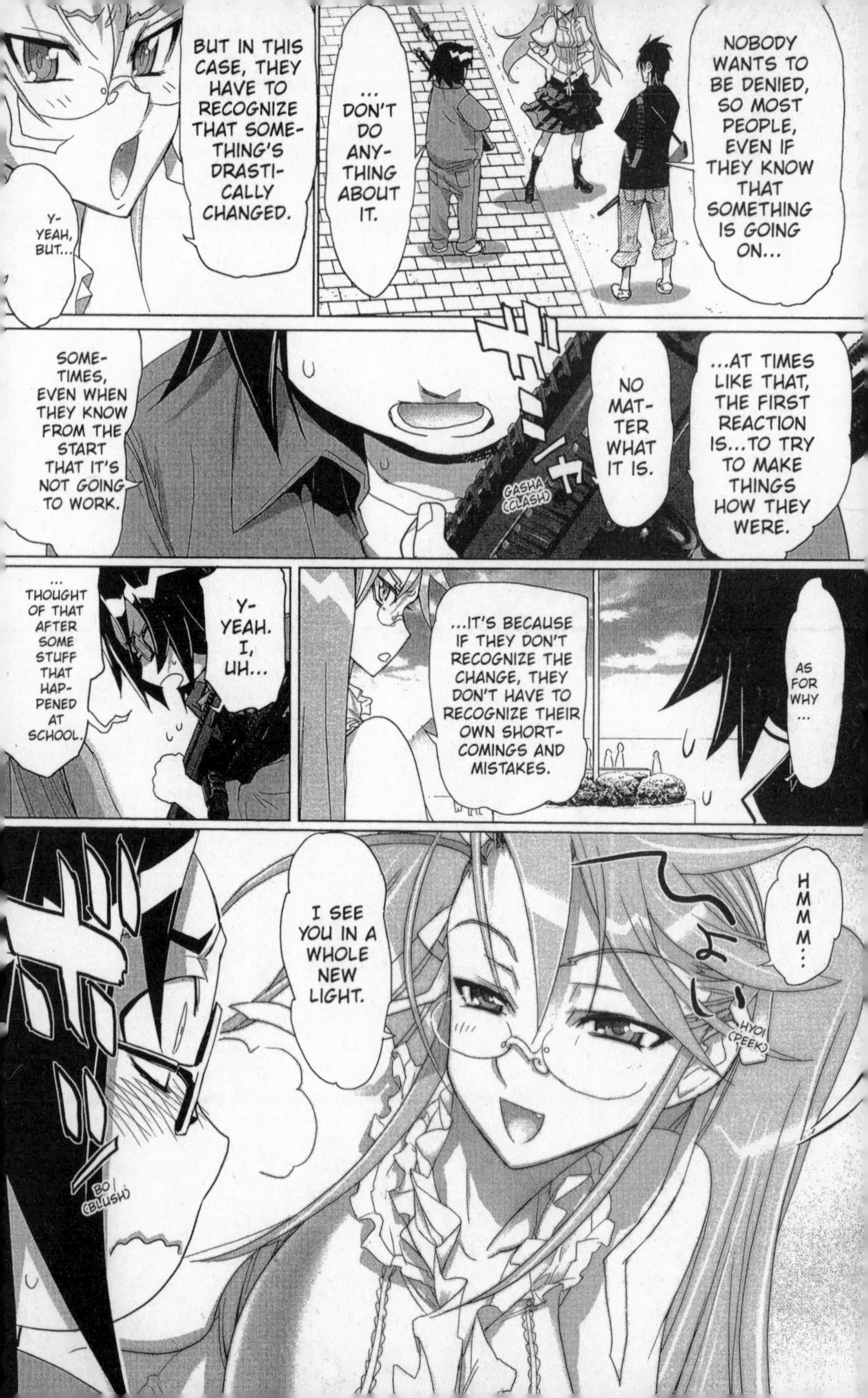
NOBODY WANTS TO BE DENIED, SO MOST PEOPLE, EVEN IF THEY KNOW THAT SOMETHING IS GOING ON...
...DON'T DO ANYTHING ABOUT IT.
BUT IN THIS CASE, THEY HAVE TO RECOGNIZE THAT SOMETHING'S DRASTICALLY CHANGED.
Y-YEAH, BUT...
...AT TIMES LIKE THAT, THE FIRST REACTION IS...TO TRY TO MAKE THINGS HOW THEY WERE.
NO MATTER WHAT IT IS.
GASHA (CLASH)
SOMETIMES, EVEN WHEN THEY KNOW FROM THE START THAT IT'S NOT GOING TO WORK.
AS FOR WHY...
...IT'S BECAUSE IF THEY DON'T RECOGNIZE THE CHANGE, THEY DON'T HAVE TO RECOGNIZE THEIR OWN SHORTCOMINGS AND MISTAKES.
Y-YEAH. I, UH...
...THOUGHT OF THAT AFTER SOME STUFF THAT HAPPENED AT SCHOOL.
HMMM...
HYOI (PEEK)
I SEE YOU IN A WHOLE NEW LIGHT.
BO (BLUSH)

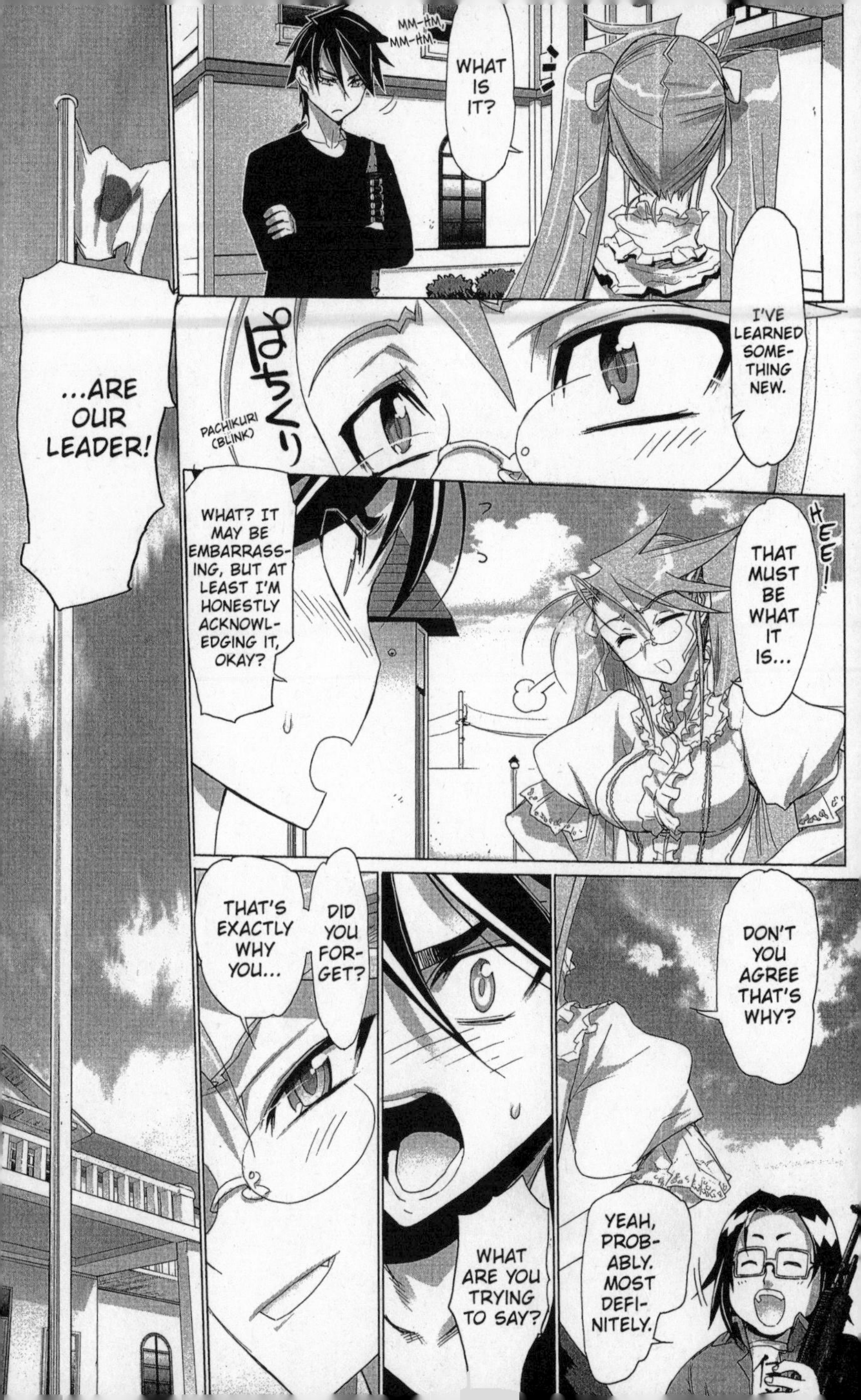
MM-HM, MM-HM.
WHAT IS IT?
I'VE LEARNED SOMETHING NEW.
ぱちくり
PACHIKURI (BLINK)
HEE!
THAT MUST BE WHAT IT IS...
WHAT? IT MAY BE EMBARRASSING, BUT AT LEAST I'M HONESTLY ACKNOWLEDGING IT, OKAY?
DON'T YOU AGREE THAT'S WHY?
YEAH, PROBABLY. MOST DEFINITELY.
WHAT ARE YOU TRYING TO SAY?
DID YOU FORGET?
THAT'S EXACTLY WHY YOU...
...ARE OUR LEADER!

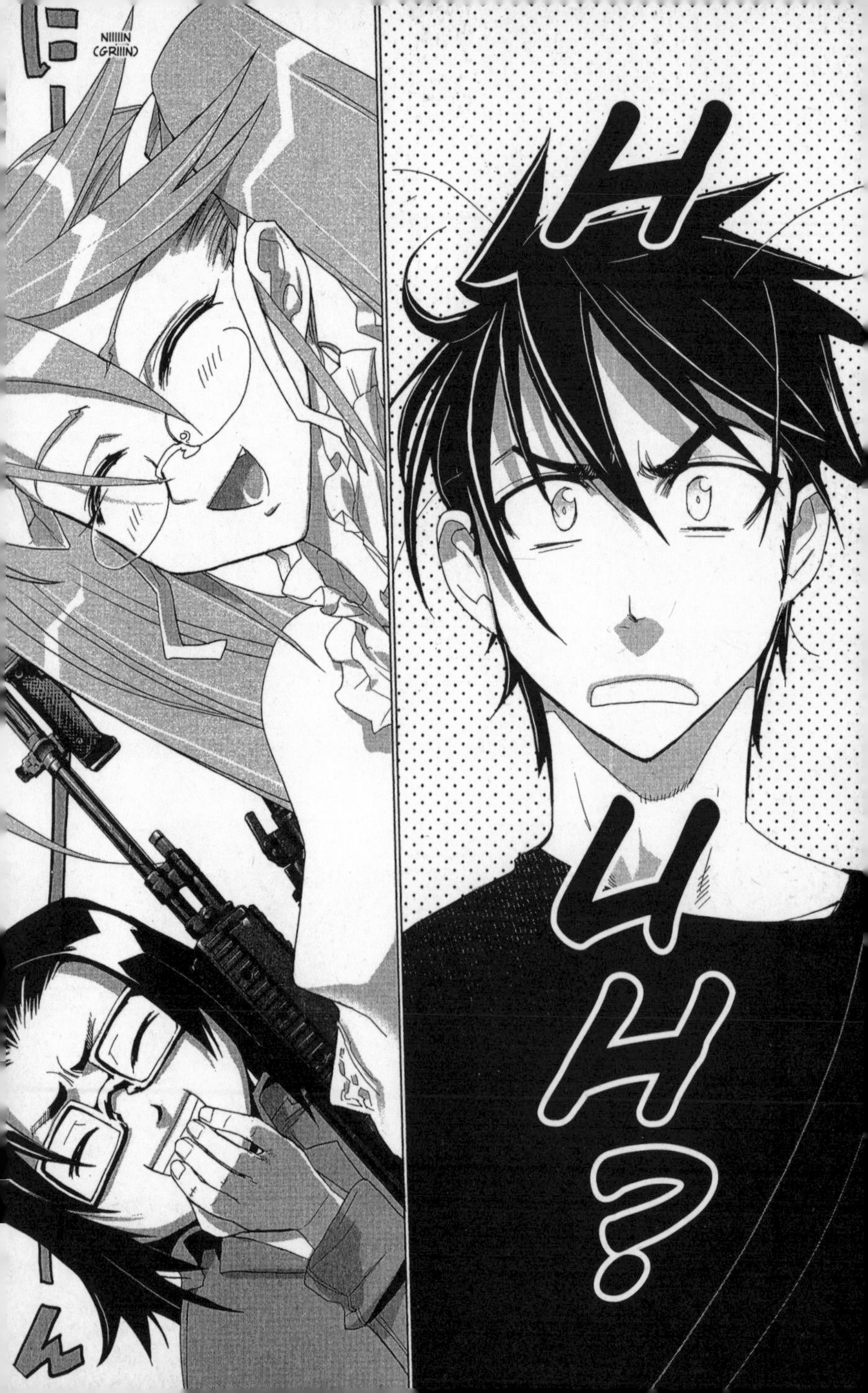
HUHH?!
ニーーん
NIIIIIN (GRIIIN)

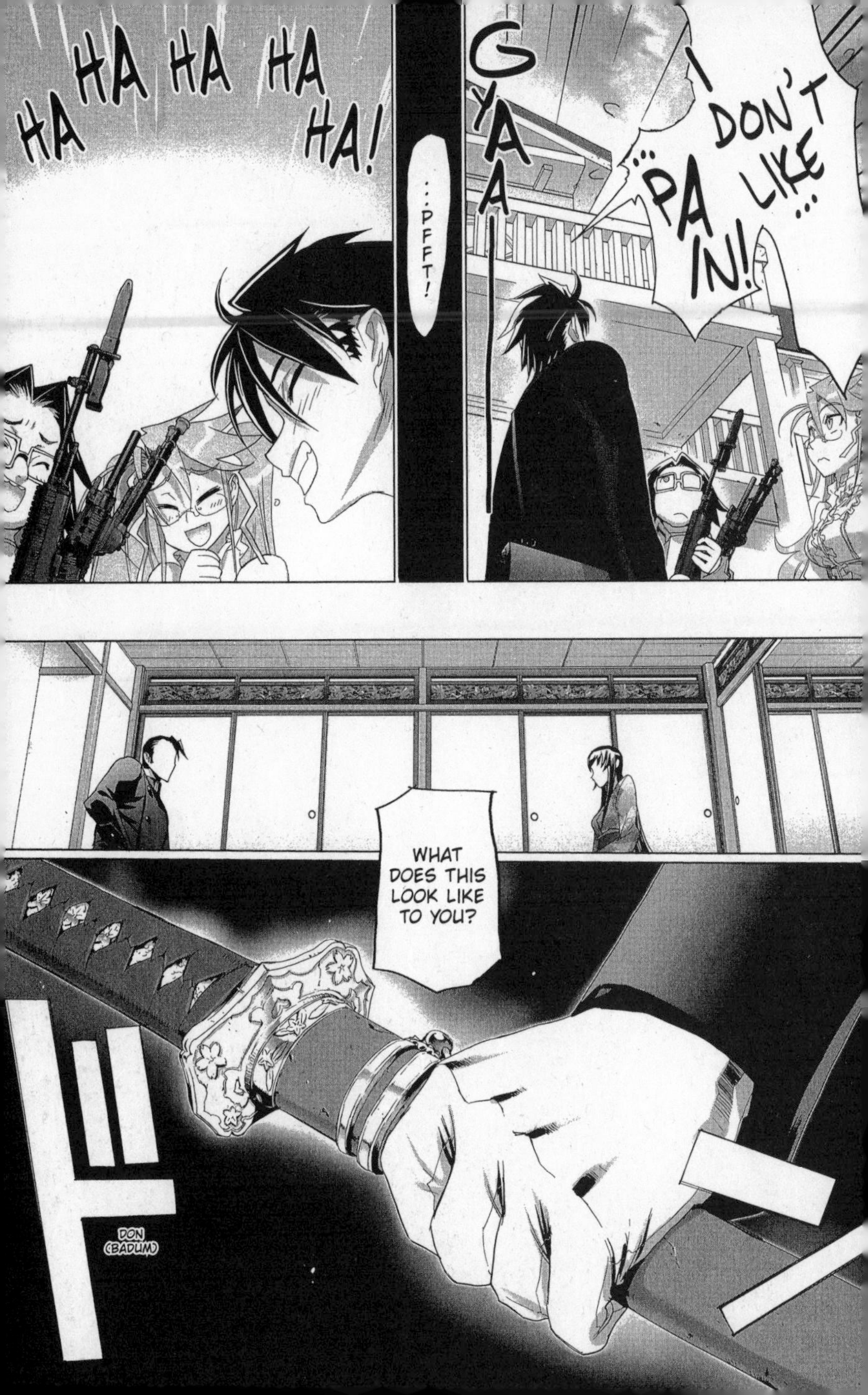
GYAA!
I DON'T LIKE ...PAIN!
...PFFT!
HA HA HA HA HA HA!
WHAT DOES THIS LOOK LIKE TO YOU?
DON (BADUM)

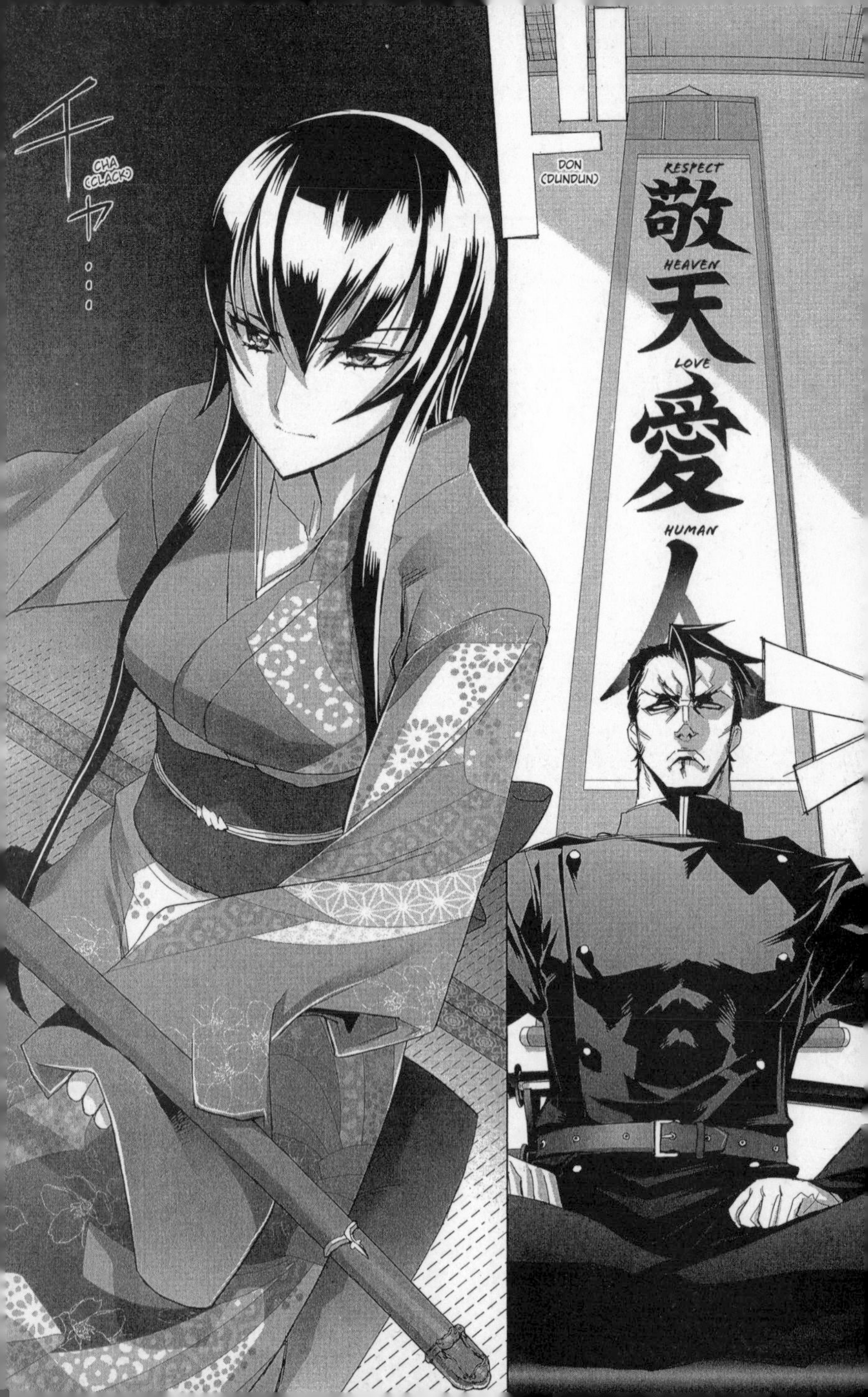
DON (DUNDUN)
RESPECT
敬
HEAVEN
天
LOVE
愛
HUMAN
人
チャ…
CHA (CLACK)

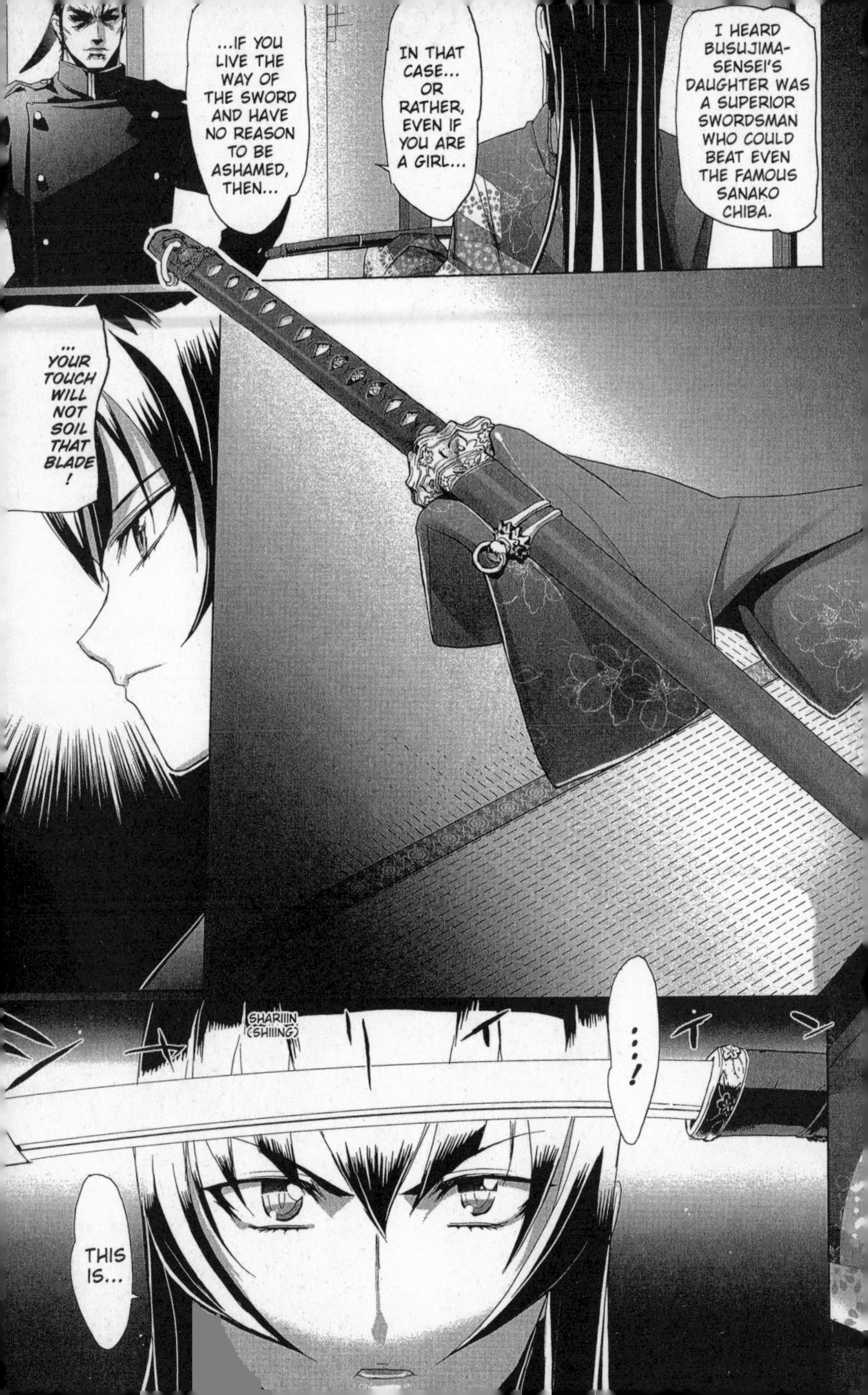
I HEARD BUSUJIMA-SENSEI'S DAUGHTER WAS A SUPERIOR SWORDSMAN WHO COULD BEAT EVEN THE FAMOUS SANAKO CHIBA.
IN THAT CASE... OR RATHER, EVEN IF YOU ARE A GIRL...
...IF YOU LIVE THE WAY OF THE SWORD AND HAVE NO REASON TO BE ASHAMED, THEN...
...YOUR TOUCH WILL NOT SOIL THAT BLADE!
...!
SHARIIIN (SHIIING)
THIS IS...

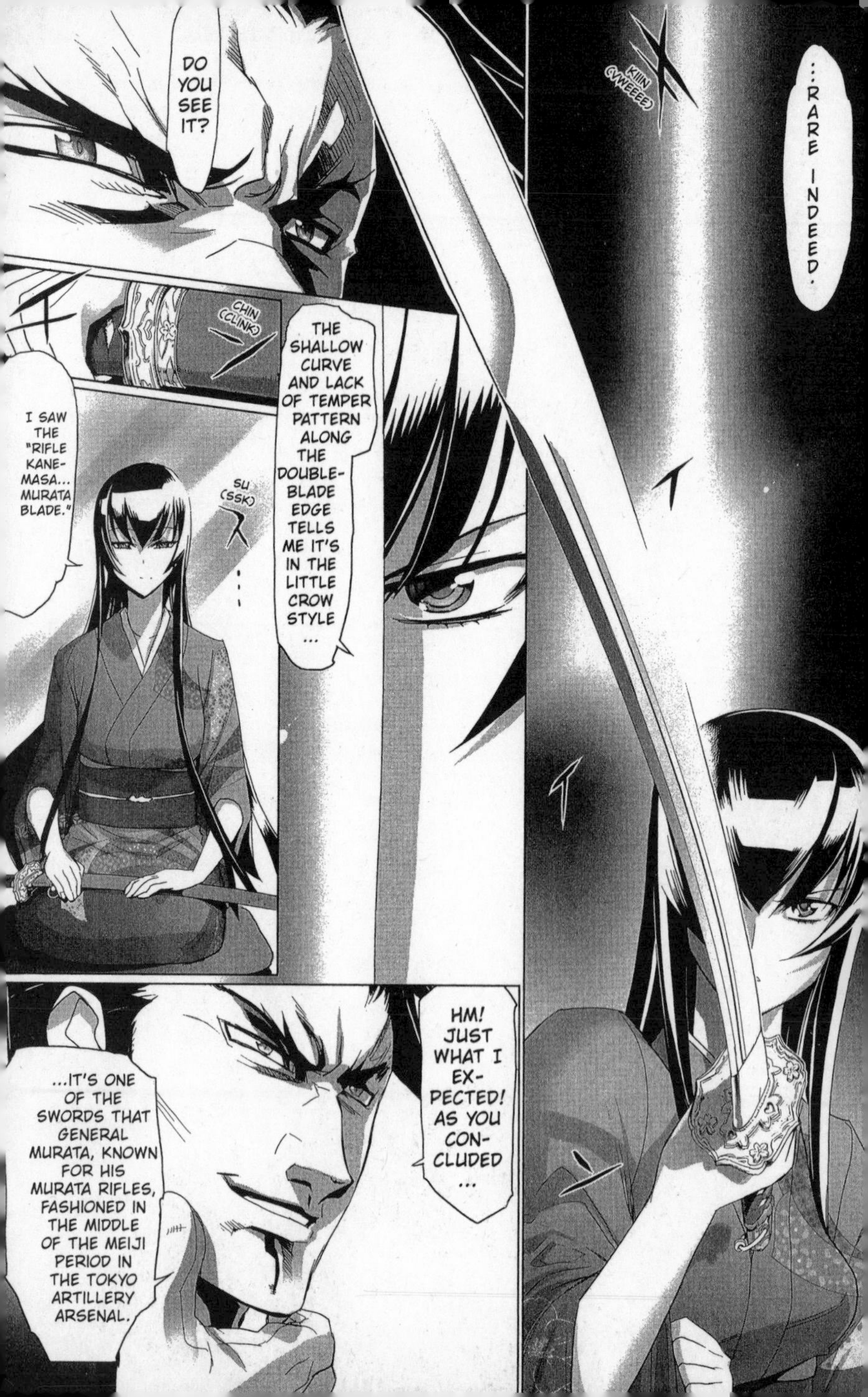
KIIIN (VWEEEE)
...RARE INDEED.
DO YOU SEE IT?
CHIN (CLINK)
THE SHALLOW CURVE AND LACK OF TEMPER PATTERN ALONG THE DOUBLE-BLADE EDGE TELLS ME IT'S IN THE LITTLE CROW STYLE ...
SU (SSK)
I SAW THE "RIFLE KANE-MASA... MURATA BLADE."
HM! JUST WHAT I EX-PECTED! AS YOU CON-CLUDED ...
...IT'S ONE OF THE SWORDS THAT GENERAL MURATA, KNOWN FOR HIS MURATA RIFLES, FASHIONED IN THE MIDDLE OF THE MEIJI PERIOD IN THE TOKYO ARTILLERY ARSENAL.

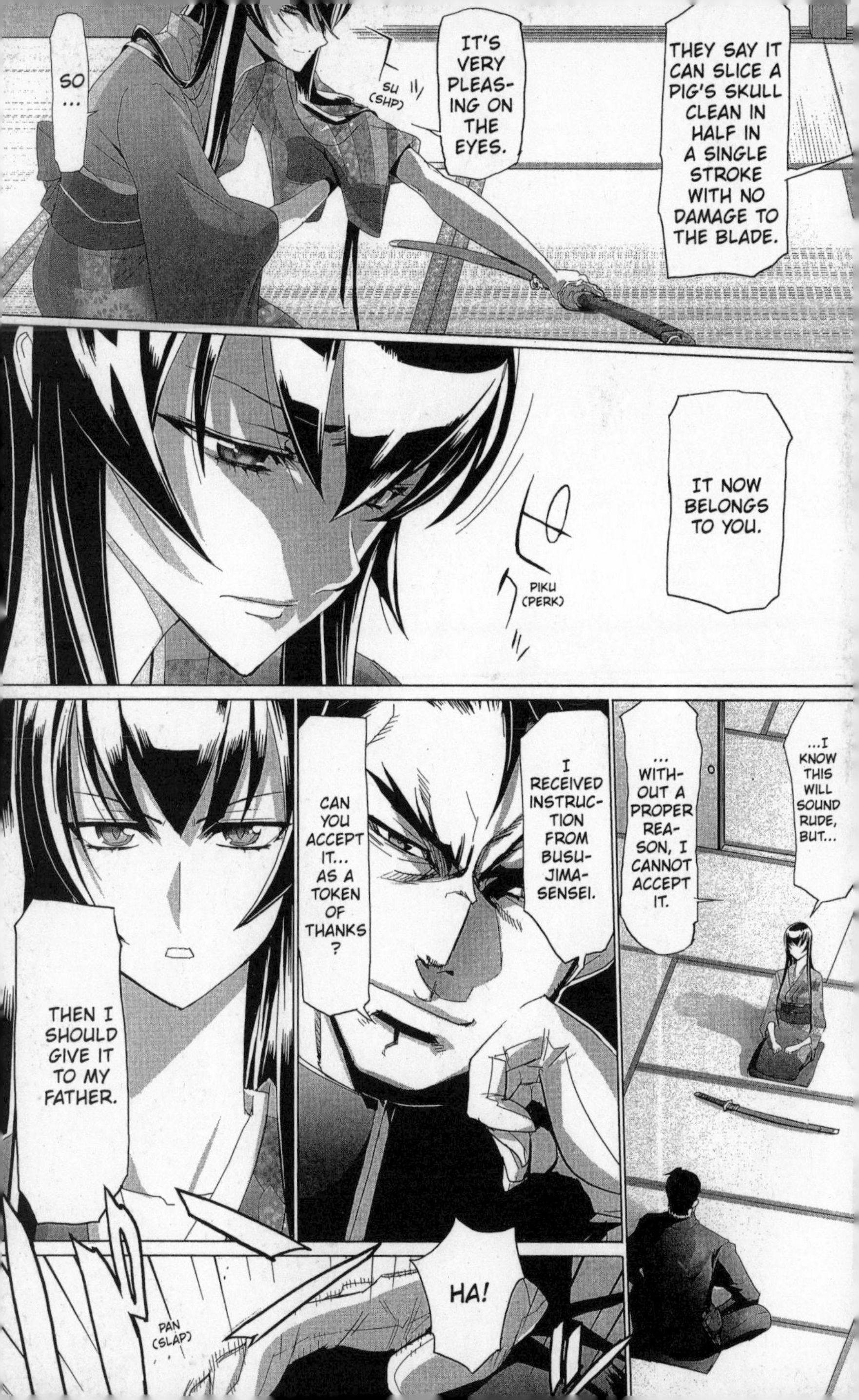
THEY SAY IT CAN SLICE A PIG'S SKULL CLEAN IN HALF IN A SINGLE STROKE WITH NO DAMAGE TO THE BLADE.
IT'S VERY PLEASING ON THE EYES.
SU (SHP)
SO ...
IT NOW BELONGS TO YOU.
PIKU (PERK)
...I KNOW THIS WILL SOUND RUDE, BUT...
... WITHOUT A PROPER REASON, I CANNOT ACCEPT IT.
I RECEIVED INSTRUCTION FROM BUSUJIMA-SENSEI.
CAN YOU ACCEPT IT... AS A TOKEN OF THANKS?
THEN I SHOULD GIVE IT TO MY FATHER.
HA!
PAN (SLAP)

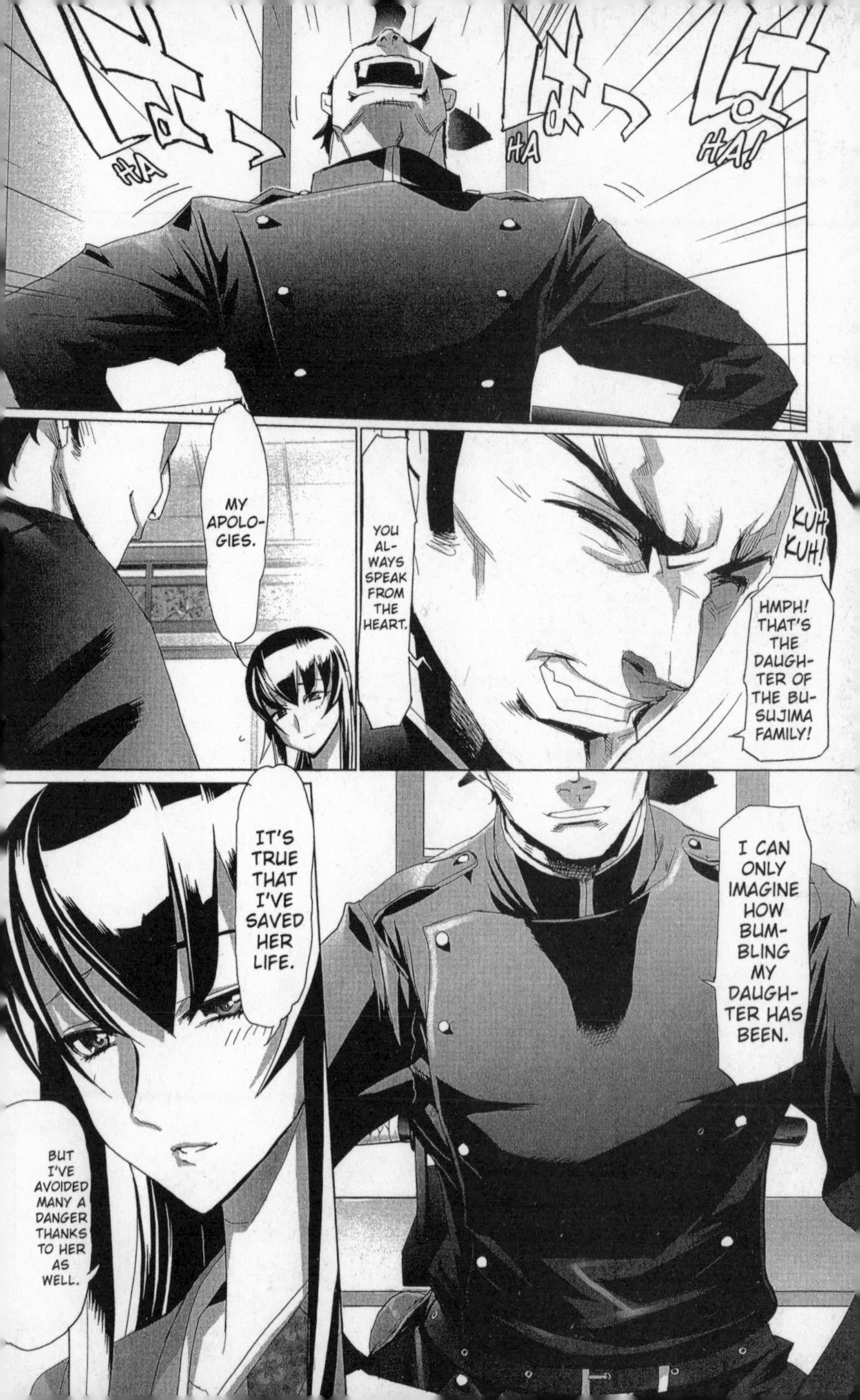
HA!
HA
HA
KUH KUH!
HMPH! THAT'S THE DAUGHTER OF THE BUSUJIMA FAMILY!
YOU ALWAYS SPEAK FROM THE HEART.
MY APOLOGIES.
I CAN ONLY IMAGINE HOW BUMBLING MY DAUGHTER HAS BEEN.
IT'S TRUE THAT I'VE SAVED HER LIFE.
BUT I'VE AVOIDED MANY A DANGER THANKS TO HER AS WELL.

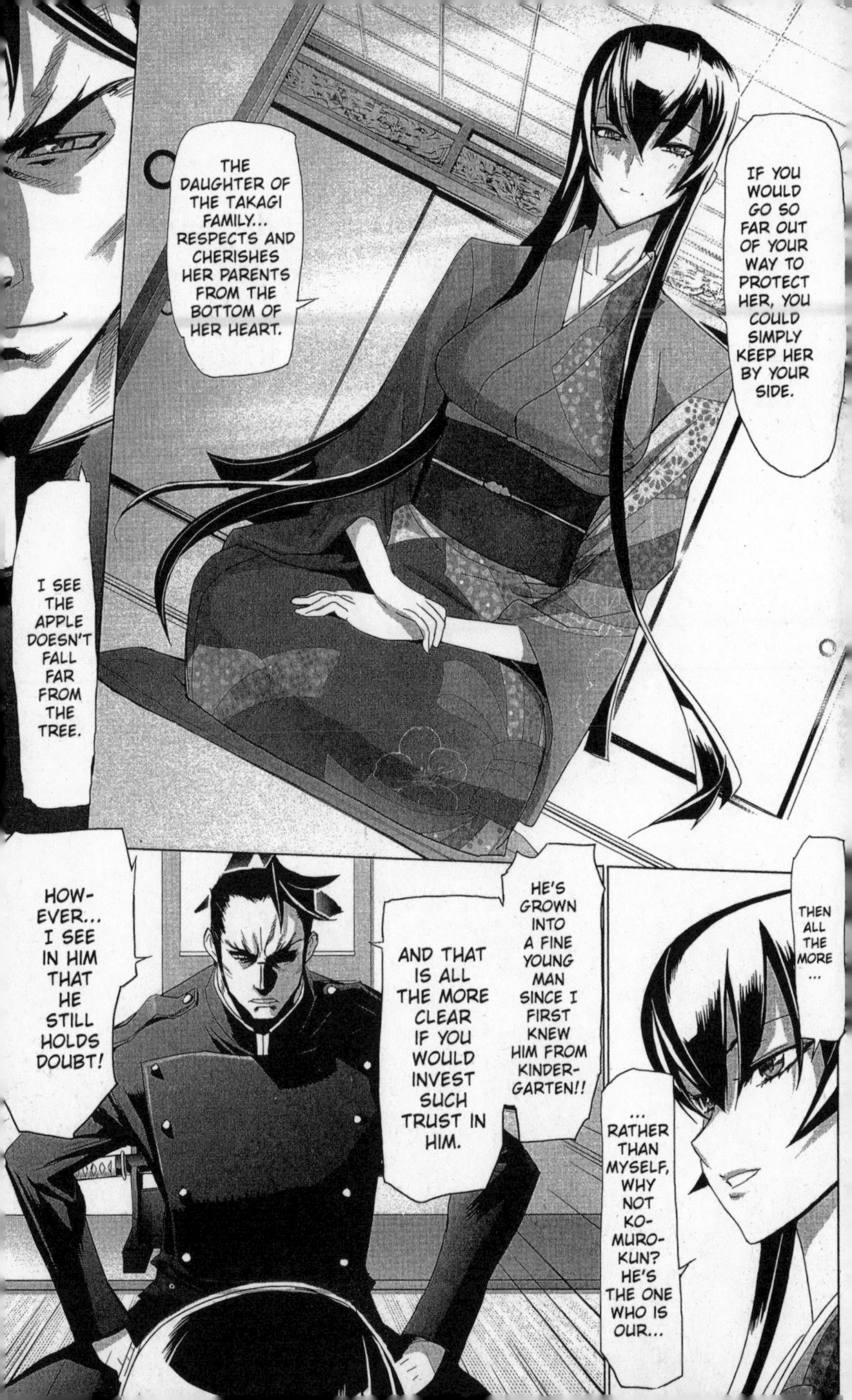
IF YOU WOULD GO SO FAR OUT OF YOUR WAY TO PROTECT HER, YOU COULD SIMPLY KEEP HER BY YOUR SIDE.
THE DAUGHTER OF THE TAKAGI FAMILY... RESPECTS AND CHERISHES HER PARENTS FROM THE BOTTOM OF HER HEART.
I SEE THE APPLE DOESN'T FALL FAR FROM THE TREE.
THEN ALL THE MORE...
...RATHER THAN MYSELF, WHY NOT KO-MURO-KUN? HE'S THE ONE WHO IS OUR...
HE'S GROWN INTO A FINE YOUNG MAN SINCE I FIRST KNEW HIM FROM KINDER-GARTEN!!
AND THAT IS ALL THE MORE CLEAR IF YOU WOULD INVEST SUCH TRUST IN HIM.
HOW-EVER... I SEE IN HIM THAT HE STILL HOLDS DOUBT!

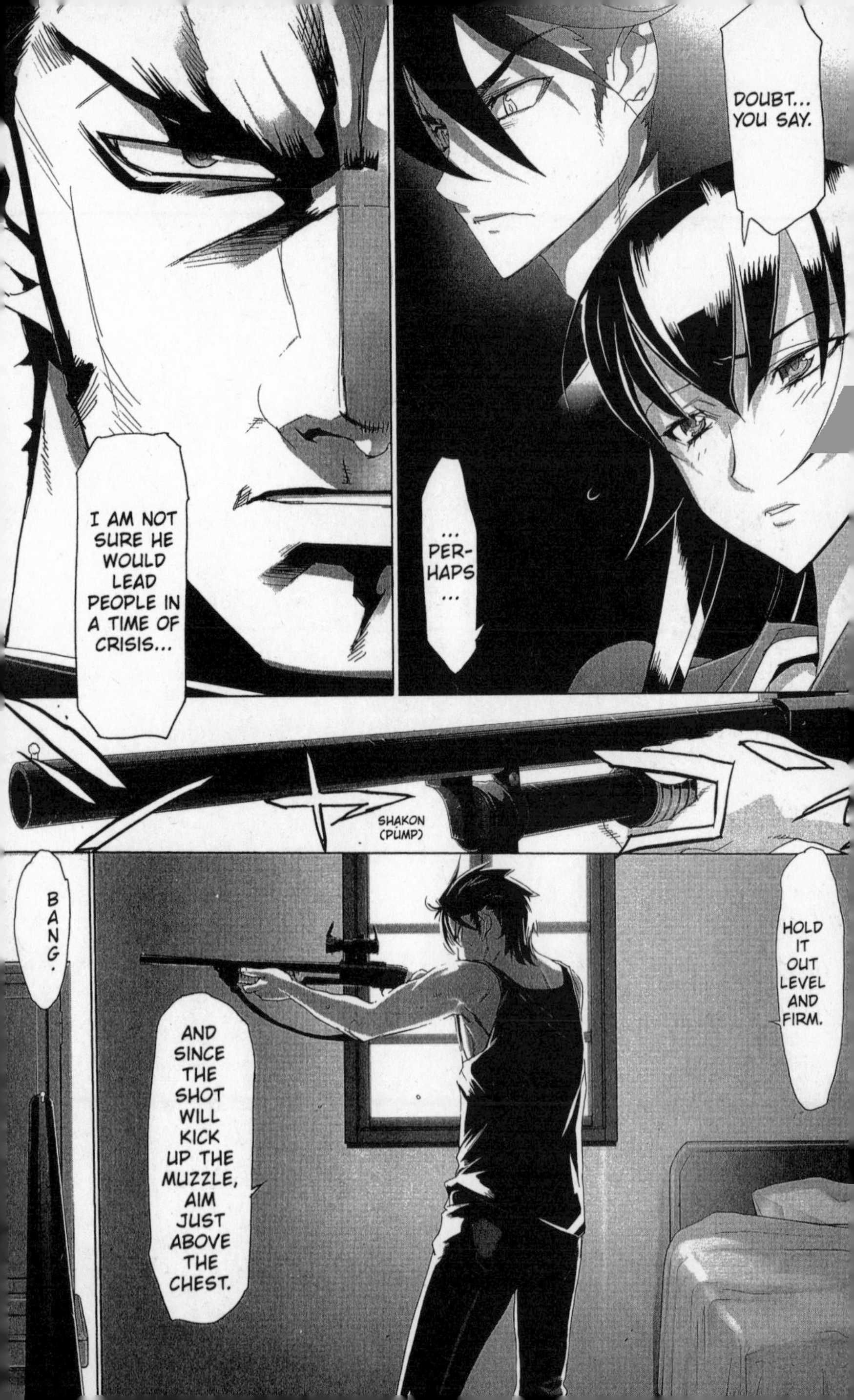
DOUBT... YOU SAY.
...PER-HAPS...
I AM NOT SURE HE WOULD LEAD PEOPLE IN A TIME OF CRISIS...
SHAKON (PUMP)
HOLD IT OUT LEVEL AND FIRM.
BANG.
AND SINCE THE SHOT WILL KICK UP THE MUZZLE, AIM JUST ABOVE THE CHEST.

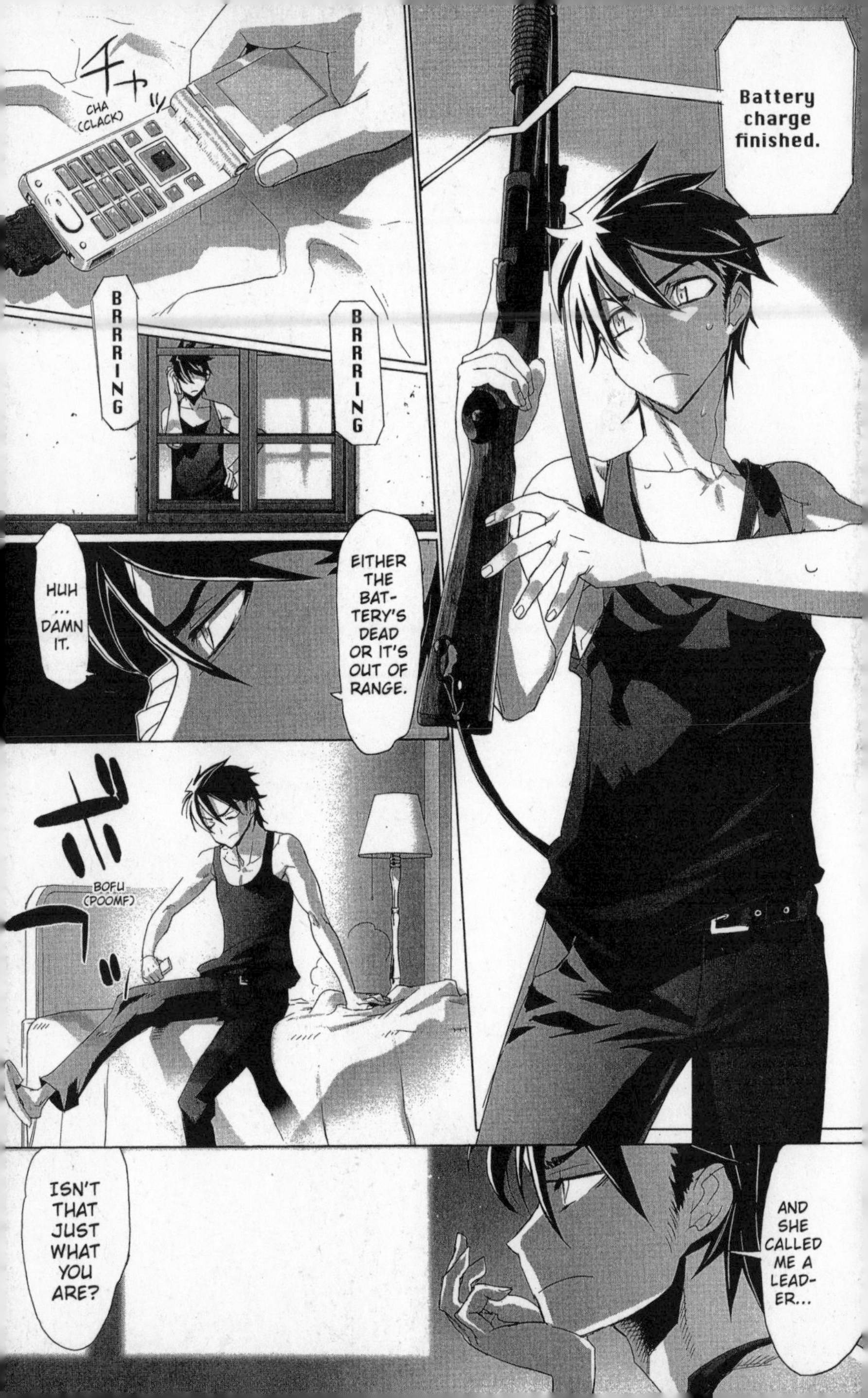
Battery charge finished.
CHA (CLACK)
BRRRING
BRRRING
EITHER THE BAT-TERY'S DEAD OR IT'S OUT OF RANGE.
HUH ... DAMN IT.
BOFU (POOMF)
AND SHE CALLED ME A LEAD-ER...
ISN'T THAT JUST WHAT YOU ARE?

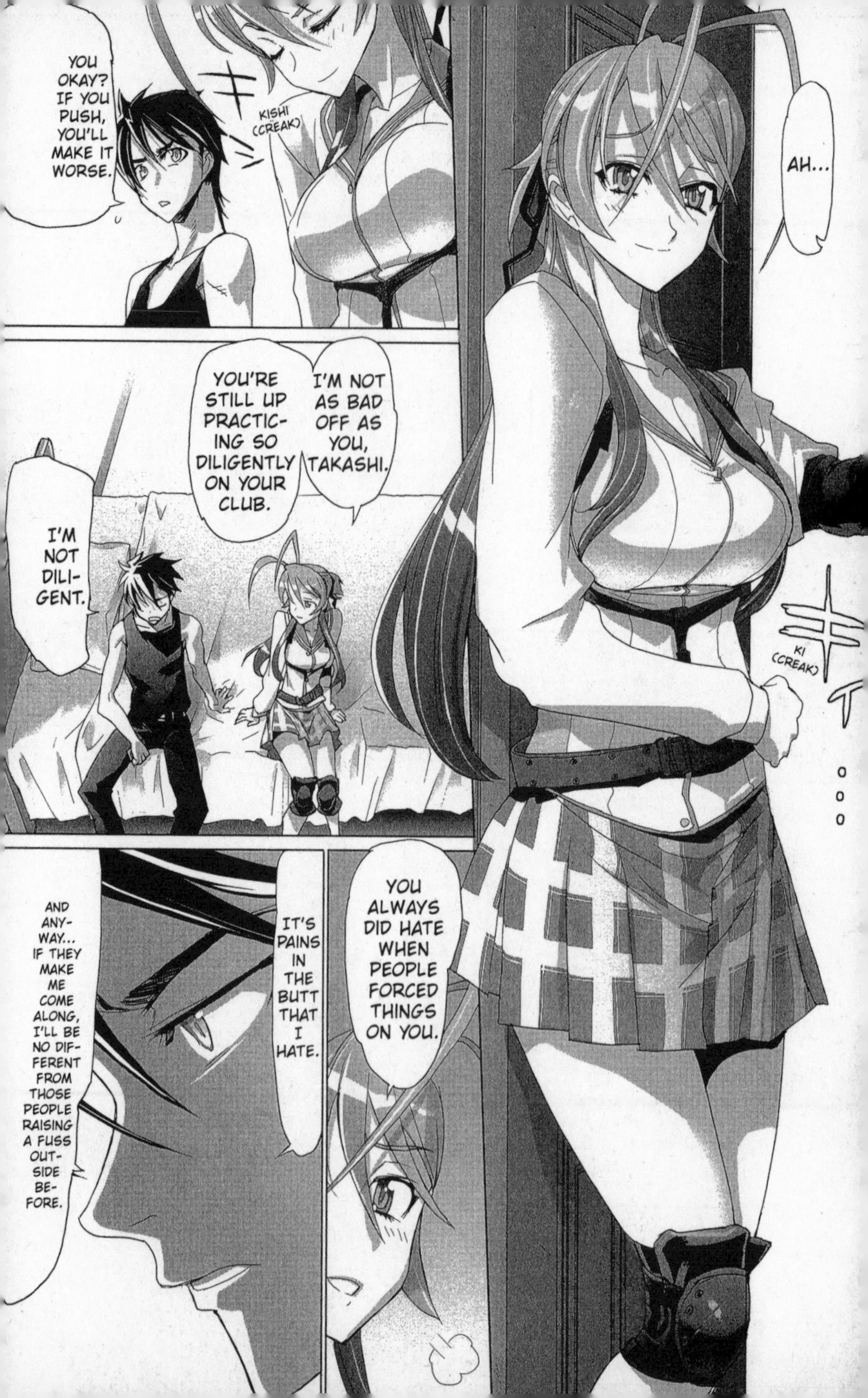
AH...
KI (CREAK)
...
KISHI (CREAK)
YOU OKAY? IF YOU PUSH, YOU'LL MAKE IT WORSE.
I'M NOT AS BAD OFF AS YOU, TAKASHI.
YOU'RE STILL UP PRACTICING SO DILIGENTLY ON YOUR CLUB.
I'M NOT DILIGENT.
YOU ALWAYS DID HATE WHEN PEOPLE FORCED THINGS ON YOU.
IT'S PAINS IN THE BUTT THAT I HATE.
AND ANYWAY... IF THEY MAKE ME COME ALONG, I'LL BE NO DIFFERENT FROM THOSE PEOPLE RAISING A FUSS OUTSIDE BEFORE.

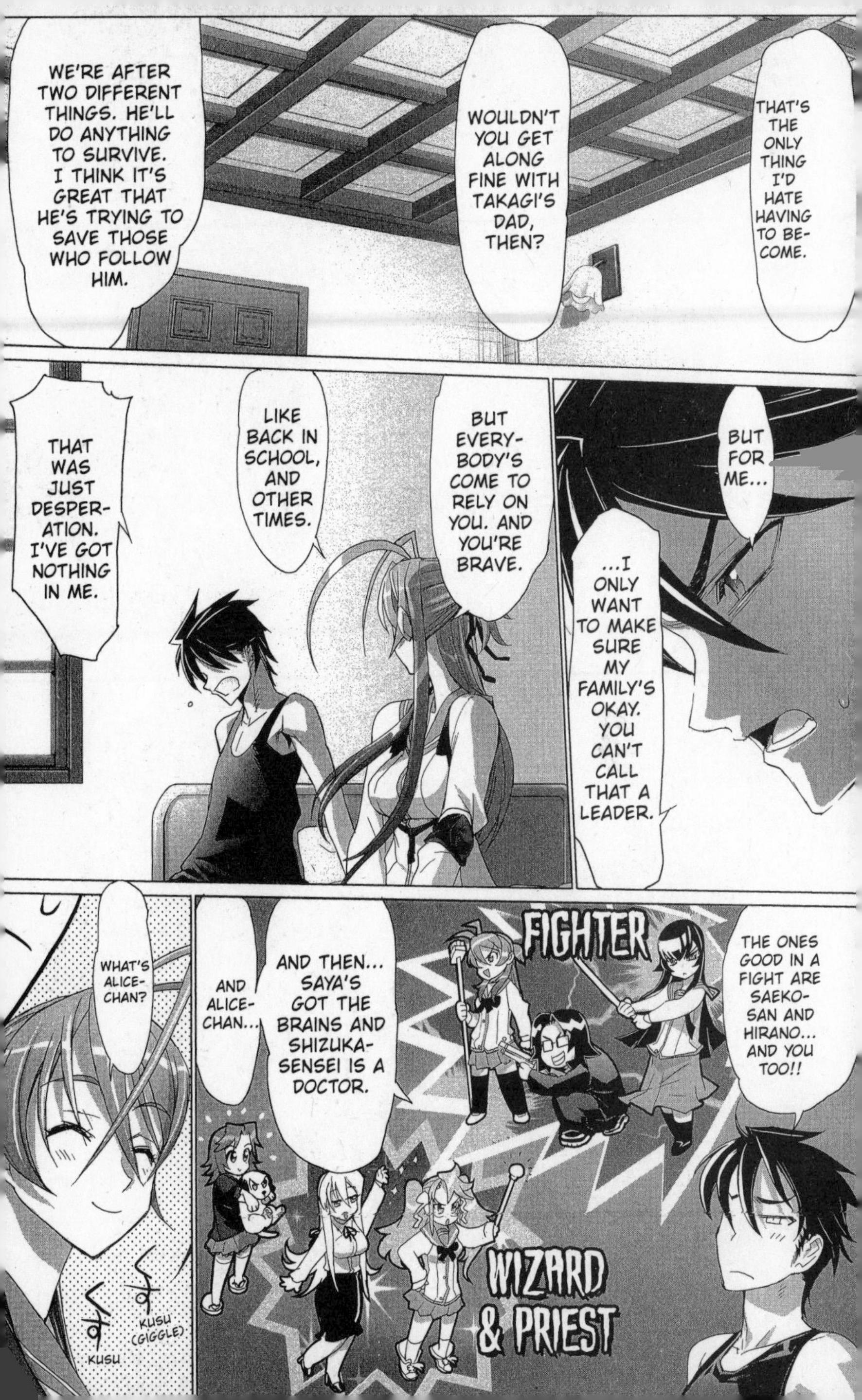
THAT'S THE ONLY THING I'D HATE HAVING TO BE-COME.
WOULDN'T YOU GET ALONG FINE WITH TAKAGI'S DAD, THEN?
WE'RE AFTER TWO DIFFERENT THINGS. HE'LL DO ANYTHING TO SURVIVE. I THINK IT'S GREAT THAT HE'S TRYING TO SAVE THOSE WHO FOLLOW HIM.
BUT FOR ME...
...I ONLY WANT TO MAKE SURE MY FAMILY'S OKAY. YOU CAN'T CALL THAT A LEADER.
BUT EVERY-BODY'S COME TO RELY ON YOU. AND YOU'RE BRAVE.
LIKE BACK IN SCHOOL, AND OTHER TIMES.
THAT WAS JUST DESPER-ATION. I'VE GOT NOTHING IN ME.
THE ONES GOOD IN A FIGHT ARE SAEKO-SAN AND HIRANO... AND YOU TOO!!
FIGHTER
AND THEN... SAYA'S GOT THE BRAINS AND SHIZUKA-SENSEI IS A DOCTOR.
WIZARD & PRIEST
AND ALICE-CHAN...
WHAT'S ALICE-CHAN?
くす
KUSU (GIGGLE)
くす
KUSU

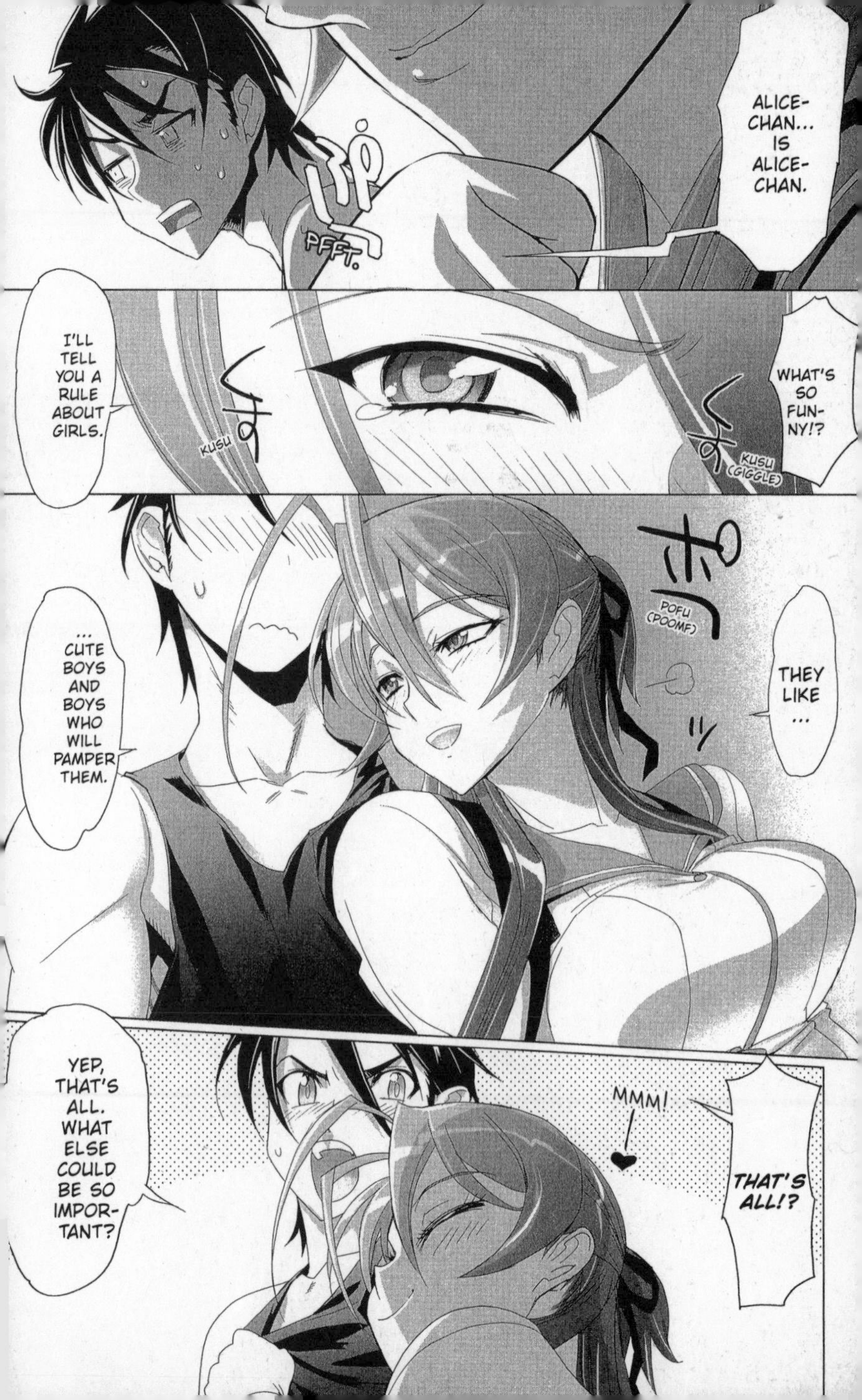
ALICE-CHAN... IS ALICE-CHAN.
ぷっ
PFFT.
WHAT'S SO FUN-NY!?
くす
KUSU (GIGGLE)
くす
KUSU
I'LL TELL YOU A RULE ABOUT GIRLS.
ぽふっ
POFU (POOMF)
THEY LIKE...
...CUTE BOYS AND BOYS WHO WILL PAMPER THEM.
THAT'S ALL!?
MMM! ♥
YEP, THAT'S ALL. WHAT ELSE COULD BE SO IMPORTANT?

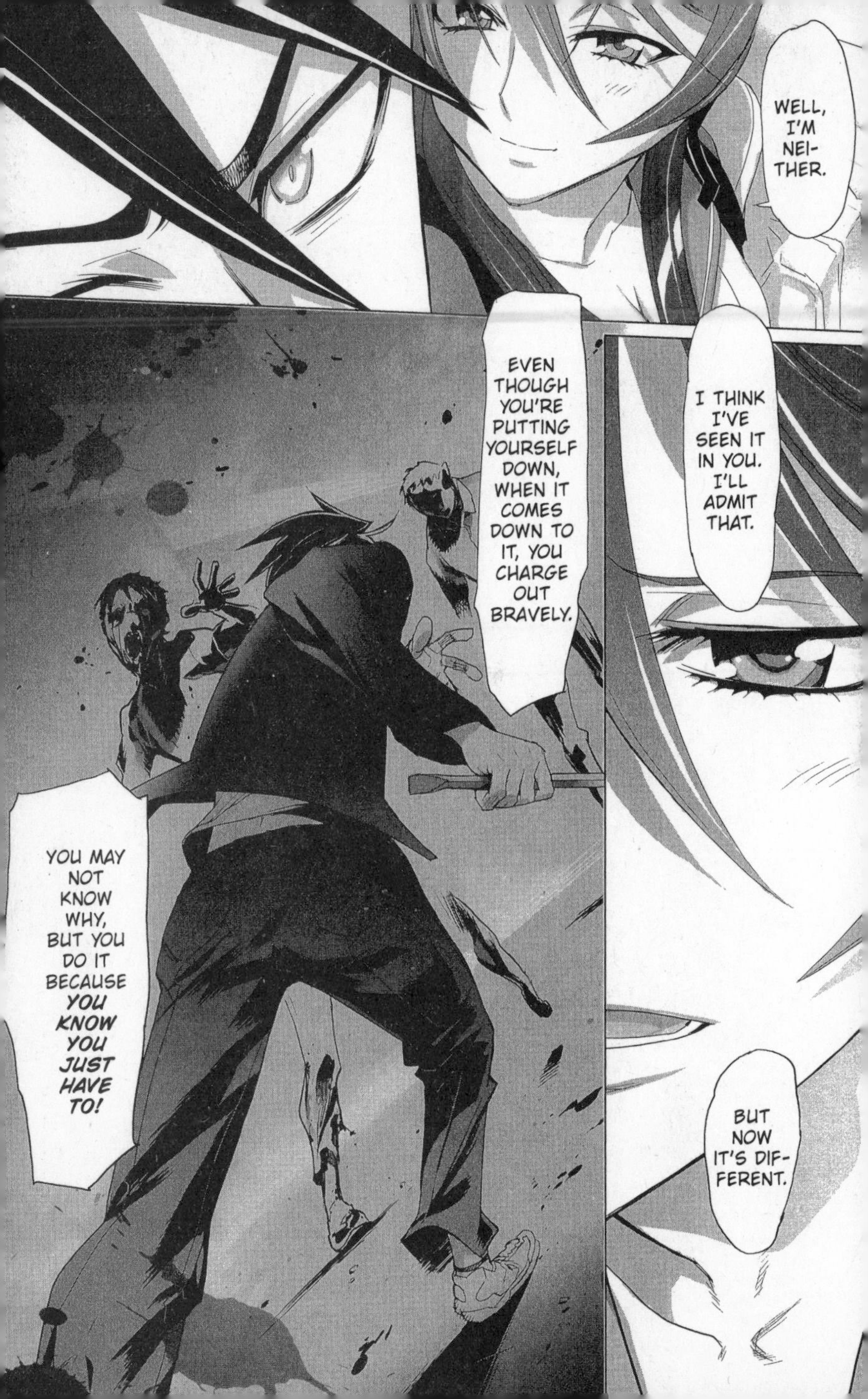
WELL, I'M NEITHER.
I THINK I'VE SEEN IT IN YOU. I'LL ADMIT THAT.
BUT NOW IT'S DIFFERENT.
EVEN THOUGH YOU'RE PUTTING YOURSELF DOWN, WHEN IT COMES DOWN TO IT, YOU CHARGE OUT BRAVELY.
YOU MAY NOT KNOW WHY, BUT YOU DO IT BECAUSE *YOU KNOW YOU JUST HAVE TO!*

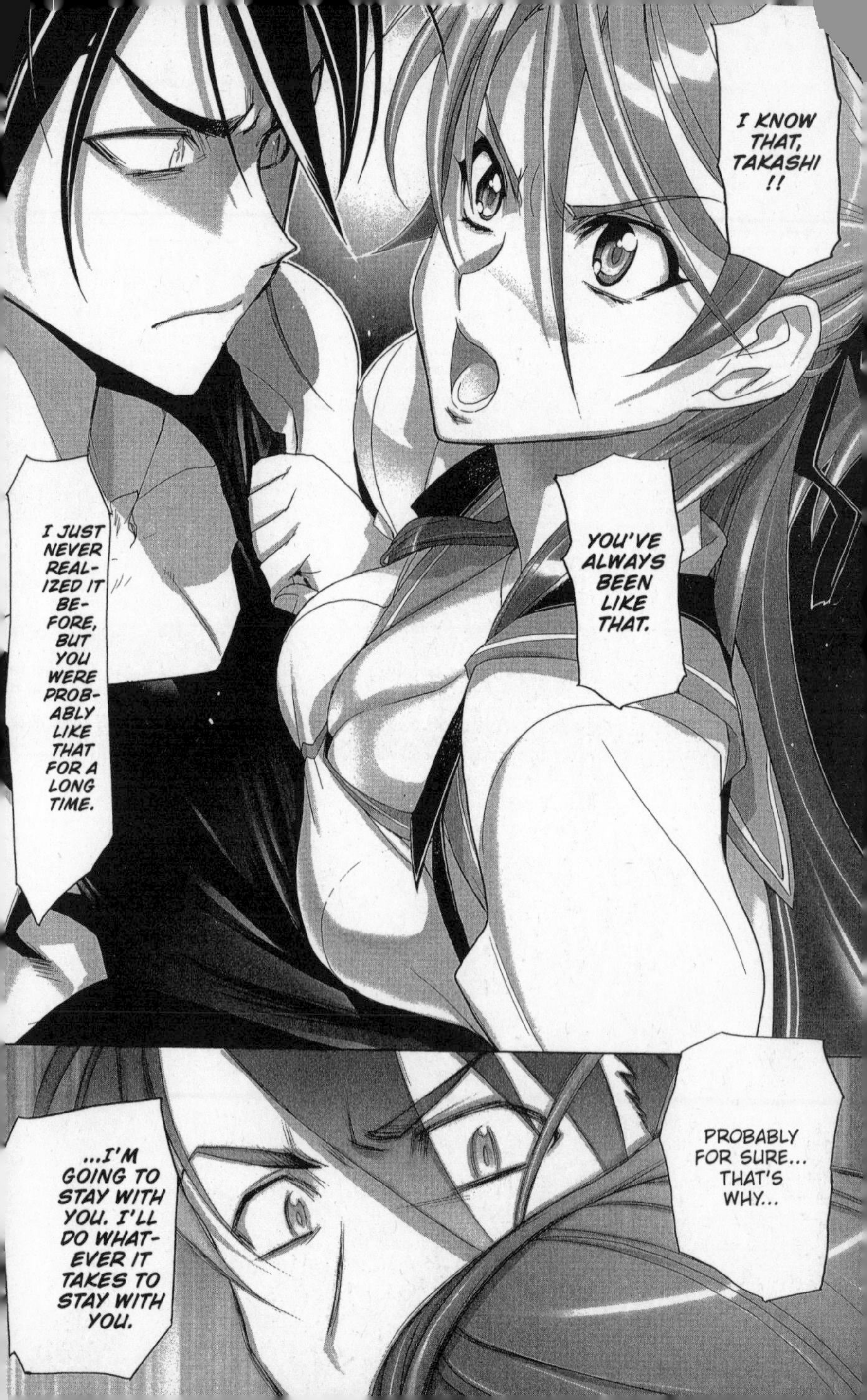
I KNOW THAT, TAKASHI !!
YOU'VE ALWAYS BEEN LIKE THAT.
I JUST NEVER REALIZED IT BEFORE, BUT YOU WERE PROBABLY LIKE THAT FOR A LONG TIME.
PROBABLY FOR SURE... THAT'S WHY...
...I'M GOING TO STAY WITH YOU. I'LL DO WHATEVER IT TAKES TO STAY WITH YOU.

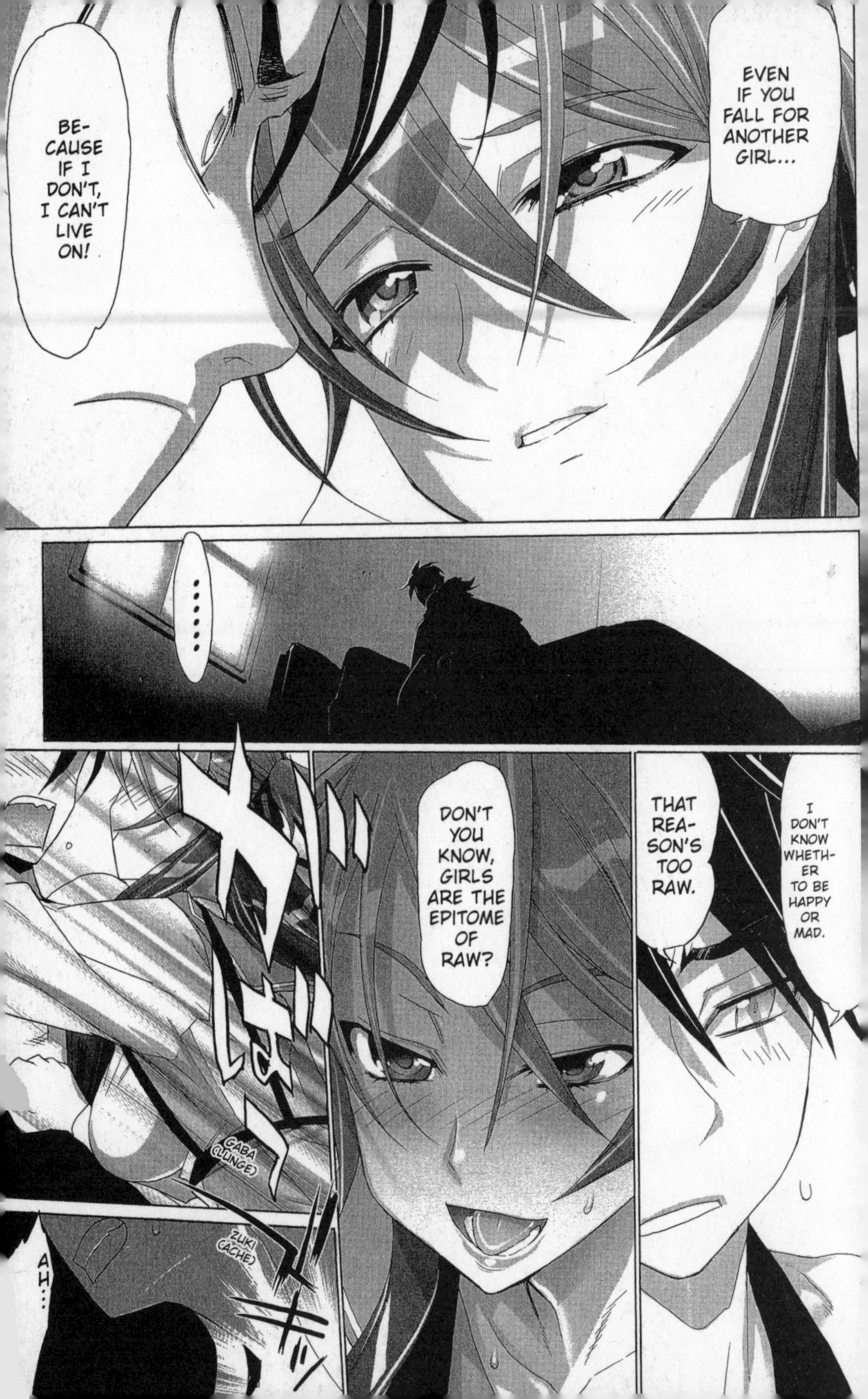
EVEN IF YOU FALL FOR ANOTHER GIRL...
BE-CAUSE IF I DON'T, I CAN'T LIVE ON!
......
I DON'T KNOW WHETH-ER TO BE HAPPY OR MAD.
THAT REA-SON'S TOO RAW.
DON'T YOU KNOW, GIRLS ARE THE EPITOME OF RAW?
GABA (LUNGE)
ZUKI (ACHE)
AH...

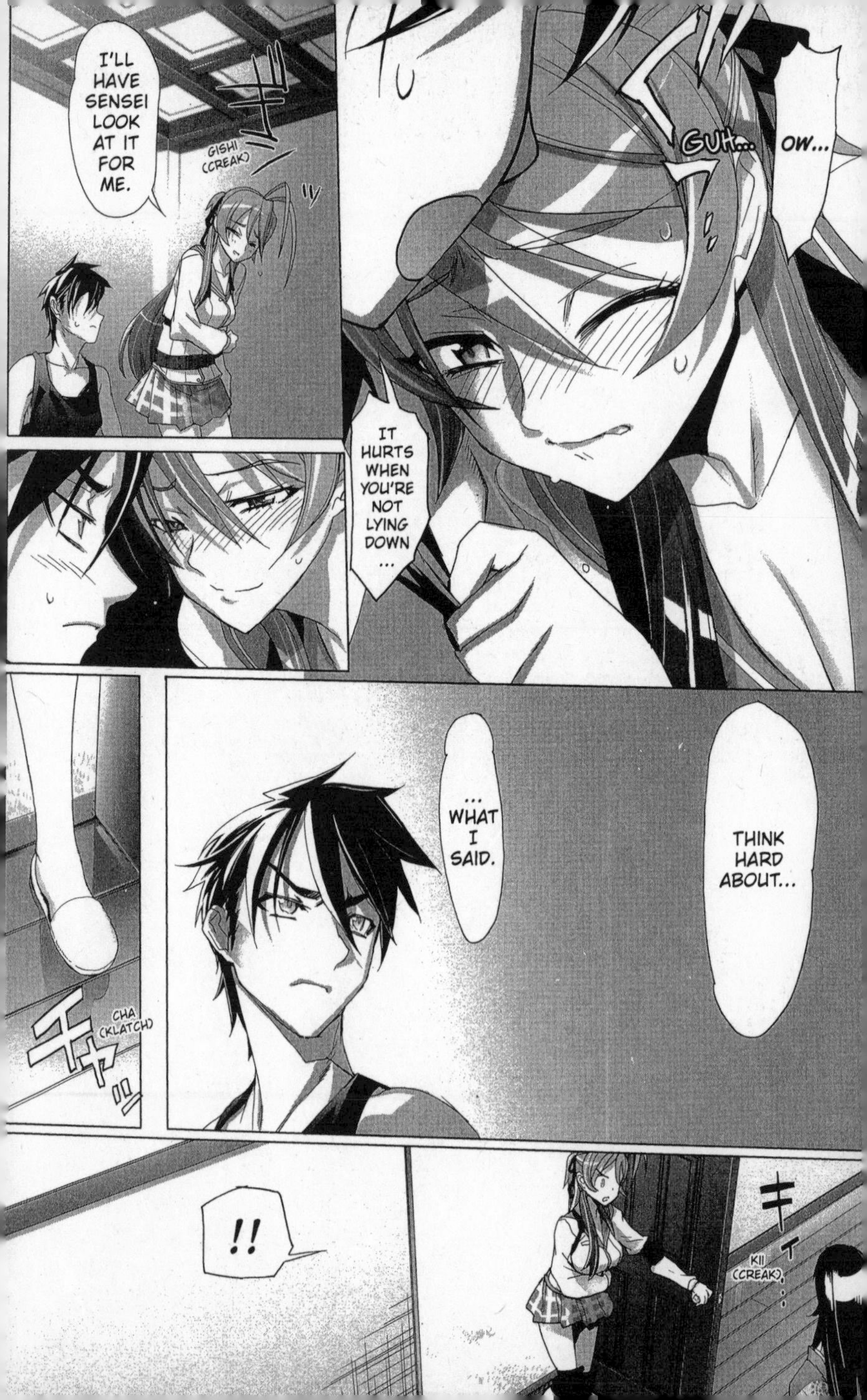
GUH... OW...
IT HURTS WHEN YOU'RE NOT LYING DOWN...
I'LL HAVE SENSEI LOOK AT IT FOR ME.
GISHI (CREAK)
THINK HARD ABOUT...
...WHAT I SAID.
CHA (KLATCH)
KII (CREAK)
...
!!

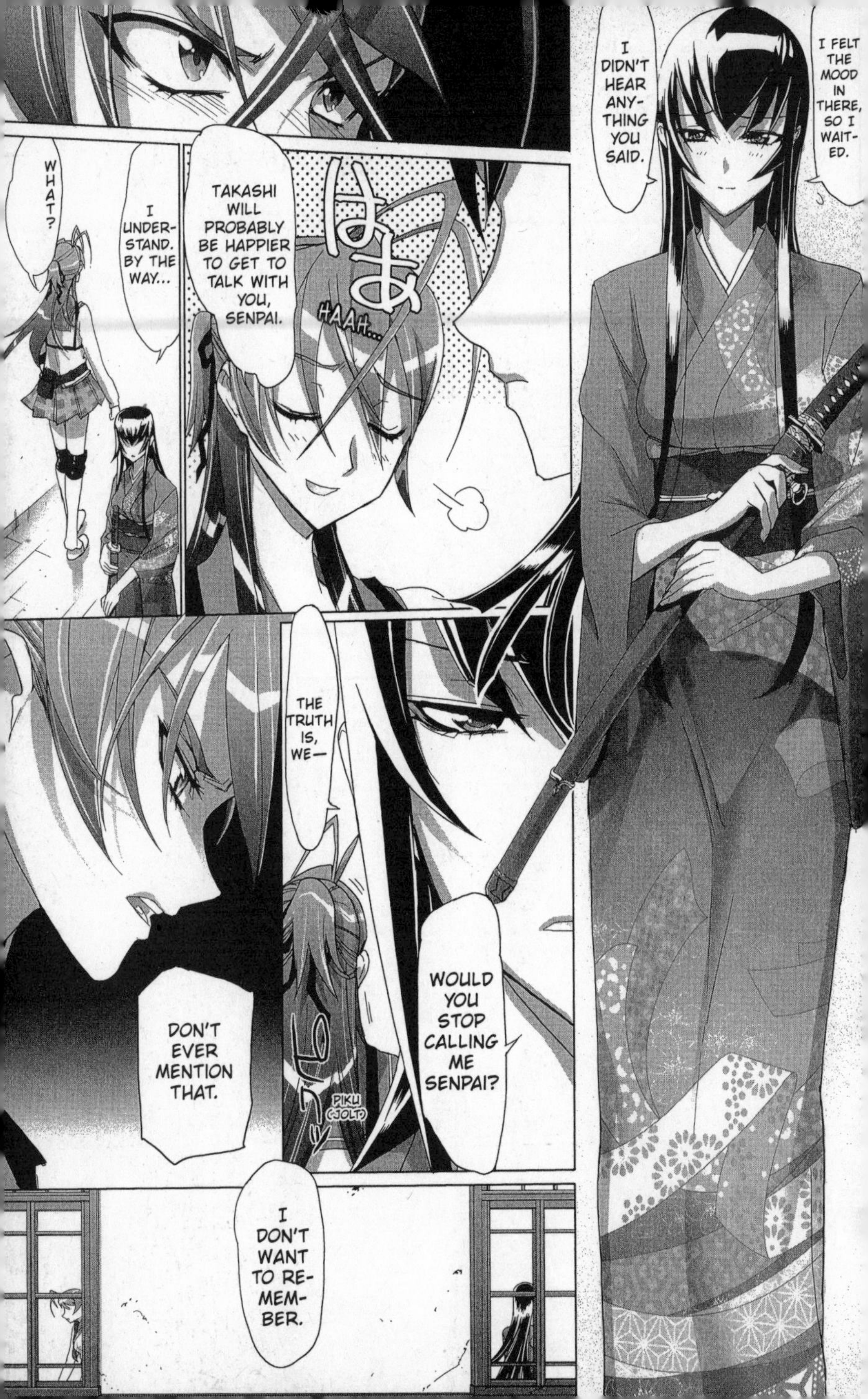
I FELT THE MOOD IN THERE, SO I WAIT-ED.
I DIDN'T HEAR ANY-THING YOU SAID.
TAKASHI WILL PROBABLY BE HAPPIER TO GET TO TALK WITH YOU, SENPAI.
はぁ
HAAH...
I UNDER-STAND. BY THE WAY...
WHAT?
THE TRUTH IS, WE—
WOULD YOU STOP CALLING ME SENPAI?
ピクッ
PIKU (JOLT)
DON'T EVER MENTION THAT.
I DON'T WANT TO RE-MEM-BER.

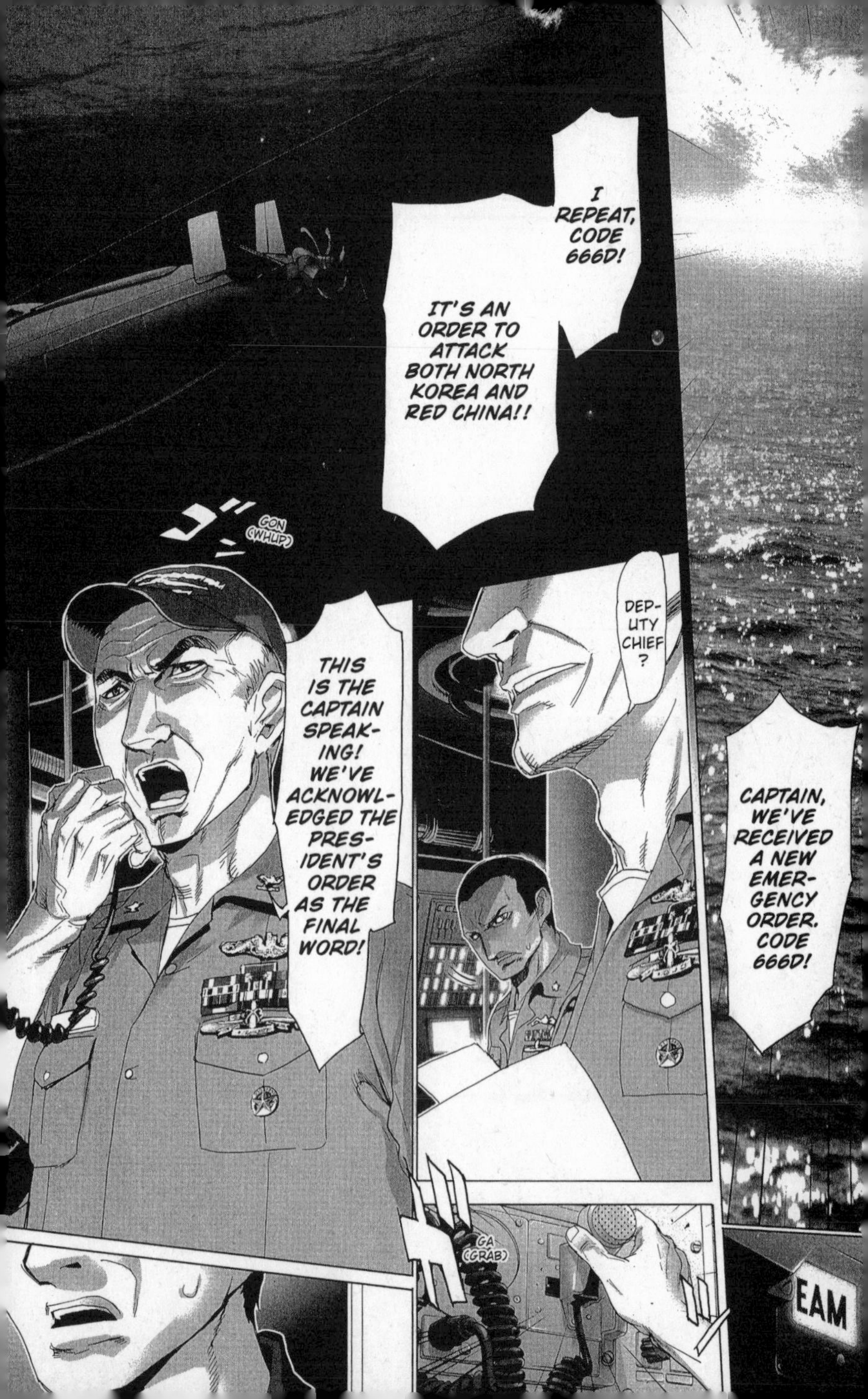
CAPTAIN, WE'VE RECEIVED A NEW EMERGENCY ORDER. CODE 666D!
DEPUTY CHIEF?
I REPEAT, CODE 666D!
IT'S AN ORDER TO ATTACK BOTH NORTH KOREA AND RED CHINA!!
GON (WHUP)
THIS IS THE CAPTAIN SPEAKING! WE'VE ACKNOWLEDGED THE PRESIDENT'S ORDER AS THE FINAL WORD!
GA (GRAB)
EAM

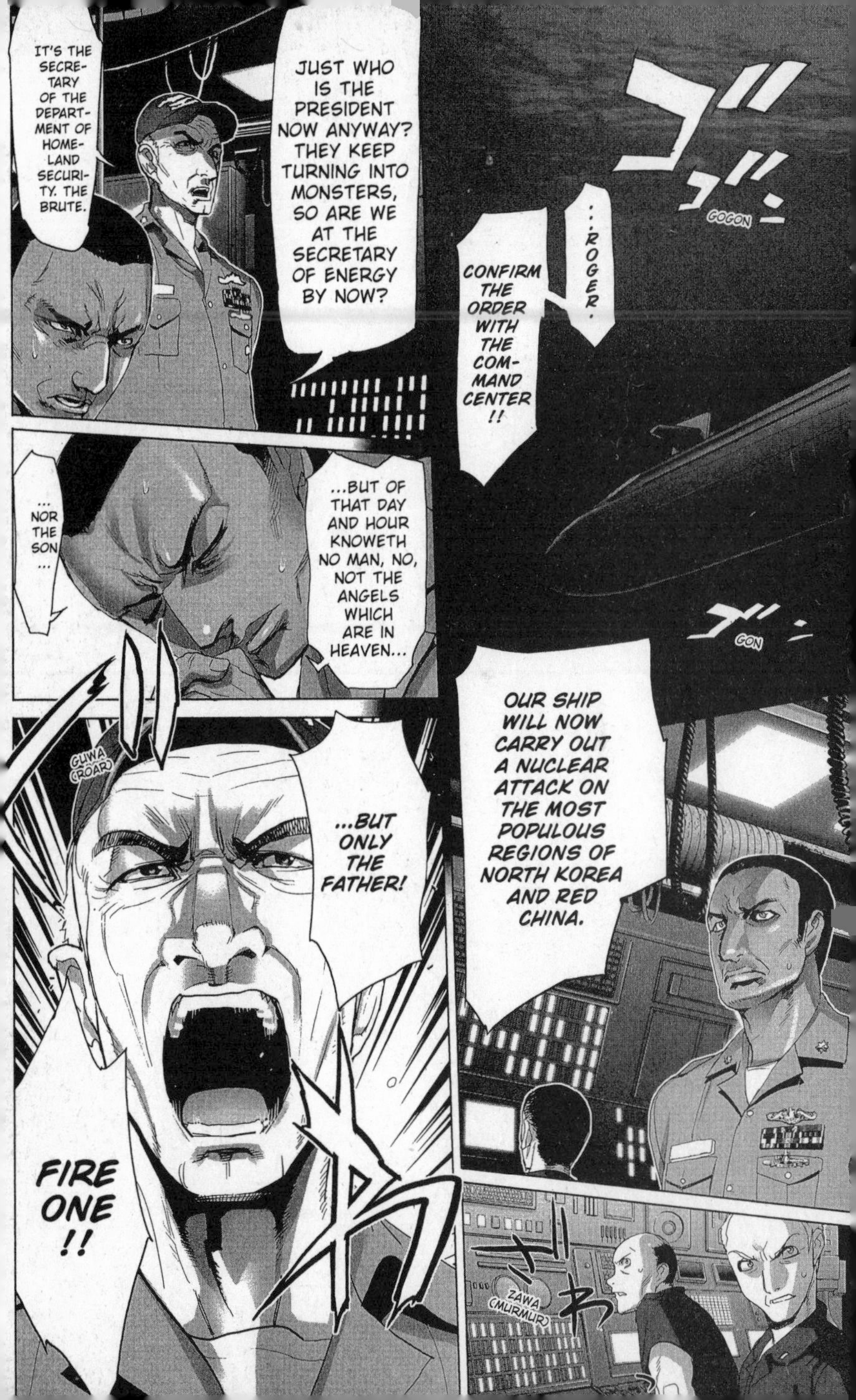

GOGON
...ROGER.
CONFIRM THE ORDER WITH THE COMMAND CENTER!!
GON
JUST WHO IS THE PRESIDENT NOW ANYWAY? THEY KEEP TURNING INTO MONSTERS, SO ARE WE AT THE SECRETARY OF ENERGY BY NOW?
IT'S THE SECRETARY OF THE DEPARTMENT OF HOMELAND SECURITY. THE BRUTE.
...BUT OF THAT DAY AND HOUR KNOWETH NO MAN, NO, NOT THE ANGELS WHICH ARE IN HEAVEN...
...NOR THE SON...
OUR SHIP WILL NOW CARRY OUT A NUCLEAR ATTACK ON THE MOST POPULOUS REGIONS OF NORTH KOREA AND RED CHINA.
...BUT ONLY THE FATHER!
GUWA (ROAR)
FIRE ONE!!
ZAWA (MURMUR)

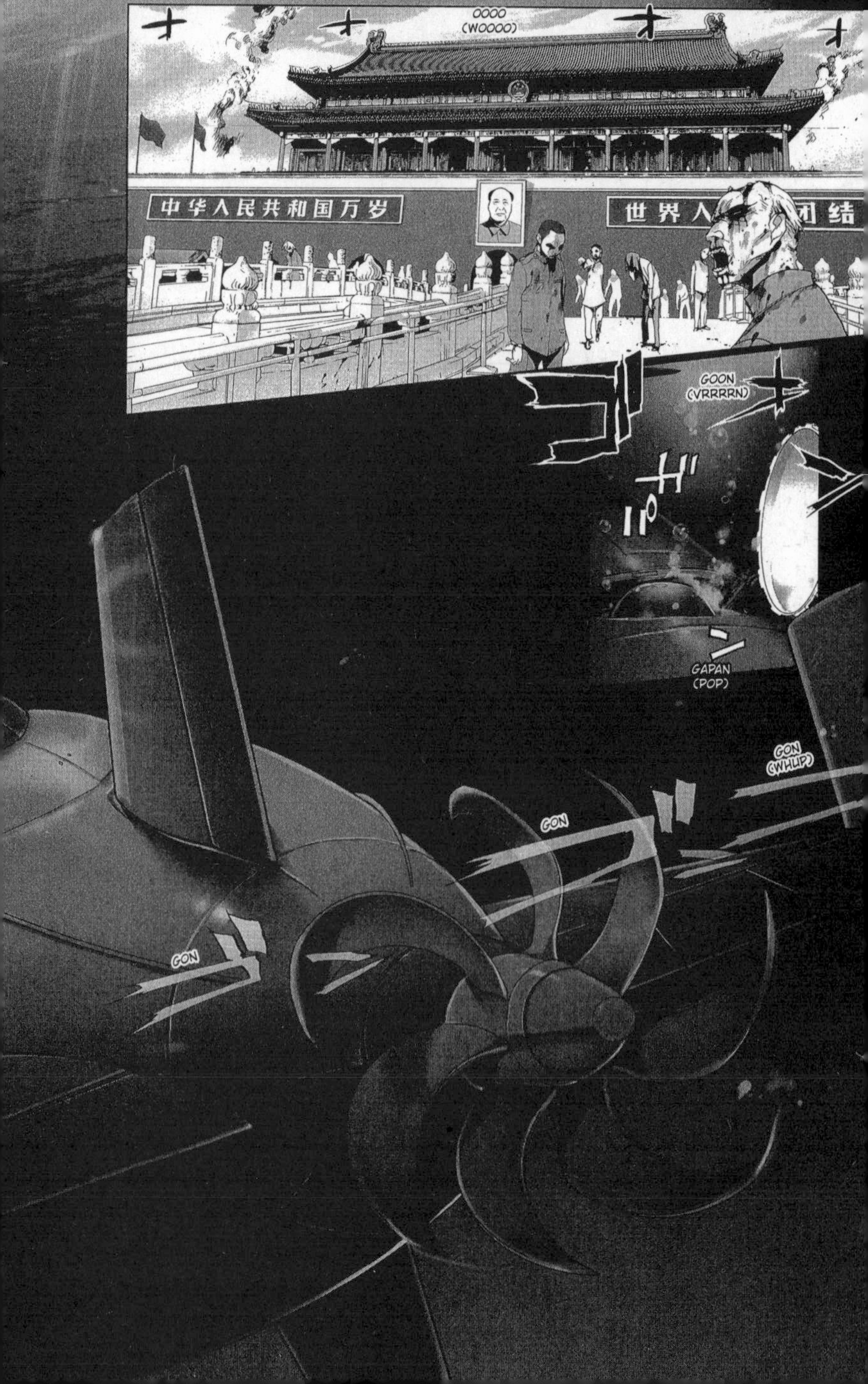
OOOO
(WOOOO)
中华人民共和国万岁
世界人
团结
GOON
(VRRRRN)
GAPAN
(POP)
GON
(WHUP)
GON
GON

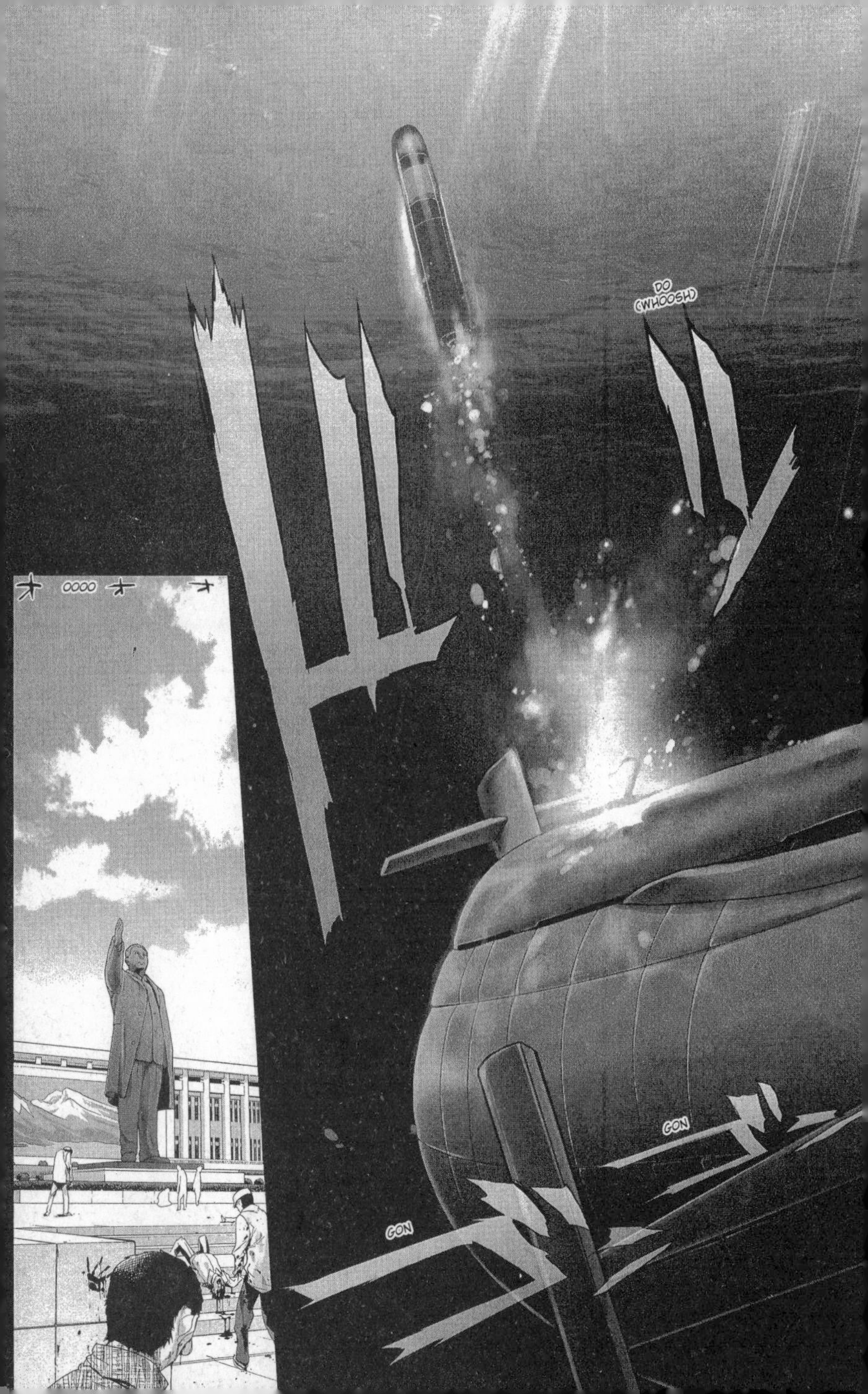
DO
(WHOOSH)
GON
GON
OOOO

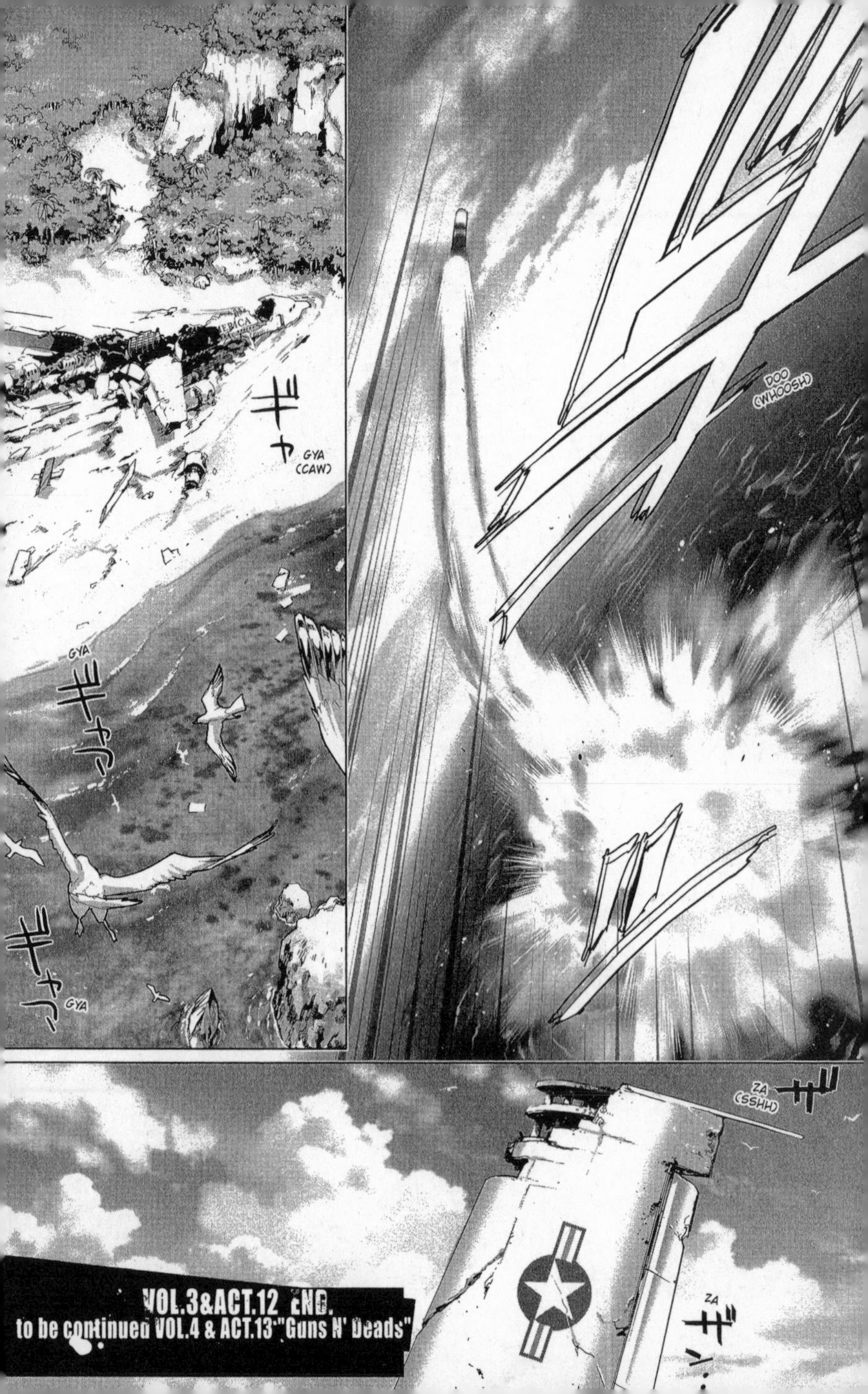
DOO (WHOOSH)
GYA (CAW)
GYA
GYA
ZA (SSHH)
ZA
VOL.3&ACT.12 END.
to be continued VOL.4 & ACT.13"Guns N' Deads"

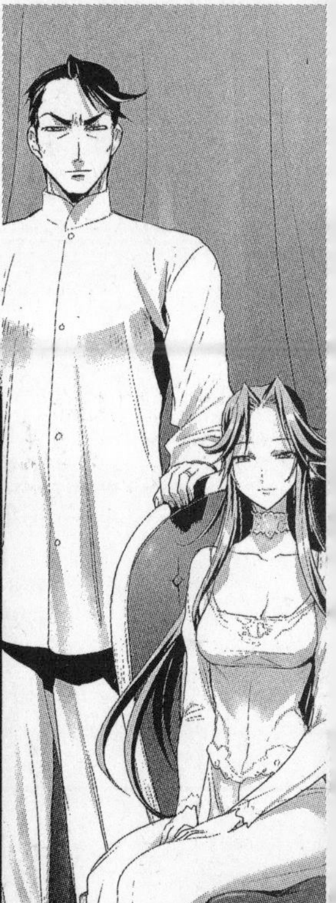

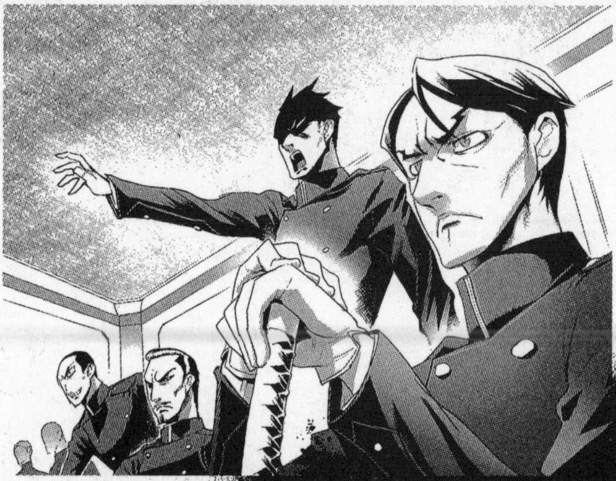

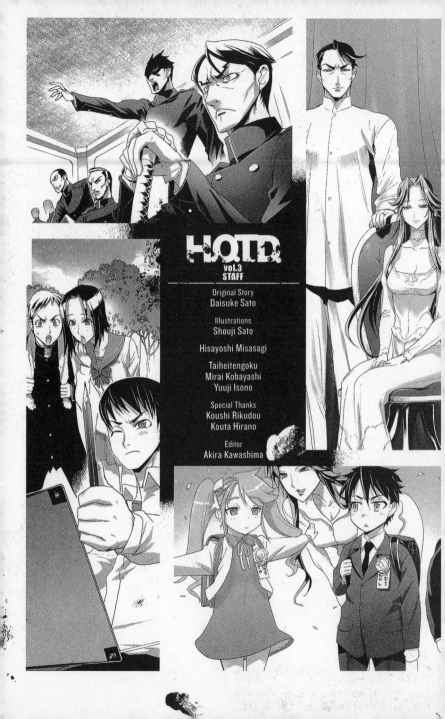

H.O.T.D.

vol.3
STAFF

Original Story
Daisuke Sato

Illustrations
Shouji Sato

Hisayoshi Misasagi

Taiheitengoku
Mirai Kobayashi
Yuuji Isono

Special Thanks
Koushi Rikudou
Kouta Hirano

Editor
Akira Kawashima

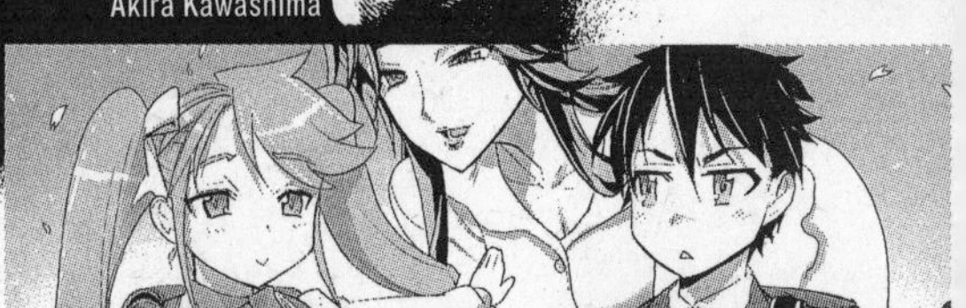

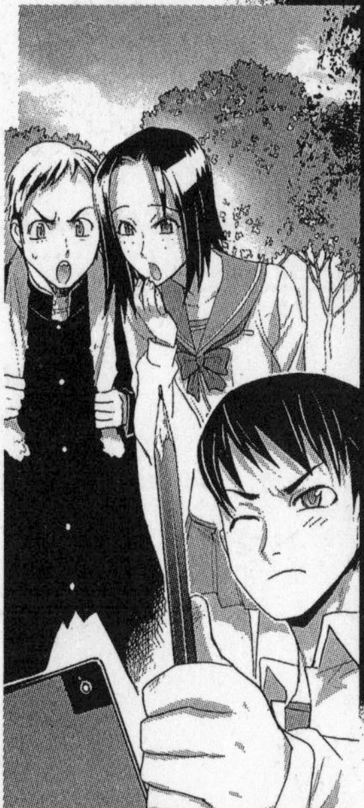

HIGHSCHOOL OF THE DEAD ❸

DAISUKE SATO
SHOUJI SATO

Translation: Christine Dashiell

Lettering: Chris Counasse

This book is a work of fiction. Names, characters, places, and incidents are the product of the author's imagination or are used fictitiously. Any resemblance to actual events, locales, or persons, living or dead, is coincidental.

GAKUENMOKUSHIROKU HIGHSCHOOL OF THE DEAD Volume 3
©2007 DAISUKE SATO ©2007 SHOUJI SATO. Edited by FUJIMISHOBO. First published in Japan in 2007 by KADOKAWA CORPORATION, Tokyo. English translation rights arranged with KADOKAWA CORPORATION, Tokyo, through TUTTLE-MORI AGENCY, INC., Tokyo.

Translation © 2011 by Hachette Book Group, Inc.

Yen Press
Hachette Book Group
1290 Avenue of the Americas, New York, NY 10104

www.HachetteBookGroup.com
www.YenPress.com

Yen Press is an imprint of Hachette Book Group, Inc.
The Yen Press name and logo are trademarks of Hachette Book Group, Inc.

First Yen Press Edition: July 2011

ISBN: 978-0-316-13242-8

10 9

BVG

Printed in the United States of America